RUNAWAY TO HEAVEN

RUNAWAY
TO
HEAVEN

THE STORY OF HARRIET BEECHER STOWE

by Johanna Johnston

Doubleday & Company, Inc.
Garden City, New York, 1963

Library of Congress Catalog Card Number 63–12167
Copyright © 1963 by Johanna Johnston
All Rights Reserved
Printed in the United States of America
First Edition

To W.W.W.

Contents

Part One BONDAGE

Part Two FREEDOM

Prologue

A compound of contradictions—deep feeling and sentimentality, laughter and melancholy, self-righteousness and humility, dark fears and clear visions—all fused at one time in one person to produce a book that shook the world.

Can we hope to understand such a miracle—such an enigma?

We can look at her century and see it full of contradictions too, see its contradictions focused in her as in a burning glass.

We can laugh at her humor, undimmed by the years. We can see well what caused her pain. We can see many things, for she wrote about many things—almost anything that caused her to wonder, rage, hope or despair.

Then we look again and see the enigma again, not to be explained.

We have here no continuing city . . .

RUNAWAY TO HEAVEN

BEECHER AND STOWE FAMILIES

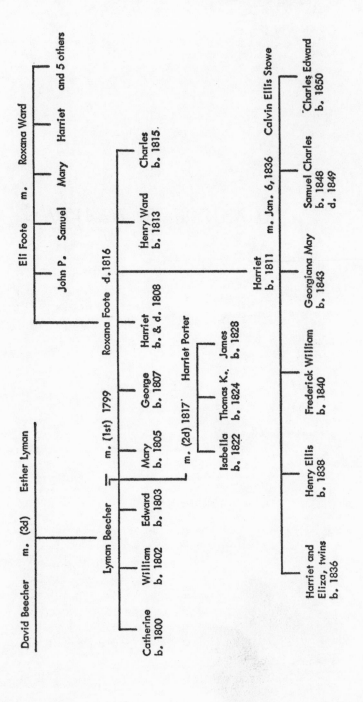

Part One

BONDAGE

In anger, Lord, do not chastise,
Withdraw the dreadful storm;
Nor let thine awful wrath arise
Against a feeble worm.

Old Hymn, early 1800s

Chapter 1

My dears, those were not onions, but the roots of beautiful flowers.

1811–1821

Her name was Harriet—Hattie they called her as often as not—and her first memory was of finding a bag of tulip bulbs in her mother's bedroom, and, with some help from her small brother, eating them all up, convinced they were onions. "My dears," their mother said sadly, when the deed was discovered, "those were not onions, but the roots of beautiful flowers." Why, even if they had been onions, Hattie felt the need to eat so many, never seems to have been remarked. But she would always have a tendency to do whatever she did to extremes, and all her life she would be leaping to conclusions as rash as the one about the tulip bulbs, and acting on those conclusions with an equal lack of hesitation.

She was a merry and affectionate child eager to make people laugh by making "monkey faces," eager for love and praise. And all her life a wild and wonderful comic sense would sparkle through both her writing and her conversation, and a deep desire to love and be loved would lie underneath everything she did.

Still, by the time she was eight or nine, she had begun to retreat now and then from her gaiety and friendliness into moods of abstraction so deep that she seemed deaf, dumb and blind to the world around her. She was a little thing, small for her age, with great gray-blue eyes, and when she ran away like that, into one of her moods, her eyes would be half-veiled by their heavy lids. "Hattie's owling about again," her brothers and sisters would say, and shrug and ignore her till the fit had passed. Her father, a man who liked to find a family precedent for everything, recalled that his father, a New Haven blacksmith, had been given all his life to fits of absentmindedness. Chuckling, he told again a favorite family story about how his father would sometimes gather eggs in the barn, put the eggs in his coattail pocket and then forget them until sometime later he chanced to sit upon them. Hattie's "owling about" was of a piece with that same behavior, he decided. So no one worried about her moods, then or later, and all her life she would suddenly vanish in spirit from the scene around her, in the same way she had as a child, never mind how important the situation, or how pressing the demand that she be present.

Outgoing and gay, moody and withdrawn, she was as contradictory a child as she would be a contradictory sort of a woman. And variable as she was, there was no hint of the one thing that would ultimately focus all her emotions into an irresistible passion of protest—a sense of bondage.

There was no hint that she might know anything about bondage personally. It seemed that she was one of a very special family, with a very special place in the world. Her father, Lyman Beecher, was minister of the Congregational Meeting in Litchfield, Connecticut, the town where she was born and spent her childhood. This by itself meant that he was a person of prestige and importance. In Connecticut, in the early nineteenth century, political affairs were still in the hands of the church, as they had been since the days of the early Covenanters, and Congregationalism was still the authorized religion of the state. But beyond Lyman Beecher's importance in Litchfield, he was a preacher well known throughout New England, famous for his periodic and passionate crusades against practices that struck him as abhorrent —dueling, drinking, Unitarianism. He was also a man who boiled with such energy and self-confidence that not one of his children could escape the feeling that he lived in an atmosphere of destiny.

"Wisht it had been a boy," he had said when Hattie was born, June 14, 1811, his and his wife's sixth surviving child. He already had three sons, and he doted on his daughters, particularly the oldest, Catherine, but still he wanted more sons to train for earth's one meaningful task, saving souls. This regret that Hattie was not a boy was one he continued to voice throughout her childhood, never dreaming of keeping it from her. "Hattie is a genius," he wrote a friend when she was six. It was an extravagant remark prompted equally by evidences she had given of a phenomenal memory, and his own inclination to find everyone connected with him unique. "I would give a hundred dollars if she were a boy."

But the young Harriet never gave any sign that being a girl laid a feeling of bondage upon her. She leaped to the challenge of piling wood and sweeping up chips at wood-chopping time, when her father said loudly, "If only Hattie were a boy now, she'd do more 'n any of 'em." And she joined her father and brothers in fishing expeditions on the pond afterward, with the same unselfconscious enthusiasm. Never in her life would she consciously rebel at a woman's role, with all the restrictions it entailed in the nineteenth century. Rather she would have an idealized vision of how important that role was, and a dreamlike picture of what a perfect woman should be.

Her mother, Roxana Foote Beecher, was the woman who represented that vision to her. Roxana had died, swiftly and suddenly, of "galloping consumption" the year Hattie was five. The grief that filled the Beecher household had laid no shadow on young Harriet. She was whisked away soon after the funeral to spend almost a year with her mother's people, the Footes, who lived in a little hamlet near New Haven, called Nutplains. And she came back to a legend of her mother, elevated to the status of a saint. Gentle, serene, talented, well educated, pious—it seemed there was no virtue Roxana Beecher had not possessed. It made little difference that soon after Hattie's return, her father came home from a trip with a stepmother for his eight motherless children. The legend of Roxana glowed as brightly as ever, and the new stepmother, young, pretty, cool and precise, had no power to combat its hold, no strength to give young Harriet some other vision of what a real, living, breathing and happy woman might be like.

But, any sense of loss because she had scarcely known her own mother did not come to Hattie until later. The years of her childhood in Litchfield would always be the happy years, the years to which her heart would return over and over again.

Church on Sundays, at the Meeting House on the Green, school
on weekdays at Miss Pierce's famous Academy, just down North
Street from the Beecher house, a loving family, and the turn of
the seasons across the beautiful hills all around—there was every
reason why her childhood should have been happy.

There were only two elements in the pattern which were somewhat unusual and prophetic, two memories burning themselves
into the consciousness of an emotional little girl, which would
influence her profoundly.

One was a legend. Legends abounded in the Beecher family,
for Lyman turned every event of daily life into a drama, and all
the Beecher children had the sense of living in a sort of saga,
which stretched back to their father's youth and to their mother's,
and still farther back to encompass their grandparents' lives and
their great-grandparents' also. There were stories of Lyman's boyhood on his "Uncle Lot's" farm; stories about how his father
and that same Uncle Lot had taken their muskets, when the
British invaded New Haven, and played their own homely roles
in the Revolution. There were stories about Lyman's days at
Yale, in the time of the great Timothy Dwight; stories of his
courtship of Roxana, and how he had wrestled with her soul to
convert her to Calvinism; stories of his first church on Long
Island, and his crusade against dueling after Aaron Burr had
killed Alexander Hamilton; and there was a dramatic set piece
relating the details of Roxana's last illness and death. But there
was one legend that had a lurid quality which made it different
from the others, one legend that was a strange and unlikely
story to find its way into the heart of a little girl growing up in
a peaceful New England village in the early nineteenth century.

The legend concerned her Aunt Mary, her mother's younger
sister, who had died in the Beecher house in Litchfield when
Hattie was only two, too young to have any memories of her
herself. But Aunt Mary's story, recalled again and again by her
father, fixed itself in young Harriet's mind, giving her her first
harsh picture of slavery, and a sense of something else, nameless
and frightening, which filled her with unease.

Mary Foote had been a happy, healthy young woman when
she fell in love with a West Indian planter named Hubbard,

visiting in the States. She had married him and sailed off with him to his island home, full of expectations of felicity. But then, at the plantation house she had been greeted by a horde of mulatto children. They were all his, her husband cheerfully informed her, and that was the end of Mary Foote Hubbard's happiness. Her husband could not understand her shock and revulsion. The Negro mothers were his property. It was as sensible to breed new servants on them as to see that his livestock was well bred. But Mary could not for a moment accept his reasoning. She sat at the window of her new home, staring out at the sea, wishing the island would sink beneath its load of shame and misery, even if she had to sink with it. Then—as it obviously was not going to do so, and as she could neither bear to touch nor look at her husband—she soon became ill enough to more than justify a return home. She had come to her sister's house in Litchfield. Lyman had slung a hammock for her across one corner of the kitchen. And day by day she had wasted away until at last she died. Probably her illness had been "consumption," and equally probably, Roxana had contracted the disease while nursing her sister. But "a broken heart" was what Lyman always called it before he concluded the story with a grim denunciation of slavery.

Slavery was still legal in Connecticut when Harriet was young, and there were some slaves in Litchfield, but only a few. They were busy, contented Negroes, working as domestic servants, coachmen or cooks. There were two young Negro girls in the Beechers' kitchen, Rachel and Zillah, who had worked for the family as far back as Hattie could remember. But they were "bound girls," not slaves. Periodically, Hattie heard her father thundering from the pulpit on the sin of slavery, and she could remember one sermon so impassioned that many women in the congregation burst into tears. But the sermons never seemed to have anything to do with the Negroes in Litchfield, and both slaves and slaveowners went on as placidly as ever. So the slavery against which her father harangued, the slavery that had broken the heart of her Aunt Mary, was obviously some kind of far-off evil, full of unimaginable horrors. As for the "mulatto children" in the Aunt Mary legend, Hattie both knew and did not know

what they signified, but they, more than anything else, gave the
story its peculiar potency.

"Oh, that this land would sink beneath its load of shame and
misery. . . ." One day, years later, when she had learned a good
deal more about all kinds of slavery, Harriet would cry out the
same words. The legend would seem like a fated thing to her,
entering her consciousness when so young.

The other prophetic element in her childhood, pointing to the
future, was her discovery of the poetry of George Gordon, Lord
Byron. This was not so unlikely as the Aunt Mary legend. From
the time she learned to read, Hattie was a bookworm, searching
avidly among the books available for anything that would yield
to a child's understanding. *Pilgrim's Progress,* the *Arabian Nights'*
Entertainment and Cotton Mather's *Magnalia Christi Americana,*
for all its staggering title a wonderful collection of tales about In-
dians, massacres, witches, and the heroism of the Puritan fathers
—these were her treasures, and she had memorized long passages
from all of them.

Then, by the time she was ten, the Byron fever had begun raging in Litchfield, and all over America, just as it had been raging
in England for eight years and more. The young ladies at Miss
Pierce's Academy were sighing over Byron's poems and portrait.
The young men of Judge Tapping Reeve's Litchfield Law School
were affecting open collars, careless curls and looks of melancholy.
And the older people of the town were equally, if less flamboy-
antly, impressed. At the tea-drinkings, Litchfield's chief form of
social life, when the conversation turned to literature, as it did
in that educated village, everyone spoke gravely of Byron's
genius, and then even more gravely and obliquely of the rumored
excesses of his life.

Given such circumstances, Hattie, always looking for something new to read, soon found a copy of *The Corsair.* Emotional
and broody, she responded instantly to the poetry. She might not
understand all the allusions and turns of phrase:

"Aunt Esther, what does it mean, 'One I never loved enough
to hate . . .'?"

"Oh, child, it's just one of Byron's strong expressions," her aunt might answer.

But the rhythms and images held her despite such mystifications. And the passion, the cynicism, the melancholy, struck deep chords in her without her knowing how or why.

Captured by the poetry, she listened to everything she heard about the poet. And learned just what everyone knew. Byron was a young English nobleman who had come home to London after a tour of the East with a book of poetry, *Childe Harold's Pilgrimage,* that had become an instant sensation. Hattie heard of how he had been lionized, how all the young ladies had fallen in love with him, and how he had finally married a beautiful young Englishwoman. Then came the part so irresistible to every romantic heart. For all his genius, Byron was a wild and reckless young man, and so he had done some wild thing that was too much for Lady Byron. Soon after their marriage, she had taken their infant daughter and left him. At this, he had fled to the continent, where he was now, and where, like one of the heroes of his poems, he was trying to forget the emptiness of his life by throwing himself into one noble cause after another, the Italian fight for independence, the Greek struggle for freedom from Turkish rule.

As soon as she heard the story, Hattie was convinced of what thousands of other girls and women also knew for sure. Whatever Lord Byron had done, Lady Byron should have forgiven him. His poetry made it clear that his heart was full of noble impulses only waiting to be released. She should have forgiven him and through all the strength of a woman's love, helped him to realize the good that was in him. She had not done it. She must have a heart of stone.

Hattie saw everything in pictures, and her imaginings all her life would be as vivid as pageants or tableaux. Now she had a brilliant new set of pictures to play with when she sat on the back steps dreaming and staring out at the hills that encircled Litchfield. Instead of the hills, she would see a tall, pale lady, her face as cold as the long, white pallor of her gown, repulsing with downthrust hand the pleas of the handsome, tortured poet

who knelt before her. Lady Byron was the villainess. Lord
Byron, wild, reckless, repentant, was the hero.

So young Harriet enshrined Byron in her heart and there he
would stay for years and years, until, by a set of curious chances,
she would meet his widow, and hear, from Lady Byron's own
lips, the story that would bring the image toppling down in ruins.
Then, in reaction, she herself would feel that she had to tell the
world why Lady Byron was not a villainess after all, but a heroine
who had suffered a long and silent martyrdom.

Of course, by 1821, when Hattie was ten, and first in love with
Byron, the story of the poet's alleged incest with his half sister,
Augusta, had long since run its course as a six-month sensation
in London's sophisticated Regency society. Everyone in London
who was anyone had heard about it and forgotten it. Only Lady
Byron could not forget the story, would not forget it, but clung
to it desperately, her one defense against collapse. She cherished
the story and nurtured it, almost as though waiting for the day
when she would confide it to, of all unlikely people, little Hattie
from America.

That Hattie had known and loved Byron's poetry so early
would seem fateful to Lady Byron then. "I feel *you* could have
understood him," she would say to her sadly and flatteringly.

But naturally there was no hint in the early days of anything
ominous to come because of her love for Byron. Hattie put her
remarkable memory to work learning whole pages of Byron's
verse, and the routine of her life went on.

And these were the years that would forever after seem washed
in sunshine. She had not yet seen or felt the shadow that was at
the heart of the seemingly peaceful, pastoral life around her.
She had had no hint of the kind of bondage that held her, her
family, and all New England in its thrall.

Chapter 2

The years Harriet was young were years all America remembered as happy, peaceful, growing years. The struggles of the Revolution were long over, already they had taken on the shape of glorious myth.

Like most boys and girls of her time, Harriet Beecher would remember the Fourth of July celebrations. Fourth of July and Thanksgiving—those were the two holidays. Christmas was frowned upon by the Congregationalists. Only that stubborn minority group, the Episcopalians, marked Christmas as a special day.

But the Fourth of July! In Litchfield, the cannon on the Green was loaded with gunpowder, and a sham battle involving all the excited boys of the town and countryside took place. There was a review of the militia, and then a lavish picnicking by Litchfield families as they laid out their cloths and foodstuffs all over the Green. Later, there were impressive ceremonies in the Meeting House, with Colonel Benjamin Tallmadge, majestic in the blue and buff uniform he had worn when he fought under Washington, reading aloud the Declaration of Independence.

All over the growing United States there were similar ceremonies on the Fourth, cannon firing, sham battles between Americans, British and Redskins, and then the honored veterans who had fought in the real battles, reading aloud the sonorous words that now were almost Biblical in their meaning and implication.

Happy years. The confused and overcharged dreams which had led to the War of 1812, the defeats and panics which had followed it, were over. The struggle between those two opposed political schools, the Federalists and the Democratic-Republicans,

was almost over too. In the beginning, it had almost seemed the
conflict between them would destroy the new nation before it
was well started, but somehow, through the troubled years of
1812, 1813, 1814, they had come closer together. The Democratic-Republicans began adopting so many Federalist theories
that the Federalist party was gradually disappearing.

In rockbound and stubborn Connecticut, men were still cherish-
ing Federalist ideals. Connecticut men of substance still abhorred
Jefferson and his ideas of mob democracy, abhorred both the
Presidents in the Jeffersonian succession, Madison and Monroe.
But by 1817, even in Connecticut, a tide of republicanism had
begun to rise.

Lyman Beecher had fought the tide to start with. A minister
of the church that was the authorized church of the state, he had
been bound to fight it. He had been still sunk in grief over the
death of his first wife, Roxana, when word had come through to
him that his church was in danger, and he had roused from his
sorrowing at once.

Men were uniting against the church control of the state all
over Connecticut. In Hartford, lawyers, no longer poorly thought
of as they had been in colonial days, but gaining new prestige
and importance every year, were rebelling against a legislature
handpicked by the rich and bewigged Congregational clergy. The
minority faiths, Episcopalians, Baptists, Methodists and Unitarians, were joining them, weary at last of laws dictated by the
Congregationalists, weary at last of paying taxes to support a
church that was none of theirs. Even those few daring souls who
were freethinkers, unbelievers or infidels, were joining the crusade, and were being welcomed. All of them, Episcopalians and
infidels, lawyers and riffraff, were gathering for a brief, unlikely
period of union under a democratic banner to elect a Governor
on the platform of Toleration. It was Litchfield's own Oliver
Wolcott, of the old, honored family of Wolcotts, a polite attendant at Lyman's own church every Sunday, who was running
for Governor on that platform.

Toleration! The word was a mockery to Lyman Beecher. To
him, these gathering forces were simply showing their intolerance

of the church through which God had given man His one great
plan of salvation.

So he had put aside his grief to fight, that year of 1817, writing
to other ministers, penning long, rousing articles for religious
papers, thundering warnings from his pulpit.

Then had come the election and the Democratic sweep.

"Well, Doctor, we're smashed. Democrats beat us all to flinders," was the way the news came to the Beecher house. "Everything has voted that could stand on its hind legs, and the hogs
are too many for us. It's a bad beat—bad beat."

All the Beecher children who were home at the time remembered their father's reaction. He slumped in a kitchen chair and
whispered, "I fear for the whole future of Christ's church." Then,
in a long, desperate prayer, he exhorted the Almighty to come
to the rescue of the vine he had brought into the wilderness.

His mood of despair had not lasted. Despair never lasted too
long with Lyman Beecher. Within a few months, he had turned
the whole thing into a victory of sorts, saying it was the best
thing that ever happened to his church, cutting it loose from state
support, "forcing its ministers and its members to greater voluntary efforts." His own increased voluntary efforts would lead him
to Boston, to "let loose his big gun" in defense of Calvinism, a
sermon on "The Bible, A Code of Law." There he would meet,
within a day or so, an admiring young lady named Harriet Porter,
who would become his second wife, the Beecher children's stepmother.

Thus with Lyman Beecher first resisting, then rejoicing, another
aspect of colonial New England vanished in the years when Harriet Beecher was young, and Connecticut began to merge with
the new republic.

Every vestige of the colonial scene was vanishing. Hattie could
remember, from her childhood, men in knee breeches, buckled
shoes and wigs. That fashion, so long established, was disappearing, and men were wearing pantaloons, once despised as a fashion
born in the blood and terror of the French Revolution. The look
all over America was becoming plainer now. The courtliness of
knee breeches had no place in the new activity that was sweeping
the country.

There was a bustle everywhere of a young nation suddenly turned to concentrate on itself, to improve itself, to build and unite. North, south, east and west, roads were stretching out to link towns and settlements once isolated, to open new territory, pave a way to new resources, provide an outlet for the products of remote regions so they could be marketed on the coast. In Maryland, a road planned as a national turnpike was slowly, mile by mile, clearing a path to Ohio and the West.

In another great preoccupation, people were talking about, planning, or starting work on canals, waterway links from region to region. The biggest was under construction in upper New York State—the Erie Canal, which would link the Hudson River at Albany with Lake Erie to the west.

In Washington, D.C., tall, handsome young John C. Calhoun was speaking eagerly for all these improvements, voting "aye" on every bill that seemed to further the interests of nationalism. A few years earlier, he had been in Litchfield, riding up there from his native South Carolina to read law with Judge Reeve in his famous Law School. Then he had been one of the War Hawks of 1812, overoptimistic, overconfident of the young United States' power to embark on aggressive war. Now he had come to his happiest years, leaving those grandiose dreams behind, come to the years when he was fired by a vision of a nation strong in itself, growing in unity, prospering in the wealth of its own resources.

Calhoun's state was prospering, growing rich from the dizzying boom in cotton, as all the states of the Deep South were. But John C. Calhoun still saw South Carolina, beloved as it was to him, as just one part of a nation that could, in unity, be greater than any of its parts. He saw no menace in the South's concentration on wonderful, wonderful cotton, no evidence yet of how this concentration would finally unbalance all its economy, leaving the South impoverished in the midst of plenty.

In South Carolina, and elsewhere in the South, the talk in those years was only of how cotton's price had risen over the last year's, and how one could get more land to plant with this greedy crop that wore out soil so quickly. And the men of the South pushed west, into western Georgia and Alabama, to clear the rich bottomlands there for King Cotton.

There was one thing the men of the South were not talking about, as they had been before 1800. Before the wonderful, dazzling boom in cotton—before a certain spindle had been invented in England, and a certain gin in America—the men of the South had talked rather generally about the possibility of slavery soon dying a natural death. Slavery was an expensive institution, and almost any thoughtful plantation owner could be brought to admit that it was a basically unprofitable system for working the land, when that land was devoted chiefly to crops of indigo and tobacco. Slavery was expensive, wasteful, and so it had been easy to see that slavery was morally unattractive as well.

Then came the spindle that made it possible to spin a fine cotton thread quickly and economically, then came the cotton gin, which did away with the tedious hand-cleaning of cotton, and the two obstacles that had stood in the way of cotton's wide use as a fabric were gone. The boom was on. Land, land and more land planted to cotton needed slaves, slaves and more slaves to tend it. Slavery was no longer a dying institution. Suddenly, slavery was indispensable.

No one really stopped to ponder the sudden reversal in moral attitudes. Everyone was too busy getting rich, raising and selling cotton.

In New Haven, Connecticut, the town where Lyman Beecher had been born, even Eli Whitney, the dismayed inventor of the gin that had worked such a miracle, was beginning to find some peace and happiness. For years he had been battling for a modicum of justice, some legal restriction on the wholesale copying of his patented machine, some financial return to himself from the states that were rocketing to wealth through its use. But beyond everything else, Eli Whitney was a man of reason. Seeing at last that his fight was hopeless, that even the United States Congress to which he took his appeal was unable to rise above the pressures of its Southern members, he had decided to abandon the struggle before it exhausted any more of his energies, and to turn to something new.

Calm, observant, reasonable, he had decided not to waste his inventive talents any longer on machines that could easily be duplicated, once their principles were known. For a long time he had been interested in a new *process*, by which any variety of things could be made. It was a process that, properly applied, might enable him to gain financial security by manufacturing some item more profitably than anyone else. The process that intrigued him, the process he was the first to introduce in America, was the system of interchangeable parts, the basis of all mass production. It would be as revolutionary in American history as his first invention had been, spurring the North to an industrial economy just as the cotton gin had committed the South to agriculture.

Whitney experimented first in making muskets by this new process, and ultimately he was given a large contract by the government, twelve thousand muskets to be delivered within two years. There had been troubles in fulfilling the contract—the time limit was unrealistic and he had difficulty in finding skilled labor —but at last he had made and delivered the muskets. His factory on the outskirts of New Haven was a smoothly running operation now, and other contracts were coming in.

Even Eli Whitney was a contented man by 1820, squire of a model workers' village, affluent enough for marriage and a family.

Happy years, growing years. Down all the new roads and turnpikes that were reaching out from the settled and civilized states of the East and South, families were moving west into the uncleared land, the land full of promise. From Pennsylvania, they were moving on into Ohio. From Kentucky, they were moving north and west into Indiana. It was 1817 when a hard-working carpenter named Thomas Lincoln took his family into the rich, wild forests of the new state. It was in 1818 that his wife died, and not much longer after that that he, like Lyman Beecher, gave his children, including a nine-year-old named Abraham, a stepmother. The new Mrs. Lincoln, unlike the new Mrs. Beecher in Connecticut, seemed to have an easy way with her stepchildren. Warmth and love flowered naturally between her and her gangly stepson, Abraham.

A certain amount of confusion was created by the expanding, the pushing out, the rush for new land. Recklessly, men agreed to pay fantastic prices for the new land that offered so much. Credit was extended until it reached the breaking point—and

snapped. For a while, there was financial panic in the new western states.

There were other difficulties. The men from the South, moving
west, took their slaves with them as a matter of course. As they
carved new states out of the wilderness they saw no reason why
these should not be slave states like the ones they had left. Suddenly there was uproar in Congress and in the East. Moral attitudes were no part of it. It was a question of power. Slave states
had congressional seats and electoral votes based on a population
reckoning that included human chattels, a situation that could
hardly seem fair to northern and eastern nonslave states. But
then there arose the question of how much power Congress itself
should be allowed in placing qualifications on the admission of
new states. Should the older eastern states control the destiny of
the West? All over the country, men debated the question.

Then, more quietly than anyone could have hoped, the Missouri Compromise solved it, or so it seemed. Missouri would enter the Union as a slave state, but to keep the power balanced,
Maine, just detached from Massachusetts, would enter as a free
state. As for the future, the remaining Louisiana Territory would
be divided, north and south, with slavery allowed in the southern
portion, but prohibited north of latitude 36° 30'.

It seemed eminently fair and reasonable. The slavery question
was answered, and North and South, men could forget it and
get on with more exciting business.

Only a few men trembled. Jefferson, a busy man of seventy-
seven, engrossed in building his cherished University of Virginia,
raised his head. He heard "a firebell in the night," which filled
him with terror. John Quincy Adams, much younger, but almost
as perceptive as the older man, shivered too, and saw the compromise as simply "a title page to a great, tragic volume."

Chapter 3

Come all you jolly sailors bold, and listen unto me,
A dreadful story I will tell that happened at sea;
The loss of the Albion ship, my boys, upon the Irish coast,
And most of the passengers and crew were completely lost.

> *Chorus: Ye landsmen all pray pity me*
> *When rolling on the raging sea . . .*

Our passengers were twenty nine, when from New York she
*   came,*
With twenty five bold sailor lads as ever crossed the main,
Full fifty four we had on board when first we did set sail
And only nine escaped the wreck to tell the dreadful tale.

So now that noble vessel, the Albion, she is lost,
Though the tempestuous ocean she so oftentimes has crossed;
Our noble captain he is lost, a man, a sailor bold,
And many a gallant life is lost, and many a heart made cold.

1821–1824

It was the disaster of the decade—the wreck of the packet ship
Albion, crack transatlantic vessel of the Black Ball line. Ballads
were struck off and hawked about the streets, the tale flew everywhere, and the fate of the *Albion* became a byword to fearful
passengers embarking on an Atlantic crossing.

The wreck was more than a distant catastrophe to the Beecher
family in Litchfield, Connecticut, far more than a ballad or a byword. The news of the disaster changed the life of one Beecher
forever, and the aftermath of the tragedy would give young Harriet Beecher her first real glimpse of the shadow that lay at the
heart of the sunshine around her. The impact of it all would

remain so vivid that years later she would write of a shipwreck
and its effects on the bereaved in a novel that thrilled thousands.
Not her most famous book—still it would be a book that, in its
own way, dealt with the same theme—bondage, the first kind of
bondage of which young Hattie was really aware.

"Tell me—what is it?—is it?—is he—dead?" she would have her
heroine gasping, years hence.

Then there would be a form "gliding like a spirit, eyes wide
with calm horror," and a "paleness becoming livid," as a fearful
story was unfolded, the story of a ship "crushed like an eggshell
against the rocks, and waves taking strong men and smashing
them like pie plates against the cruel stone."

And after that:

*"Gone—gone, and his spiritual state unknown? Oh, God, I can-
not bear it. I cannot, will not be resigned!"*

Hattie's sister Catherine was the focal figure in the real-life
tragedy. Laughing, self-confident, casual, Catherine had always
been important in young Harriet's life, next most important, probably, to her dramatic, eloquent father. It was Catherine, eleven
years older than Hattie, who had taken over a mother's role after
Roxana's death, dressing and undressing the younger ones, seeing
them to bed and hearing their prayers. It was Catherine to whom
Hattie turned when another in the endless parade of kittens died,
asking for an "epithet" for its tombstone; Catherine who made
up funny poems and stories about the rats that raced through
the garrets of the Beecher house in the winter, immune to cats,
traps and guns; Catherine who shone, if anyone did, as the favored one in the family, her father's pet, everyone's admired
big sister.

Then one summer, Catherine acquired a beau. He was a remarkable young man named Alexander Metcalfe Fisher. Gifted
with prodigious intellectual powers, he had swept through Yale
reaping honors on every hand, until at twenty-five he was already
a full professor at the college.

Every week the professor made the trip from New Haven to
Litchfield to attend the service in the Meeting House, sitting in
the Beecher pew. After the service, pacing sedately up North

Street to the Beecher house for a cold, light meal, Catherine and her beau would talk gravely but animatedly of many subjects— astronomy, mathematics, natural history, poetry. Most of all they talked about poetry, for Catherine fancied herself a poet, and in the beginning it had been some poetry of hers, published in a religious paper, which had caused Professor Fisher to seek out her acquaintance on a visit to Litchfield. After lunch they would play duets on the old piano, for Professor Fisher was an accomplished musician as well as everything else. Then he would go with them all to the afternoon service, and after that, there would be more talking and talking and talking.

Hattie found all of this only moderately interesting. Professor Fisher with his long, thin scholar's face, his long, sensitive scholar's hands, was no figure of romance to her, looking nothing like Byron. If she was especially concerned about any family matter just then, it was more likely her father's health. Since spring he had been in the throes of a mysterious misery. His face was pale, his long, mobile mouth was set in lines of suffering, even his cockatoo crest of hair seemed to have flattened on his head. And he went about muttering that he feared his end was near, his symptoms surely meant "consumption or cancer internal." But Catherine, more used than Hattie to their father's periodic hypochondria, was untroubled, and her courtship went on in its quiet, dignified way.

Catherine left in the fall for New London, where she had been teaching in a girl's school for a year. But at the New Year she was home again, more cheerful, more blooming than ever. She was through with teaching, which was a bore anyway—she was engaged to be married to Professor Fisher.

Lyman Beecher was delighted that Catherine should have made such a fine match. He was no longer ailing. He had almost forgotten the long months of suffering. The cure had been effected well-nigh overnight by a new diet and a regular program of exercise, and the one reminder of his long depression was his unremitting enthusiasm for brisk outdoor activity.

The Beecher house hummed with renewed optimism. Lyman was charging about again. Catherine was taking over housekeeping chores with new authority, readying herself for the role of

matron. It was going to be a year before she and Professor Fisher
could be married, because he was leaving in April for a long tour
of Europe, engaged in various scholastic missions. But though
she would miss him, Catherine was not depressed. She sang as
she moved about the house, showing how capable she could be.
Mrs. Beecher was glad of the help. She was pregnant and feeling
poorly. Because of her condition, and the generally overcrowded
state of the house, it was decided to send one of the younger
children for a stay with the Foote relatives in Nutplains.

Hattie had already spent almost a year there after her mother's
death, with Grandmother Foote and Aunt Harriet (for whom
she had been named), and Uncle George, one of her mother's
brothers. She was pleased when she was the one chosen to go
this time, for she had loved Nutplains. She traveled off on the
stage, to enjoy for a few months the quiet orderliness of the farmhouse at Nutplains, kept so meticulously by her efficient spinster
aunt. She liked being petted by her grandmother, liked showing
Aunt Harriet her progress in sewing and knitting; and as an
added treat, she became acquainted with another of her mother's
brothers, Uncle Samuel. He was a sea captain, home for a few
months from his voyaging, and he was full of stories that fascinated young Harriet—tales of strange ports, storms at sea, and
adventures with pirates and Turks—that made all the *Arabian
Nights* tales leap to life again in her imagination.

Then it was spring, time to return to Litchfield and see the
new baby half sister, Isabella, in her cradle. All was well and
happy in the Beecher house. Catherine was as cheerful as ever,
tossing her curls back from her cheeks when she lifted her head
from her sewing to speak or laugh. Professor Fisher had sailed
on April 1, but she had his letter, written before sailing, tucked
in the bosom of her dress, and she was counting the weeks until
she could expect another letter from England.

Then came the news of the shipwreck.

Lyman Beecher, who had ridden to New Haven to discuss
some church matters with his friend Dr. Taylor of Yale, heard of
the disaster first. Stunned and shocked, he learned that the *Albion*, on which Professor Fisher had sailed just a few weeks be-

fore, had been wrecked off the coast of Ireland. Only a few lives had been saved. His was not one.

Lyman had to write the letter that would break the news to Catherine:

"My dear child,
On entering the city last evening, the first intelligence I met filled my heart with pain. It is all but certain that Professor Fisher is no more. . . ."

"Tell me—what is it?—is it?—is he—is he dead?"
In Litchfield, scanning the letter, heart stopping and then beginning to race, Catherine must have felt the question crying in her mind. Attempting to break the news gently, her father had buried any details of what had happened under mountains of rhetoric:

"Thus have perished our earthly hopes, plans and prospects. Thus the hopes of Yale College, and of our country, and I may say, of Europe, which had begun to know his promise, are dashed. The waves of the Atlantic, commissioned by Heaven, have buried them all. . . ."

Catherine's were the eyes growing "wide with calm horror," Catherine's was the form "gliding like a spirit," as she came to her family and choked out the news. All the Beechers felt the shock reverberate through them. What could they do? What can a family ever do in such a moment? Catherine, merry, confident Catherine, with her tossing curls and her happy plans, was standing in a desolate world, her lover gone and all her hopes gone with him.

But the grief, the sudden sense of loss and emptiness were only the beginning, in Litchfield, Connecticut, 1822.

"Gone, gone—and his spiritual state unknown?"
Lyman had touched on what was even more fearful than Professor Fisher's death in his letter:

". . . with respect to the condition of his present existence in the eternal state, I can only say that many did and will indulge the hope that he was pious. . . ."

After the letter, he rushed through his business with Dr. Taylor in New Haven and hurried to Litchfield to help Catherine face what had to be faced. It was very possible—it seemed more than possible to Lyman, quite probable—that Professor Fisher had gone from his death to the tortures of Hell, and was even now suffering the most terrible, total punishment that an omnipotent God could devise, which punishment he would continue to suffer through all eternity.

"We can hope," he said to Catherine as he held her to him. "We can hope that in the last terrible moments, the wind howling about him, the storm raging, eternity opening—that the miracle happened, and he knew and accepted the sublime goodness of God."

"Hope!" It was such a feeble word. Hattie, watching and listening, heard the lack of conviction in her father's voice as well as Catherine did. It was a completely changed Catherine who beat at her father's chest, who clutched at his hands as she pleaded with him, or who turned from him to walk back and forth, distracted. Her mind was filled with visions that hundreds and hundreds of sermons had made unbearably clear. Her beloved was burning, endlessly burning, but was still unconsumed. He was racked and tortured, but still sustained for further torture by a God who had only one use for him now, that he be strengthened to endure tortures otherwise intolerable.

"But he was so good—so good in every way. His mind was all nobility."

It was no use. Lyman could only allow "hope." If he was cruel, it was not because he wanted to be, but because he had to be, caught as he was by the demands of the doctrine he preached, pushed to its logical extremes.

Three hundred years earlier, John Calvin, in Switzerland, reacting against a Catholic Church that had become corrupt and soft, had turned to the Bible itself and wrested from it the doctrine that held Lyman—a doctrine that had a strangely wide and irresistible appeal, considering its harshness and ferocity. God was not a Being whose indulgence could be won by the intercession of priests or saints, as the Catholic church was teaching. Man could not buy or pray his way into Paradise. God was omnipotent and implacable, and He had created all mankind "under His wrath and curse."

All her life Hattie Beecher had been hearing about this God, listening dreamily and without comprehension as her father preached about Him in the Meeting House, elaborating on His mysterious demands upon men. Now, as tragedy struck at Catherine, and the workings of this God were the cause of such anguish, she still did not wholly comprehend the logical structure that her father was trying to force her sister to accept. But she did begin to realize for the first time, in a vague but overpowering way, that all men were prisoners, bound, long before their birth, to an inexorable destiny.

In His great plan for the world, the plan that preceded creation, all, all had been known beforehand, all preordained. God had *known* that the very first man, Adam, would sin, and in his fall carry with him the whole human race. God had known that all mankind thereafter would be born full of such depravity that the tortures of Hell would be the only fitting punishment. Still, in His immense goodness and pity, He had elected that *some* souls should be spared those tortures to enjoy Paradise with Him. It was all done—done and finished and over—before Adam first woke in the Garden of Eden . . . "eternal life . . . fore-ordained for some, and eternal damnation for others. . . ." There was nothing man could do.

And yet there was something man *had* to do. And if this dilemma of everything being settled and yet not *quite* being settled was bewildering to young Hattie Beecher it was not surprising. Seventy-five years before, the whole church of New England, built on Calvin's doctrine, had almost floundered on the contradiction. But then brilliant Jonathan Edwards had bent his immense intellect to the problem and woven a new web of logic so firm and tight that the church had felt a new surge of life, and two generations later, Lyman Beecher was still bound in its network.

There was something man *had* to do, sealed as his destiny was since before creation. Every individual had to descend agonizingly to a full acceptance of God's plan and be willing to rejoice even in his own damnation, if that was what God had willed for him. Only then, if he *was* one of those God had elected, would Divine Grace come to his assistance and inform him of the fact. Then, with a sense of joy and rapture, he would know he was saved. It was a knowledge that was somehow required before salvation was certain, in spite of everything having been settled before creation.

This was where the agony lay for Catherine Beecher. Professor Fisher had never admitted to any such knowledge or "conviction" of his own salvation. Professor Fisher had never even, so far as anyone knew, begun to work his way to an acceptance of God's will. His mind filled with science and poetry and music and history, he had neglected the matter that should have been his chief concern, the matter that was surely the chief concern of every living mortal. This was why Lyman could only offer a *hope* that he might have compressed into those last, few hectic moments of shipwreck and onrushing disaster the intensive reflections and surrenders that usually took weeks, months or years to achieve.

"But he was so good. . . ."

But "natural goodness" was heresy to Calvinist logic. Could puny man, created in wrath, have a *natural* goodness of his own to move a Creator who had infused him with depravity through every part of his being? Lyman had fought out that point with Roxana, years and years before, when he was courting her, but had determined he could not marry her unless he could wrest her from her family faith, Episcopalianism. Could he yield to his daughter in her extremity, much as he loved her, any more than he could have yielded to Roxana, even more dearly loved, twenty-three years before?

By 1822 many people had turned at last in horror from the logic of this Puritan God. In some churches of Europe, a totally opposite doctrine was being preached, and had been, almost since the days of Calvin himself—a doctrine called Unitarianism. Its creed denied that God was three persons (Father, Son and Holy Ghost) as the Calvinists believed, and held that God was one—

hence the name, Unitarianism. But its special charms to those appalled by Calvinism lay in everything else about Calvinism that it rejected. By the late eighteenth century the relief it offered had begun to be accepted in some places in America. In Boston, especially, a tidal wave of Unitarianism had begun to build. By 1822, a young Oliver Wendell Holmes had learned from his gentle mother that God was not a God of wrath, but a God of love, a Father who had created men as His children, and that men were not essentially evil but essentially good.

But Unitarianism was and always had been to Lyman "a fire in his bones," an arrogant attempt by man to minimize God's majesty. And there were thousands and thousands more like Lyman Beecher, all over America, held fast by the old faith, held by the hairsplitting logic its ministers preached, and gripped even more surely by visions of the literal Hell's fire that logic made so inevitable.

When Harriet wrote later about the particular kind of anguish that could follow a sudden, tragic death, there would be thousands to thrill to the reality of that suffering, its details piled page on page. They too had known it and envisioned loved ones, snatched into eternity before conviction, burning and tortured in Hell. In the 1820s, when they had been young, like Hattie, rebellion against it was unthinkable to most of them.

When Hattie was eleven and her sister Catherine's life broke in two, rebellion was still unthinkable to Hattie. It was incredibly shocking when Catherine did at last cry out:

"*I cannot—I will not be resigned!*"

How could Catherine utter such words? They would only damn her as Professor Fisher was undoubtedly damned.

"I can never love such a God—never praise Him."

Harriet watched the struggle between her father and sister. Tirelessly, Lyman reasoned with Catherine, trying to save her soul in this crisis. Sometimes it seemed she listened to him and would go away, quieted. She would sit at the table, composing an elegiac poem to Professor Fisher, or writing letters to his family, begging them to think if they had not noticed some signs of conviction in their son. Or she would write to her brother Edward, the second oldest Beecher boy, off at Yale, and planning to be a minister himself, asking him to tell her there was more than hope for Professor Fisher's soul.

Then Catherine would be up again, running to her father's study, over one of the ells of the house, crying out again the rebellion she could not suppress.

"What if a father should act so to his child—making it certain he should be an abandoned wretch, while giving him the illusion of free will? Oh, it is not right. It cannot be right. I cannot be resigned!"

Finally, to the benefit of everyone else's sanity, Catherine went away for a while to visit Professor Fisher's family in Massachusetts. It seemed hardly the place to benefit her own sanity and to help her in some measure to forget. But Catherine did not want to forget. Her rebellion, having begun, had caught her in a whirlwind. As relentlessly as her father and all his Calvinist forebears had worked out their logic of damnation, she was going to work out some logic to refute it.

It would take a long time. She would be completely changed from the breezy, cheerful girl she had been by the time she had achieved it, but the search had begun.

By the middle of the century, thousands of Americans would have taken the same path, rejecting the Puritan God of wrath to find a God of love, modifying the Calvinist doctrines so they could find a loving God in their own churches. When Harriet wrote for them, "I *cannot* be resigned," they would hear the echo of their own desperate voices. Harriet would long since have taken the same path herself, but Catherine was the first of the Beechers to tread it.

With Catherine's departure, there was a sigh of relief in the Beecher household. Life could resume its normal course, not quite so wracked with emotion. And there were, it turned out, one or two reminders of Professor Fisher that were not wholly distressing.

He had made Catherine his heir. This meant, for one thing, that she had a legacy of two thousand dollars. He had also left her his library and all his notes and papers. While she stayed on, month after month, with his family, she packed up his books and sent them to Litchfield to be held for her there.

Lyman opened the boxes in his study. The doubts that had been raised about Professor Fisher's orthodoxy, made Lyman think it wise to look over the books before allowing his children access to them. He soon discovered there were novels among them, and contemporary novels had always been forbidden to the young Beechers. But then he saw that some of these novels had been written by an author whom he had heard praised by various thoughtful men and women. He decided to glance through them before putting them away.

He plunged down the stairs from his study, a few hours later, hair on end, face alight, to announce to one and all that the ban on *one* writer's novels had been lifted.

And so the books of Sir Walter Scott came into young Harriet's life, to be read and reread and almost memorized as the other treasures had been, and to add their deposit of rich Gothic adventures to the other melodrama stored in her mind. With books like these to read, with school to attend, chores to do, and her own private dreams to dream, the shadow that Catherine's tragedy had revealed to her began to retreat a little.

Catherine was different when she finally returned home. She talked very little about her loss. The problem of refuting the God of wrath had become a private one. Her conversations with her father concerned her plans for the future. She had decided to use the legacy Professor Fisher had left her to start a girl's school. She did not like teaching but it was the only "sphere of usefulness" open to a woman.

Hartford was the town she chose as the site for her new venture. Edward, graduated from Yale in June, was headmaster of a boy's school there, and various inquiries had shown the city was a likely place for a girl's school. Arrangements progressed rapidly. Mary, the second Beecher daughter, pretty, quick and popular, and in her last year at Miss Pierce's Academy, would leave that school and go with Catherine to Hartford, to be the first and, at the moment, only member of the teaching staff. By spring, both of them were gone.

But the problem of the soul and what happened to it after death had entered Hattie's consciousness never to leave. However calmly the routine of her life went on, thoughts about that mystery kept recurring. And when, two years later, she suddenly distinguished herself in the eyes of her family and the whole town, this was still the subject that was engaging her.

Afterward, she liked to remember that during the course of the school year previous she had paid particular attention to the lessons of the English instructor at Miss Pierce's Academy, John P. Brace. He taught the older girls but Hattie remembered listening from the back of the room as he spoke to them about style, construction and the value of having something definite to say before one embarked on a composition. Whether these precepts had anything to do with it or not, at the end of the school year she made her first appearance as a writer—a writer winning public recognition for her efforts.

The closing exercises of Miss Pierce's Academy were a town event in Litchfield. Her father sat on the platform along with Miss Pierce, John Brace and other teachers and local dignitaries. A portion of the program displayed the accomplishments of the Academy's students. And suddenly, as this part of the program proceeded, Hattie heard someone reading aloud one of her own compositions.

When the reading was over, Hattie saw her father, with a pleased look on his face, turn to Mr. Brace and ask a question. Mr. Brace smiled and pointed in her direction. Then Hattie was basking in one of her father's proudest, most radiant smiles. For once she had captured all his attention and shown herself capable of doing something that singled her out from the others. From now on, writing would always be the thing *she* could do, the talent she could turn to when she sought to discover just who she was.

The future of the soul was the subject she had dealt with in this fateful composition. Still, in spite of the terrors evoked at the time of Catherine's tragedy, she had not written a gloomy piece. Running away from the spectacle of souls moving inexorably to damnation, she had found a happier aspect on which to dwell, and turned to that part of the Calvinist doctrine which counter-

balanced the grim despair of the "unelected." Jesus was the figure
of hope, the one through whom men knew God's goodness and
pity, "in Whom" men were elected. The Gospels of the New
Testament revealed His message of salvation to the "elected."

The title of her essay sounded formidable enough. "Can the
Immortality of the Soul Be Proved by the Light of Nature?"
But Hattie knew exactly where the question would take her. All
her life she had been listening to supper-table debates, started
and kept bouncing from argument to counterargument by Lyman, who hoped to sharpen his sons' wits for the ministry.
Many themes were tossed about in this forum, topics Lyman had
debated when he was a fledgling at Yale. "Has Christianity really
benefited civilization?" "Can war be condoned on any grounds?"
"Are the abilities of the sexes equal?" And, yes, "Can the immortality of the soul, etc." had been one of the topics too. Hattie
had heard the question argued many times, listening as her father
chopped down any proofs of immortality that came from outside
the Bible with the same logic that proved predestination. Still,
she had arranged the arguments in her own fashion for her composition, had neatly balanced argument and rebuttal, and had
chosen lively examples.

"The first argument which has been advanced to prove the immortality of the soul" she wrote, "is drawn from the nature of the
mind itself. It has (say the supporters of this theory) no composition of parts, and therefore, as there are no particles, is not
susceptible of divisibility and cannot be acted upon by decay,
and therefore if it will not decay it will last forever."

She countered this argument with the rebuttal that even if the
mind did not decay in the ordinary way, that offered "no proof
that that same omnipotent power which created it cannot by
another simple exertion of power again reduce it to nothing."

She took up the argument that the benevolence of the Creator
would not have formed man "with such vast capacities and
boundless desires . . . and given him no opportunity of exercising
them," and disposed of that one as an attempt to arraign "the
'All-wise' before the tribunal of his subjects to answer for the
mistakes in his government." The great desire of the soul for immortality, its innate horror of death, the theory that the mind

was constantly progressing in its powers, the activity of the mind at the moment of death, the fact that all nations had some conceptions of a future state—these arguments were advanced in turn and briskly refuted.

At last, she arrived at the one aspect of religion that one could contemplate in joy:

"The sun of the Gospel has dispelled the darkness that has rested on objects beyond the tomb. In the Gospel man learned that when the dust returned to dust the spirit fled to the God who gave it. He there found that though man has lost the image of his divine Creator, he is still destined, after this earthly house of his tabernacle is dissolved, to an inheritance incorruptible, undefiled, and that fadeth not away, to a house not made with hands, eternal in the heavens."

Already, at thirteen, she was striking the theme to which she would return all her life—"this earthly house" was a fleeting one, man was destined for "a house not made with hands." And already she was writing with surprising clarity, power and command of language. Lyman had reason to kiss her proudly.

So Hattie banished the shadow of predestined damnation and had a public triumph as well, and was, for a while, a little girl astonishingly pretty, her cheeks flushed, her big, gray-blue eyes bright and sparkling.

The shadow fell across the sun again a little later that same month. Her father brought the news, and when he spoke it seemed to her his voice tolled like a bell.

"Byron is dead—gone!" he said.

It was a sharper blow than the news of Professor Fisher's death. Byron was more real to her than Professor Fisher, his image the central one in her heart.

"I am sorry," her father said. "I did hope he would live to do something for Christ. What a harp he would have swept!" Lyman stood silent and thoughtful, seeing nothing incongruous in a vision of that mocking cavalier sweeping a golden harp. He sighed and went on, "Oh, if Byron could only have talked with Taylor and me, it might have got him out of his troubles."

Hattie looked at her father and she saw nothing absurd in the statement either. If only Byron could have come to Litchfield and sat quietly in her father's study, with its view out over the folding Berkshires, if only he could have listened while her father spoke to him eloquently and pleadingly, indeed his soul might have been saved and he in Paradise, instead of—where?

Hattie was thirteen. The fear and dread the shadow inspired would retreat once again. But then they would come back to lie across her soul for a long, long time.

Chapter 4

There was a restlessness in the air. A time of transition was coming to the country. The long, placid period that had followed the War of 1812 was over. The growing was not over. The growing, the expanding, would go on even more swiftly and dramatically. But the placidity was gone. The serenity of the scene where everyone had been able to labor harmoniously for one common goal—unifying the nation—had been disrupted. With each outthrust of growth, new elements entered the picture—new needs, problems, loyalties. New states in the Union had brought new types and faces to Washington, D.C., to speak for those needs and loyalties—men from the west, Kentucky, Indiana, Illinois, men from the frontiers, both north and south.

In 1824, two decades influenced by Jefferson, the first Democratic-Republican, were ending. Everyone in the Presidential race that year was still *calling* himself a Republican, still publicly holding to the creed of nationalism, but the very attempt to pretend nothing had changed and that one party could contain all the new and varying points of view that had arisen, turned the campaign into a bitter, bruising battle of personalities. The new faces, the new types, were part of a Presidential campaign for the first time. The governmental dynasty of aristocratic gentlemen and Virginia planters that had existed since the birth of the nation was almost over. Henry Clay—"young Harry out of the West"—handsome, eloquent, audacious Henry Clay from Kentucky, was one of the candidates, a new sort of Presidential contender altogether. So was General Andrew Jackson, rough, self-educated product of the frontier. Only William Crawford represented the Virginia dynasty. Only John Quincy Adams, son of the second President, and a man cold, stiff, but devoted to duty and country, repre-

sented the old New England line. John C. Calhoun from the
rough hill country of inland South Carolina, had hoped to be one
of the candidates too, but outmaneuvered, he had fallen back
to try for the Vice-Presidency.

New types, wrought in new environments, wrestled for power,
and in the end, after the election, the confusion the whole country was beginning to feel about its future was manifest. No candidate had a majority. There were indications of how the wind
was blowing. Andrew Jackson, the backwoodsman, plain-spoken,
plain-thinking, had the most electoral votes, fifteen more than
Adams, the runner-up. Then when the unsettled election was
turned over to the House of Representatives for a decision, Henry
Clay, the Speaker of the House, and chief wielder of its power,
threw his vote to Adams. He thought Adams would not be too
popular and, as a result, it would be easier to win victory himself
in 1828.

And so, in 1825, John Quincy Adams was inaugurated President, and for four more years the country would know the cool,
careful administration of a New Englander. Adams made no
friends among Jackson's supporters by naming Henry Clay his
Secretary of State (and he did not help Clay's chances in 1828
either). And it would only increase the tension and the restlessness of the next four years for Adams to hold to the course of
nationalism, already threatening to special interests, South, West
and East.

Trouble was simmering. The tariff, cement to the Union, was
gravel to the South, putting a premium on the manufactured
goods no one had time to produce there, so busy was everyone
raising and selling cotton. Adams had plans to use Federal funds
for all kinds of national benefits, not only for the building of national roads and canals, but to finance scientific expeditions and
establish centers of learning and research. The South, already
feeling a jealous nervousness about slavery, began to wonder if
granting Federal powers of such scope might not lead in time
to the possibility of Federal interference with its "peculiar institution."

But pride and optimism in the achievements of the young
nation were there also. In 1825, Governor De Witt Clinton of

New York presided at "The Wedding of the Waters," when the Great Lakes were united to the Hudson River, and the Atlantic Ocean, by the Erie Canal. "May the God of the heavens and the earth smile propitiously on this work and render it subservient to the best interests of the human race," he intoned. And he poured five gallons of water, brought in a keg by flatboat from Lake Erie, into the Atlantic.

Digging for other canals was still going on. The Cumberland Road was stretching farther and farther to the West. An experiment in laying railroad tracks across a mountain was undertaken west of Baltimore, though few people elsewhere had any clear idea of what a railway was. Everywhere, the stretching out, the reaching forth, were continuing as eagerly as ever. New lands might indeed bring new problems, unsettling much that had been taken for granted before, but that deterred no one from moving on.

Amid so much that was new, so much bustle and building, some ties with the past still held. America, the growing young nation, remained under the shadow of Europe so far as art, music and literature were concerned. A few native writers had appeared— James Fenimore Cooper, Washington Irving—to picture for their fellow Americans, and curious Europeans, the new American scene. A few painters were at work, in Boston and Philadelphia and in Washington, D.C., turning out heroic portraits of America's great men. But most books still came from England, or Germany, or France. Here and there in America, men, and women too, tried their skill at versifying. But all *real* poets were overseas, or so everyone felt. America was still very young indeed when it came to the arts and was content to listen to the voices from abroad.

When young Harriet Beecher grieved for Byron in 1824, all America was grieving for him. It did not harm his legend that the Greek cause, for which he had been fighting when he died of fever in Missolonghi, was very popular in America. The French Revolution had roused bitter partisan feeling, but almost everyone in the United States was united in sympathy for Greece, struggling to throw off the yoke of despotic rule.

"The mountains look on Marathon—
And Marathon looks on the sea;
And musing there an hour alone,
I dream'd that Greece might still be free;"

Byron's lines could bring tears to thousands of American eyes, so easy was it to compare the Greek struggle to America's own fight for independence.

Sympathy for Greece invaded all aspects of life. Architecture, something that very few people had had time or money to consider previously, suddenly became a more general concern when it was discovered how simple it was to add a "Grecian" influence to a building. Colonnades were slapped onto the fronts of houses everywhere, onto farmhouses as well as more pretentious town buildings. The Grecian Revival was under way.

Settlers, moving out on all the new roads to the wilderness, took their sympathy with Greece along with them and christened their raw new villages with Greek names like Ypsilanti or Chios. And the study of Greek was revived in schools.

In 1824, the year of the election that ended the tenure of Presidents in the Jeffersonian succession, Thomas Jefferson, eighty-one years old, was putting the finishing touches on his "academical village" in Charlottesville, Virginia. Colonnades had been part of his original design for the university buildings long before they took America by storm. Jefferson, as steeped in the arts as he was in politics, had been aware of architecture since the days of his young manhood. But the chief beauty to him of the beautiful university he was building was still in the idea it embodied. It was to be a school supported by the state, not the church, a school that could be free of the overpowering emphasis on theology that characterized every other institution of higher learning in the country. Young men could study all the sciences at the University of Virginia, agriculture too, he hoped. They could study everything, letting their minds roam the world. "And ye shall know the truth and the truth shall make ye free," was the motto he had chosen for his University, to be engraved over the classic colonnade that fronted his domed central building.

Jefferson would be dead in 1826—dead on the same day as his

long-time friend and enemy, John Adams, in Massachusetts, once President himself, father of the current President. The men who had presided at the birth of the new nation were almost all gone now. Only their ideas would still live on, to be followed eagerly by some, and quarreled over bitterly by others.

In 1824 in Weimar, Germany, another very old man was embarking on a work that would also leave its mark on the thinking of the new century and the new country across the sea. At seventy-five, Goethe was starting work on the final sections of his masterpiece, *Faust*, the sections that would build to a climax his great theme that man found immortality for his soul by doing good for others.

It was not a theme that Lyman Beecher in Litchfield, Connecticut, stubbornly resistant to any belief that "natural goodness" could help man, would find congenial. But his daughter, Catherine, fighting the doctrine of damnation, would welcome it. And so, in time, would all his other children, growing up along with the century.

So would the whole new nation, growing and expanding and building on the American continent. For busy as it was, restless as it was, with little time for philosophy at home, it would still heed the paternal voice in these matters, coming from overseas.

Chapter 5

Then has a new flower blossomed in the Kingdom this day....

That Harriet should have been full of contradictions was hardly surprising. Her father, Lyman Beecher, lived in contradiction, serenely unaware of it most of the time, completely blind to the fact that he often was holding two opposing points of view at once.

He saw nothing funny about himself, and yet he was always seeing something funny about himself. He might find nothing incongruous in declaring he could have saved Byron's soul. And yet, when someone mentioned how loudly he had spoken during one sermon, he could say, "Oh yes, the less I have to say the more I holler." And he was forever making similarly pungent remarks that were fondly quoted not only by his parishioners but by a wider audience as well.

"Once I threw a book at a skunk," he said, when someone challenged him to answer an attacker, "and he had the best of it. I made up my mind never to try it again."

His talk was peppered with analogies from the woods and streams. Bursting with life himself, dedicated to saving souls for eternal life, he was at the same time passionately addicted to hunting and fishing, dealing out death to deer, rabbits, birds and fish with the excitement of a boy. Hunting and soul-saving seemed confused in his mind. He "took aim and fired" at sinners in his congregation. And he said, "I don't mind when I see tail feathers fly. It means I've hit my bird."

There were also times when he neatly transformed the awful God of whom he preached into a folksy friend of the family, seeing no incongruity in that either. "He sent the ravens to feed

Elijah. He won't forget us now," he would say cheerfully when
the proprietor of the General Store started pressing for some payment on the minister's grocery bill. It did not seem unlikely to
him that an omnipotent God, lost in majestic contemplation of
the universe He had created, should take time out to make sure
Lyman Beecher, in Litchfield, Connecticut, would be able to pay
a little something on account.

So it was only in the pattern of her own contradictions and
her father's that when Hattie came to her own conversion it was
anything but the fearsome, mystical business most people made
of it, and her father accepted it as lightly and easily as she
achieved it.

She had had a very happy year before it happened, a year
full of new experiences, new scenes, new pleasures. In the summer of 1824, Catherine and Mary came home from Hartford
pleased to report that after a year's existence Catherine's school
appeared to have every prospect of success. Catherine had
rented a couple of rooms over a harness store. Fifteen young
ladies had enrolled for the school's first session. More had enrolled in the fall, and more still were expected in the coming fall.
The only difficulty was in the heavy teaching load it meant for
Catherine and Mary. With each student paying only six dollars
tuition a quarter, it would be a while before Catherine could hire
more teachers.

Catherine's eye fell on Harriet. Perhaps Hattie should come
with her and Mary to Hartford in the fall to attend the new
school. There they could train her intensively so she would be
able to teach a class or two herself by the next year.

Small, shy, and only a schoolgirl herself, Hattie made no protest. Catherine had been telling her what to do for years. Since
her bereavement Catherine had become even more authoritative.
So, in September, a small trunk was packed for Harriet, and she
was with her sisters, Kate and Mary, in the stagecoach when it
started for Hartford, thirty miles away.

Hattie was impressed by Hartford, a city of five thousand, with
all sorts of shops lining its main street and the imposing State
House rising above them. She was excited when she saw the sign

of the two white horses over the harness store. Above that store
with its sign was Catherine's school. Even more pleasing was the
room where she was going to stay, boarding with a Mr. and Mrs.
Bull. It was a room she would occupy by herself, for the first time
in her life, and so she never noticed that it was small, with a
minimum of necessities, bed and bureau, table and chair. It was
spankingly neat and clean, and all her life Hattie would remember the pleasure she took in keeping it so, making up her bed
each morning and smoothing down the coverlet with "awful satisfaction."

The school was something else again, at least at first. The chat-
ter, the giggling, the general commotion raised by twenty-five
"young ladies" was alarming to a shy stranger. But Catherine,
managerial though she might be, was not without sympathy.
While they were still in Litchfield, she had written to two of her
students, asking them to write her young sister letters of welcome.
This they had done, and now the same two students detached
themselves from the general twittering group to introduce themselves to Hattie.

One of them was named Catharine Cogswell. She was the pret-
tiest girl in the school, the gayest and most popular, and Hattie
at once felt nothing but blind adoration. It was the first of a series
of crushes the emotional Hattie would have throughout the rest
of her school days, and now and then throughout all her life.
The other girl was plainer and quieter than Catharine. Her name
was Georgiana May, and though initially she made the lesser
impression on Hattie, it was she would become Hattie's real
friend.

Having a friend was the best part of the first year at Hartford
for Hattie. Catharine Cogswell added the glamour, dancing from
one group to another, finding time for Hattie every so often. But
Georgiana was there beside her whenever Hattie wanted her, offering a kind of friendship Hattie had never known, loyal, interested, admiring.

As a result, Hattie shone for Georgiana. When lessons were
over (and there were long hours of lessons for Hattie, who was
being crammed with Latin to prepare her to teach it, as well
as following the regular schedule of courses), then she and Geor-

giana went walking together, oftenest finding their way to the quiet, tree-bordered banks of Hartford's Park River. Hattie talked and talked as she had never talked to anybody in her life, telling Georgiana of the books she had read, the poetry she had loved, the genius of Byron, and how her father might have saved him had things been ordered differently. And it was to Georgiana she confessed the ambition that had been hers ever since the triumph of her essay. Some day she was going to be a great writer, a poet, most preferably.

Georgiana agreed to everything without question. She also agreed, during these walks by the river, that this sylvan setting was a perfect place for a home. Some day when she and Hattie were both famous, they would return here and build their homes.

Some forty years later, when the first part of Hattie's ambition had come true beyond her most extravagant dreams, Harriet would do just that. She would come back to the grove by the Park River—though it would no longer be quite so unspoiled—and she would insist on making that part of a childhood dream come true, building a rich and elaborate home there.

Still a schoolgirl, Hattie set to work to become a writer. Alone in her bedroom at Mrs. Bull's, she embarked on a heroically-scaled tragedy in verse. Night after night, she sat at her small table, the candle flickering, and her pen raced along as she filled page after page of her notebook with rocking iambic pentameters.

The scene of her drama, no trouble at all for her to imagine, was Nero's court in ancient Rome. Her hero gave her no trouble either. Who should he be but Byron, her first love? He was Byron disguised as a rich Athenian and Olympic champion named Cleon, a favorite of Nero's, and a man who, for all his gifts, was spending himself in dissipated, luxurious living:

"Diversion is his labour, and he works
 With hand and foot and soul both night and day:
 He throws out money with so flush a hand
 As makes e'en Nero's waste seem parsimony."

Harriet was pleased by the ease with which the rhythms came to her mind, but she was exalted by a new power she was discovering. In writing she could do what her father had not been

able to do in real life. She could convert this Greek Byron to
sweep a harp for Christ. She took on the task eagerly, inventing
an aged Greek Christian to wrestle and reason for Cleon's soul.
At last she was leading Cleon from his "luxurious slough" down
the slopes of anguish and torment she had heard described so
often, until finally, in a moment of blinding joy, he became "utterly convicted."

But this was only the beginning. Nero had to discover the
shocking change in his onetime favorite, had to send him to the
torture chambers in a rage, and then relent a little and try persuasion on the martyr, persuasion which the redeemed Cleon
would nobly and righteously resist. How was it all going to end?

Harriet never found out, for just as Cleon was about to sweep
his harp for Christ, Catherine paid an unexpected visit, discovered the notebooks, and stopped the whole literary endeavor.

"If you have this much leisure," Catherine said, "you may use
the time better by beginning the study of Butler's *Analogy of
Religion* and preparing yourself to teach it next fall."

It was the clearest sign yet of the new Catherine, who was
emerging from the wreck of her young dreams to build a different sort of world for herself, stern, revolutionary, ceaselessly
active. Gradually, in spite of the endless details of managing and
teaching school, she was formulating a new concept of God, a
God who had not arbitrarily doomed nine-tenths of mankind to
damnation, but a God who was moved by good character and
good works (as He *must* have been moved by the good character
and good works of Professor Fisher). It was an almost heretical
softening of the old creed, but in working her way toward it
Catherine's own character had hardened. She forgot her own
early joy in writing poetry. She had no pang of sympathy for
Hattie's efforts or hurt eyes. If God was not a God who had
foredoomed man, but a God willing to allow every man to prove
himself worthy of salvation, then it behooved everybody to be up
and stirring, making himself worthy. Enough of dreaming. The
watchword was work, work to achieve one's own election!

Harriet saw Nero's court dissolving, her handsome hero vanishing, his greatest chord for Christ unswept. She did not even
close the notebook to put it away, but began dutifully right after

the abrupt fracture in her drama to make notes on Butler's *Analogy* as instructed. And that was the end of Cleon.

But Georgiana was still there to talk with and walk with in the few free moments Catherine allowed Hattie. There was even a certain satisfaction for Hattie in seeing how well she could master the intricacies of Butler. In Latin, she had progressed so rapidly that although she had begun with basic grammar in the fall, by spring she was writing her own translation of Ovid. This achievement Catherine greeted with approval, deeming the verses good enough to be read at the school's closing exercises in June.

Hattie said good-bye to Georgiana and Catharine Cogswell and her other new friends, and, with Kate and Mary, boarded the stage for Litchfield. It was in the next month, in Litchfield, that she came so lightly and impetuously to her conversion.

Litchfield was at its summer best, full of the scent of hay and roses. The great trees dappled North Street with spangles of sun and shade as Harriet walked beneath them on her way to the Meeting House one Sunday. She knew it was a Communion Sunday, the one Sunday of the month that always separated the elect from the unconverted—only those who had been "under conviction" of their own salvation could go up to the communion table, spread with its white cloth, and partake of the bread and wine laid out there. She felt a recurring regret that she was still among the outsiders and wondered when the hour would come that she would be overwhelmed by a conviction of her sins, the necessary first step to discovering if she had been elected. She sighed. She had put Cleon through all these paces but had never had any glimmerings of the same feelings herself.

In the Meeting House, she sat half-listening, as always. Then something about her father's voice caught her attention. He was not speaking in his usual didactic manner as a teacher, pursuing some intricate thread of reasoning back and forth to its conclusion. His voice was suddenly soft and warm, and Hattie knew he was preaching what he called a "frame sermon," not a sermon written out in advance, but one that was springing spontaneously from some deep feeling.

She began really to listen. Her father was talking about Jesus as a *friend*, a soul-friend, and returning again and again to his text, "Behold, I call you no longer servants, but friends."

Was it because the word "friend" had meaning for her at last that it caught her so? At any rate, as her father spoke on and on, telling his congregation of how patient Christ was with man's errors, how compassionate with his weakness, and how ready he was to supply every need, Hattie's heart began to swell.

"Come then, and trust your soul to this faithful friend!" her father cried.

Yearning to answer, "I will," Hattie had what seemed like a blinding revelation. If Jesus could supply her every need, he could supply her sense of sin as well. He could supply her "conviction." It was the same as done. It was done. With a deep breath, she realized she had passed the mystic moment and was among the saved.

That afternoon she hurried shyly up the stairs to her father's study, ran over to him as he sat at his desk by the window and fell on her knees beside him.

"Father, I have given myself to Jesus and He has taken me."

Lyman looked down at her. Then, as she always remembered it, he said softly, "Is it so? Then has a new flower blossomed in the Kingdom this day." He caught her to him and kissed her, and Hattie saw tears in his eyes—happy tears, shed for *her!*

How was it that Lyman, so unyielding in Catherine's great sorrow, so ruthless in exacting the last ounce of torment from Roxana years ago, when she strove for "conviction," was ready to accept young Harriet's announcement so easily? How was it, for that matter, that he could preach most of the time of a terrible God of wrath, and then turn to talk so winningly of a gentle Jesus? It was his own secret.

He thought of himself as one who would "follow Truth if it took him over Niagara." Still he could be both for and against free will, a believer in both predestination and immediate repentance, and could straddle, on various stilts of logic, all the issues that were soon going to split the Presbyterian Church (allied so closely with the Congregational Church in those days that a minister in one was a minister in the other, at will).

Whatever it was that moved him to accept Hattie's conversion so instantly, though others of his children might moan and pray for days, it was done. His kiss, his tears, wiped away any doubts Hattie might have had. It did not even trouble her that Catherine was skeptical. Catherine spoke sharply and skeptically about many things these days.

Catherine looked at Hattie, raised her eyebrows, and wondered aloud that a lamb could so easily be brought to the fold "without being first chased all over the lot by the shepherd." This observation simply caused Lyman to raise his eyebrows in return at his rebellious oldest, whom he loved as dearly as ever, but whose remarks were daily becoming more questionable.

Harriet's conversion inaugurated a cheerful summer, even though there were more chores with a new baby in the Beecher cradle. The previous fall, Mrs. Beecher had given birth to a son, christened Thomas, and Harriet had to help with his care, as well as with that of Isabella. But she was fourteen years old, and there were various festivities to which she might go, along with Mary, when chores were over. Horseboat excursions were a new kind of entertainment on Bantam Lake in the valley below the Beecher house. Then there were hayrides and country suppers and picnics with hams and chickens and pickles and cake to eat.

It was the last unclouded summer Harriet would know in a long time. In the fall would come the reaction, a reaction that would sweep away her self-assurance for years. Her conversion had been the business of the tulip bulbs all over again. She had not been eating onions, as she thought, but something else entirely.

Hattie returned to Hartford in September, with Catherine and Mary, eager to see her friends, and not too alarmed that this fall, young as she was, she would be teaching as well as studying, imparting some of last year's crammed knowledge to girls older than herself. Before she left home, her father had suggested that she join the First Congregational Church in Hartford, since she was going to be away from home so much in the future. So, with

Georgiana May and Catharine Cogswell to keep her company on
the way, Hattie had gone to the church, and made her way to
the pastor's study to present her application for membership.

The divine listened to her gravely as she told him of her conversion, was silent a moment, and then gazed at her.

"Tell me, Harriet, do you feel that if the universe should be
destroyed, you could be happy with God alone?"

Hattie felt a premonition of disaster. She had been listening to
questions like this all her life, but the minister's voice was so
solemn as he asked her that it was as though she had never heard
such an idea before. The universe destroyed? Could she really
imagine it?

"Yes, sir,"she said.

"You realize, I trust," the preacher went on, "in some measure
at least, the deceitfulness of your heart, and that in punishment
for your sins God might justly leave you to make yourself as miserable as you have made yourself sinful?"

"Yes, sir," Harriet whispered.

At this answer, the preacher nodded, smiled, and welcomed
her into the church.

But it was all a dream to Hattie by then. In a dream, her eyes
wide, her face pale, she went out to join Georgiana and Catharine, and the preacher's questions had changed the whole look
of the day. It seemed bleak and chill, and she had no answers to
Georgiana's questions about how it had been. "You realize, I trust,
in some measure, at least, the deceitfulness of your heart . . ."
The words echoed and reechoed and filled her with growing
alarm.

Why? What was so fateful about the questions? They *were*
familiar. She had been raised with them. Was it because deep
inside she was aware of some "deceitfulness of heart" in allowing
her conversion to be so easy? "In punishment for your sins . . ."
She had been relying on Jesus, her soul-friend, to give her a conviction of those sins, but somehow or other, she had never felt
any such conviction and had actually forgotten the matter. Was
it just an awakening to questions she should have asked herself
before that tumbled her so abruptly from happiness to misery?
Or was it simply because she was fourteen?

Whatever the reason, the terrible years had begun, years
that Harriet would never write about in any of her books, skip-
ping all her heroines lightly from happy girlhood to serene young
womanhood, or else wafting them to Heaven while they were
still in the bloom of childish innocence. The writing that told anything about those painful, adolescent years was done while she
was in the midst of them, in the letters she wrote to anyone she
thought would listen to her outpourings of woe.

Chapter 6

I wish I could die young and let the remembrance of me and my faults perish in the grave, rather than live, a trouble to everyone.

1826–1828

Once really devoted to looking for sin in oneself, it was not so difficult to discover it. Every gesture one made, every thought one thought, could be traced to some sinful origin.

"My whole life is one continued struggle," Hattie wrote to Edward, kind, handsome brother Edward, now at Andover Theological Seminary, finishing his training for the ministry.

Catherine's school was doing so well that a move had to be made from the rooms over the harness store to larger quarters. Hattie helped erratically.

"I do nothing right. I yield to temptation almost as soon as it assails me. I am beset before and behind. . . . But that which most constantly besets me is pride. I can trace almost all my sins back to it. . . ."

The school routine swept on, and Hattie was part of it without being part of it. Up at dawn, she was busy all day, with classes in which she was a student and classes which she taught. She was smaller than most of her pupils, younger than several, and the teaching could have been a kind of nightmare. But her mind was so preoccupied with her own feelings—dizziness, weakness, pounding of blood in her ears, her sin in speaking sharply to someone, her sin in not having been aware of it sooner—that the teaching ran along on a different plane. "Now, Miss Cogswell" and "Please try that again, Miss Wilcox" were almost automatic.

Dramatic news came from Litchfield. After seventeen years as minister of the Congregational meeting there, seventeen years of trying vainly for a salary that would enable him to feed and clothe his family decently, Lyman Beecher had decided to leave. He was a preacher famous throughout New England, and he was still making only eight hundred dollars a year. Then, the hand of the Lord never faltering in his affairs, he had scarcely made the decision to look for a new church when a call came from the Hanover Street Church in Boston. The congregation there was willing to pay him two thousand dollars a year.

Boston! Hattie was briefly jarred from her preoccupations. How sad to think that lovely Litchfield would not be her home anymore. What would Boston be like? It was the scene of so much history, but it was also the cradle of that fearful heresy, Unitarianism, which roused her father to such passion. And then, with the vaguest thought of religion, she was back on her sins again, the sins that took away all her happiness.

The projected move was causing an upheaval in Litchfield. A large family was being uprooted, and there was also Aunt Esther to be considered, Lyman's half sister, a kindly, nervous, helping-out spinster aunt who had always been part of the clan. The prospect of change filled Aunt Esther with alarm. Perhaps she should stay on in Litchfield for a while, taking care of the younger boys while the family got settled in Boston. Perhaps she should go to Hartford and keep house for Catherine and Mary and Hattie so they would not have to board. Finally, all the decisions were made. Aunt Esther joined the schoolteaching sisters. The clothing and furniture in Litchfield were packed and shipped off by wagon. The departure for Boston was a reality.

Taking an unfamiliar stage that summer, greeting her family in the new home on Sheaf Street in Boston, Hattie wondered if her father could help her in her misery and give her again the vision of a forgiving Jesus, the soul-friend, whom she had known on her conversion Sunday. But Lyman was busy in his new post, involved in all sorts of church activities, rallying his energies to raise the banners of Calvinism in Boston again, Boston now so indoctrinated with Unitarianism that Harvard had, to all purposes, become a Unitarian school. He had little time for Harriet's anxious questions.

The summer brought a surprise. Edward, graduated from Andover, had at once received a call to a Boston church. Lyman was delighted. Edward was the first of his sons to join him in the hunt for souls. Hattie was briefly cheered by Edward's arrival. He was busy with the problems of his first church, but he found time to talk to her anyway, patiently trying to help her bridge the gap between the God of wrath and Jesus, the soul-friend. Talking with Edward, Hattie could feel a surge of hope for herself. Then she would leave Edward and go back to the house on Sheaf Street, and in no time the comfort would have gone cold.

She stayed on in Boston that fall, but the release from the long hours of studying and teaching was no help. She was as miserable as ever.

Her father had developed what he liked to call a "clinical theology," whereby he claimed he could tell if a parishioner were suffering from "dyspepsia or piety." He had learned to fight his own hypochondria with physical exercise. There being no room in Boston to exert himself in farming activities, he had a huge pile of sand dumped in the cellar of the house. Whenever cramped muscles or a fatigued mind demanded relief, he went down and shoveled sand from one side of the cellar to the other. He installed parallel bars in the yard for further stimulation, and not only chopped the wood for his own house, but offered to chop the neighbors' wood as well.

Somehow, it never occurred to him to practice his "clinical theology" on his pale and troubled daughter, or to urge her into some kind of brisk physical activity. So Hattie muddled around the house, mooning and moody, until Mrs. Beecher spoke out sharply to her. Then she burst into laughter, too loud, too long, and spoke in a voice too high, too shrill. Whenever Lyman did happen to notice her, he was annoyed by her behavior more than anything else. Being morbidly sensitive to everyone's reaction, Hattie knew this, and it only made her behave worse.

Finally she was penning her desperate letter to Catherine: "I wish I could die young, and let the remembrance of me and my faults perish in the grave. . . . You don't know how perfectly wretched I often feel; so useless, so weak, so destitute of all energy. Mama often tells me that I am a strange, inconsistent being. Sometimes I could not sleep, and have groaned and cried till midnight, while in the daytime I tried to appear cheerful and succeeded so well that papa reproved me for laughing so much. I was so absent sometimes that I made strange mistakes, and then they all laughed at me, and I laughed too, though I felt as though I should go distracted. I wrote rules; made out a regular system of dividing my time; but my feelings vary so much that it is almost impossible for me to be regular. . . ."

Catherine was dismayed by the letter. She had moved her expanding school again and even so had a hundred students crammed into rooms in a church basement. She was working on a grand scheme for incorporating her own Academy, selling stock, and building proper quarters for the school. She had enough on her mind, but she was ready to deal with Harriet's unhealthy state as well. It had been a mistake for her to remain in Boston. She wrote the family there that Hattie should return to Hartford.

"If she could come here, it might be the best thing for her, for she can talk freely to me. I can get her books, and Catharine Cogswell, Georgiana May, and her friends here could do more for her than anyone in Boston, for they love her, and she loves them very much."

Books and friends, friends especially—they had made Hattie's first year in Hartford very happy. How had they slipped away from her, become unreal, like everything else except the state of her soul?

Harriet was hardly the first adolescent in the world to drive herself and her family nearly to distraction, nor would she be the last. But the harsh demands of Calvinism, and its endless contradictions, could make the agonies of growing up uniquely painful for an emotional young person. All over America, other young people of sensitive natures were going through similar difficulties. Some were driven to desperate measures. Boys ran away to sea, or to the city, or, despairing of victory over their inherent "depravity," flaunted their sinfulness. Girls, cut off from such active escapes, became prone to hysteria and fainting fits. When, somehow or other, girls and boys managed to creep through the worst of their confusion to some kind of peace, they had an iron in their souls to hold them firm against most self-doubt in the future.

Twenty-five years before Harriet's turmoil, young John Calhoun had been absorbing Calvinist views of life from his father, a roughhewn frontier farmer. "Life is a struggle against evil," he had learned. In the solitude of the South Carolina backcountry and in long hours of hard physical work on the farm, his nature had grown stern, unyielding, and fiercely individualistic, and it would remain so all his life.

Twenty-five years before, in England, young George Gordon, who would become Lord Byron, had also been stamped with the seal of Calvinism. Not by his mother, erratic and emotional, not by his father, the dissipated "Mad Jack" Byron, but by a dour Scotch-Irish nurse. He already knew he was bad. When his mother fell into one of her tempers, she always told him that the clubfoot with which he had been born was proof of his badness. To hear then from his nurse that God had *created* him full of sin was enough to fix his heart toward hopelessness from the beginning. What was the use of trying to be good when he was foredoomed anyway? He was inexorably set on a path of wickedness.

Young Harriet Beecher, in New England, was more fortunate than he. She could remember a happy childhood. A loving family was all around her. Still, her struggle against the sin within her and the punishing God above would go on for years, and even when she felt she was through with it, the melancholic cast of mind it had induced would leave her periodically expecting, even wishing for death.

She went back to Catherine's school and improved a little, but not much. So Catherine sent her, along with Georgiana, on a visit to Nutplains in the summer. But Nutplains could not work its usual magic. Aunt Harriet and Grandmother Foote, calm and assured, had settled their doubts by another system than the one she was struggling to accept.

Hattie could remember how, when she was five, her aunt had started her religious training by teaching her the Episcopalian catechism, untroubled by the fact that Lyman Beecher considered the Episcopalian doctrine to be heresy. Hattie had enjoyed the Episcopalian primer much more than the instructions the Congregational Church offered the young. The Episcopalian catechism had started with a simple question, "What is your name?"—much easier for a child to answer than the first question in the Westminster catechism, "What is the chief end of man?" The five-year-old Hattie had liked the services at the Episcopalian church near Nutplains, too, and had been quite overjoyed by the Episcopalian celebration of Christmas.

But none of that was any good now.

It did not even help that Uncle Samuel, the glamorous sea captain, was at Nutplains during this visit. Uncle Samuel had recently been married, and at his bride's insistence he had retired from the sea. So there were no nautical adventures to hear. Instead, Uncle Samuel was full of talk about a long trip into America's West from which he and his bride had just returned. They had been looking for some inland spot in which to settle, and had traveled through Pennsylvania and Virginia, on into Ohio. In Ohio, that far-off state across the Appalachians, they had found what they were looking for.

"Cincinnati!" Uncle Samuel said enthusiastically. "A beautiful spot, right on the river, and growing by leaps and bounds! Nothing but a wilderness twenty years ago, and now it's a real city. Steamboats coming in and going out every day, all kinds of businesses prospering."

Hattie scarcely listened as Uncle Samuel went on about Cincinnati. It was remote and unimaginable, a weird jumble of activity in the wilderness. It would be four years and more before the name of that city would begin to assume importance to her and all the Beechers. Cincinnati still meant nothing to her father. Busy with his battles in Boston, he had no idea that one day he would gather the clan for a full-scale migration there.

Hattie's misery unabated, she and Georgiana left Nutplains. Sister Catherine's new school, subscribed for by the residents of

Hartford, was in the process of construction. Hattie trailed in Catherine's wake to inspect it, trying to be interested in window openings and beams, but consumed by her own wretchedness.

Sister Mary announced her engagement to a promising and well-to-do young Hartford attorney, Thomas Clapp Perkins. She was aglow with pleasure and plans for the future. They were to be married in the fall, and she was already furnishing her new home. In the atmosphere of Mary's happiness, Catherine relaxed briefly to recall her own romance with Professor Fisher. Thomas Perkins was an excellent young man, but no one would ever compare with Professor Fisher.

Harriet was sixteen, at an age to enjoy plans for a wedding, and to think and talk about romance herself, but she never did, except in a mocking, scoffing way. It was strange, for she was an attractive young lady, with a small, delicate figure, softly falling brown curls and great eyes. But unless Harriet was happy or interested in something, her natural prettiness was extinguished. Being happy about nothing and interested in no one but herself, she gave no young man the impulse to look at her twice. The brothers of her schoolmates and pupils, being introduced, might speak politely, and Harriet would either mumble shyly, or find herself making a sharp, unplanned remark.

The only young men who paid attention to her were her brothers, and her heart filled with love for them in consequence. Dear Edward, so patient with her and so helpful, dear Henry Ward, her playmate in childhood, still speaking with the curious thickness in his speech that he had had since he was a baby, but so good-natured and loving, dear George, dear Charley, with his talent for music, even dear William, her oldest brother, the bumbling and slow one, for whom nothing seemed to turn out right—these were the only young men and boys in whom she felt any interest.

"I love to hear sisters speak well of their brothers," she wrote in one letter. "There is no pride I can so readily tolerate as pride of relationship."

So she allowed herself pride in her brothers, and kept a cool eye for other young men, and looked at herself in the mirror and thought she was beyond measure plain and unattractive.

Then she hated herself for her concern with anything so worldly and vain and flung herself down on the bed to cry.

School began again. Mary was married in November. Catherine's new school building was opened with appropriate ceremonies, and the classes moved themselves into the pleasant, fresh-smelling rooms. And Hattie drudged along, teaching Latin, learning French, and spending long hours drawing and painting.

"I am very comfortable and happy," she wrote falsely to Grandmother Foote. "I propose, my dear Grandmama, to send you by the first opportunity a dish of fruit of my own painting. Pray do not now devour it in anticipation, for I cannot promise you will not find it sadly tasteless in reality. If so, please excuse it for the sake of the poor young artist. I admire to cultivate a taste for painting, and I wish to improve it; it was what my dear mother admired and loved, and I cherish it for her sake. I have thought more of this dearest of all earthly friends these late years—I sometimes think that, had she lived, I might have been both better and happier than I now am, but God is good and wise in all his ways."

Winter came, and spring. "Dear Edward," she wrote in March, "do you think, my dear brother, that there is such a thing as so realizing the presence and character of God that He can supply the place of earthly friends? . . ."

"Dear Edward," she wrote in April, "it seems to me that my love to Him is the love of despair. . . . All through the day, in my intercourse with others, everything has a tendency to destroy the calmness of mind gained by communion with Him. One flatters me, another is angry with me, another is unjust to me. . . ."

In one answer to her, Edward wrote that "predilections for literature had been "a snare" to him.

Oh, Edward, "I have found it so myself. I can scarcely think, without tears and indignation that all that is beautiful and lovely and poetical has been laid on other altars. Oh, will there never be a poet with a heart enlarged and purified by the Holy Spirit, who shall throw all the graces of harmony, all the enchantments of feeling, pathos and poetry, around sentiments worthy of them? . . ."

She was trying to forget the lure of a dark, handsome face that she had studied in a finespun line engraving, and trying to forget the lure of the poetry associated with that face—Byron. She was trying to find some stimulation in her old dream of being a great writer some day.

"Dear Edward . . . I do not mean to live in vain. He has given me talents, and I will lay them at His feet, well-satisfied if He will accept them. . . ."

At last, in Boston for the summer vacation, with Edward nearby, she could talk to her brother in person instead of writing her long letters of appeal. She could talk to her father too, if she ever found him free. But Lyman was busier than ever this year. He had embarked on a political fight against the Unitarians, so entrenched in Boston that they controlled the primaries and were excluding Congregationalists from any influence at all.

The challenge stimulated Lyman. "Fight!" he cried to the young men of his congregation. "We must fight!" Rallied by his spirit, the young men had organized the Hanover Street Church Young Men's Association, and taken a hand in the primaries themselves, with cheering results. Congregationalists were back in the political swim again. The young men were full of ideas for using their new political power. Other similar organizations were formed, at Edward's church and various Congregational and Presbyterian churches. Working together, the young men were achieving all sorts of victories. The lotteries and booths for the sale of liquor on the Boston Common were prohibited. Sunday steamboat excursions—wicked violation of the Sabbath law—were stopped. A project to complete the Bunker Hill Monument through funds raised by a lottery was stopped. But not all their activity was prohibitive. They started a popular lecture series, of the sort called lyceums, with a daring innovation. Women were admitted as well as men. They appointed a committee to welcome young men to the city and help them get in touch with the right people—Congregationalists.

The young men carried out the battles, but Lyman's advice, Lyman's influence and inspiration were needed everywhere. Instead of seeing more of her father, Harriet simply seemed to be forever opening the door to one or another of his ardent young crusaders.

She never noticed any of them specifically. A short and stocky young man, with beetling brows and twinkling eyes, went as unnoticed as the rest.

The young man did not notice her either. Hers was not the type of beauty that caught his eye. He preferred a more conventional prettiness, and would, within a year or so, find a young woman of just that type, whom he would marry and adore.

Neither of them noticing the other, Hattie would open the door to him and he would step in and nod politely, like all the others, and she would go tell her father that Mr. Calvin Stowe was there, and that would be that.

Chapter 7

1828–1829

The restlessness, the awareness of the nation's growing strength had come to a climax.

Who spoke for this new nation? Whose was it? Should its destiny still be guided by the aristocratic gentleman-farmers, the thoughtful, educated New Englanders, who had presided at its birth?

All the men who had helped to make it bigger and stronger gave their answer. The men who had moved out on the new roads to the wilderness and chopped down trees there and put plows to virgin soil; the men who fought and trapped along the frontiers, who kept the small shops and stores, who dug the canals and poled flatboats on the Western Waters, the workers in the new factories of New England, the small farmers of the South—all of these spoke, rallying behind the man they had almost made President in 1824.

In the election of 1828, they left no doubt. It was their country, they had helped to make it what it was; they spoke for it, and Andrew Jackson spoke for them.

Jackson's inauguration in March 1829 was a fantastic free-for-all. The men who had made him President thronged the streets of Washington and milled through the White House, gawking at its glories—their own now—spitting on the carpets, resting their muddy boots on brocade chairs, wolfing down the food and drink set out in a grand buffet.

It was settled. All honor to the Founding Fathers, but the child that had been sired was speaking for himself now—not so lettered as the fathers, speaking from instinct rather than sophistry. But let the world take notice of how much truer instinct often was than elaborate consideration. Let the world take no-

tice of how great and strong the new nation would become
now.

This was what the Founding Fathers had planned for, surely.
This was what Jefferson had meant when he wrote, "All men are
created equal. . . ."

"The duties of all public offices are . . . so plain and simple
that men of intelligence may readily qualify themselves for their
performances. . . . No one has any more intrinsic right to official
station than another," Andrew Jackson would proclaim, sweeping out government officeholders who had grown rooted to their
desks in the long Republican years.

Voices were raised in protest. It was not so simple as it
seemed. What of minorities, when the majority ruled? Surely the
Founding Fathers had thought of them too and provided for
their protection in the Constitution? Even plain people, so much
the same everywhere, must take differing roads to security and
happiness.

It was curious and fateful that in 1828, the year when the
plain people spoke and claimed the country for their own, John
C. Calhoun, the burning-eyed Calvinist from South Carolina,
took his first steps down another road, pursuing his own dream
of what he thought Jefferson had meant.

Calhoun still loved the idea of union as he believed Jefferson
himself had envisioned it, a union of states banded together for
the protection of their liberties. But what happened when the
very union itself, with its Federal powers, threatened the liberties of one state or another, one class or another? What happened
when one state, or one section, stronger than another by reason
of population or resources, pushed laws onto the union that actually damaged some other section?

The trouble simmering in the South, in South Carolina especially, had become acute by 1828, and John C. Calhoun and a
great many fellow South Carolinians saw it all as the fault of
the North. The North, committed to industry and stronger than
the South both in money and population, was pushing through
one tariff bill after another to protect its manufactured goods

in the market. The smaller, less powerful South, with its one crop
of cotton, which it sold well enough, chiefly in England, had to
buy every other necessity of life at prices kept high by protection.
In South Carolina, where land was already exhausted by cotton,
this was making for hard times.

How could the Union be preserved under such circumstances?

Brooding on his farm in South Carolina, John C. Calhoun
worked for the answer, based on what he was convinced the
Founding Fathers had intended. Each state, each section, reasoned Calhoun, when obviously threatened by some Federal law
or act, should have the power to nullify that act within its own
borders, at least for a period of time long enough to put the law
or act to a referendum of all the states.

It was the one theory he could devise that might ultimately
save the Union, the union of great and small, plain and rich,
farmers and manufacturers. It was the one means he could discover whereby the South could escape from the burden of tariff
that was ruining it.

Calhoun did not see—few Southerners did—that some of the
trouble in South Carolina might arise from the cotton-slave economy itself—cotton, wearing out land so quickly, demanding new
land, new land demanding new slaves to work it, new slaves adding to the costs and responsibilities of plantation owners, and so
demanding the planting of more cotton, requiring more land,
requiring more slaves. . . .

Calhoun saw only the tariff, selfish shield of the fat, prosperous
North, against which the South was beating itself to death. "The
ground we have taken," he wrote a friend, "is that the tariff is
unconstitutional and must be repealed, that the rights of the
South have been destroyed, and must be restored, that the Union
is in danger, and must be saved."

In the fall of 1828, he shared his new theories with his fellow
South Carolinians, who welcomed them with joy. They were the
only ones to know them just then. But it did not matter. By
another curious chance, the same election that made Jackson,
the man of the people, President, also made John C. Calhoun,
the man who had made himself guardian of its minorities, Vice-
President again.

The growing, expanding new nation had made its decision. It belonged to the people who lived in it and worked for it. But the conflicts that existed between them were still to be discovered.

Chapter 8

Well, there is a Heaven—a heaven—a world of love, and love after all is the life blood, the existence, the all in all of mind.

1829–1832

One day Harriet would look back in a kind of wonder to the time when her "mind lived only in emotion," and all her real "history was internal." Still, there were external events that impinged now and then. Reports of a series of events in Boston, involving their father, so convulsed every member of the family, including the brooding Hattie, that the story quickly became a valued part of Beecher legend.

It all began when Lyman decided to launch the year 1830 by delivering on six successive Sundays his famous Six Sermons on Temperance which had previously caused a sensation in Litchfield. His congregation in Boston found them equally stirring, and neither he nor his audience gave a thought, just then, to the fact that even as Dr. Beecher railed at rum, they were all sitting on top of kegs of the stuff. The cellar of the church had been rented for months to a liquor merchant who used it as a warehouse for his spirits. The rent so received was very helpful in meeting church expenses, including Lyman's salary.

This inconsistency, so easy for Lyman to ignore, might not have mattered had it not been brought to the whole town's attention shortly after.

On a February day, the Hanover Street Church caught fire. In no time, the casks down in the cellar were bursting and shooting out fine blue alcoholic flames, while the whole scene took on the look of a vast plum pudding.

Lyman had caused a good deal of unrest among the unorthodox, the freethinkers and more liberal elements of Boston with his temperance sermons. They wondered if he really would be able to reimpose the old morality of the Puritans on the city. And so the firemen, summoned to the burning church, did not even try to control their surprise and delight at what they saw. There was Dr. Beecher's church, from the pulpit of which he had thundered against liquor, burning brightly amid the intoxicating fumes of gallons and gallons of alcohol. Soon, to add to the slapstick charm of the scene, the explosions in the cellar shook up a room in the church that had been rented to a tract society, and showers of white tracts began falling onto Hanover Street.

The firemen were enchanted. So was the happy mob that gathered. Soon they were all singing together:

"While Beecher's church holds out to burn,
The vilest sinner may return . . ."

There was also many a joke about Beecher's "broken jug."

In this carnival atmosphere, the church burned to the ground.

Lyman was dismayed for a while, but by the next day, when a gloomy committee of church members assembled to discuss the disaster, he had bounced back. He arrived at the meeting announcing cheerfully, "Well, my jug's broke, all right. Just been to see it."

So the catchphrase, "father's broken jug," entered family history, and since Lyman had followed his lighthearted opening remarks with earnest and encouraging words about setting to work at once to finance, plan and build a new church, and since he had proceeded to do just that, there was no flaw in the comedy.

Such a tale could not fail to strike Harriet's sense of the ridiculous. But her "real history" was concerned with far different matters. She had made a new friend the year before, a new teacher in Catherine's school, and from the beginning this friend had become another focus of admiration as Catharine Cogswell once had been, but much more rewarding. Mary Dutton was her name, and she was as small as Harriet, but so intelligent, Harriet felt her mind the equal of "any college-trained male's." For a year, Hat-

tie had roomed with Mary and two other teachers, and that had
made it a pleasant year. Harriet suddenly found herself more
interested in Catherine's ceaseless attempts to improve the
standards of female education. Her decision to stop giving prizes
for excellence and to appeal instead to each girl's desire for
higher entertainment, her inauguration of weekly teachers' meetings to discuss each pupil individually, her introduction of a
new kind of class for physical exercise (an activity that would
soon be called "calisthenics")—all these were far more stimulating to Hattie when she could discuss them later with Mary.

But then, the next fall, Mary Dutton had decided not to return to Hartford to teach, but to remain in New Haven with
her family. Catherine had felt Mary's departure as a blow too.
Just then Catherine was slowly recovering from a nervous collapse—even her iron determination to act and do and advance
had broken down for a while—and she regretted the loss of Mary
Dutton's help and good spirits. But Harriet felt the loss far more
than Catherine.

She had to content herself with long letters to Mary, which
she tried to make as amusing as possible, since Mary had always
enjoyed her humor. She wrote about the horseback riding Catherine had prescribed as a prebreakfast ritual for herself and Hattie,
and her own John Gilpinesque adventures. She wrote about the
books she was reading, *Rasselas*, for one, and how she was trying to write an imitation of Dr. Johnson, who wrote as if "some
fairy had spellbound him and given him the task of putting
every word in his great dictionary in his book." Sometimes she
could not refrain from touches of jealousy. Writing a newsy item
about one of Mary's former pupils, there was a memory of the
way Mary, unlike herself, had always attracted masculine attention. When she reported, "Miss Fisher says, 'Tell her I hope she'll
enjoy herself and get a husband into the bargain,'" Hattie could
not resist adding, "If such an acquisition would be to you the
summum bonum of earthly felicity, I heartily join in the request.
I think you spoke to tolerable purpose on the felicity of the
wedded state, Mary; suppose you try." Marriage, to Harriet, was
not the *summum bonum* of earthly felicity, at least not that she
would admit.

She wanted love, she was desperate for love, and knew it. She could write to Edward, "This desire to be loved forms, I fear, the great motive for all my actions. . . ." But as the months and the years went on and there was no young man asking permission to come calling, how could she admit, even to herself, that she might have a deep yearning to love and be loved by a man? It was impossible. Her desire for love had to be channeled into a straining to understand the mysterious love of God, into friendships so intense the friends themselves could scarcely bear the burden, into affection for her brothers, appearing briefly in Hartford now and then on their way to various schools, into love for all her family.

But other external events were occurring that would ultimately have an effect even on a mind that "lived only in emotion."

It was while his new church was still in the planning stage that Lyman Beecher went to a General Church Assembly in Philadelphia and first heard talk about a new theological seminary that was being established in the West, in Cincinnati. The talk became especially interesting to Lyman as one person after another harked back to the same theme. If this new school, which was to be called Lane Theological Seminary, was to really become the great institution everyone hoped—the Yale of the West—there was surely only one Calvinist minister in the East who could give it the prestige and impetus it needed, Lyman Beecher.

Lyman began to smell the challenge that lay across the Appalachians in the wilderness. Cincinnati—and the West! Samuel Foote and his wife had long since made the journey out there, settled down near another Foote brother already in Cincinnati, and written back glorious reports of the city. Like Aaron Burr, whom he had once decried so violently in his sermons against dueling, Lyman too began to see the possibility of an empire in the West, but this one an empire under God's scepter, not man's.

Hattie, at home in Boston for the summer again, saw her father curiously abstracted, and heard him launch forth now and then in unexplained perorations about the West. Catherine, in Hartford, had a letter from him. "While at Philadelphia and since, my interest in the majestic West has been greatly excited and increased. . . . The moral destiny of our nation, and all its institutions and hopes . . . turns on the character of the West."

But it was all vague, grand, theoretical. There was no reason to think that this talk would affect any of them personally, no reason for Hattie to think the stale routine of her life was about to change. The summer was just another summer like any other. Her brother William was there, getting married, and Hattie was the bridesmaid. But William, pessimistic by nature, was hardly cheered even on his wedding day, and there was little festivity about the event.

Then the shocks began. The West became more real to Harriet than any of Uncle Samuel's stories had made it. Brother Edward provided the first shock when he received an invitation to be the first president of a new college in Illinois, in a town called Jacksonville. For several days, Edward was frequently at Sheaf Street, shoveling sand with his father in the cellar, or swinging on the parallel bars in the backyard, debating the question. Should he make such a drastic move? There were reasons enough to hesitate, but there were also factors that made it tempting. Young Edward, untried in the ministry, had been having his troubles with the congregation of the Park Street Church. The troubles had abated, under Lyman's advice, but still Edward wondered if he was accomplishing as much in Boston as he might be able to in the West.

Edward decided to accept the invitation from Jacksonville. Hattie was back in the routine of classes and studying in Hartford when he left Boston for Illinois. And by that time, all Lyman's vague talk about the West had crystallized too.

He had a firm offer to come to Cincinnati and head the new Lane Theological Seminary. A member of the board of trustees of the new school had come East, first to New York, where he had won the promise of an endowment from a wealthy merchant, Arthur Tappan, provided Lyman Beecher would become the school's president. Then the trustee had come to Boston and put the offer before the Reverend Beecher.

Cincinnati—and an empire—which might be won for God if he accepted! It was a long distance from all that had always been home. Lyman was in his fifties, no longer young as Edward was, and there was no foretelling the difficulties. Still, if he refused, suppose the post went to a man who did not, like himself, believe in the mighty power of revivals to stimulate repentance and salvation? Could the West be won without revivals? Lyman debated the question with his family. He took the problem to his congregation.

"The question whether the first and leading seminary in the West shall be one which inculcates orthodoxy with or without revivals is a question, in my view, of as great importance as was ever permitted a single human mind to decide," he cried to his parishioners.

His own "single human mind" having grappled with the problem, he went on to indicate that the fateful decision had been made. It was up to him to settle the question and "give a complexion probably forever to the doctrine and revivals of that great world."

Came the stumbling block,—his congregation, perfectly willing to believe the future of the West did depend on its minister, still was listening to him in temporary church quarters. He had promised it, had he not, to see it safely and triumphantly to a brand-new church after the destruction of the old one. Surely he was honor-bound to stay with his congregation until the new church was finished and dedicated.

The crusade for the West, already bright with banners in Lyman's mind, was suddenly halted. In Cincinnati, Lyman's name was put down on the records of the new school as president, but in Boston, Lyman was abruptly quiet about the matter, publicly at any rate. He was "undecided."

This meant another dull year for Harriet in Hartford, a year in which she tried intermittently and without too much success to improve her character according to Catherine's advice. She would try not to be so critical of others, try not to expect so much and be more pleased with what she found. She tried and failed and tried again. And 1830 was a waste of books and lessons and sharpening pupils' quills and hearing recitations.

The next year dragged along promising no more. In the sum-

mer, Catherine tried again to get Mary Dutton to leave New
Haven and join them at Hartford. Harriet added her pleas, but
Mary was immovable.

Then, rumblings from Boston in the fall of 1831 indicated
that the western move was again under consideration. The new
church was built and dedicated, but that had not been the pre-
cipitating factor. A Dr. Wilson, out in Cincinnati, had brought
the project to life again, chiefly by suddenly suggesting that Dr.
Beecher might *not* be the man for the presidency of Lane. It
had come to Dr. Wilson's attention rather belatedly that Dr.
Beecher was not an Old School Calvinist like himself, but of the
New School, which, naturally, allowed Dr. Wilson to hint at that
handy, all-purpose charge of heresy.

Lyman was not especially alarmed. All the other trustees of
the Seminary in Cincinnati, dazzled by the idea of having such
an eminent Easterner as Dr. Lyman Beecher at the head of their
new school—all of Cincinnati, in fact, excited by the prospect
of having a famous preacher from the East in their growing city
—sprang to his defense, and cried down the Reverend Doctor
Joshua Lacy Wilson.

Soon they were sending letters and emissaries east to renew
and reinforce their original invitation to Dr. Beecher. Finally,
Lyman, hemming and hawing, now that he had become such a
sought-after character, decided he would go out to Cincinnati
in March and look over the situation, preparatory to making up
his mind.

Catherine had been tantalized from the beginning by her
father's talk of the "majestic West," and now she was full of
excited speculation. She had been saying for months that she was
weary of all the responsibilities that fell on her as head of the
Hartford Female Seminary. There were not only her duties in
managing its teaching staff and teaching policies, but also the
endless problems of financial administration, and a teaching load
as well. For months she had been seeking an endowment for the
school to relieve her of the business responsibilities, but her in-
novations in curriculum and character building had made the
conservative elements of the community reluctant to help her.

With her father poised for a leap, Catherine thought how

wonderful it would be to abandon those labors and take her educational theories to the West. There, in that vast, new region, she could establish another school, but this time a school where she would make sure she was merely a supervisor, leaving the exhausting details to others.

Almost as soon as Lyman decided to go to Cincinnati on an exploratory visit, Catherine announced her plan to go with him, to see what the prospects were for the success of her scheme. By the latter part of March 1832, they were off!

In May, Hattie was interrupting the drudgery of another Hartford school day to read a letter from Catherine, a letter that brimmed with reports on that far-off city, Cincinnati.

The reports were almost rapturous. Catherine, full of optimism at the promise of something new, described the city on its terraced cliffs above the Ohio River, told of how they were staying with Uncle Samuel in his home in the upper part of the city, which commanded a fine view of the whole lower town and river, and wrote: "I never saw a place so capable of being rendered a paradise by the improvements of taste as the environs of this city." Walnut Hills, the site some two miles from the city, where the Seminary was located, was "so elevated and cool that people have to leave there to be sick, it is said." On and on, she rhapsodized, describing the spot she and her father had chosen as a homesite, in case they made the move, and "you cannot find a more delightful spot for a residence," she declared.

She spoke of the various people with whom she had become acquainted and how she had found them "intelligent, New England sort of folks." Even more to the point, "the folks are very anxious to have a school on our plans set on foot here. We can have fine rooms in the city college building, which is now unoccupied, and everybody is ready to lend a helping hand."

The details piled up, and reading them, Hattie could only feel a curious, breathless sense of how very imminent the whole move sounded. If her father was going, and Catherine too, obviously she would be part of the migration as well. Was she glad or sorry? She did not know.

Catherine and her father were back in the East by June, and Hattie's twenty-first birthday, and the decision was definite. They

were going. An offer from the Second Presbyterian Church in
Cincinnati, offering Lyman a very pleasant financial consideration for preaching there whenever he had free time from the
Seminary, was the clinching factor. Lyman would actually be
making more money in Cincinnati than in Boston, as well as
winning an empire for God and setting forever the "complexion
of its doctrine."

Catherine flew into action, settling matters for the school in
Hartford. Her side curls bounced, her steps and tone were brisk,
and she spent long, busy hours at the desk. She wanted to find
just the right person to take over the management of the school.
Perhaps she could persuade Mary Dutton. But no, Mary Dutton
was not to be lured. Finally it was John P. Brace of Miss Pierce's
Academy in Litchfield, who was offered and accepted the
management of the school, that same John Brace to whom Hattie
had listened as a young student, and who had chosen Hattie's
essay to read aloud at those closing exercises long ago.

Hattie said good-bye to Hartford, to sister Mary and Mary's
husband, Thomas, and everyone else she knew. There was a
long good-bye to Georgiana May, the best of all friends really.
And then she went to spend the summer at Nutplains.

In the familiar order and quiet there, knowing there would
be only a few weeks before the strange, almost unimaginable
leavetaking from all that was dear, Hattie felt suspended between past and future.

Uncle Samuel and his wife were at Nutplains also, visiting in
the East for the summer. It would have been a good opportunity
for Hattie to ask questions about Cincinnati and build up some
sort of picture to put alongside the one Catherine had painted.
But Hattie was not interested.

She was twenty-one—surely it was time once again to examine
her spiritual state and to think of who and what she was. So
she went "owling about," doing the few chores there were to do
at Nutplains, and walking down to the brook that tumbled over
its stones so near the house and out through the sunny mead-
ows. What did she really think and feel, after all the years of
anguish and misery, wavering between the God of wrath and

the gentle Jesus? Had her prodding, resistant, stubborn mind at last allowed her to accept one or the other?

Her mind was stubborn, but her emotions were more so. She had not answered half the questions her mind had presented to her. She had not worked out the logic that made a choice inevitable. Still, it was plain that somehow, sometime during the last years, she had simply run away from the God of wrath, who answered "the lamentations of Job with the whirlwind," and fled to the figure who had first seemed to hold out his arms to her on that Sunday when she was "converted" long ago—the gentle Jesus. Perhaps she would answer all the questions later, and work out the logic. It was enough now to realize that, whatever the answers, only love made life bearable.

When she did talk to Uncle Samuel it was more in an attempt to cope again with her critical approach to other people, and those easily wounded sensibilities that made any casual look seem a look of scorn, any light word, a word of reproach. Uncle Samuel was a large, tolerant man. His years of voyaging and meeting people in ports around the world had given him a quality of acceptance, both of people and of life, that suddenly seemed very enviable to Harriet.

"Horas non numero nisi serenas," Uncle Samuel quoted to her. It was an inscription he had copied fron a sundial he had seen in Venice. "I only number the hours that shine." Hattie was delighted with it as a motto, and wondered if she could put it into effect in her own life.

". . . the hours that shine." She could remember a few,—the hours with Mary Dutton, the walks and talks with Georgiana. And envisioning both those friends receding from her, she saw them both through a glow of love.

She wrote Georgiana pouring out her conclusions and resolutions.

"The amount of the matter has been, as this inner world of mine has become worn out and untenable, I have at last concluded to come out of it and live in the external one." She quoted Uncle Samuel's motto, "Horas non numero nisi serenas," and her own resolve to follow it, and she added:

"I am trying to cultivate a general spirit of kindliness towards everybody. Instead of shrinking into a corner to notice how other people behave, I am holding out my hand to the right and to the left, and forming casual or incidental acquaintances with all who will be acquainted with me. In this way I find society full of interest and pleasure—a pleasure which pleaseth me more because it is not old and worn out. From these friendships I expect little; therefore generally receive more than I expect. From past friendships I have expected everything, and must of necessity have been disappointed. The kind words and looks and smiles I call forth by looking and smiling are not much by themselves, but they form a very pretty flower border to the way of life. . . ."

She had an answer from Georgiana in a week or so, and again rushed for her writing pad and pen to tell her friend the emotions her letter had aroused.

"It touched me with a sort of painful pleasure, for it seems to me uncertain, improbable, that I shall ever return and find you as I have found your letter. Oh, my dear G.—, it is scarcely well to love friends thus. The greater part that I see cannot move me deeply. They are present and I enjoy them; they pass and I forget them. But those that I love differently, those that I *love:* and oh, how much that word means! I feel sadly about them. They change; they must die; they are separated from me, and I ask myself why I should wish to love with all the pains and penalties of such conditions? I check myself when expressing feelings like this, so much has been said of it by the sentimental, who talk what they could not have felt. But it is so deeply, sincerely so in me, that sometimes it will overflow. Well, there is a Heaven—a heaven—a world of love, and love after all is the life blood, the existence, the all in all of mind."

No, she would not be sentimental. And if later generations would call her sentimental all the same, not seeing how real everything she wrote seemed to her, they might not have known any concept of sinfulness quite like the one she had struggled through to reach this haven at last—a world of love that was heaven enough.

Chapter 9

1832

For the nation, its awkward age was just beginning.

The plain people had spoken. It was their country. In 1832 they spoke again, reelecting Old Hickory. Was he not breaking that moneyed monopoly that called itself the Bank of the United States? Had he not given hundreds of jobs to his loyal followers, who were proud to be called Democrats?

But the country was so big, so much bigger than anyone was able to grasp. It was all arms and legs seeming to have wills of their own, defying any principle of coordination. North, South, East, West—every section had different resources, different needs, and galvanic impulses were beginning to run through them, twitching each into independent uncoordinated activity.

In 1830, in the Senate, Daniel Webster of Massachusetts had tried to spell out a principle of coordination. And John C. Calhoun had watched and listened, his brows lowered. Webster was answering *him*, really, denying his great theory that individual states had a right to nullify acts that were threatening to them, that arms or legs feeling pain from some other part of the body might somehow withdraw themselves from the pressure.

When it came time for the doctrine of Nullification to be presented to the nation, Vice-President Calhoun had to let a fellow South Carolinian speak for him. But everyone knew whose doctrine it was, and everyone was listening as Webster tried to refute it.

Hour after hour Webster spoke, in the interminable oratorical style of the time, his voice rising and falling, sonorous, majestic, but lightened now and then with humor, too, so no one in the packed Senate Chamber could lose interest for a moment. Then, in his final peroration he had given the nation a rallying cry.

What was needed was an ensign inscribed, "not Liberty first
and Union afterwards, but everywhere, spread all over in characters of living light, blazing on all its ample folds, as they float
over the sea and the land, and in every wind under the whole
heavens, that other sentiment, dear to every true American
heart—Liberty *And* Union, now and forever, one and inseparable."

The cry echoed from the Senate Chamber across the nation,
full of impelling magic. This *was* what the new nation was all
about.

But to John C. Calhoun, and to many another South Carolinian,
Webster, with his spellbinding eloquence, was simply a mouth-
piece for the moneyed interests of the North. It was easy for
Webster to say "Liberty *And* Union," when the North could have
both with profit. And Calhoun counted on Old Hickory in the
White House, a Carolinian by birth himself, a slave owner, and
an advocate of States' Rights, to help the South protect its liberties, so union would not mean death.

Then had come the Jefferson's Birthday Dinner, with a series
of toasts carefully planned to imply that Calhoun's theory of Nullification was a theory that Jefferson himself, with his belief in
a "loose federation of states," would have approved. After the
programmed toasts, there had come Jackson's answer. Glaring
at Calhoun with his sophisticated theories, the President spoke:

"Our Federal Union—it must be preserved!"

The hall was silent, waiting for Calhoun's reply. Gathering
himself together—was he not fighting for the Union too, against
the swallowing of one section by another?—Calhoun did his unyielding best.

"The Union—next to our liberty, the most dear!"

Still, it would be two years before South Carolina openly put
the doctrine to the test.

In the summer of 1832, when Harriet Beecher was dreamily
assessing her spiritual state in Nutplains, Henry Clay gave South
Carolina the provocation it could not resist. A new tariff bill
with some abominations removed, but some brand-new ones
added, was pushed through the Senate.

The Beecher clan was already on its way West, in November 1832, when the South Carolina legislature issued its defiance of the tariff act by declaring it null and void within that state. No customs duties were to be collected by Federal officials within South Carolina's borders. If the Federal Government attempted to make sure such duties were collected, by force or otherwise, South Carolina would have no choice but to leave the Union.

From Washington, President Jackson sent an outraged proclamation to South Carolina. Its decree was based "on the strange position that a state might retain its place in the Union, and yet be bound only by those laws it might choose to regard as constitutional." He ordered the army forts near Charleston reinforced and made provision for revenue cutters to collect the duties if customs officers were resisted.

Meantime, a committee was appointed in Congress to reduce the tariffs most abominable to South Carolina.

After that there was no need for the force that Jackson dreaded to use. But he emerged from the crisis shaken. A precedent had been established. One state had set itself up against the Union.

And, "the next pretext," said Jackson fearfully, hearing the same firebell that had aroused Jefferson, "will be the negro, or slavery question."

How pressing was the slavery question, really? The North was against slavery, on principle, having no need for it. But how urgently?

Not very urgently, in 1832—no more urgently than various slaveowners in the upper tier of Southern states, where cotton was not the staple, slaves not so indispensable, and the difficulties inherent in the institution somewhat clearer.

There were some fanatics on the subject. Visionaries, zealots and reformers had been lifting their heads here and there, since the 1820s. In 1830 an intense young man had shown up as a member of Lyman Beecher's congregation in Boston. William Lloyd Garrison was his name, and Lyman had been much impressed by him at first, since Garrison was a firm New School Calvinist, with an ardent belief in revivals and immediate repentance.

Then the young man came to him, and with burning-eyed insistence urged Lyman to join him in a crusade for the immediate abolition of slavery.

Immediate abolition? Lyman's long, quirking eyebrows shot up. What kind of talk was this?

"Is not slavery a national sin?" the young man inquired.

"Yes, yes, to be sure," said Lyman. Had he not preached on and off for years, on that very theme, reducing some of his parishioners to tears?

"Well then," the young man cried, "in accordance with your own doctrine of immediate repentance is it not the duty of this nation to repent immediately of the sin of slavery and emancipate the slaves?"

"Oh, Garrison," Lyman said then, mildly and humorously, seeing where the young man's logic had taken him. "You can't reason that way. Great economic and political questions can't be solved so simply. You must take into account what is expedient as well as what is right."

The young man had not been pleased with Lyman's answer. He had stormed away and—with no blessing from Lyman, not many blessings from anyone—had started to crusade for immediate abolition by publishing an antislavery journal called *The Liberator*.

"I am in earnest—I will not equivocate—I will not excuse—I will not retreat a single inch—and I *will be heard*. . . ." he announced in his first issue.

But was Lyman, inconsistent in a hundred ways, looking to an omnipotent God to help him pay grocery bills, preaching on temperance while standing above kegs of liquor, being equally inconsistent in his answer to young Garrison? There were thousands who would not have thought so, in 1830. Slavery was a sin, admitted. But to do away with that sin could only create hideous new problems. Millions of Negroes, uneducated, totally inexperienced in providing for themselves, suddenly freed and cast adrift in the world—was not such an abandonment almost a sin in itself?

There were other ways to solve the problem. There was, for instance, the American Colonization Society, founded as long ago as 1817, and supported by many Southerners. The Society had

purchased land in Liberia and was engaged in transporting as
many freed Negroes as possible to the colony it had started there.
Like many another who hated slavery, Lyman thought this was
the reasonable way to attack the problem.

But "I will be heard!" Garrison had shouted.

And he was. With fury in the South, which was shocked and
terrified by a rare and unlikely slave uprising in August 1831,
just a few months after Garrison had begun publishing *The Liberator*. In Baltimore, in the twenties, Southerners had already put
Garrison into jail for his attacks on slavery—a jail from which he
had been rescued by the same New York merchant, Arthur Tappan, who was endowing Lyman's presidency of Lane. Now the
South blamed Garrison and his inflammatory writing in *The Liberator* for the fact that a mystic and visionary Negro preacher
named Nat Turner had rallied half a hundred slaves around him,
and, after various heavenly omens, such as a solar eclipse and
lesser phenomena, massacred more than sixty white people.

Yes, Garrison was heard in the South. And in the South men
were demanding that the North, if it thought so much of union,
should do something about the citizens there who were deliberately inciting slaves to riot.

He was heard in the North, too. Heard by many with an outrage almost equal to what the South felt, for there were those in
the North with a vested interest in the South's cotton economy,
and these were pleased enough when mobs gathered to attack
men like Garrison, inflamed by nothing more than anger at the
thought of free Negroes roaming the country, taking their jobs.

But Garrison was also heard by a few who were converted to
his way of thinking. There was one in particular, a tall, handsome
young evangelist named Theodore Weld. In the summer of 1832,
when Henry Clay was pushing through his new tariff bill, Theodore Weld read a denunciation of the colonization system for
ending slavery, written by Garrison, and became as ardent an
Abolitionist as Garrison.

Garrison, Theodore Weld, Nat Turner—in the months and years
to come, all of them would have their impact on Hattie's life,
as well as America's, though Garrison's *Liberator* and the Nat

Turner Insurrection were only names to her in 1832, and of Theodore Weld she had not heard—as yet.

North, South and West, there were other pulls and tugs, strains
and stresses, resisting any principle of coordination.

In the West, the vast, wide-open, hardly charted West, there
was a land boom as full of promise, almost as fraught with peril
of imminent financial collapse, as the South's cotton boom. And
North and West, there was a population boom. From England,
Ireland and Germany, immigrants were beginning to pour in,
not just twice as many as had come in previous decades, but
three, four, five times as many. "Liberty and Union"—yes, it was
a resounding motto to float on every wind, but even more appealing, if not so majestic, were the banners the immigrants seemed
to see floating over America—"Liberty and cheap land," "Liberty
and plenty of jobs"—helping to build the canals, roads and railroads that were still creeping out in all directions.

Not all the immigrants were peasants or downtrodden serfs.
Artisans, intellectuals, political refugees from European revolu-
tions were swelling the tide, and though one day all of these—
peasants and intellectuals, artisans and refugees—would be absorbed in the great new country, and in the absorption enrich it
immeasurably, the sudden flood of their arrival could not help
causing upheavals, dislocations, various spasms all over the body
politic.

There were also those, not so many, but enough, who came
from overseas, stayed for a while, and then returned to their
native lands, to report on what they had seen.

A great many Americans were reacting, in 1832, to the reports
of one such visitor, Mrs. Fanny Trollope, who, after coming to
America to find her fortune and failing in the goal, had gone back
to England to write a book about the people and the customs she
had observed. The reactions everywhere were unfavorable. People's emotions ranged from simple hurt to incoherent fury.

In Cincinnati the reactions were most extreme because it was
there that Mrs. Trollope had spent most of her time. Her plan
had been to build a bazaar, which was to have incorporated
many refinements she thought Americans needed and would pay
for—a department store, a dance hall, an ice cream parlor and a

saloon, not to mention an art gallery, a cyclorama exhibit and a stock exchange, were all to have been part of it. But her elaborate plans had been halted midway by lack of funds, and *that*, said Cincinnati citizens, was why she wrote so spitefully. Still, they could not quit talking about her book, and plainly the most irritating thing about it was the difficulty everyone had in finding any one particular detail that was altogether false.

It was probably unfortunate that energetic, bright-eyed, curious Fanny Trollope and her children who accompanied her, should have entered the United States through the southern port of New Orleans. An arrival in the East, where they might have been greeted by the metropolitan graces of Boston or Philadelphia, or even the somewhat provincial New York, would surely have created better first impressions. Mrs. Trollope was generous in her praise of the East in the latter part of her book.

There was little grandeur in the low, misty, swampy Louisiana coastline as her ship approached, little that seemed remarkable to her in New Orleans. After that, there had been the trip by steamboat, up through the flat desolation of the lower Mississippi. There had been an embarkation at midnight, in drenching rain, at Memphis, and a hair-raising excursion into the Tennessee wilderness to visit a European friend, Miss Frances Wright. Miss Wright was launching a school for Negro children there in the forest, a visionary project that had totally bogged down in mud and confusion. Then it had been back to the Mississippi and another steamboat for Mrs. Trollope, as she pursued her way to her goal, Cincinnati. No, it had not been the best possible way to arrive in America.

Above all, it was the primitive manners that shocked Mrs. Trollope, as she witnessed them in boardinghouses, hotels and on the steamboat. In amazement, the cultured lawyer's wife described the manner of eating in the dining saloon—"the voracious rapidity with which the viands were seized and devoured, the strange uncouth phrases and pronunciations, the loathsome spitting, from the contamination of which it was absolutely impossible to protect our dresses; the frightful manner of feeding with their knives, till the whole blade seemed to enter into the mouth;

and the still more frightful manner of cleaning the teeth afterward with a pocket knife."

It was all true enough. Other European travelers mentioned the same things. But somehow Mrs. Trollope's account was the most infuriating to Americans, who might know, in their hearts, that what she described was true, at least of some of their fellow citizens, but who asked why she had to dwell at length on such details, when there was so much in the way of accomplishment in this great, new land to praise. And what was so wrong with that way of eating anyway, if some people chose that style? America was the land of freedom.

Mrs. Trollope did find some things to admire in the West, but even in these there was some lack, some way in which they did not approach the European ideal of beauty or convenience. She had been delighted when the steamboat left the murky Mississippi for the clear waters of the Ohio. This was indeed La Belle Rivière, as the French had named it. But then as she described the scenery of the river banks, the cliffs, the wild intervals of forest, the occasional meadow or clearing, and pretty dwelling, she could not forebear remarking on how much the scene would have been improved if, here and there, there had been a ruined abbey, or a feudal castle to blend the romance of real life with that of nature.

Cincinnati, of which she had heard reports as enthusiastic as Catherine's letter to Harriet, was "finely situated." It had a "noble" landing place for steamboats, where one could sometimes see fifteen steamers lying at once, but she missed the Gothic touch here, too. The city wanted "domes, towers, steeples."

Alas, it did *not* want pigs. She was as amazed by the prevalence of those creatures, wandering in droves up and down the streets, as she had been by Mississippi steamboat table manners. The pigs, it seemed, were destined ultimately for one of Cincinnati's many slaughterhouses, where they would be turned into sides of bacon, ham, or salt pork, and shipped off to the East or the South. Meantime, the pigs grew fat and healthy and served as a municipal benefit by taking care of Cincinnati's garbage, thrown out in the street for them.

Mrs. Trollope went on, recounting in wonder and amazement

one thing after another, in which the people of Cincinnati saw no reason for wonder or amazement at all. She had a great deal of difficulty in getting a domestic servant, or "help" as she found it was called in Ohio. She discovered it was "more than petty treason in a Republic to call a free citizen a servant" and she wondered that girls would prefer to work in factories at half the wages they could receive in domestic service, feeling in some way that their equality was less compromised by the former.

Mrs. Trollope was amazed also by the number of Cincinnati's churches, by the multiplicity of sects, and by the way Cincinnati's citizens seemed to find their chief means of entertainment in those churches, with throngs gathering in them almost every night. She heard a great deal about a phenomenon known as a "revival," when enthusiastic members of the clergy, traveling about the country, entered a city or town and held meetings for a week or more, preaching and praying all day and often for a considerable portion of the night. Curious, she pressed for more details, but what she heard in this instance she absolutely refused to believe.

She did attend one ordinary, run-of-the-mill Presbyterian service, at which the minister gave a long, passionate dissertation on Hell, describing it in minute detail. When he concluded, "the perspiration ran in streams down his face; his eyes rolled, his lips were covered with foam, and every feature had the deep expression of horror it would have borne, had he, in truth, been gazing at the scene he described." The acting, Mrs. Trollope felt, was excellent, but she was appalled at the effect of this on the audience, the young girls especially, who were reduced to sobbing and convulsions.

It was not too strange that most Americans should have reacted as they did. Church meetings such as these were the very backbone of life. The freedom to indulge in them had been one of the things their forefathers were seeking when they turned their backs on Mrs. Trollope's England. As for the pigs, the table manners, the "help" that was so hard to get, and all her other comments and criticisms, she exaggerated, she distorted, she took pleasure in seeing only the worst. She was angry because her

foolish Bazaar had cost so much she was unable to complete it
(and who wanted it or had asked for it, anyway?). She was spiteful because none of the best people in Cincinnati had really noticed her. She was, above all, unprincipled, unreliable, and well
away from America.

A young person, all arms and legs, fumbling and awkward as
he attempts some grand new project, does not care for criticism.
Neither does a young country, bursting with new projects, strange
impulses and unaccustomed growth.

Chapter 10

I will put out my hand to the right and to the left. . . . I will live in the external world. . . .

If ever the shy and morbid Hattie had a hope of holding to such a resolution, it was now, as the Beecher clan prepared for the move west. Nervous excitement filled all the Beechers. Even Mrs. Beecher felt it, agitated as she was by nameless forebodings of what lay ahead. Even Aunt Esther felt it, faithful Aunt Esther, who was as fearful as Mrs. Beecher, but who would go where Lyman and his family went all the same. As for Harriet, her letters as the journey began were full of a bubbling gaiety.

The Beechers' first stop, after the turmoil of leaving Boston, was New York City. A host in themselves, they bore down on the city with their trunks and luggage in October 1832, a host even though five Beechers were no part of the hegira. Edward was already in the West, in Jacksonville. William was busy with his first pastorate in Rhode Island. Safely-settled Mary was remaining in Hartford with her husband, and young Henry Ward and Charley were both staying in the East to continue their schooling. But even with five missing, there were nine of them—Lyman, Mrs. Beecher, Aunt Esther, Catherine, Hattie and George—and the three little ones, the second Mrs. Beecher's children, Isabella, Thomas and James, born during the Boston years and already four years old. Nine of them, to be distributed among hospitable families who had offered to be their hosts while they stayed in New York.

"Well, my dear, the great sheet is out and the letter is begun," Hattie scribbled on her writing pad, sending back the first report to the family in Hartford. The Beechers were lingering in New York because there had been a provision attached to the generous endowment Arthur Tappan was offering to Lane Seminary. Two more professorships of twenty thousand dollars each had to be raised by the Seminary itself, so Lyman, eloquent and persuasive Lyman, was adding his help to the fund-raising.

"He is begging money for the Biblical Literature professorship," Hattie wrote, and added, with no thoughts about the matter either way, "the incumbent is to be C. Stowe"—the short, stocky young man who had been one of her father's earnest protégés during the summer of 1828. Since then, the young man had gone on to win a small but solid reputation as a professor, first at Bowdoin, then at Dartmouth. But Hattie had only a passing mention for him. Lyman's activities were the chief news.

"Father is all in his own element," she wrote, "dipping into books; consulting authorities for his oration, going round here, there, everywhere, begging, borrowing and spoiling the Egyptians, delighted with past success and confident of the future."

Hattie was feeling the glow of it herself, even feeling some confidence about her own future.

"Wednesday: Still in New York," she continued, a couple of days later. "I believe it would kill me dead to live long in the way I have been doing since I have been here. It is a sort of agreeable delirium. There's only one thing about it, it is too *scattering*. I begin to be athirst for the waters of quietness."

It was the proper thing to say, but New York was full of novelty and interest, new things to see and do, new people to meet. "I will put out my hand to the right and to the left. . . . I will live in the external world. . . ."

After New York, the next stop was to be Philadelphia, where Lyman was scheduled for more fund-raising and preaching. Still excited by everything, Hattie reported on the minor trials and frustrations of the departure from New York, the trunks delivered to the wrong wharf, the long, fruitless wait aboard the Philadelphia steamer, George left behind, finally, to find the baggage and bring it on to Philadelphia the next day, Mama and Aunt Esther in despair because they had no clean caps.

Then the Philadelphia Congregationalists were welcoming the

Beechers even as the New York faithful had, and a Philadelphia newspaper was printing a long editorial eulogizing Lyman
Beecher and his family, who had "torn themselves from the endearing scenes of their home," to go forth into the wilderness like
Jacob and his sons. Hattie thought the prose unduly florid. That
was speaking with entirely too much of a flourish. A number of
pious people in Philadelphia were going to hold a prayer meeting
for the success of the Beecher journey and its objective. "For
this, I thank them," Hattie wrote primly.

After Philadelphia they were really away at last, into strange,
new country. And that heady sense of excitement that marks the
real beginning of a journey rose within them all.

George, as boyish and high-spirited at twenty-five as he had
been at five, ten and fifteen, started the singing. Soon all the
Beechers were singing, lining out psalms and hymns as they
rolled through the peaceful Pennsylvania countryside. Then
George, who had provided himself with a quantity of religious
tracts in New York and Philadelphia, had another exuberant idea.
Distributing the tracts among the younger children, he and they
began tossing them from the coach to any startled farmers or
wayfarers they passed. "*Peppering* the land with moral influence," cried Hattie, laughing at their display.

The singing, tract-tossing coachload had traveled thirty miles
from Philadelphia by nightfall. At an inn in Downington, Harriet took out her writing pad to tell Georgiana about it. "Here we
all are,—Noah and his wife and his sons and his daughters, with
the cattle and creeping things, all dropped down in the front
parlor of this tavern, about thirty miles from Philadelphia. If today is a fair specimen of our journey, it will be a very pleasant,
obliging driver, good roads, good spirits, good dinner, fine scenery, and now and then some 'psalms, hymns and spiritual
songs. . . .'"

But stimulating as everything had been so far, a reaction was
beginning to set in. There had been a honeysuckle vine growing
by the tavern where they had stopped for lunch, a honeysuckle
that reminded Hattie of the one that grew back at Nutplains.
She sighed as she described it for Georgiana. The singing had
brought back memories too, of how she and Georgiana used to

sing while riding along the rough North Guilford roads near Nutplains.

"Well, my dear, there is a land where we shall not *love* and *leave*," she wrote. "Those skies shall never cease to shine, the waters of life we shall *never* be called upon *to leave*. We have here no continuing city, but we seek one to come—."

Already the distance from home and those she loved was growing too great. And the next day it was up and out onto the road again. At Harrisburg the mountains began, and Lyman, thinking it would be faster and cheaper, decided to hire horses and a private coach for his family. So they started on the winding road that led over the Appalachians. The horses, it soon turned out, were not so fast as Lyman had hoped. They strained on the slopes, grew winded and halted. Progress was slow, continually being interrupted.

But if the scenery had been fine before, it was spectacular here. The mountain forests were flaming in autumn coloring; there were cascades, gorges, precipices. For Hattie, it was the first mountain scenery she had ever seen.

Was she impressed? The wild fall beauty around her must have left its imprint on her, as everything did. But her letters were oddly silent about any grandeur of nature she was witnessing. Was she falling back into her moods again, putting a screen between herself and the world, now that the journey had taken her so far into the wilderness? Or was she, like many another romantic of her time, inclined to be careless of landscapes that were without historical interest, unsoftened by tradition? Like Mrs. Trollope, she might have been more thrilled if a ruined abbey or Gothic temple or old monk's cell had appeared here and there in the midst of the wild, almost virgin territory.

The coach bounced and lurched, the horses panted and slipped and halted, and the miles wore on, day after day. Finally, eight days after leaving Harrisburg, the Beechers had completed a trip that the mail-stages made in forty-eight hours, and their coach rolled into the town of Wheeling, on the Ohio River.

Lyman had planned to halt there only briefly. A steamer was down at the wharf. The plans were for the family to board it next day and go the rest of the way to Cincinnati by water. But

as the Beechers disposed themselves among the Wheeling homes
that were welcoming them, there was dismaying news. Cincinnati, that lovely, healthful garden spot of the West, which people
had "to leave in order to get sick and die," was in the throes of
a terrible epidemic of Asiatic cholera.

Frightened passengers coming upriver on the steamboats, fleeing the stricken city, were telling dreadful stories. Coffins were
stacked in doorways in Cincinnati, and the deaths mounted daily.
The city was covered by a pall of smoke from open street fires
of bituminous coal. The smoke was supposed to suppress the
spread of the disease, but so far it seemed to have little effect.

Trying to suppress their own panic at these tidings from their
new home-to-be, the Beechers consulted on what they should
do. Plainly, they decided, it would be wiser to stay on in Wheeling until the epidemic had abated.

The Wheeling people were delighted. Dr. Beecher could
preach again and again while the family lingered, and give them
further benefits of his Eastern background. So Lyman did preach
for them, night after night, expounding all the points of the
New School doctrine of immediate repentance, that same doctrine which the eminent divine of Cincinnati had tried to have
branded as heresy just a year before. But the people of Wheeling had never heard the doctrine questioned, and knew little
enough about the whole New School-Old School controversy,
and so were pleased and edified.

After almost two weeks of this, the reports from down the river
began to sound more encouraging. The plague was slackening.
The Beechers could resume their journey.

Lyman had changed his mind about going by steamboat and
decided they should continue by land. He chartered a stagecoach,
the luggage was piled on the roof, the family settled inside,
and they were off. They crossed the Ohio River at Wheeling and
then rode south, along the river on the Ohio state side, south and
west, mile after mile. The singing began again. A few more tracts
were tossed to natives as they passed, and spirits rose generally.

Then, the river began its deep loop that would take it miles
south before it turned north and west again to Cincinnati, and

the Beechers turned away from the river road, to travel due west inland across Ohio toward their goal.

Harriet would write years later, about Ohio's corduroy roads, sending a hero forth over "an Ohio railroad of the good old times," which she would then describe in detail, telling how, in certain regions of the West, "where the mud is of unfathomable and sublime depth, roads are made of round, rough logs, arranged transversely side by side, and then coated over with earth, turf, and whatsoever may come to hand." This construction was then called a road, which "the rejoicing native straightway essayeth to ride upon."

Jolted and jarred, flung from one side of the coach to another, the Beechers essayed it in their turn. Cheerily, Lyman tried to distract everyone from the bumps, bruises and total disarrangement of clothing and possessions, by declaring such a road was good for dyspepsia. But there were worse hazards than the general buffeting to encounter. "Western travelers," Harriet would write, still on the same subject, "who have beguiled the midnight hours in the interesting process of pulling down rail fences to pry their carriages out of mudholes, will have a respectful and mournful sympathy with our unfortunate hero. We beg them to drop a silent tear and pass on."

Finally even this leg of the journey, mud-splashed and bonewrenching, was over. On November 14, 1832, they bounced their last bounce on corduroy and the coach rolled out onto the relatively well-paved streets of Cincinnati.

The city was big, much bigger than Hattie had imagined. Hundreds had died in the plague just past, and the smoke-blackened facades of the buildings were a reminder of that epidemic, and so were all the new graves in the cemeteries. Still, by 1832, Cincinnati had a population of almost thirty thousand. It was a city, there in the wilderness, a boom city that had attained its metropolitan size in less than twenty years.

There were the fine buildings of which Catherine had written on her first visit. There was the "noble" landing place. There were the thousands of busy, hurrying citizens. And there, up above the lower city, were the slopes on which Uncle Samuel and Uncle John had their homes. Beyond that upper city, screened by the

great trees that covered and crowned the heights, was Walnut
Hills, where the Seminary was located, Lyman's new headquarters. They would see Walnut Hills and the Seminary tomorrow.
For the weary travelers, who had been five weeks on their journey, it was enough to ride as far as Uncle Samuel's and Uncle
John's, where they would stay temporarily, and there disembark,
dirty, disheveled, and eager only to bathe and go to bed.

The novelty of it all entertained Hattie for a while, and she
was able to look with more humor than Mrs. Trollope did, on the
pigs in the streets.

"I have much solicitude on Jamie's account," she wrote to sister
Mary in Hartford, "lest he should form improper intimacies, for
yesterday or day before we saw him parading by the house with
his arm over the neck of a great hog, apparently on the most
amicable terms possible; and the other day he actually got on the
back of one, and rode some distance. So much for allowing these
animals to promenade the streets, a particular in which Mrs.
Cincinnati has imitated the domestic arrangements of some of
her elder sisters, and a very disgusting one it is."

She could also report humorously on the trials of their temporary home, the "most inconvenient, ill-arranged, good-for-noth-
ing, and altogether to be execrated affair that was ever put
together. The kitchen," she wrote, "is so disposed that it cannot be
reached from any part of the house without going out into the
air. Mother is actually obliged to put on a bonnet and cloak every
time she goes into it. In the house are two parlors with folding
doors between them. The back parlor has but one window, which
opens on a veranda and has its lower half painted to keep out
what little light there is. I need scarcely add that our landlord
is an old bachelor and of course acted up to what lights he had,
though he left little enough of it for his tenants."

She was still trying to hold fast to her resolutions—to count
only the unclouded hours—but the interlude of the journey was
over. She was set down in Cincinnati now, to pick up the daily
routine of life in a setting that was strange and bewildering.
And for her it would always be strange, no matter how long she

lived there. It would never become dear and familiar, cherished
even for memories of sufferings endured.

One day she would write movingly of those in exile, would
bring tears to the eyes of her readers as she wrote of Uncle Tom,
banished to the cotton plantations of the Deep South and dreaming of his cabin back in Kentucky, or of beautiful young Negro
girls, ravished and despairing, but still wistfully remembering
the happy security of their childhood.

It would not be odd that she could write so feelingly on the
subject and that it would be almost a joy to pour out the emotions of loneliness, homesickness and despair that it brought in
its train. She had begun to feel an exile as soon as she arrived in
Cincinnati, and so long as she lived there would feel, underneath
every other emotion, a longing for the New England where she
had been born.

Homesick or no, her days in Cincinnati were busy. Part of the
time there were domestic chores to do, helping Mama and Aunt
Esther with the endless sewing and mending required by a large
family ("Having finished the last hole on George's black vest, I
stick in my needle and sit down to be sociable."). Part of the
time, just as in Hartford, she trailed around after Catherine, who
was energetically making arrangements for her new school in
Cincinnati. This entailed talking to a great many people, expounding her plans for the school, getting subscriptions and en-
rollments, looking at various rooms where the school might be
located, shopping for equipment and supplies, or finding sources
where she might obtain them free. Harriet was of minor help in
such organizational activities, but Catherine liked to have someone to argue with as she made up her own mind.

A much more interesting project filled Harriet's spare time. At
last, after so many years of nothing but long, long letters and
required compositions for school, she was writing something. It
was her first serious writing project since the days of *Cleon*, that
grandly envisioned tragedy, so rudely interrupted by Catherine.
But the current project was something Catherine had suggested,
a useful and practical item, as anything Catherine suggested
would be. Catherine had decided there was a need for a new
geography for young children, and appointed Harriet to write it.

Modest though the assignment was for someone who had once planned to be a great writer or poet, Hattie was enjoying herself. It was her idea to make an interesting narrative text out of the miscellaneous information generally offered as geography, and she had begun it the summer before they started West.

Now, there was a pleasant sense of continuity with the past in getting to work on it again and finally finishing it. When the manuscript was completed, Catherine took it to a Cincinnati publishing firm, Corey, Fairbank and Webster, and not too much later there was the news that the book had been accepted for publication. Harriet's share of the purchase price was one hundred and eighty-seven dollars and it was a far more meaningful sum to her than any of the money she had ever received from Catherine in payment for her teaching efforts.

The Cincinnati newspapers carried an advertisement for the book in March.

A NEW GEOGRAPHY FOR CHILDREN
Corey & Fairbank have in the press,
and will publish in a few days, a
Geography for Children
with numerous maps and engravings,
upon an improved plan.
By. Catherine E. Beecher.

It was a small shock to Harriet to see only Catherine's name listed as author, but she accepted it stoically. Catherine was the Beecher daughter who was known in Cincinnati as a brilliant young educator from the East. It was only logical that the publishers would wish to take advantage of her name.

Another cheerful prospect filled Hattie with anticipation. Mary Dutton, her dearest "duck," the friend who had made one year at the Hartford Female Seminary so happy, was coming to Cincinnati!

Catherine's plans for her school had been advancing swimmingly. In the early winter she had written to Mary Dutton, still the most admired of the teachers who had worked for her in Hartford, to tell her how she was planning to "start a school of the first-rate order, which shall serve as a model to the West, and which shall gradually grow into a large institution as its conductors gain experience and public confidence." As she had determined long before, she was not going to be burdened with teaching cares herself, but was simply going to found the school, give it the prestige of the Beecher name, and then supervise its policies. So the real reason she was writing to Mary Dutton was to ask her to come West and be the new school's principal.

Why this proposal should have lured Mary, who could never be tempted from New Haven to Hartford after the first year, no one knew exactly. But after a few more letters, it was decided. She was coming West.

May was the month when all the plans and projects flowered. Mary Dutton arrived during the last of April, and it was almost as wonderful to see her again as Hattie had hoped. On May 1, the Western Female Seminary opened its doors for its first term, and if it was not quite so splendid as Catherine had originally planned—"handsomely furnished, with a carpet, curtains and each pupil with a desk and chair of her own. Also a piano to render Calisthenics interesting. Also recitation rooms, as many as necessary, furnished with blackboards . . ."—still it looked very well. In May, too, the *New Geography for Children* was published and began at once to sell briskly.

Accordingly, Hattie began a letter to Georgiana in a tone full of good cheer. She told her of how Cincinnati's Bishop had visited the school and spoken admiringly of her "poor little geography," thanking her particularly for "the unprejudiced manner" in which she had handled the Catholic question in it. It did indeed speak well for Hattie's objectivity, since her father held Roman Catholics to be almost as dangerous as Unitarians. She told Georgiana how flattered she had been that the Bishop knew of the book at all. Then, so buoyed up was she, she launched into a lyrical passage about Walnut Hills, where the Seminary was, and where the new Beecher house was being built: ". . . the road to it is as picturesque as you can imagine a road to be without 'springs that run among the hills.' Every possible variety of hill and vale of beautiful slope, and undulations of land set off by velvet richness of turf and broken up by groves and forest of every outline of foliage, make the scene Arcadian. . . . Much of the wooding is beech of a noble growth. The straight, beautiful shafts of these trees as one looks up the cool green recesses of the woods seems as though they might form very proper columns for a Dryad temple."

But: "There! Catherine is growling at me for sitting up so late; so 'adieu to music, moonlight, and you.' I meant to tell you an abundance of classical things that I have been thinking tonight, but 'woe's me.'"

When Hattie took up the letter again some days later, her mood had changed. Her brief brightness had vanished. She was the miserable Hattie of the drudging Hartford days, with the new loneliness of exile added.

"Since writing the above my whole time has been taken up in the labor of our new school, or wasted in the fatigue and lassitude following such labor. . . . About half of my time I am scarcely alive, and a great part of the rest, the slave and sport of morbid feeling and unreasonable prejudice. I have everything but good health."

She remembered—she told Georgiana how she remembered—her vow to speak cheerfully even to people who were not agreeable, and to say something when she had nothing to say, but it was no use.

What had happened? Was it simply the business of teaching, which she never liked, that threw her back into despondency? Or had the friendship with Mary Dutton, so idealized during the years of absence, proved somehow disappointing, now Mary was there in person? Pretty, poised, and popular at once with all the young ladies of the Seminary, perhaps Mary was too busy with her new duties as principal to pay much attention to Hattie.

The black moods were back whatever the reason. Georgiana, a thousand miles and more away, loomed again as the one faithful friend.

"Thought, intense emotional thought, has been my disease," Hattie cried out to Georgiana across the miles. "How much good it might do me to be where I could not but be thoughtless."

Recently Hattie had been reading the life of Madame de Staël, that extravagant French apostle of "enthusiasm" and "emotion," who practiced her theories as passionately as she preached them, taking unto herself one brilliant man after another as a lover, taking unto herself as an enemy none other than Napoleon Bonaparte himself. Remote as this sort of behavior was to a New England Calvinist like Hattie, was it strange that she felt "an intense sympathy with many parts of that book, many parts of her character"? Not really. Hattie was a creature of emotion herself.

"But," she wrote Georgiana, "in America feelings vehement and absorbing like hers become still more deep, morbid and impassioned by the constant habits of self-government which the rigid forms of our society demand. They are repressed, and they burn inward till they burn the very soul, leaving only dust and ashes. It seems to me the intensity with which my mind has thought and felt on every subject presented to it has had this effect. It has withered and exhausted it, and though young I have no sympathy with the feelings of youth. All that is enthusiastic, all that is impassioned in admiration of nature, of writing, of character, in devotional thought or emotion, or in the emotions of affection, I have felt with vehement and absorbing intensity,— felt till my mind is exhausted, and seems to be sinking into deadness. Half of my time I am glad to remain in a listless vacancy, to busy myself with trifles, since thought is pain, and emotion is pain."

She was twenty-two, young in years as she said, but perhaps she did have reasons for such an outburst, distracted and worn out by passions that had no channel for emergence, as Madame de Staël's did. "Withered and exhausted," she was in exile. And she had no inkling, and neither did anyone else, that the city that just happened to be the site of her exile, would provide her with the theme to release all her passions one day, in a flood of writing incredibly healing to her, incredibly inflammatory to the world.

Chapter 11

It is true that Master James had an uncommonly comfortable opinion of himself, a full faith that there was nothing in creation that he could not learn and could not do; and this faith was maintained with an abounding and triumphant joyfulness that fairly carried your sympathies along with him. . . .

1833–1834

Who could dream that Lyman Beecher, charging out to the West to win an empire for God, might possibly fall short of his goal? He had an aura of success about him that made such doubts unthinkable. Who could dream that Catherine, equally possessed of missionary zeal, might not accomplish all she planned? Catherine carried a conviction of her own infallibility too.

But the Cincinnati years were full of upsets. And the ultimate irony would be that Hattie, who had gone along because there was nothing much else to do, would be the one to emerge from the western sojourn with the greatest achievement.

In Cincinnati, across the river from the slaveholding state of Kentucky, she could not help observing, day after day, year after year, the particular kind of activity that was constantly going on along such a borderline between slave states and free. One way or another, and all unplanned, she would become acquainted with many kinds of Negroes, both slave and free. She would become involved with the plights of runaway slaves, and would hear, in the midst of conflicts that almost destroyed her father, every argument there was on either side of the slavery question, arguments for the civilizing benefits of slavery as well as arguments for and against every scheme for abolishing it. She would, because her exile had placed her at such a midpoint, be able to temper her indictment of slavery in a way no outright Northern Abolitionist was able to, dramatizing "something of the best" of the system, as well as "something approaching the worst." The South might never admit that she had shown any of "the best" of it and might be furious to hear the way she presented its own rationale, but the fact remained, she would have heard the defensive arguments of the South, however weak she might have found them. And in the dialectical style she had learned at her father's supper table, she was willing to let the South damn itself with its own theories.

She could never have done what she did if her life had left her in the comfortable patterns of her well-loved New England. Slavery would not have presented itself with the immediacy that made it such a unique emotional outlet for her own passions. Even if she had become theoretically dedicated to the cause of the slave, she could not have written a book that held the tension of "best" and "worst" without the years in Cincinnati.

The new proximity to slavery brought few immediate reactions from her and her family. Hattie noticed, as they all did, the advertisements for runaway slaves in the Cincinnati papers. "One hundred dollars reward . . . will be paid by the subscriber for the apprehension and delivery of Humphrey, a slave, who is about 17 years of age, and who made his escape from the undersigned in Boone County, Ky. on the 22nd ult. . . ."

She read similar signs posted in public buildings around the town, and, like the rest of her family, frowned and felt distressed. The evil she had heard about all her life was no longer far-off but close at hand. Then she began to read editorials in the Cincinnati *Journal* that made the evil even more real and immediate. The editor of a paper in a city located as crucially as Cincinnati, with its dependence on river traffic to and from the South as well as the East, had no thought of being Abolitionist, or even a spokesman for gradual emancipation. He had plenty of excuses for his Southern neighbors, helpless heirs of a system that left them in possession of, and responsible for, human property. Still, the sight of a steamer at the wharves, with a cargo of chained slaves on their way to market in New Orleans, could only provoke a protest against abuses of the system. However one might defend slavery, one could not defend the practice of raising slaves as a marketable commodity, and then sending them, herded like animals, to any fate that might befall. Reading about such specific instances of callousness and brutality, occurring so close to her, filled Hattie at first with a kind of incredulity, and then a sense of suffocating oppression. Slavery was even more dreadful than she had imagined. It was all around, and there was nothing she could do but shudder and look away.

Hattie's life had assumed a familiar pattern after the opening of Catherine's school. Day after day, she was busy preparing lessons, hearing recitations, going to teachers' meetings, making lists of matters to bring up at such meetings, "about quills and paper on the floor; forming classes, drinking in the entry (cold water, mind you); giving leave to speak; recess-bell, etc., etc." At the end of the school day, she slumped with fatigue and let her mind go blank.

Summer vacation brought a brief respite. There was even a holiday trip, in the summer of 1833. One of the students of the Western Female Seminary who lived across the river in Kentucky, had invited the school's popular principal, Mary Dutton, to visit her and her family. Mary asked Harriet to go along. It was a pleasant trip, down the river by steamboat fifty miles or so to Maysville, Kentucky, then a stage ride back into the country for a dozen more miles to the little town of Washington. And there they were, Mary and Hattie, two young ladies from New England, visitors for the first time in a region where slavery was the law of the land.

What impression did it make on Hattie? Her hosts lived in the village of Washington, in a comfortable house that was no plantation. They lived an easy, open-handed sort of life, quite different from the ordered thrift of New England, and there were domestic slaves to handle all the household chores.

Then one day during their visit, they rode to visit friends of their hosts out in the country, friends who did live on a plantation, a farm of some size and pretension, with a big, pillared house and a cluster of slave cabins out back. The master of the place was a genial fellow, kind to his Negroes, but when he asked one of them to perform for the company after dinner, he laughed at the small Negro's antics with the same unself-consciousness he would have shown at watching a monkey.

Was Harriet shocked? She gave no sign of it. In fact, throughout most of the visit to the plantation, she was lost in one of her fits of abstraction, and was "owling about," seemingly unaware of anything around her.

Mary Dutton looked at her and wanted to shake her for removing herself in such a fashion from this unusual experience. But much later, when Mary read Harriet's famous book, she would find a description of a pleasant plantation in Kentucky and recognize with a shock the place they had visited that day. The very essence of it had been imprinted on Hattie's memory, although she had seemed so far away.

Another scene stamped itself on her memory during this Kentucky visit. Their hosts took them to church. Seated a few pews away was a young woman of unique and puzzling beauty. She had brownish skin with a lovely flush to her cheeks, soft, rippling hair, great dark eyes with sweeping lashes. She was a quadroon, her hosts told Hattie, property of such and such a neighbor.

A quadroon! All that loveliness was simply the exotic flower of —what kind of liaison? Harriet tried not to think any further, tried not to picture some lustful white master, with no scruples as to sin or the need for self-control, inflicting his will on some helpless black woman, who had no hope of resisting, since she was only a piece of property. Had she fought her seducer anyway? As he came toward her had she— Hattie shut her eyes and her mind against the pictures her imagination presented to her so vividly and swiftly. But holding her mind shut against that sequence of pictures, another one simply rose in its place, an old and familiar one that had been part of her since childhood. The Aunt Mary legend. There was Aunt Mary suddenly confronted by a whole family of mulatto children, sired by her own husband—Aunt Mary with her heart breaking, sitting at the window of her island home, wishing the island would "sink with its load of misery, even if she sank with it." Harriet would have preferred not to think about Aunt Mary. Even a glancing recollection of her story brought back sensations that had filled her adolescent years with misery, curious tremblings and empty fainting feelings. She had fought her way through those, she liked to think, to some kind of calmness, however "withered and exhausted" the fight had left her. She would not look at the quadroon or think about her. She would not think about Aunt Mary either.

She fought such thoughts away, but they kept returning not just for the duration of the visit in Kentucky, but month after month, year after year. And when, one day, she came to write her book about slavery, her heroine, Eliza, would be just such a beautiful quadroon as she saw that Sunday. Nor would Eliza be the only product of illicit sex in the book, for an awareness of slavery as an invitation to sexual license—an equation of slavery with a release for all man's darker passions—would throb through it from beginning to end.

But that book, which would release so many burdens from Harriet's soul, was far in the future. And it was a blessing that soon after she and Mary returned to Cincinnati, Harriet was diverted by something that gave her an opportunity to look at the world as "a world of love" again. She found a new friend, one who seemed capable of taking the place Mary Dutton was not filling as she once had.

Calvin Stowe arrived in Cincinnati in the last part of August —"C. Stowe," the stocky, stubby young man who had been chosen as the incumbent for the chair of Biblical Literature at Lane Theological Seminary. With him he brought his young bride, the former Eliza Tyler, daughter of Dartmouth College's President Tyler. Dr. Tyler was a Calvinist of the Old School, whose warrings with Lyman's old friend, Dr. Taylor of Yale, had already polarized the conflict in the church into a Taylor-Tyler controversy. None of that mattered to Harriet. She took one look at Eliza Stowe, and "fell in love with her directly."

"Let me introduce you to Mrs. Stowe," Harriet wrote eagerly to Georgiana, "a delicate, pretty little woman, with hazel eyes, auburn hair, fair complexion, fine color, a pretty little mouth, fine teeth, and a most interesting simplicity and timidity of manner."

"Simplicity and timidity of manner . . ." They gave Harriet, so conscious of her own smallness and weariness, an assurance she lacked most of the time. At once, she and Eliza Stowe were

the best of friends, going to church together, and going to the
Presbytery meeting together, where Calvin Stowe was to present
his papers. Brother George was a focal figure at the same meeting. Having finished his theological studies with a few final
courses in the spring term at the new Lane Seminary, George
was applying for a license to preach. The restlessly hostile Dr.
Wilson, who had resented Lyman's coming to Cincinnati in the
first place, had plotted to make George's examination as difficult
as possible, hoping that any unorthodoxy proved against the son
would weaken the father's position as well. But George held his
own with the same aplomb that he had shown tossing tracts to
the natives of Pennsylvania. A true son of Lyman Beecher, he
answered and parried and resisted every attempt to shake him.
Warmed by her new friendship, full of that one pride she found
most forgivable, "pride of family," Hattie had been delighted.

When school began that fall, she was feeling much less "withered and exhausted" than before. She and Catherine were boarding in town close to the school. Eliza and Calvin Stowe were
living in Walnut Hills, near the Seminary and the Beechers' new
brick house. But the Beecher carryall was forever making the
two-mile trip down from Walnut Hills to the city and back again,
carrying Lyman to meetings, to preaching engagements, or to do
the family marketing. Often Eliza Stowe rode down in it, or Hattie rode back in it, to pay a visit to Eliza, and drop in on her
family.

Walnut Hills was a cheerful place to visit, for the fall term had
opened auspiciously for Lane Seminary, and Lyman was in tearing spirits. There had been a great influx of students, almost a
hundred, and Lyman saw his dream of a school that would train
ministers and missionaries by the score to win the West for
Calvinism already turning into a reality.

Almost all the new students had come in a body, under the
leadership of a tall young evangelist named Theodore Weld. Enrolled as a student, Theodore Weld was so self-assured and had
such influence over the young men who had followed him to
Lane, that he spoke and acted a good deal as though he were
running the Seminary. But Lyman only laughed. What did it
matter if it had been young Weld who brought the students?

They were there, and his own magic would keep them and mold
them as they should be molded. As for Weld's fine air of authority, Lyman was sure the young man would settle down in time
and see the folly of his arrogance. After all, he could be excused
for it. Already, at his early age, he had been an itinerant preacher
and lecturer, traveling through the South. It had given him a
precocious habit of command. But Lyman could handle him, or
so he thought.

Down in the city, Hattie was finding life not so burdensome
either. There was a brand-new social diversion to keep her from
morbid introspection—a literary club, which met weekly, generally at Uncle Samuel Foote's comfortable and expansive home.
Its name—the Semi-Colon Club—was the result of a labored bit
of punning, something to do with "Colon" being Spanish for
Columbus, and "he who discovers a new pleasure" being "certainly half as great as he who discovers a new continent," hence
"Semi-Colon." But the name was the only absurd thing about the
club. Some of Cincinnati's most distinguished citizens were members—Judge James Hall, a writer and the editor of the new *Western Monthly Magazine,* which Cincinnati residents regarded as
the equal of any eastern publication, young Salmon P. Chase,
already a leader in civic affairs, Caroline Lee Hentz, Cincinnati's
chief "literary lady"—and all of these added luster to the evenings. Harriet was most pleased because when she and sister
Catherine were asked to join, so were Calvin and Eliza Stowe.

Harriet found the Monday evening meetings a fine blend of
seriousness and frivolity. At each session a member was chosen
to read contributions, which could be either signed or anonymous.
After the reading, the work would be discussed, and then came
refreshments and a few rounds of the Virginia reel. Shy in general company as always, Hattie made sure her contributions were
anonymous, and at first she confined herself to humorous or satirical trifles. Once again she burlesqued the writing style of Dr.
Johnson, whose pen was "spellbound by fairies." She compiled a
set of legislative enactments against too much joking about "old
maids and bachelors," and she spent a good deal of time faking
a set of letters to make them look old, smoking them and tearing

them, sealing them and then breaking the seals, for another contribution.

And then she was suddenly caught up in something a great
deal more real than such schoolgirlish projects. It began as a character sketch, no more—a brief word-portrait of "Uncle Lot"
Benton, on whose farm her father had been raised and about
whom there had been so many family legends. But once involved
in describing that crusty, crochety, good-hearted character, once
transported in fancy to the New England she missed so constantly, Harriet found the sketch growing far beyond her original
plans for it. Facet after facet of the New England scene had to
be added.

She found herself with a plot on her hands, a young man, suing
for the affections of Uncle Lot's daughter, but needing to win
Uncle Lot's difficult confidence first. What sort of New Englander should the young man be? Without making any conscious
decision about it, Harriet began describing her father as she envisioned him when he was young—"one of those whole-hearted,
energetic Yankees, who rise in the world as naturally as a cork
does in water."

Harriet had grown up more than she knew. She was charmed
by the young man she was picturing, but she was not taken in
by him. "Master James," she called him, and, "Master James had
an uncommonly comfortable opinion of himself," she wrote, "a
full faith that there was nothing in creation that he could not
learn and could not do; and this faith was maintained with an
abounding and triumphant joyfulness that fairly carried your
sympathies along with him, and made you feel quite as delighted
with his qualifications and prospects as he felt himself."

She still felt a fierce and swelling pride in her father's activities
and achievements, felt that of course Lane Seminary would soon
be the great Western bastion of faith that he declared it would
be, felt a passionate rejection of Dr. Wilson, or anyone else who
contested her father's beliefs. At the same time she was now
able to write about the young "James Benton" with a small,
pleased smile on her lips, as she enumerated "a saucy frankness
of countenance," "a knowing roguery of eye, a joviality and
prankishness of demeanor that was wonderfully captivating, es-

pecially to the ladies." Young James was not the conceited sort of person who took no notice of other people's accomplishments. He was quick with praise and pleasure for other people's talents. But "his own perfections being more completely within his knowledge, he rejoiced in them constantly."

The words spun from Harriet's pen with ease. "James understood every art and craft of popularity, and made himself mightily at home in all the chimney corners of the region round about; knew the geography of everybody's cider barrel and apple bin, helping himself and every one else therefrom with all bountifulness; rejoicing in the good things of this life, devouring the old ladies' doughnuts and pumpkin pies with most flattering appetite, and appearing equally to relish everybody and thing that came in his way. . . ."

How had she come to see him so clearly, this man who had spent little enough time relishing the talents of his sixth child, but whose smile had been all the reward she needed when her essay had been read at the school exercises? Had the miserable adolescent years, when there had been so few smiles, forced a knowledge of him on Hattie in spite of herself? Or was her pen writing from a knowledge of which she herself was not wholly aware?

At any rate, there was "James," or Lyman, as robust a character as ever leaped into life on a scrawled page, and there was Uncle Lot, called "Uncle Tim Griswold" in the story, and he was wonderfully believable also, in his cross-grained petulance that forever belied his generous behavior.

His daughter, Grace, whom James was courting, had a request to make of him. In one scene "Uncle's" character came clear.

"Father," said Grace, after dinner, "we shall want two more candlesticks next week."

"Why, can't you have your party with what you've got?"

"No, father, we want two more."

"I can't afford it, Grace—there's no sort of use on't—and you shan't have any."

"Oh, father, now do," said Grace.

"I won't, neither," said Uncle Tim, as he sallied out of the house, and took the road to Comfort Scran's store.

In half an hour he returned again; and fumbling in his pocket, and drawing forth a candlestick, leveled it at Grace.

"There's your candlestick."

"But, father, I said I wanted *two.*"

"Why, can't you make one do?"

"No, I can't; I must have two."

"Well, then, there's t'other; and here's a fol-de-rol for you to tie round your neck." So saying, he bolted for the door, and took himself off with all speed. It was much after this fashion that matters commonly went on in the brown house. . . .

Writing the story was pure pleasure, but it was something else again when she had to turn it in, with proper precautions for secrecy, at the beginning of a Semi-Colon Club meeting. It would be read anonymously, but even so, how could she bear it if it were criticized? She wilted under criticism. No one else would know it was her work that was under discussion, but it was enough that *she* knew.

Then the story, "Uncle Tim," was read, and the whole membership of the Semi-Colon Club was captivated, as well it might have been. Suddenly, amidst the foolery, the bombast, or even the easily professional sentiment or reflection that pleased the time, it was hearing a true voice, a voice with a clear New England accent, informed by a shrewd, amused New England eye.

Harriet sat quietly, cheeks flushed, lids drooping over her eyes, as the chorus of praise rang around her. She did not quite know how she had done what she had done, nor if she really deserved such acclaim. And still there was more triumph to come.

Judge Hall, as everyone knew, had announced a prize story contest in his *Western Monthly Magazine,* as long ago as August. Hattie had never thought of entering it, not with all the professional writers living in Cincinnati who would surely be competing. Then, in November, because of the disappointing quality of the entries he had received, Judge Hall had extended the contest until February.

Now, charmed by the story he had just heard, he wondered why no story of its merit had been submitted. That very one should be entered, he declared, and he looked around the circle, alert for any telltale signs of authorship.

Did Harriet confess, now that success had made it safe? Or did Judge Hall guess by looking at her—guess, first of all, that it must have been one of the Beecher girls, so recently from New England, so steeped in its lore, and then guess from Hattie's flushed silence in the midst of the clamor, that it must have been she? One way or another, the secret was out. Then, nervously and eagerly, Harriet was insisting that she must polish the story before submitting it to the contest. Nervously and eagerly, she took it back to the room where she and Catherine were living, and worked over it as she had never worked over any writing before, and as she would rework very little of her writing in the future.

Finally she was satisfied. The story was submitted in proper order, and the announcement came as promptly as even the sensitive Harriet could wish. She had won the story contest, and the fifty-dollar prize. The schoolgirl dream of becoming a "great writer" might be a long way from fulfillment, but no one would have guessed it from the Beecher family reaction. Everyone had always known Hattie was a genius. Now here was public proof of it. She would go on to greater and greater achievement. Harriet felt a new sense of purpose. With this fifty-dollar prize, and the hundred and eighty-seven dollars that had been her share of the sale of the *New Geography*, she was actually earning money with her writing.

She set to work on another story, another character sketch, since the first had been so successful. Having taken her inspiration from her father for the first one, this time she turned to her mother. But now she was looking at a dream picture. She had few memories of her mother, could remember the "tulip bulb incident" and that was almost all. There were only legends of Roxana Beecher to help her, sentimental tales of a woman whose gentleness and serenity and understanding were so great that she made people good as though a spell were upon them. It was no sort of knowledge from which to build a real character, but convinced of her vocation as a writer, Harriet rushed ahead.

Finishing this one, she titled it "Aunt Mary," and it too was read before the Semi-Colon Club and hailed with delight. In critical retrospect, it seems nowhere near the equal of the story about Uncle Lot, its only sparkle provided by the character of a young boy, forever falling over things or dropping things or bungling things somehow, whose sense of awkwardness and shame was banished by the tender influence of "Aunt Mary." All her life Harriet would have similar troubles with women as heroines, any woman whom she wished to characterize as "good" evolving at once into a saint. But this view of women would not be displeasing to her audience later. It was not displeasing to the members of the Semi-Colon Club in the winter of 1834. Judge Hall was again so impressed that he bought "Aunt Mary" for later publication in his magazine. Two stories, bought for publication in the West's most eminent magazine! Small wonder if Harriet was happier that winter, able to forget sometimes, for hours, the sense of exile that still lurked within her.

The story about Uncle Lot finally appeared in the *Western Monthly Magazine* in April 1834. Retitled "A New England Tale," and signed by Miss Harriet E. Beecher, it filled the whole front half of the issue. It was part of the irony characterizing so many aspects of the Beecher sojourn in the West that the very month when Harriet achieved her first public success, Lyman Beecher met the defeat that was the beginning of the slow collapse of all his dreams.

Lyman did not recognize what happened that April as a turning point. He was too optimistic and self-confident to see doom for himself in any kind of setback. Besides, in his mind, the whole issue that was suddenly concerning him that spring could not possibly hold elements of disaster for him. Slavery! His stand on that had been clear for years. It was a sin, a moral evil. Gradual emancipation of the Negroes of the South, arrangements for their colonization in Africa, would have to cleanse America of this stain on its soul. The citizens of the South would have to awaken to their duty in this respect sooner or later. Meantime, he had not come West, to a city living in perilous confrontation of the evil, to create increased bitterness by belaboring his stand or the evil itself. "Great political and economic problems are not solved that way," he had told young Garrison in Boston; one had to consider what was expedient.

He had thought he could stay clear of the slavery issue. But he was reckoning without Theodore Weld.

Lyman knew that young Weld was an ardent Abolitionist, but full, even at fifty-nine, of that same "buoyant cheerfulness of mind" he had always known, he saw no threat. He knew that Weld, converted by Garrison's fiery *Thoughts on Colonization*, was talking immediate emancipation among his fellow students. But he did not see how that could cause any real trouble either.

Did he know, as well, that his and Lane's chief benefactor, Arthur Tappan of New York, had also been converted by Garrison's tract? Did he know that young Weld had been in New York for several weeks before coming to Lane in the fall, and had met and talked with Tappan and won Tappan's blessing for "introducing" antislavery sentiments at the Seminary? It hardly seemed likely.

Happily innocent, Lyman had busied himself all year with the multifarious concerns of managing the Seminary and teaching and preaching. And all the while Theodore Weld was single-mindedly pursuing his course of agitation. It was midwinter when the young man wrote to Tappan to tell him that Lane Seminary was not as hospitable to Negro students as it should be. It had a Negro student, a former slave, true enough, but though this in itself was unique, Weld had noticed that the Negro had not been present at the levee that Dr. Beecher had given to warm his new home. Was this an attitude of which Tappan could approve?

Lyman did not enjoy having to write a long, defensive letter to Mr. Tappan as a result of Weld's report, explaining that of course all the students had been invited to the levee. If he had known the Negro student was too shy to attend he would have gone to him personally and insisted that he come.

While this was rankling in Lyman's breast, young Weld came to him and announced he was ready to turn the Seminary into an Abolition Center. As a matter of form he was requesting permission to hold a debate on the subject to dramatize the fact, but his attitude made it plain he needed permission from nobody.

Controlling the various emotions aroused by the bland request,

Lyman urged the young man to postpone any such debate and attempted to convince him of how unwise it would be. The young man listened to his arguments, remained unconvinced and withdrew.

Lyman had reason for urging caution. There were in Cincinnati, because of its proximity to the South, a great many businessmen whose financial interests committed them completely to the status quo and slavery. There were also, in Cincinnati, a shipping center, any number of rough, transient characters who frequented the wharves—roustabouts, deckhands, drifters—all the elements that go to make up a mob. And there was, in Cincinnati a fair-sized colony of free Negroes, a focal point if a mob did collect and become violent. And there had been mobs and violence in the past.

But Theodore Weld was going ahead calmly with plans for the debate over abolition.

All Lyman's experience with young hotheads told him that an outright prohibition would only make matters worse. To keep the business in hand and convince the conservative elements in the city that all was still well at the Seminary, Lyman determined to uphold the negative in the debate himself. Abolition was not the answer to the problem of slavery. He would tell the students, and the city, why.

And so he did, as only Lyman could. For eighteen evenings, the debate raged. Night after night, students and faculty and a variety of other interested parties, filled the Seminary hall, and followed the play of the argument. Lyman poured into his talks all the eloquence, the charm, the passion, that had captivated thousands of audiences, and freely granted to the students that their sentiments did them credit.

"Boys, you are right in your views but impracticable in your measures. Mining and quiet strategy are better as well as safer methods of taking a city than to do it by storm . . ."

But Theodore Weld had eloquence and charm and passion too. And he also had some facts. Colonization, so highly regarded as a cure for slavery by Dr. Beecher, was completely inadequate as a remedy. The American Colonization Society, after fourteen years of valiant effort, had managed to return to Africa not quite fifteen

hundred Negroes, about as many as were born into slavery in the
United States every four months. Colonization as a means for
ending slavery was about as practical as trying to empty the
ocean with a pail.

A vote was taken at the end of all the debating. Unanimously
the students voted for a resolution to advocate the immediate
emancipation of slaves.

It should have alarmed Lyman more than it did. But Lyman
was a man "full of faith that there was nothing in creation that
he . . . could not do," and that included a full faith that he
could easily cope with this kind of insurrection among his students. He would watch, he would wait, he would give them their
heads for a while. Then, when and if it became necessary, he
would step in.

He watched as the students formed the Lane Seminary Anti-
Slavery Society. He watched and said nothing as the Society
drew up a declaration of principles and had the declaration published in the Cincinnati papers. And he watched as the young
men of the Society prepared to put their principles into action.

His daughter Harriet was watching too, and with growing uneasiness. She could not disagree with the principles the students
had declared, stating their belief in "social intercourse according
to character, irrespective of color." And certainly it was commendable of the students to establish a Lyceum for the Negro
colony in Cincinnati, commendable of them to start free evening
schools for teaching illiterate Negroes to read and write.

But she was there to see the angry looks Cincinnati citizens
were casting on the divinity students from the hill, as they prome-
naded the streets with groups of Negroes, both male and female.
She was there, to hear the mutterings about the way students
were eating with Negro families, spending the nights with them,
even boarding with them. The mutterings grew louder when a
group of young Negresses hired a carriage and rode up to the
Seminary for a picnic given for them by the students.

Lyman decided it was time for a warning. "Boys, if you go on
this way, you will be overwhelmed." He also decided to reassure
the city fathers of his own stand, and preached a ringing sermon
in the Second Church on the merits of Colonization. Hattie went

with Eliza Stowe to hear a lecture by Calvin on the same subject, further pounding home the Seminary's official stand.

But that seemed enough. And so, reassured by her father's
faith that all would be well, Harriet turned her thoughts from the
subject to something much more exciting.

Henry Ward, the younger brother who had always been Harriet's pet, was being graduated from Amherst in June. Mary Dutton was going east for the summer to visit her family. Why should
not Harriet go east with her, attend Henry's graduation, and then,
after visiting all the family and friends in Hartford and Nutplains
and elsewhere, return to Cincinnati with Henry?

Harriet grew giddy with anticipation. She dipped happily into
the funds of the Western Female Seminary for money to buy
lengths of cloth for a new dress. (Catherine never paid her a
regular salary. Hattie had no idea how much she took erratically
from the treasury, but surely it was very little. Her wants were
few. Certainly there was more than enough to her credit to pay
for this journey and a new dress as well.)

She and Mary Dutton set forth, by stagecoach to Toledo, then
steamship across Lake Erie to Buffalo, and stage again to Albany and Massachusetts.

Harriet's letters back to Cincinnati bubbled as they had at the
beginning of the journey west. She was full of witty descriptions
of her fellow passengers, amusing about the events of the trip.
The East was all that she hoped too. At Amherst, Henry Ward
was handsome and lively and wonderfully improved in one most
important way. Following the example of Demosthenes of old, he
had tried various remedies for his persistent thickness of speech,
and managed to completely cure it. Harriet was proud to bursting of his accomplishments and his popularity. Then after the
week at Amherst, she was off with Henry on the round of visits
she had promised herself.

Word arrived from Cincinnati that Lyman was coming east,
and Catherine also. With the Seminary officially closed for the
summer, Lyman was confident the antislavery flurry of the spring
would die down. He felt free to undertake a grand fund-raising
tour. Catherine had a goal of her own—recruiting more teachers
for the Female Seminary. Soon they were on their way.

Disaster struck in Cincinnati while all of them were in the East.

Harriet was the one most appalled by the news brought by a letter in August. Cholera had broken out again in Cincinnati. She knew that from the letter that had heralded her father's trip east. There had also been word that Eliza Stowe was not so well, but no hint that the ailment was anything serious.

And then Eliza Stowe was dead! Eliza! pretty Eliza Stowe, with her "little mouth, fine teeth," and her "simplicity and timidity of manner," gone, with the same shocking suddenness as so many others—Harriet's own mother, Catherine's lover, and others not so near, but near enough. The rest of the summer was darkened for Hattie.

Lyman was most affected by the other disaster in Cincinnati, but it took him some time to even realize anything was wrong. Convinced that his worries about the Lane Anti-Slavery Society were over, at least for the summer, he was preaching here, there and everywhere, expounding on the need to keep the West free from Catholics and infidels. One letter after another from Cincinnati related the mounting difficulties there, but he took little heed of them.

Lane Seminary had closed for the summer, true enough, but he was forgetting about fifty or sixty students whose homes were distant and whose funds were low, who were staying on in the dormitory. Freed from the restraints of classwork, they were devoting all their time to their self-chosen task of elevating the Negro. There had been another picnic for a group of young Negresses. This time, the displeasure down in the city, which had only been a muttering before, grew to a clamor. There was an outraged editorial in one of the papers, and other expressions of indignation.

The protests so alarmed the members of Lane's Board of Trustees who were left in the plague-troubled city, that they quickly assembled, and in a thoughtless panic adopted a resolution to abolish the Lane Anti-Slavery Society. They also decided on a resolution to prohibit any further discussion of slavery in the Seminary.

Not content with merely passing such resolutions, eager to

quiet the sense of outrage in the city, they had their resolutions published.

Now, as the Cincinnati papers went out across the country in exchanges with other papers, this ringing prohibition of free speech was seized on everywhere as an item worthy of reprinting. Lane Seminary was winning a notoriety it had never known before.

It *was* disaster—as Arthur Tappan, the fervent Abolitionist, read that slavery might not even be discussed in the school he had helped to found; as men and women everywhere read the item and leaped to the conclusion that Lane Seminary was not only a proslavery school, but an institute of oppression as well.

Lyman realized at last that all was not well in Cincinnati, and he stopped his lecturing and hurried westward. But by the time he got there, Theodore Weld had already walked out of the school, taking his followers with him, and they were camping in the countryside nearby, while Weld looked for a school "where free discussion would be tolerated"—a haven they would eventually find in the new and radical Oberlin College.

Lyman Beecher would not recognize it, or admit it, for years, but the school that was to have given a "complexion, probably forever, to the West" was doomed. He would keep it alive by his indomitable will for a long, long time, but the empire of the West was lost to him. The slavery issue, on which his daughter would unexpectedly ride to fame, had just as unexpectedly trapped him, full of "abounding and triumphant" faith as he was, and moral and sensible as all his views were.

Chapter 12

1835–1838

The bewildering years were beginning, years full of a bustle and commotion that would somehow blur in later history books, leaving a time that would seem unfocused and unromantic to later generations.

A few figures would stand out, lovable and understandable enough for legend. Jackson was one of those, Jackson who was President until 1838. He was not a man whom the politically conservative Lyman Beecher could approve ("Oh, Lord, grant that we may not despise our rulers—and grant that they may not act *so we can't help it*," Lyman prayed very seriously one Sunday in Cincinnati). Jackson was insisting that Peggy Eaton, an ex-barmaid who had finally married a senator after what some people were sure was an interlude of dalliance, be accepted socially in Washington. His only reason for this insistence was that his beloved dead wife had liked and defended the cheerful, flighty creature. But the quixotic sense of gallantry that would lead to a "Peggy Eaton crisis" in his cabinet and an irrevocable split with John C. Calhoun (whose wife would *not* receive Mrs. Eaton) would seem very human and endearing—later. Jackson, blunt, plain, honorable, would stand out above the bewildering hubbub.

But after Jackson there came Martin Van Buren. People called that short, shrewd man "The Little Magician," for he knew how to play politics, and how to handle Jackson, using Old Hickory's dismay about the Peggy Eaton scandal to further his own ends. But there any legend ended, and there was little about him to excite the imagination and sympathy of a later time.

People were beginning to concern themselves with such curious things—or so it would seem, later. The energetic building and expanding were still going on—canal building, railroad building, the establishment of new businesses and factories. But reformers, always a vaguely unsympathetic lot, were beginning to pop up everywhere.

Many of their causes were admirable. Some would even remain understandable. Catherine Beecher gave up teaching entirely in 1834 to travel about the West, crusading for higher education for females and the employment of women as teachers not only for girls but also for boys. And it would not be difficult to salute her later, and give her credit as a pioneer. Then there was Lucretia Coffin Mott, joining her husband in the Abolitionist movement, and beginning to fret about the restraints laid on women, so they could not speak in public, however informed their views —a pioneer in the cause of women's rights. There were the two beautiful Grimke sisters, Sarah and Angelina, of Charleston, South Carolina, coming north and being converted to the Quaker faith and the Abolitionist theories, and then going south to free their slaves. In 1838, Angelina would marry the zealous Theodore Weld and join her efforts to his in the Abolitionist cause. It would be easy to salute and admire all of these, and many others, dedicated and active toward the same worthy goals.

But there were thousands more, dedicated to causes less comprehensible, all designed to rescue the United States from its awkward age. Theodore Weld, before he became committed to the Abolitionist movement, had been engaged in proselytizing for Manual Labor Institutes. A sufficient number of these, dotted across the country, would have a marvelous missionary effect, it was believed. Plans for Utopian colonies were engaging many serious, intelligent thinkers. The social theories of the French reformer, François Marie Charles Fourier, were having their impact on Americans. Society should be reorganized into small, cooperative groups—phalanxes—of a thousand people or more, each group living autonomously and working and loving in an atmosphere of freedom, enthusiasm and harmony. The colony of New Harmony, out in Indiana, had already collapsed in discord. But Brook Farm, bright vision of the intellectuals of Boston was still to come. "Utopia in patty-pans," Ralph Waldo Emerson would call it, but the young writer, Nathaniel Hawthorne, the sage Bronson Alcott, and dozens of others were eager to experiment with a way of life designed to bring out all that was finest in everyone.

Or perhaps it was not cooperation that was lacking, but culture. A few pioneers were crusading in that field. In New York, an art lover named James Herring was planning an art gallery, adding the lure of a lottery to make it more palatable to the masses. A five-dollar membership might win one a "large and costly Original Engraving from an American painting." In Boston, the brilliant and erratic Margaret Fuller was crusading to make Americans aware of European literature, as though they had ever really known any other kind.

Naively earnest as such activities might sound later, there were others still more naive.

"What a fertility of projects for the salvation of the world!" Ralph Waldo Emerson would write. Beginning his own career as a Unitarian minister, he had lost God entirely in that faith and turned finally to a philosophy that found man infinitely perfectible—Transcendentalism. Still he had an amused smile for the proliferation of ideas that might lead man to perfection. "One apostle thought all men should go to farming; and another that no man should buy or sell; that the use of money was the cardinal evil; another that the mischief was our diet, that we eat and drink damnation. These made unleavened bread and were foes to the death of fermentation. . . ."

Bewildering years—and also, somehow, years that were embarrassing to remember. Perhaps that was why they appeared to blur so.

People had such odd visions in those years. Visions, trances, superstitious dreads, unlikely manifestations—they were, if not universal, quite taken for granted.

Later, after Lincoln had become a legendary figure, his melancholy, his strain of backwoods mysticism, his belief in dreams as omens, would become hallowed. Men would look back at him as he was in 1832—a gawky storekeeper and would-be legislator in the ramshackle settlement of New Salem, Illinois, and the melancholy that alternated with his humor would seem unique. They would read his account of his brief service in the Black

Hawk War, and how he and his company had arrived at the
scene of a skirmish in time to bury the dead—read of how young
Abraham Lincoln had seen the dead strewn about the prairie,
and "painted all over" by the red sunset. And the mystic strain
in the writing would seem wholly prophetic, wholly his own.

Lincoln's mysticism would indeed lead him to visions and per-
ceptions profound enough to guide a nation. But others were
having mystic experiences. Margaret Fuller, clever and erudite
as she was, had visions and walked in her sleep. And no one
suggested she might be curiously troubled or even ill. Young
Joseph Smith, of Palmyra, New York, had a vision in the twenties,
a vision of an Angel of the Lord, who told him to go to a certain
hill where he would find golden tablets engraved with "the ever-
lasting gospel," along with magic spectacles that would help him
read the tablets. By 1830, with the aid of the spectacles, he had
deciphered the tablets and was founding the Mormon Church,
with himself as prophet of a new dispensation.

Bewildering years, the 1830s and 1840s, full of a bustle that
would seem only half comprehensible to later generations,
haunted by visions that would be hardly comprehensible at all.

But it all seemed natural to young Harriet Beecher. Returned
to Cincinnati, with Henry, in the fall of 1834, she was involved as
a matter of course with Catherine's crusade for reforming female
education. And it was the recently bereaved Calvin Stowe who
unfolded a strange story of visions, not only to Harriet, but to the
entire Semi-Colon Club.

Round, moonfaced and generally rumpled, Professor Stowe had
a fine pulpit air of authority all the same, as he stood up one
Monday evening in the early winter of 1835 to read a paper to
the club that might have been one of the most surprising in its
history. Except that nobody in that time or place was that much
surprised by the sort of story the paper revealed.

Mr. Stowe, a vastly learned scholar of Hebraic languages, a
sober and respected Professor of Biblical Literature, and Lyman's right hand at Lane Seminary, had, he was now confessing,
been since childhood, subject to a variety of visions, hallucina-
tions and delusions.

He approached his revelation as objectively as possible. "The facts," he said, by way of introduction, "appear to me to be curious and well worth the attention of the psychologist." He continued, saying that he found them the more remarkable since he felt he had no talent whatsoever for creating fiction or poetry, and was barely able to enjoy the works of others in that department of literature—a frank enough confession to a literary club of which he had been a member for a year and more. His only talents, he believed, were for accurate observation of men and things, and a certain broad humor and drollery.

All that notwithstanding, he saw things. Or, as he told the Semi-Colon Club: "As early as I can remember anything, I can remember observing a multitude of animated and active objects, which I could see with perfect distinctness, moving about me, and could sometimes, though seldom, hear them make a rustling noise, or other articulate sounds; but I could never touch them. They were in all respects independent of my sense of touch, and incapable of being obstructed in any way by the intervention of material objects; I could see them at any distance, and through any intervening object. . . . I could see them passing through the floors, and all the ceilings, and the walls of the house, from one apartment to another, in all directions, without a door or a keyhole or crevice being opened to admit them. . . . These appearances occasioned neither surprise nor alarm, except when they assumed some hideous and frightful form, or exhibited some menacing gesture, for I became acquainted with them as soon as with any of the objects of sense."

It was tantalizing, even in a day when visions were not unlikely. *What* were these appearances that came and went so freely and casually? Harriet Beecher, with her own reputation for being "odd," her own trances of abstraction, her own vivid mental pictures, was sitting on the edge of her chair in Uncle Samuel's parlor, her great eyes wide, her lips parted, as she listened.

Calvin Stowe grew more specific. He had been a boy of four, in Natick, Massachusetts, when the family moved to a low, one-story house. His bedroom, just off the kitchen, had also held the staircase to the garret, a staircase only half enclosed. Every night,

after he had gone to bed, and the candle had been removed, a
very pleasant-looking human face would appear over the top
board of this enclosure, and "gradually press forward his head,
neck, shoulders, and finally his whole body as far as the waist,
through the opening," smiling at the little boy all the while with
great good nature.

"He was a great favorite of mine," said Calvin, "for though we
neither of us spoke, we perfectly understood, and were entirely
devoted to, each other. It is a singular fact that the features of
this favorite phantom bore a very close resemblance to those of
a boy older than myself whom I feared and hated; still the resemblance was so strong that I called him by the same name,
Harvey."

Other visions were not so kindly. One night Harvey appeared
"with an expression of pain and terror on his countenance." Turning his eyes to the far wall of the room, the little boy saw it
suddenly transformed into a vista of Hell, where a band of small,
resolute devils, all ashy-blue in color, and hairless and glossy, were
busy torturing a certain "unprincipled and dissipated man in the
neighborhood"—a man, as it happened, whom the little boy also
hated and feared. The persistence and cruelty of the devils, who
began forcing the unfortunate victim through some sort of huge,
iron press, ultimately alarmed the young Calvin so that he fled
to his parents' room for comfort. But it never occurred to him to
tell them what he had seen. Nor did he tell them another time,
when he woke one night to find a full-sized, ashy-blue skeleton
in bed with him.

Then he returned to happier visions. At one time, he told the
spellbound club members, "I saw upon the window-stools companies of little fairies, about six inches high, in white robes, gam-
boling and dancing with incessant merriment. . . . They took the
kindest notice of me, smiled upon me with great benignity, and
seemed to assure me of their protection." Still, there had been "a
sort of sinister and selfish expression in their countenances which
prevented" the boy from placing implicit confidence in them.
Another time, he seemed to see a meadow and a grove, and
across the meadow "a charming little female figure" advancing,
"about eight inches high and exquisitely proportioned, dressed

in a loose black silk robe." She advanced, smiled at the boy, and
then ran away.

Devils, skeletons, visions of Hell, a pleasantly transformed version of a daytime enemy, another daytime enemy being punished
cruelly—where had they all come from?

Calvin Stowe gave a brief account of his emotional nature as a
boy. He had loved "solitary rambles," especially at night. "Moonlight was particularly agreeable to me, but most of all I enjoyed
a thick, foggy night." Sometimes he would be oppressed by a
deep feeling of melancholy, a conviction that "friends at home
were suffering some dreadful calamity," so vivid that he would
rush home to see what had happened. He also confessed he had
"a morbid love for my friends that would almost burn up my
soul and yet, at the least provocation from them, I would fly into
an uncontrollable passion and foam like a little fury."

He also referred to the books he had read as a child. Even
fewer had been available to him than to young Hattie Beecher.
He had found "intense delight" in the books of Job and Revelation, in the Bible. There had been a book containing extracts from
Milton and Shakespeare. But of all the books that he read none
compared to Bunyan's *Pilgrim's Progress*. He took it to bed with
him and hugged it to his bosom while he slept.

There it was. He had read the same books every child read
who grew up in the early years of the nineteenth century and
had heard the same kinds of sermons. If he was really lacking in
imagination, as he said, he certainly was not lacking in emotionalism. And he had visions.

There were no theories then to consider the ways in which a
small boy, oppressed by internal fears and anxieties, might ex-
ternalize those fears into visions and phantoms so they would be
more bearable and easier to escape.

Calvin Stowe gave his one explanation, "I became satisfied that
it was all a delusion of the imagination"—never mind how lacking he was in that quality—and sat down.

The members of the Semi-Colon Club were fascinated by the
whole story and made neither frightened nor uneasy. It was indeed a curious tale, quite remarkable, but there was no fathom-
ing these things, no way on earth one could explain them.

Later, Harriet learned that the visions were not all things of
the past, as Calvin Stowe had indicated in his paper, but still
continued. She heard that even now, seated in his study of an
evening with his books before him, he might look up and see—
almost anything. Sometimes, he would see the lovely and beloved
young wife whose death had been such a blow to him. She would
not say anything. He could not touch her or speak to her, but it
was a comfort all the same just to see her, gentle and smiling
as she had been in life.

What more did Harriet need to start looking at Calvin Stowe
with new eyes? She had felt an enormous sympathy with him in
his grief over Eliza's death. Since her return from the East, her
sympathy and his need to talk of his dead wife had brought them
into much more frequent conversation. With these revelations
that added such a strangely exotic element to his character, Calvin Stowe, round and rumpled though he might appear, became
almost a figure of romance.

Chapter 13

*Well, here comes Mr. S., so farewell, and for the last time 1
subscribe   Your own, H.E.B.*

1834–1836

He was hardly the man of whom she had dreamed, she who
had loved Byron all her life, and the novels of Sir Walter Scott.
A plump, already balding widower, first drawn to her because of
her willingness to talk interminably about his dear, dead wife, he
was in no way like any of the heroes who would, years later,
move through her novels. He was not handsome, reckless and
cynical like Augustine St. Clair, the Byronic hero of *Uncle Tom's
Cabin*. He was not handsome, earnest and dedicated, like Edward Clayton of *Dred*. He was not even curly-haired, merry and
buoyant like the Master James of her first story, "Uncle Tim."

But Calvin Stowe was far from unlovable. There were endearing aspects of his character that she discovered gradually, as they
saw each other more and more frequently.

He was a friendly, eager sort of man. His classmates at Bowdoin College, in Maine, from which he had been graduated in
1824, had liked him. The classmates had been, by and large, a
worldly lot, skeptical in religious matters where Calvin was pious
to an extreme. Calvin had known scraping poverty all his life,
and many of the boys came from wealthy and cultured homes.
Just the same, they had liked him, in spite of his piety, rusticity
and tendency to grind. When graduation day came, it was inevitable that he should be valedictorian, but there was pleasure
in it for everyone. There were, among his classmates, and in the
classes below him, various young men who would know fame
one day. They had all congratulated him and parted from him

fondly. Franklin Pierce, one day to be President, had laughed
after the exercises and said, "You know I only made it because
I sat next to you, Stowe." There had been good wishes from a
young man with a taste for poetry, Henry Longfellow, and from
an intense undergraduate with a gift for writing, Nathaniel Hawthorne.

Gradually, Harriet began to see for herself why Calvin might
have been popular with his classmates, why all his students at
Lane liked him, why her brother, Henry Ward, taking up theological studies at the Seminary, found Professor Stowe's course
the most satisfying and admired the man extravagantly.

Calvin was preoccupied with his grief for Eliza. Even so, he
showed a flash of droll Yankee humor now and then. Harriet
liked the colloquialisms of country folk, had enjoyed them ever
since childhood days in Litchfield. She was appreciative when
Calvin Stowe showed his own pleasure in these. And there were
times when he could tell a New England anecdote with even
greater effect than Lyman himself.

Calvin Stowe was also a man without guile or envy. Prodi-
giously learned, author of a highly praised work on Biblical literature even before he finished college, he put on no airs about his
erudition, and was full of genuine admiration and respect for the
talents of everyone else. Lyman Beecher, under whose spell he
had fallen in the late 1820s, was still one of his idols, a leader
whose guidance he never thought of questioning. Obviously, this
could only endear him to Hattie.

And then there was the way he reacted, as emotionally as she,
to tales of human drama, heroism or suffering.

Circumstances threw them together in the fall of 1834, when
their acquaintance was still somewhat general and impersonal,
so that they both caught a glimpse of just the kind of drama that
excited them, and heard a tale that neither one of them would
ever forget.

The Cincinnati Synod of the Presbyterian Church was meeting
in Ripley, a little town some miles down the Ohio from Cincinnati. Harriet had decided to go with her father. Calvin Stowe
was also attending the meeting. As matters were arranged, Lyman, Harriet, and Calvin Stowe were all three the guests of a

certain Reverend Rankin for the duration of their stay. And it was this same Reverend Rankin, a modest, amiable man, whom they had known previously simply as a worthy minister, who astonished them all one evening with the revelation of a secret life quite at variance with his mild public character.

The Reverend Rankin's home crowned a high bluff overlooking the river and the opposite Kentucky shore, while the town and his own church were invisible beneath, at the foot of the cliff. Every evening, they noticed, he carefully lighted a lantern and placed it in one of the windows overlooking the river.

Why? one of them asked at last. Was there some reason for this nightly ritual?

There was a pause before the Reverend Rankin answered, for the answer was one that could doom him if it were repeated in the wrong quarters. But plainly he had more confidence in Lyman Beecher's antislavery sentiments than the intransigent Theodore Weld. All of a sudden he was telling them in a quiet voice that the light did have a meaning over on the Kentucky shore, where it was visible as a faint twinkle. Whether any white Kentuckians realized its significance, he did not know, but every slave along that stretch of shore knew it as a beacon of freedom. Any slave who had the resolution and courage and good fortune to run away from his bondage and to arrive safely at the river and then cross it, knew that at the top of the bluff where the lantern glimmered, he would find food and clothing and help in hurrying on toward the next such clandestine aid station on the way to Canada.

Hattie and Calvin and Lyman could only stare at the Reverend Rankin with wondering eyes. They had heard of these secret routes from the slave states to the North and Canada (routes that would soon be called the Underground Railway). They had heard of the brave and quiet men who maintained them, men as violently opposed to slavery as any William Garrison or Theodore Weld, but men who chose to express their opposition in secret acts that at least rescued some individuals for freedom. Oftenest, it seemed, such men were Quakers, committed by their faith to this kind of quiet resistance. But here was their host, admitting that he also was one of the few.

Then the Reverend Mr. Rankin went on to make the revelation even more vivid by recalling some of the fugitives he had
helped. It was 1825 when he first lit his beacon, he told them,
and there had been many to make their way across the river and
up the bluff to his home. Still, to the Reverend Rankin, the most
memorable runaway of all was one who had accomplished the
dramatic feat of making her way over the river on foot, across
the winter ice. She had been a young Negro mother, fleeing a
cruel mistress in Kentucky. Her baby bundled to her breast, she
had slipped away into the woods one cold March afternoon and
hurried toward the river. It had been dark when she reached the
Kentucky shore, and the Ohio could hardly have looked more
forbidding and treacherous. For a month and more it had been
frozen solid, due to an especially bitter winter, then a March thaw
had brought a thin film of water to the surface and started cracks
forming here and there. There was no way of telling where it
might already be too weak to support any weight, no telling
when the whole icy mass might suddenly break.

Still, the desperate woman had started out across the river,
clutching her baby against her. She had slipped and fallen, soaking her clothes in the icy water, struggled up and gone forward
a few more yards, only to slip and fall again. But slipping, falling, struggling up and on, she had made her way across the river
at last, and then toiled up the steep bluff to Rankin's house. He
had given her dry clothing and food, and when she was warmed
and rested a little, he had driven her and the baby some miles
into the back country of Ohio, where another dedicated foe of
slavery was ready to shelter her until she was strong enough for
the long trip to Canada.

That was not all the story, the Reverend Rankin said. When
he had returned from his hurried and secret journey, some time
after midnight, he had heard a sudden thunder and rumble from
the river. The ice was breaking up. It had held just long enough
for the fugitive mother to make her escape, and then it had begun cracking everywhere, moving, heaving, starting its rush down
the river on the icy current flooding up from the river depths.

Mr. Rankin's listeners were all thrilled, but to Harriet it had
been as though she were fleeing with the desperate woman. Her

heart had gone faster and faster as she envisioned the slippery ice, the stumbles, the falls, and above all, the need to escape—the straining to run at whatever peril, from nameless dangers threatening from behind. She had sighed with overwhelming relief at the picture of Mr. Rankin opening his door to the runaway. The fugitive was safe. She had made her escape. She was free. Inevitably, the imagined scenes of the story printed themselves in Harriet's memory to remain there, vivid and compelling, waiting for her to describe them in her famous book.

The story was also another bond between her and Calvin Stowe. Together, they had lived through the drama in imagination. Later that evening, in the Rankin front yard, standing by the picket fence at the edge of the bluff and gazing out over the dark river, she and Calvin could murmur their wondering reactions to each other. They could express their admiration of the daring mother, of the brave Reverend Rankin, and speak once again of their mutual hatred of slavery. In the soft autumn dark, caught up in the mood of the story, Harriet could forget her shyness, and Calvin could see her more as she really was, emotional, passionate, full of unchanneled love. In the same dark, Harriet could see Calvin better too, see him as more than the husband of her late friend, more than a scholar and preacher and teacher and disciple of her father. She could see him as a gentle man, profoundly touched, as she was, by heroism and kindness and fate's mysterious ways.

After they returned to Cincinnati, various occasions brought them together—church services, functions at the Seminary, Harriet's visits to the Beecher house up in Walnut Hills, the Monday evening meetings of the Semi-Colon Club.

Then came the Monday evening when Calvin Stowe read of his singular psychic experiences to the club members, and Harriet saw still another aspect of this kind, clever, funny man. He claimed he had no imagination. He modestly said that if he had any talents they were for accurate observation and broad humor and drollery. But Harriet made her own interpretations. He was more colorful and dramatic than she had dreamed. There was in him, as his visions testified, that dark strain of melancholy she always found so irresistible. With melancholy and humor intermingled, with simple kindness joined to great learning, he had some of her own contradictions, and there was an appeal in that too.

Reasons for them to meet multiplied. Calvin undertook a series of Sunday evening sermons at Lyman's Second Church, sermons drawing on his immense knowledge of the origins of the Bible. One way or another, Harriet had herself delegated to report the sermons for the newspaper. Plainly, this called for conferences both before and after the sermons, to discuss technical and intricate details. Calvin Stowe became a regular visitor to Hattie's rooms down in the city.

Once the habit was established, there were many excuses to maintain it. Calvin was compiling a series of lectures for publication. He needed Harriet's help. Harriet was eager to ask his advice about school problems, about Catherine's latest educational theories, about her own activities in connection with the church missionary society.

Drawing them together even more than any of these subjects, even more than their grief for Eliza, was another topic of conversation. This was the succession of troubles besetting the man they both loved—Lyman Beecher. The fuse that Theodore Weld had lighted with his Abolitionist activities had not gone out with that young man's departure from Lane Seminary and Cincinnati. Instead, it continued to sputter along, setting off one explosion after another. These threw Harriet and Calvin together in mutual outbursts of rage and helpless sympathy for Lyman.

William Garrison, in Boston, finally got around to commenting on the events at Lane Seminary in the summer of 1834, when the Anti-Slavery Society had been outlawed and any discussion of slavery prohibited. When he spoke at last, Garrison, immoderate in all his utterances, and remembering Lyman Beecher's refusal to support his antislavery magazine in 1830, was even more immoderate than usual.

It made no difference to Garrison that Lyman Beecher, on his hasty return to Cincinnati, had done what he could to modify the Board of Trustees' restrictive rulings—any suppression of societies, or of free speech was to be left to the discretion of the faculty, and so on. Garrison was not interested in equivocation.

The techniques of compromise in which Lyman was adept revolted him. As a result, Lyman Beecher and his family and Calvin Stowe and anyone else who was interested, could read in the January issue of *The Liberator* that "Lane Seminary is now to be regarded as strictly a Bastille of oppression—a spiritual Inquisition." Lest anyone should doubt the grounds for such a conclusion, Garrison published both the damning resolutions of the Board of Trustees and the protesting statement of the seceding students.

It made bitter reading for Lyman. And Harriet and Calvin could wax righteously indignant for hours. It was not Lyman who had put the ban on the Anti-Slavery Society. His stand against slavery had been clear for years.

Then came another explosion. Arthur Tappan, whose support had helped found Lane, and on whose bounty Lyman depended for his salary, had been much impressed by Garrison's remarks about the Seminary. Accordingly he joined with other New York Abolitionists to have the editorial attack reprinted in a pamphlet, which was then circulated by the thousands.

Harriet could rage again, but at this news Calvin was almost more frightened than angry. Enrollment at the Seminary was down badly this year. After the exodus of Weld and his followers, that had been expected. But what of the future? Would it ever pick up, with a pamphlet like this circulating among the very people who might be sending their sons to a theological seminary?

Another firecracker went off, in an area no one had suspected before. It was their host of the previous fall who attacked this time, none other than the amiable Reverend Rankin whose clandestine slave smuggling had so impressed them. Now it seemed he had reviewed the evidence in the affair of "Lane versus Weld" and had been so dismayed by the actions and attitudes of the board and the faculty that he was moved to write a long letter of protest to the Cincinnati *Journal*.

It was too much for Calvin. Someone had to defend the Seminary, so he sat down and penned a long letter in reply. This provoked an answer from Rankin, and so, intermittently for months after that, the debate continued. Naturally Harriet and Calvin found this a stimulating subject for discussion.

More trouble rained on Lyman, trouble finally that had nothing to do with Theodore Weld, but which could only keep everyone in a state of agitation. It was a shock to Harriet personally
that it was Judge Hall who attacked her father now, that same
delightful editor who had so praised her writing and given her
her first publication. Judge Hall was not taking advantage of
the antislavery difficulties at Lane. He had new complaints of
Dr. Beecher and was accusing him in the *Western Monthly Magazine* of bigotry, intolerance, and incitement of religious hatred
against the Catholics.

As it happened, the charges were not without facts to back
them up. In the East, that fateful summer of 1834, when Theodore Weld was stirring up his own brand of trouble at Lane, Lyman had become somewhat carried away in his fund-raising
sermons and speeches. A great and steady influx of Irish immigrants into Boston had caused an enormous increase in the Roman Catholic population there. Anti-Catholic sentiment was high,
and it was fatally easy for Lyman to seize on public moods and
emotions, to use them for his own purposes. "Help us to save the
West from Popery," he had cried, and donations for Lane had
poured in. It was the poor timing of the Sermons on Temperance
all over again, for even as he harangued one audience, a mob was
sacking a Catholic convent just outside of town. Still, Lyman had
not been responsible for inciting that particular mob, as Judge
Hall charged, so once again Lyman could feel unfairly attacked.

That storm blew over quickly. It was a **time** when there might
be various stands on the slavery question, but it was not a time,
even in the West, to appear to favor Catholicism. A dozen other
western publications rushed to attack Judge Hall for his criticism
of Dr. Beecher, and to denounce the *Western Monthly Magazine* as a Catholic organ. In the end, it was Judge Hall who suffered, not Lyman, and before long his magazine, which had begun so promisingly, had ceased publication.

Hardly had the attack by Judge Hall faded into unimportance
before new trouble erupted. If Lyman had been anyone but Lyman, surely this new threat, coming as it did on the heels of such
a procession, would have found him groggy. Instead, he rose to

the new challenge as though it were just what he had been waiting for.

Perhaps he had been. For at last his old enemy, Dr. Wilson, who had opposed his appointment to Lane, and dogged him ever since his arrival, waiting for a chance to strike, decided the moment had come. With Lyman's prestige already damaged by the antislavery repercussions, Dr. Wilson filed formal charges with the Presbytery, accusing Lyman Beecher of heresy and assorted ecclesiastical crimes.

As before, there were some grounds for the charges. Following the New School line of Calvinism, Lyman had been preaching for years a somewhat different doctrine of original sin and Christian perfection than the Old School Dr. Wilson. Dr. Wilson had his own supporters in the Presbytery and was sure they would indict Lyman at his trial.

Harriet might worry, all the family might worry, Calvin Stowe might worry too, but Lyman was untroubled. In a debate about Abolition with Theodore Weld he might be worsted. In any theological argument he felt himself more than the equal of any man alive.

Cheerfully he rode down from Walnut Hills to Cincinnati to face the trial. And this time his optimism was justified. Dr. Wilson attacked with all the ammunition he had. Then Lyman arose from the pulpit steps where he had been sitting, surrounded by piles of documents, and the rout was on. First there were the pyrotechnics of proving this, that and the other, with quotations from Church Fathers before and after Calvin's day. Then there was the passionate, half-sobbing peroration as the martyred Lyman begged Dr. Wilson to tell him why, why he had first lured him from his loving congregation in Boston if he had only planned to meet him later with a club.

There was a sigh of relief through the family when Lyman brought home the news. The vote for acquittal had been twenty-three to twelve. True, the defeated Dr. Wilson had announced he was going to carry the case upward, through the Presbyterian church organization to the Synod. But after this victory it was difficult to be alarmed by his threats any longer.

And then Mrs. Beecher, who had been ailing for months and

had been lying in bed gravely ill all through Lyman's trial, took a turn for the worse. Fate had still another blow for Lyman this year. By the early part of July, Harriet Porter Beecher, Lyman's second wife, was dead.

She had been "a cool, neat, precise stepmother," so far as Harriet was concerned, a Mama in name only. Years before, when Harriet had been a little girl, she had appeared, pretty and smiling, but gradually the smiles had vanished. She had become a Mama "naturally hard, correct, exact and exacting," a Mama consumed by nervous dread as the great western trek began, and then a Mama as disappointed, dismayed and crushed by the West as she had feared she would be.

Harriet could know the melancholy that the arrival of death always brought, but it was impossible to feel great grief. None of Roxana Beecher's children could feel deep sorrow for this Mama who had become more and more a shadow, counting her sins in jealous solitude. But it was a sad time, even so. There were the second Mrs. Beecher's children, left motherless—Isabella fifteen, Thomas thirteen, and James who was only seven. For Harriet, all the old thoughts of life's brevity were wakened as she and the family followed the coffin to the little graveyard on the Seminary grounds, where Mrs. Beecher was interred not far from the grave where Eliza Stowe was buried.

Eliza had died not quite a year before. After putting flowers on the new grave, Harriet had to join Calvin Stowe in putting flowers on Eliza's, and they stood awhile, talking of her who lay there, so recently full of young perfection. Shared melancholy made them feel very close to each other.

Then after a year starred by one kind of trouble after another for Lyman—criticism, attacks, a heresy trial, the death of his wife —and only a month or so after the funeral, the whole Beecher family soared with Lyman into a joyous mood of festivity and celebration.

The occasion was a reunion of all the Beecher children, and the impetus for the great ingathering of the clan had been given by Edward. On his yearly trip to the East from Jacksonville, Illinois, that summer, Edward had persuaded Mary Perkins to

return west with him for a visit. When sister Mary's plans for
the trip were announced, brother George, who was preaching at
his first church, in Batavia, New York, and brother William, who
had a church in the West now, decided to make their way to
Cincinnati too. Catherine was at home, for a change, and so, suddenly, there they all were—Catherine, William, Edward, Mary
and George, Harriet, Henry Ward and Charley, and, of course,
the three younger ones, Isabella, Thomas and James—eleven of
them altogether.

Lyman had never seen all eleven of his children together before, and it was the first time the children had ever seen themselves together in one group, the first time sister Mary had ever
laid eyes on the youngest, Jamie. Such an occasion filled everyone's heart to bursting, and the three-day celebration that followed not only had the big brick Beecher residence in Walnut
Hills packed with people laughing, crying and singing, but echoes
of the festivities drifted out all over the city of Cincinnati. Forgotten were the criticisms of Lyman Beecher's blunders and mistakes. Remembered only was the fact that he was a great Eastern
preacher, famous across the land, with an almost apostolic number of children, several of them already winning renown in their
own right.

Now, instead of letters of attack, the Cincinnati *Journal* was
filling column after column with rapturous reports of the reunion
in Walnut Hills.

"There were more tears than words. The doctor attempted to
pray but could scarcely speak. His full heart poured itself out in
a flood of weeping. He couldn't go on. Edward continued, and
each one, in his turn, uttered some sentences of thanksgiving.
They then began at the head and related their fortunes. After
special prayer, all joined hands and sang 'Old Hundred,' in these
words:

"'From all who dwell below the skies.'

"Edward preached in his father's pulpit in the morning, William in the afternoon, and George in the evening. The family
occupied the three front rows on the broad aisle. Monday morning they assembled, and after reading and prayers in which all
joined, they formed a circle. The doctor stood in the middle and

gave them a thrilling speech. He then went round and gave them each a kiss. They had a happy dinner. . . ."

And the account had hardly begun! Guests filled the house in the afternoon, bringing gifts. In the evening, there was a general examination of character, when "shafts of wit flew amain." Tuesday, all eleven children assembled again and formed into a circle for another speech from their father. Then he kissed and embraced them all, and "each took from all a farewell kiss." There was another hymn, another prayer.

Hattie, small and emotional, caught up in the midst of such solidarity, listening as first one brother, then another, recounted his tale of valiant efforts for the Lord, felt an irresistible surge of her "pride of family." There was an inspiriting sense of confidence and assurance, too, just in being part of such a clan. Alone, she might be moody, irritable, absentminded, even "withered and exhausted," but in her own place in the family circle, holding hands with Henry Ward on one side, with George on the other, she felt strength flow into her from all of them.

Calvin Stowe, a welcome guest during the celebrations, stood outside the circle watching, and the sight was one to fill his eyes with tears also, and swell the heart of one whose "morbid love" for his friends could "almost burn up his soul." He had been an only child, with little but strange visions and apparitions to keep him company. His father had died when he was six. He had been raised by an anxious, fretful mother, and two strong-minded spinster aunts, none of whom was inclined to displays of affection. It had been work, work, work, through the days of his boyhood, work in the paper-mill at Natick, to earn money not only to help support his mother, but to send himself to college. Working, studying, taking "solitary rambles," it had been a lonely, drudging time all the way, until at last, in college, he had tasted friendship, and then, after college, won the boon of Eliza Tyler's love. Now he saw what a real family was, a family vibrating with love and mutual esteem and admiration. How wonderful it would be to be a Beecher, part of that handfast circle, he thought. Harriet glowed with a new aura of importance and desirability. One of her beautiful moods flushed her cheeks, gave her eyes a sparkle

and her soft, sensuous mouth a happy curve. By now, Calvin
knew he wanted to marry her.

After all the farewell kisses and prayers, the clan began to
disperse. One by one, they departed, Edward toward Jacksonville to take up again his struggles to win appropriations for his
college from the Illinois legislature, William to his church, George
to his, Mary to husband Thomas, in Connecticut.

The school year began. And at Lane Seminary, the prospect
was not encouraging. All Calvin Stowe's fears, which had begun
blooming as one Weld repercussion followed another, seemed
more than justified. There were so few new students that most
classes averaged only five each. What was the future for Lane?

The Western Female Seminary, on the other hand, was prospering. A more than adequate number of young ladies was enrolled as the fall term began. Catherine hurried about, giving all
sorts of instructions to Mary Dutton, before she departed on another tour.

Harriet had her own reasons for contemplating the beginning
of the school year with pleasure. She was not going to be part of
it for long. She was not going to have to teach all her life, fine
as it might be to help in revolutionizing the educational field
for women, and to proselytize, along with Catherine, for a worthy
new profession for women.

Calvin Stowe had proposed. She was going to be married.

She left no record anywhere of what the proposal was like. In
her books, later, she would always draw the curtain as soon as
two lovers had come close enough to understanding for the heroine to blush and look away, the hero to stretch forth a hand,
saying, "You know what I mean, Grace."

The engagement too, she kept as secret as possible, telling
only her family and her very closest friends, Mary Dutton, and
far-off Georgiana May. There were some quiet talks with Catherine, when she was home and Catherine could once again sigh
as she remembered her own blighted romance. But after a few
tender moments, Catherine was her brisk self again, considering
how Hattie's withdrawal from the teaching staff would affect
the Seminary. She would have to hire another teacher, and

there must be an announcement in the newspapers that *both*
Miss Beechers had retired from any active connection with the
school.

Harriet and Calvin planned a very short engagement, decid-
ing to be married early in 1836. There were not many other plans
to make, for the wedding was going to be simple, with only the
family present and Mary Dutton as an attendant.

Then strange terrors began to assail Harriet. It was one thing
to read of love and passion in the pages of Madame de Staël,
one thing to confess, almost impersonally, to Georgiana that she
was full of such intense feelings that, lacking an outlet, they
burned her soul to dust. It was quite another thing to have an
actual event rushing toward her, an event that might, in who
knew what manner, stir those burned-out feelings into some new,
unlikely and sinful sort of life. Hattie would not have been Hattie
if she had not spent those last two months before her marriage
in a state of nervous panic and dread. The day was upon her—
January 6, 1836.

"Well, there is a Heaven—a heaven—world of love . . ." So she
had written to Georgiana May in 1832, when the only loves she
knew were the love of family, of friends, and of a gentle Jesus.
Any other kind of love had been a vague dream.

Now she was at her father's house, dressed in her wedding
gown, high-waisted, slim-skirted as gowns had been all her life,
but fashionably up to the minute with its great, puffed leg-of-
mutton sleeves. Her hair was arranged in proper curls. She was
all ready, simply awaiting the arrival of Calvin Stowe.

The other members of the family were busy with last minute
tasks, but for Harriet there seemed nothing to do in those last
endless moments. Then suddenly there was something. She hurried to the desk, got out her writing portfolio, and wrote to
Georgiana May:

"Well, my dear G., about half an hour more and your old
friend, companion, schoolmate, sister, etc., will cease to be Hatty
Beecher and change to nobody knows who. My dear, you are
engaged, and pledged in a year or two to encounter a similar
fate, and do you wish to know how you shall feel? Well, my
dear, I have been dreading and dreading the time, and lying

awake all last week wondering how I should live through this overwhelming crisis, and lo! it has come, and I feel *nothing at all*.

"The wedding is to be altogether domestic; nobody present but my own brothers and sisters, and my old colleague, Mary Dutton; and as there is a sufficiency of the ministry in our family we have not even to call in the foreign aid of a minister. Sister Katy is not here, so she will not witness my departure from her care and guidance to that of another. None of my numerous friends and acquaintances who have taken such a deep interest in making the connection for me, even know the day, and it will be all done and over before they know anything about it.

"Well, it is really a mercy to have this entire stupidity come over one at such a time. I should be crazy to feel as I did yesterday, or indeed to feel anything at all. But I inwardly vowed that my last feelings and reflections on this subject should be yours, and as I have not got any, it is just as well to tell you *that*. Well, here comes Mr. S., so farewell, and for the last time I subscribe

Your own,
H.E.B."

Chapter 14

And now, my dear, perhaps the wonder to you, as to me, is how this momentous crisis in the life of such a wisp of nerve as myself has been transacted so quietly.

1836

Three weeks after her marriage, Harriet was continuing the letter she had begun to Georgiana May on her wedding day. "My dear," she wrote, "it is a wonder to myself. I am tranquil, quiet, and happy."

She liked being a wife. It might never be quite the euphoric state she described in later books. In those, every heroine passed on her wedding day "into that appointed shrine for women, more holy than cloister, more saintly and pure than church or altar,— *a Christian home.* Priestess, wife and mother, there she ministers daily in holy works of household peace, and by faith and prayer and love redeems from grossness and earthliness the common toils and wants of life." Obviously, in such passages, it was the ideal Harriet would be describing. Her readers would recognize it as such and find comfort in it, even as she.

"Ministering daily in holy works," Harriet was not always too successful in redeeming "common toils" from "grossness and earthliness," for she was not especially adept as a housekeeper. She wanted to be. She had great admiration for the kind of housekeeping talent that New Englanders called "faculty," meaning such a genius for organizing and accomplishing household chores that no work ever seemed necessary or even in progress. Long ago, Aunt Harriet, in Nutplains, had exhibited "faculty" to an extreme degree, and Harriet knew many another New England housewife with the same talent. But she herself had almost none of it. Later on, in books, she would pay tribute to all those good housekeepers, over and over again, writing long, loving passages describing their clean, homely kitchens with white scrubbed floors and big dressers lined with scoured tin and pewter. But no matter how she flung herself at it in periodic bursts of resolution, Harriet never managed to sustain that kind of shining peace for long. Trances of abstraction, fits of moodiness would suddenly intervene on days when the schedule called for washing or ironing or baking, and she would "owl about" while her plans for a well-regulated home went glimmering, just as her plans for ordering her days into peace and accomplishment, when she was an adolescent, had always gone glimmering too.

Still, she might rebel at many things, but the nineteenth-century idea that a woman must at least give lip service to the worldly superiority of the male was never one of the chains that irked her.

In due time, she discovered several things about Mr. Stowe that were not so endearing as his humor, so impressive as his learning, or so exotic as his visions. She knew, even before she married him, that he was subject to moods of gloom and depression and hypochondria. But it took living with him to discover that these moods were often more extreme and dramatic in their manifestations than her own. Overcome by a sense of hopelessness and despair, Mr. Stowe would sometimes take to his bed and stay there for days.

He was unbelievably awkward and inept at anything that required physical coordination. Hattie soon found that out too, found out that if furniture were to be moved, curtains hung, or even nails hammered in, it was simpler and better for her to do the task herself, rather than hope he could achieve the desired results for her. Inept physically, he was also without any talent for organizing or planning or charting any course toward worldly success for himself, despite his great learning.

This last incompetence did not reveal itself at once. Listening to and reporting his Sunday evening sermons all through the winter of 1835, Harriet had noticed proudly how many people of importance, like William Henry Harrison, for instance, hero of Tippecanoe, and an Ohioan of note in national politics, had

bowed to Calvin's erudition and eloquence. With the support and
encouragement of people like these, Harriet could feel, for the
first year or so of her marriage, that her husband was destined
for great things.

Their wedding journey had been a trip to Columbus, where
Calvin had been asked to address the Western Teachers College
on methods of Prussian education. It was a subject of increasing
interest all over the United States those days, as one new state
after another grappled with the problem of public schools and
German methods and techniques loomed as the ideal. But this
speech Calvin was making was only part of a much larger recognition of his ability to stand as an authority in these matters.

Harriet had heard Calvin and her father talking for some time
before her marriage, about the possibility of Calvin making a
European tour, to buy books for the Lane Seminary library.
Funds for buying such books were available, part of the money
Lyman had raised in the East. But the cost of the European
trip would in itself diminish the amount available for books, and
so the plans remained vague. Then William Henry Harrison took
a hand in the project. He had arranged for the Columbus address, and as a result, the Ohio legislature was soon passing a
resolution requesting that C. E. Stowe, on his contemplated tour
of Europe, should collect information on public instruction
abroad that might be helpful in Ohio's organization of its public
school system.

Calvin's trip abroad was no longer just a vague possibility. It
was a planned reality. A month after Harriet's last addition to the
letter to Georgiana, she was taking out the unfinished letter to
add a few more lines. Postage being expensive, one did not send
off brief notes lightly, but waited till a letter had become meaty
with news. The lines she added now made it a portentous letter
indeed, covering her wedding day sentiments, her trip to Columbus, her reflections on how marriage affected a "wisp of nerve"
like herself, and finally the news that "He sails the first of May!"

She could only envision an important future for a husband
who was being so honored at the very outset of their life together.
She planned to travel east with him, as he began his journey, to
go to Boston and New York and to stop over in Hartford, and

see Georgiana in person, before returning to Cincinnati after his
sailing. And this prospect of visiting in the East, along with her
pride in her new husband, made it easier to bear the fact that
she was not going along with him to Europe, a trip she would
have dearly liked to make.

Then, as they were making ready to pack for the trip east
she found she would not be able to go along for even that part
of the journey. It was the last of March, not three months after
her marriage, but there was no doubt about it. She was going
to be a mother. The long journey by steamboat and jolting
stagecoach and even some miles on the new and terrifying railway cars was not to be considered when she was in such a delicate condition. Years later, when she had become inured to cop-
ing with difficulties that would have made her adolescent head
swim, she would make the journey east while pregnant and
never think twice. But now she was a brand-new wife, a brand-
new mother-to-be, and the idea was dismissed at once.

Instead of having a holiday, she would have to stay behind
in Cincinnati, moving from the small house where she and Calvin
had lived together so briefly, down the road to her father's big
house. It would be hard to say good-bye to Calvin, hard to think
of the trip east she was missing, not to mention the long months
when he would be away. Still she sat down privately, before
Calvin left, to write a gay and loving note for him to read "at sea."
She smiled fondly as she began it, remembering Calvin's depressions, already a sort of joke between them, and remembering too,
a certain ridiculous book called *Kemper's Consolations*, which
was one of the few things that could make him laugh, however
gloomy his mood. Then, in her fine, dashing script, she wrote the
greetings for him to read on the watery deep.

"Now, my dear, that you are gone where you are out of reach of
my care, advice and good management, it is fitting that you
should have something under my hand and seal for your comfort and furtherance in the new world you are going to. Firstly,
I must caution you to set your face as flint against the "cultivation
of indigo," as Elizabeth calls it, in any way or shape. Keep yourself from it most scrupulously, and though you are unprovided
with that precious and savory treatise entitled "Kemper's Conso-

lations," yet you can exercise yourself to recall and set in order
such parts thereof as would more particularly suit your case, particularly those portions wherewith you so consoled Kate, Aunt
Esther, and your unworthy handmaid, while you yet tarried at
Walnut Hills. But seriously, dear one, you must give more way to
hope than to memory. You are going to a new scene now, and
one that I hope will be full of enjoyment to you. I want you to
take the good of it.

"Only think of all you expect to see: the great libraries, and
beautiful paintings, fine churches, and, above all, think of seeing
Tholuck, your great Apollo! My dear, I wish I were a man in
your place; if I wouldn't have a grand time!"

"I wish I were a man in your place; . . ." It was an echo,
of the long-ago years when Lyman was forever wishing she had
been a boy, the years when she had eagerly put on a little black
coat to "look more like the boys," and carried and piled wood
till she was almost exhausted, to show she could do as much as
any boy. "Women," as the supper table debates in those days
always concluded, might "excel in piety; their abilities equal the
male." Still males did seem to have all the prerogatives.

But she was not really depressed. Marriage was pleasant. Being
on the way to motherhood gave her a sense of importance. To
be home again at her father's house, in the new and respected
role of young matron and mother-to-be would not be bad. So
she sealed the letter and gave it to her husband, and kissed him
good-bye for a journey that would last almost a year.

And with what did she occupy herself, as she waited for her
child to be born? Once again it was the slavery question, which
always seemed to erupt with new violence in Cincinnati in the
summertime. In the slave states themselves, slavery was established, and over the years men had developed ways of living
with it. In the North and East, a few men might feel a passionate
concern over the issue, and from time to time, mobs, impelled
by various motives, might arise and harass them. But it was only
along the border between slave states and free, in cities and
towns like Cincinnati, that people could never escape from the
tension. Mobs were always a possibility. Free Negroes and fu-

gitives mingled constantly, bewildering and confusing the issue
for everyone, making almost any incident the cue for a new
crisis.

The trigger for the crisis in the summer of 1836 was the arrival in town of a certain James G. Birney, the publisher of
an antislavery paper which he called the *Philanthropist*. It was
just one more small irony, so far as the Beechers were concerned,
that this latest crusader was still another consequence of the
activities of young Theodore Weld. Mr. Birney had been a well-
to-do lawyer and cotton planter in Huntsville, Alabama, a conscientious man who disapproved of slavery but saw Colonization
as the only solution. Then Theodore Weld had come to Huntsville, in those roaming, lecturing days before he descended on
Lane, and he had convinced Mr. Birney of the hopelessness of
Colonization. He had, in fact, so thoroughly converted him to
Abolitionist views, that the lawyer had liberated all his own
slaves and come North to devote his life to the Abolition cause.
Now, after various troubles in publishing his paper elsewhere,
he had come to Cincinnati to publish it there.

The city did not welcome Birney's arrival. It made that clear
by holding a mass meeting to condemn Abolition and all those
who supported the theory. But Mr. Birney went doggedly ahead,
finding an obliging Quaker with a press who was willing to print
the *Philanthropist*, finding also, a supporter in Cincinnati as
devoted as himself to Abolition and ready to join him as assistant editor. He was a young doctor, named Gamaliel Bailey.
With both of them determined to issue their paper each week,
the stage was set for the troubles of summer.

Lyman Beecher had left before the troubles started. This
year he had traveled east to answer the charges that Dr. Wilson
had taken, as he had promised he would, to the General Assembly of the Church. With Lyman went the editor of the
Cincinnati *Journal*, so close a friend of the Beechers by now, that
he had left his newspaper in the charge of twenty-three-year-old
Henry Ward during his absence.

This new activity of Henry's was very stimulating to Harriet.
Living at her father's house she could hear about everything as
Henry Ward took over his editorial duties. She and Henry, always

very close, shared many qualities. They were both all emotion, passionate children of a passionate father, but Henry found it far easier than Harriet to express and release his emotions publicly. Henry had fought his way past an early shyness and "dread of strangers," to a wonderfully open-handed, open-hearted way of getting along with almost everyone, quite different from Harriet's diffident approach. When Henry had fallen in love, almost three years before, everyone had known about it. And he had briskly set about conquering the objections of the young lady's parents, raised because of the extreme youth of the couple. He and Eunice Bullard were engaged now, and Henry was counting the months and the days till he could bring her from her home in the East to join him in his efforts as "missionary in the West." He was having his difficulties preparing for that role. Like Harriet, Henry could not help turning from the harsh Calvinist God of their childhood and yearning toward a gentle Jesus and a Gospel of Love. But though he was still struggling through thickets of dogma, just as Harriet once had done, his religious doubts did not darken every moment of his days and nights. Most of the time he was as buoyant and active as Lyman himself, confident all would be well, and his Eunice would be with him before long.

Now he was delighted with this opportunity to run a newspaper and speak his mind in public. Harriet must write for the newspaper too. With brother Charles contributing an occasional article on his great interest, music, the *Journal* could fairly become a Beecher family newspaper.

Harriet reported it all to Calvin, in a diary-letter she was keeping to mail to him once a month. In the first issue of the newspaper under Henry's editorship, he had written a long editorial preaching temperance and attacking the theater. In later issues, he was holding forth on other themes, arriving in due time, of course, at the question of slavery. He handled that well, Harriet thought. He wrote one editorial sternly denouncing the "peculiar institution" as an unmitigated evil. Then he wrote another editorial just as sternly denouncing the fire-eating Abolitionists. "We are partizans of neither side," Henry Ward concluded with the firm, brisk optimism of youth.

Then came the semiannual arrival of buyers from the South, filling the town with men whose way of life depended on slavery. Another big convention was being held, this one focusing on Cincinnati's greatest civic excitement of the year—the establishment of a railway to link Cincinnati with Charleston and the South.

Still, Mr. Birney and his friend, Dr. Bailey, kept churning out their paper, full of sentiments that could only enrage Southern visitors, and only alarm the solid citizens of Cincinnati, so eager for the new railway to the South and the new trade it would mean, so dependent on the goodwill of these Southerners for every sort of trade and commerce.

On a humid July night the tension burst. A mob broke into the building where the *Philanthropist* was printed and damaged some of the presses. More alarming was the fact that the mob involved was not composed of the riffraff from the wharves but almost completely of young men of the better classes. Further, as Harriet wrote to Calvin, "many of the respectable citizens are disposed to wink at the outrage in consideration of its moving in the line of their prejudices."

An excited Henry Ward quickly wrote an editorial condemning this kind of mob action which violated all the most cherished American ideals of freedom of speech and the press, and the sanctity of private property. An excited Harriet scribbled a piece of her own for the paper, "a conversational sketch," as she wrote Calvin, "in which I rather satirized this inconsistent spirit, and brought out the effects of patronizing *any* violation of private rights. It was in a light, sketchy style, designed to draw attention to a long editorial of Henry's." Then, as Henry hurried down to the city with both their pieces, she waited eagerly for further news. *Would* Birney be frightened out of town by this show of violence? She hoped not.

Harriet was not disappointed in Birney, who kept on printing his paper. Then for a period of ten days, fear and the threat of violence, and finally violence itself mounted in Cincinnati, while every evening Harriet sat down to relate the day's events to far-off Calvin.

"A meeting has been convoked by means of a handbill, in which some of the most respectable men of the city are invited by name to come together and consider the question whether they will allow Mr. Birney to continue his paper in the city . . . many . . . gave out that they should go. . . . I wish father were at home to preach a sermon to his church, for many of its members do not frown on these things as they ought. . . ."

Next day, there was more to report: "The mob madness is certainly upon this city when men of sense and standing will pass resolutions approving in so many words of things done contrary to law, as one of the resolutions of this meeting did. . . . Mr. Hammond (editor of the 'Gazette') in a very dignified and judicious manner has condemned the whole thing, and Henry has opposed, but otherwise the papers have either been silent or in favor of mobs. . . ."

The discomforts of her pregnancy were forgotten, the depressing effects of the summer heat were ignored. She was caught up, alongside Henry, in a battle for law and order.

But then she had to report to Calvin that none of Henry's editorials was having any effect. After the meeting of "respectable citizens," which had included, to her consternation and Henry's, their own Uncle John Foote, a new mob had collected. Encouraged by resolutions that practically authorized mob action, it broke into the printing establishment again, broke the presses and carried their remains to the river. It then went searching for the printer himself, and failing to find him, turned, as a pack, to flush out Mr. Birney and deal with him as best suited its mood. Guns were flourished. Shouts and oaths filled the air. "Get the damned Abolitionist!" "Run him out of town." Mayhem and murder were imminent.

At this point, young Salmon P. Chase, Hattie's friend from the Semi-Colon Club, and Henry Ward's partner in forming a Temperance Society for Cincinnati, played a hero's role. Although he was an aspiring lawyer, most of whose clients held proslavery views, Salmon Chase foreswore self-interest, rushed to defend Birney, and standing before the mob, held it at bay. So Birney was saved. But the disorders went on. The printing plant was invaded again, and this time the furniture was carried to the river and dumped in.

"For my part," Harriet had already noted to Calvin in her diary-letter, "I can easily see how such proceedings may make converts to Abolitionism, for already my sympathies are strongly enlisted by Mr. Birney." So, obviously, were Henry's. So, by now, were those of quite a few others who had paid him little heed before.

It was not sympathy for Birney that put a check on the rioting. The "respectable citizens" who had originally sanctioned the mob action now grew frightened by the lawlessness that was getting out of hand. The Mayor hurried to swear in volunteer policemen to patrol the streets and preserve order. Henry Ward was a prompt volunteer.

Hattie found him in the kitchen at the Walnut Hills house, pouring melted lead into forms. "I am making bullets," he told her "to kill men with." A little later, her heart filled with mingled alarm and pride, Harriet watched him start off down the hill toward the city, pistols at his side.

Henry Ward did not have to kill men with his pistols. With the responsible citizens awakened to their folly, the disorders began to subside. "The mob, unsupported by a now frightened community, slunk into their dens and were still," Hattie wrote to Calvin. In the quiet after the rioting, James Birney finally did decide to leave town. But Harriet and Henry were glad to hear he had not been frightened away. He had simply made up his mind to preach his message from the lecture platform. And the *Philanthropist* would continue publication, under the editorship of Dr. Bailey.

Harriet and Henry Ward, though neither of them could admit it yet, were moved much closer to Abolitionist sentiments than they were before by the events of recent days. They were not converts. They were still repelled by the intransigent activities of men like Theodore Weld and William Garrison, and inclined to go along with their father in his description of them as "mixtures of vinegar, aqua fortis, and oil of vitriol, with brimstone, saltpetre and charcoal to explode and scatter the corrosive matter." But if a gentle and soft-spoken man like Birney could be so nearly martyred for declaring that slaves should be freed, surely one could not ally oneself with his enemies. Where *should* one make one's stand?

The question hung suspended, as it was beginning to suspend itself in the minds of various other thoughtful Americans, aroused by the activities of the extreme Abolitionists. But in Walnut Hills it could almost be forgotten for a while as attention turned to the arrival of Lyman Beecher, returning from the East with both good news and a bride.

The good news, reported with Lyman's customary gusto, was that Dr. Wilson had been unsuccessful in his last and final attempt to charge him with heresy. At the General Assembly, the Old School adherents had been outnumbered, and Dr. Wilson had finally withdrawn his charges. Lyman chuckled and lifted his eyebrows wickedly as he told his family how he had pretended, at the last moment, to debate whether or not he would accept the withdrawal or perhaps make some charges of his own against Dr. Wilson. It had been great sport.

The bride was proof that it was impossible for Lyman to live without a woman beside him for any longer a time than social sanction required. He had managed, despite the demands of the trial, and other official concerns, to meet a pleasant widow in Philadelphia, to woo her, win her and marry her. There she was beside him now, along with the two youngest of her own children.

Hattie and Henry Ward, Charley, Isabella, Thomas and James, all greeted her civilly. She seemed an agreeable woman. Harriet, Henry Ward and Charley had already had one stepmother, and they were beyond the age when another would have any effect on them one way or another. Isabella, Thomas and James, Harriet Porter Beecher's children, were somewhat aloof, as Hattie and all of Roxana's children had been when Harriet Porter was introduced to them as their new Mama. So the third Mrs. Beecher settled in, and if Pa was happy that was all that really mattered.

Harriet's time was approaching. Calvin seemed very far away, though there were fairly frequent letters. He not only wrote private letters for her, but open letters that were published in the *Journal* and still other letters that he suggested be read for the members of the Semi-Colon Club. He was in Germany, where the universities seemed the very models of institutions of higher learning. Everything about Germany pleased and thrilled Calvin, the industry, the thrift, the sentimental *Gemütlichkeit* of German

families. In Berlin, he worked up a great case of hero worship
for Frederick William III, the King of Prussia. He saw the King
taking a turn in the royal gardens one day, saw him out riding
in his carriage, heard the gossip about the royal family from his
friends and acquaintances in Berlin. In no time, his letters
sounded as though he actually knew the King, good, solid, re-
liable old Fritz. Full of great names, studded with names of
romantic places, his letters caused Harriet's pride in her new husband to mount. He might be no Byron in looks, but it was even
better to realize he was a man of such learning and importance
he could be the familiar of kings.

Then, as the last days of September were bringing cooler
breezes to Walnut Hills, and the trees on the hills were changing
from green to red and gold, Harriet forgot Calvin and kings and
slavery and every other outside concern, as her hours of labor
came upon her, sooner than she had expected, but just as frightening.

Finally, the struggles were over and she lay back, limp and
exhausted on her pillows, to start adjusting to the greatest surprise of her marriage so far. She had been safely delivered not
of just one child, but two, both girls. Unbelievable as it might
seem to her, little Hattie Beecher Stowe was not only a mother,
but the mother of twins!

It would be four months and more before their father saw them.
Fall storms on the Atlantic delayed letters to him that bore the astonishing news, so he was not even aware that he was the father
of two until he landed in New York City in January 1837. Business matters delayed him further, so it was another week before
he could hurry west to Cincinnati and see his two young daughters for himself.

Hattie, he discovered, had already named the baby girls. Tactfully bowing to the first great love of her husband's life, remembering that their mutual grief for Eliza had been the first link
between them, Harriet had named one of the babies Eliza Tyler.
The other she had named Isabella.

Calvin might not look romantic, but his nature was chivalrous
all the same. He proved it now. He did not object to naming

one of his daughters after his first wife, but if one little girl was to be Eliza Tyler Stowe, then the other must bear the name of one who had achieved an equal place in his heart, Hattie herself. So the name Isabella was abandoned, and Harriet's twins became Eliza Tyler Stowe and Harriet Beecher Stowe. And family life could go on in that "appointed shrine for women, more holy than cloister, more saintly and pure than church or altar," confused now by identical names and identical babies, as well as all the less exotic, more usual confusions that generally beset a "priestess, wife and mother."

Chapter 15

Well, Georgy, this marriage is—yes, I will speak well of it after all; for when I can stop and think long enough to discriminate my head from my heels, I must say that I think myself a fortunate woman both in husband and children. My children I would not change for all the ease, leisure, and pleasure that I could have without them.

1837–1843

The twins were two-year-old toddlers, and there was a new baby boy in the cradle, Henry Ellis. It was 1838, and Harriet was writing to Georgiana May, still the confidante for whom she tried to give the most faithful picture of her life.

Money was scarcer than it had ever been. Looking back over the last year and a half, remembering events outside the nursery, Harriet could remember money difficulties without end. Still, she hardly mentioned these in her letter to Georgiana.

She might have written pages about the difficulties besetting her father. Even thinking about all that had happened to him caused Harriet to marvel afresh at Lyman Beecher's resiliency and courage. It had been July 1837 when financial disaster struck him, a result of the panic that was sweeping the whole country as Martin Van Buren became President—and heir to the consequences of Jackson's fight with the Bank of the United States. The disaster had come directly on the heels of a gala at Lane Seminary when the books Calvin had brought back from Europe were on exhibition, and an optimistic feeling about Lane's future had prevailed. But the bright mood had been shattered abruptly when the draft for Lyman's salary came back from New York— unhonored. Arthur Tappan, guarantor of Lyman's salary, had

failed in the business crash. His note, underwriting his endorsement of Lane, was just another of his debts. It had looked for a
while as though Lyman, a man in his sixties now, was to be left
with nothing but the minuscule amount paid him by the Second
Presbyterian Church. But then friends and family had rallied
around. The church had raised his salary as much as it could.
Lyman was managing to sustain life for himself and his family.
And fortunately, Calvin's salary had not been affected by the
failure of Tappan's firm.

Only fifteen students had registered when Lane had opened
for its fall term. Fifteen, and Lyman and Calvin had dreamed
of hundreds!

The Western Female Seminary had started fading in the fall,
lacking support in those hard times. The redoubtable Catherine
had rushed in from her last tour of the East, but she had little
money to contribute from her latest fund-raising efforts. Mary
Dutton began to talk despondently about giving up and going
back east.

Uncle Samuel Foote, generous, easy-going Uncle Samuel, had
failed in the general collapse of everything, and he closed the big
pleasant house where the Semi-Colon Club was wont to meet.
He and his family were living in rooms over a store down in the
city, while he went to work, as hopefully as possible, to recoup
his losses.

Yes, so far as money was concerned, there had been nothing
but trouble for the last year and a half. But Harriet ran away
from any more thoughts about that while writing to Georgiana.
It was not what was most important. She would write to Georgiana about what was important.

"Now, today, for example, I'll tell you what I had on my mind
from dawn to dewy eve. In the first place, I waked about half-
after-four and thought, "Bless me, how light it is! I must get out
of bed and rap to wake up Mina, for breakfast must be had at
six o'clock this morning." So out of bed I jump and seize the
tongs and pound, pound, pound over poor Mina's sleepy head,
charitably allowing her about half an hour to get waked up in,—
that being the quantum of time it takes me,—or used to. . . ."

Besides the money troubles, there were other difficulties that

Harriet might have written about. The ugly aspects of slavery and the struggles of the Abolitionists had once again thrust them-selves into the center of Harriet's life, anxious as she might have been simply to forget about them and enjoy her new babies.

There was the alarm caused by the young Negro girl she had hired as a household helper after Calvin's return from Europe and the reopening of their house in Walnut Hills. The girl had seemed convincing to Harriet when Harriet had questioned her as to whether she were free or not, and she had insisted she was free. Then, one evening, after an afternoon off, she had come home breathless and terrified. She was not free after all, she con-fessed, but a fugitive from a Kentucky owner. Down in the city she had learned her master was in town looking for her. Mrs. Stowe had to help her.

After that Harriet had been caught up in the rushed, fearful arrangements for spiriting the girl away to a safer place, calling on memories of the Reverend Rankin's smooth-running "under-ground" procedures to guide her. Fortunately Henry Ward had been home at Walnut Hills at the time, for Calvin was all agita-tion and misgiving in a crisis like this. Henry had hurried over to the Stowe house and taken charge. Near midnight, Calvin and Henry, armed and determined, had bundled the frightened Ne-gro girl into a wagon and started out over the rough back roads to the farm of a man Henry Ward knew made a practice of shelter-ing fugitives—John Van Zandt. Harriet had waited up, tense and alert, till their return, hours later. It was one thing to hear about aiding fugitive slaves, and another thing altogether to be in-volved in the risky, illegal business oneself, fearful of any knock on the door as one made ready, listening to the sound of any wagon or horse going by after the fugitive was started on her way. But what else could one do? It was impossible to abandon the girl and leave her to the risk of her master finding her, beating her perhaps, and then taking her back across the river to a life of slavery.

That one episode, real and immediate as it was, had not been the worst of the difficulties due to slavery. Through the summer of 1837 there had been the usual tensions and explosions down in the city—this time revolving around a case that Hattie and

Calvin's friend, Salmon P. Chase, was trying, defending the always hard-pressed James Birney against charges of sheltering a
fugitive. Then Harriet, feeling ill in the first months of her pregnancy with the new baby, conceived soon after Calvin's return,
had taken the twins and gone to visit with brother William and
his wife, in Putnam, Ohio. She had found William and his wife
already fully committed to Abolition. For Harriet, it revived the
worries that had beset her when Henry Ward was fighting the
mob a year before. Where *could* one take one's stand? If only
the Abolitionists were not so fervent, so radical, so *ultra* in their
tactics.

"It does seem to me that there needs to be an *intermediate*
society," she had written Calvin from Putnam. "If not, as light
increases, all the excesses of the abolition party will not prevent
humane and conscientious men from joining it."

She was back in Walnut Hills very near her time, when the
dreadful news came from Illinois. For some months Edward had
been giving sympathetic aid to the Reverend Elijah Lovejoy, a
fervent Abolitionist who was agitating in the area around Jacksonville. Like Birney, like Garrison, Lovejoy had his own explo-
sive antislavery paper. Like them, he published it under constant
threat of attack by mobs. The news, when it came from Alton,
Illinois, told of a mob storming the warehouse where Lovejoy's
press was stored (it was the third storming, the third press the
indefatigable Lovejoy was defending), and how, in the struggle,
both Elijah Lovejoy, and Edward Beecher, who had been helping
him, had been killed.

Edward, the Beecher's own brilliant, lovable Edward, the victim of the same kind of mob that had racked Cincinnati the year
before. It was hardly to be borne.

Relief came with the news that Edward was all right. It was
true that he had been helping Lovejoy move his press into the
warehouse, but after that, thinking all was well, he had gone
home. Edward was alive and unhurt. So then one grieved still
more for Lovejoy in the guilty reaction to one's relief—Lovejoy,
another martyr to the simple, decent belief that it was *wrong*
for human beings to own other human beings as property.

Harriet might still hesitate to commit herself to the Abolitionist movement and its excesses, but one simply could not "have the system of slavery brought before him without an irrepressible desire to *do* something." One could not see those who *were* trying to do something, however extreme it might seem, being martyred, without one's sympathies growing stronger and stronger.

Those concerns, and the fretful concern over money, slipped into the background, as her baby was ushered into the world, in January 1838. When it came to telling Georgiana what life was like for her, what really filled her days, it was of him she preferred to write:

"Well then, baby wakes—quâ, quâ, quâ—so I give him his breakfast, dozing meanwhile, and soliloquizing as follows: 'Now I must not forget to tell Mr. Stowe about the starch and dried apples'—doze—'ah, um, dear me! why doesn't Mina get up? I don't hear her'—doze—'ah, um—I wonder if Mina has soap enough! I think there were two bars left on Saturday'—doze again—I wake up again. 'Dear me, broad daylight! I must get up and go down and see if Mina is getting breakfast.' Up I jump, and up wakes baby. 'Now, little boy, be good and let mother dress, because she is in a hurry.' I get my frock half on, and baby by that time has kicked himself down off his pillow, and is crying and fisting the bed-clothes in great order. I stop with one sleeve off, and one on to settle matters with him. Having planted him bolt upright and gone all up and down the chamber barefoot to get pillow and blankets to prop him up, I finish putting my frock on and hurry down to satisfy myself that breakfast is in progress. Then back I come into the nursery, where, remembering that it is washing-day and that there is a great deal of work to be done, I apply myself vigorously to sweeping, dusting, and the setting-to-rights so necessary where there are three little mischiefs always pulling down as fast as one can put up. . . ."

All sorts of things might be happening outside the nursery. Lyman Beecher was having mixed reactions to the news that the Presbyterian Church, in assembly at Philadelphia, had split permanently into New School and Old School groups, which were organizing separate assemblies. It was bad to have the church's strength divided, even worse to see the Old School group placating Southern Presbyterians by a proslavery stand. Still, with the lines firmly drawn, there might be less dissension within one's own ranks, and the Seminary might begin to attract the students it deserved.

Henry Ward was married to Eunice, and was pastor of a small church in Indiana. Henry and Eunice had embarked on marriage with even less money than Harriet and Calvin had had—sixty-eight cents to be exact—and had furnished their rooms in Law-renceburg with furniture begged from the family. But Henry was radiantly happy, making friends and converts by the score with his charm, his eloquence, and his faith, firmly achieved at last, that God is love.

Brother Charles, for the last few years engaged in the tradi-tional Beecher struggle with religious doubts, had left home in Cincinnati and gone South, to New Orleans, and was working in a brokerage house, an equally unlikely place for a specialist in church music.

Sister Catherine was in one of her more irritably autocratic moods, being forced to realize that the Western Female Seminary was a lost cause. Mary Dutton had already departed for the East and from there had written to further aggravate Catherine by informing her that the school still owed her money.

But in her letter to Georgiana, Harriet was ignoring that and concentrating on what filled life with laughter in spite of the cares.

". . . there are Miss H—— and Miss E——, concerning whom Mary will furnish you with all suitable particulars, who are chat-tering, hallooing, or singing at the top of their voices, as may suit their various states of mind, while the nurse is getting their break-fast ready. This meal being cleared away, Mr. Stowe dispatched to market with various memoranda of provisions, etc. and baby being washed and dressed, I begin to think what next must be done. I start to cut out some little dresses, have just calculated the length and got one breadth torn off, when Master Henry makes a doleful lip and falls to crying with might and main. I catch him up and, turning round, see one of his sisters flourishing the things out of my workbox in fine style. Moving it away and looking the other side, I see the second little mischief seated by the hearth chewing coals and scraping up ashes with great apparent relish. Grandmother lays hold upon her and charitably offers to endeavor to quiet baby while I go on with my work. I set at it again, pick up a dozen pieces, measure them once more to see which is the right one, and proceed to cut out some others, when I see the twins on the point of quarreling with each other. Number one pushes number two over. Number two screams: that frightens baby, and he joins in. I call number one a naughty girl, take the persecuted one in my arms, and endeavor to comfort her by trotting to the old lyric:—

> So ride the gentlefolk,
> And so do we, so do we.

Meanwhile, number one makes her way to the slop-jar and forthwith proceeds to wash her apron in it. Grandmother catches her by one shoulder, drags her away, and sets the jar up out of reach. By and by the nurse comes up from her sweeping. I commit the children to her, and finish cutting out the frocks.

"But let this suffice, for of such details as these are all my days made up. Indeed, my dear, I am but a mere drudge with few ideas beyond babies and housekeeping. As for thoughts, reflections, and sentiments, good lack! good lack! . . ."

"Good lack!" she wrote, but she smiled as she made a comic saga of her activities as "priestess, wife and mother." And:

". . . this marriage is—yes, I will speak well of it, after all; . . . I must say I think myself a fortunate woman both in husband and children."

The letter was finally finished and folded for posting, and Harriet got ready to climb into bed beside Calvin and sleep till another dawn brought back the same round. Four years before, she had been "withered and exhausted," her emotions all burned out. Marriage and motherhood had been marvelous restoratives. But somehow Harriet, quick to laugh at the mischief of her children, quick to see humor in many aspects of life, was never one to look back and view her past self with mocking humor. She was like her father in that. Lyman never looked back, never felt amusement or embarrassment at the grandiloquent statements he had uttered at one time or another, statements ultimately proved to be somewhat exaggerated at the least.

Whether he should leave Boston and go out to the West, "to settle forever its complexion and doctrine," had once been the largest question ever "given a single mind" to grapple with. Now there was no longer any talk of settling the complexion of the West. The problem was simply whether Lane Seminary could be kept alive.

Harriet might avoid such problems in her letter to Georgiana, but Lane's difficulties affected her husband's and her family's future, as well as her father's. Soon, the situation was critical. Calvin came home from the first day of the Seminary's fall term in 1838 to tell her that no new students had registered. Ten old ones who were finishing their courses were the only students Lane had.

The dismal news imparted to his wife, Calvin made for his bed, his face settled into lines of despair. Now and then, in the days that followed, when Hattie came in, bearing tea or rallying words, he would rise from his pillows and cry out at the fate that had brought him and his family to such a pass. Had he not won fame with a work on Hebraic literature while still a student in college? Had he not become known all over the country as an authority on the Bible? Had he not traveled across Europe, hobnobbing with the learned and mighty? How was it then he was trapped in such a fashion, caught in a dying institution that might as well close its doors at once and have done with it?

Hattie listened and sighed and murmured sympathy. It was difficult for her to understand too. Calvin's future, had once loomed with promise in her mind. Now there he was, her admired and learned husband, lying in his bed and "fisting the bed-clothes," as angrily, as senselessly, as the baby himself.

But however despairing Calvin Stowe might be, Lyman Beecher was not giving up. If no new students came to Lane of their own accord, he would go out and find some, "bagging" students as he had always liked to bag sinners. Off he went, on a trip around Ohio and down into Kentucky to see what personal persuasion could do.

And Harriet suddenly discovered, out of necessity, that when Calvin ran away in defeat from a problem, she had a surprising strength and resolution. Calvin's running away, it turned out, was

the one thing that seemed to free her instantly from any need
to run away herself.

Things were *not* hopeless, as he insisted. They were *not* going
to the poorhouse, she told him. She was a writer, was she not?
She had already earned money from her writing. She would put
her pen to work again for pay, and they *would* eat, they *would*
keep a roof over their heads.

Now, in spite of the unending demands of housekeeping and
motherhood, she made time for "thoughts and reflections," considering what markets there were for the products of a woman's
pen and how she might approach them. There were, first of all,
the "annuals," sentimentally decorated and full of romantic stories and poems. *Token, Keepsake, Affection's Gift*—dozens were
published every year in the East, for the volumes were immensely
popular. A little magazine called the *Souvenir*, containing the
same sort of material, had recently been started in Cincinnati.
There were also religious papers to which she could contribute.
She thought of themes and story ideas.

Lyman returned from his hunting trip for students, after a week
or so, weary but triumphant. He had visited Marietta College
and managed to persuade a few of its students to transfer to
Lane. In Louisville, he had recognized an old parishioner from
Boston, now owner of a hardware store. Somehow, using his magic
eloquence, Lyman had convinced the man to give up his store,
study the ministry and become a preacher. Here, there and everywhere, he had snatched at any sort of prospect and dangled any
sort of lure. Now he came storming into the Stowe house, his hair
in a floating crest, his eyes alight, and marched into the bedroom where Calvin lay heaped in misery in his bed.

"Get up, Stowe," Lyman said. "I've brought ye twelve students.
Get up and wash and eat bread, and prepare to have a good
class."

Groaningly, Calvin got up and did as he was bid. And the
agony of Lane's collapse was prolonged awhile longer.

Harriet managed to write some stories and reflections and send
them forth to this paper and that. Fortune was with her. Editors
read her little pieces and accepted them and sent money. Within
a few months, things had brightened enough so that she could

write to Mary Dutton in the East and report happily on her
success.

"I have realized enough by writing, one way and another, to
enable me to add to my establishment a stout German girl who
does my housework, leaving to Anna full time to attend to the
children, so that by method in disposing of time, I have about
three hours per day in writing: and if you see my name coming
out everywhere, you may be sure of one thing—that I do it for
the pay."

A stout German girl and a governess in the nursery—it sounded
very lavish for a family that had just escaped bankruptcy, but
household wages were small in those days. A dollar or two a
week and a good Christian home were considered sufficient pay.

"I have determined not to be a mere domestic slave, without
even the leisure to excel in my duties. I mean to have money
enough to have my house kept in the best manner and yet to
have time for reflection and that preparation for the education
of my children which every mother needs."

She was feeling hopeful and strong as the new program began.
But then came Catherine. A review of the accounts of the Western
Female Seminary had shown that perhaps the school did owe
Mary Dutton some money, as she was insisting. The reason why,
Catherine now informed Harriet, was because Harriet obviously
had dipped too frequently into the treasury, in the casual way
she had of making it a substitute for salary. Catherine presented
Hattie with a bill for $114.

Harriet had been saving some of her money to buy furniture.
Paying this bill of Catherine's would use up almost all those sav-
ings. She could not imagine how she had managed to draw out
so much more money than had been agreed upon, but Catherine
had the slips with her initials on them. It was no use arguing
with Catherine.

Harriet buckled down to her writing with new urgency, fitting
it in where she could. In spite of her brave words to Mary Dutton,
she was discovering that it was easier to talk about having "three
hours per day" for writing than to find those three hours. She
looked after her children, she supervised the activities of the
"stout German girl," and Anna, "the governess," she ministered

to Calvin—glum and melancholy as he trudged out to the Seminary each day, and as he trudged back home each noon and night—and she wrote when she could.

Years later, one of her friends from those days, a friend who helped her sometimes with her literary labors, wrote a sketch about Harriet's writing habits when her children were small.

The friend had arrived saying, "Come, Harriet, where is that piece for the 'Souvenir' which I promised the editor I would get from you and send on next week? You have only this one day left to finish it, and have it I must."

The sketch proceeded with Harriet's explanation of why it was impossible to do any writing that day. There was housecleaning to do, the baby was teething, and there were kitchen affairs besides. But the friend persisted and finally they were settled in the kitchen where Harriet was to dictate the final scenes of the story while supervising the servant's work at the stove.

"Now this is the place where you left off: you were describing the scene between Ellen and her lover; the last sentence was; 'Borne down by the tide of agony, she leaned her head on her hands, the tears streamed through her fingers, and her whole frame shook with convulsive sobs.' What shall I write next?"

"Mina, pour a little milk into this pearlash," said Harriet.

It was only the first in a series of absurd rejoinders.

"I am ready to write again," said the friend. "The last sentence was: 'What is this life to one who has suffered as I have?' What next?"

"Shall I put in the brown or the white bread first?" said Mina.

"The brown first," said Harriet.

"'What is this life to one who has suffered as I?'" repeated the amanuensis.

Harriet brushed the flour off her apron and sat down for a moment in a muse. Then she dictated as follows:

"'Under the breaking of my heart I have borne up. I have borne up under all that tries a woman,—but this thought,—oh, Henry!'"

"Ma'am, shall I put ginger into this pumpkin?" inquired Mina.

"No, you may let that alone just now," replied Harriet. She then proceeded:

"'I know my duty to my children. I see the hour must come. You must take them, Henry: they are my last earthly comfort.'"

"Ma'am, what shall I do with these egg-shells and all this truck here?" interrupted Mina.

"Put them in the pail by you," answered Harriet.

"'They are my last earthly comfort,'" repeated the amanuensis.

"Thus we went on," the friend concluded, "cooking, writing, nursing, and laughing, till I finally accomplished my object. The piece was finished, copied, and the next day sent to the editor."

Years later Harriet laughed, remembering how it had been. And fortunately she was laughing at the time too. It was distracting, it was nerve-racking, but there was a sense of accomplishment in it as well, and "this marriage is—yes, I will speak well of it. . . ."

When Calvin went east to deliver an address at the Dartmouth College commencement, somehow there was enough money for Harriet to go along. A holiday in the East, visiting the family and friends there, was always a delight to her. Calvin was less gloomy, away from the depressing atmosphere of Lane. He was full of his old-time pulpit authority, delivering the Dartmouth address, and she was able to feel fond pride again. Afterward, they joked together and conversed cheerfully on all manner of subjects, and enjoyed each other as they had not done for months.

The new frame house the Seminary had been building for them was ready when they returned to Cincinnati. They moved in, and despite the inconveniences that moving occasioned, Harriet was buoyed up enough by her holiday to write a couple of New England stories. They were not the trifles she had been writing recently, but stories in the vein of her first New England tale. She was rather proud of these. Then she discovered she was pregnant again.

She did not feel well during this pregnancy. A variety of aches and pains plagued her. She struggled along through the fall and winter, caring for the children and Calvin, trying to do some writing. Her fourth child was born in May of 1840, another boy.

She and Calvin named him Frederick William, in honor of the Prussian King, "old Fritz," who had so impressed Calvin during his European stay.

But the pace she had been sustaining called for some respite. After Freddie's birth, Harriet could not get up, for a long time, but lay in a darkened room, while Anna, the "governess," coped beyond its door with the clamor and commotion of her brood.

The retreat had to end. She rose, took a deep breath and grasped the reins. There was nothing else to do. The children needed her, Calvin needed her, but it was too much to try to write as well. In December she was confessing to Georgiana, "For a year I have held the pen only to write an occasional business letter such as could not be neglected. . . ." Still she did not complain. "I have had so many counterbalancing mercies that I must regard myself as a person greatly blessed. . . . My children have thriven, and on the whole 'come to more,' as the Yankees say, than the care of them. Thus you see my troubles have been but enough to keep me from loving earth too well."

As the baby grew older, she grew stronger, and by the next spring and summer, she even had energy enough to begin writing again "for the pay."

She had developed the way of writing that would be hers all her life. There was little lingering to search for a perfect word or an exact phrase, and no time at all for reworking a piece to give it a unity of style or approach or plot. When she wrote she was a woman talking about any subject in which other women might be interested, or men, for that matter; any subject that crossed her mind. She talked, in ink, about the servant problem, and how difficult it was in America to get any kind of competent help—the same problem that had exercised Fanny Trollope a decade before—and she talked about temperance and how thoughtless it was for fashionable people to serve wine at dinner, a temptation to weaker brethren, and she talked about Sabbath keeping, fallen into such disrepute in these lax and careless days, and she talked about her brother, Henry Ward, once so thick-tongued and slow, now winning such success in his new church in Indianapolis, a golden-tongued man, vibrant with friendliness and conviction. She talked and she talked, in ink.

And all at once, it seemed that this talking in ink might have some rewards other than the immediate pay. Sister Catherine, traveling about the country, took thought of the little sister for whom she liked to feel responsible. Hattie's stories and sketches had piled up, over the years, in spite of the interruptions. Surely there were enough New England stories in the vein of her first one to merit a collection in a book. Catherine spoke to her publishers in New York about the possibility of a book by Harriet, and then wrote to Harriet that they would consider one.

It gave Harriet an excuse for another trip east in the summer. Accompanied by one of the twins and leaving the other children in the care of Anna, she took off, with New York City as her first goal. In New York, it was pleasant to discover that the Harper brothers were indeed interested in bringing out a collection of her best New England stories, and very stimulating to talk with two or three other editors of magazines and annuals and find them eager to publish any future work of hers.

After that, happily visiting with Mary and Isabella in Hartford, she was very capable and professional as she wrote home to Calvin, reporting on her interviews.

Calvin, good, kind man that he was for all his moaning and groaning, was as pleased as she. He had always known all Beechers were remarkable, and his wife as talented as any of them. He might be imprisoned in a hopeless job in a nearly defunct Seminary because of the stubbornness of the oldest Beecher, but that did not diminish his admiration of Lyman nor shake his faith in his wife. He wrote Harriet.

"My dear, you must be a literary woman. It is so written in the book of fate. Make all your calculations accordingly. Get a good stock of health and brush up your mind. Drop the E. out of your name. It only incumbers it and interferes with the flow and euphony. Write yourself fully and always Harriet Beecher Stowe, which is a name euphonious, flowing, and full of meaning. Then my word for it, your husband will lift up his head in the gate, and your children will rise up and call you blessed."

Harriet read his earnest advice and agreed. She "made her calculations" and wrote him the results. She must have a room of her own, if she were to write. "All last winter I felt the need of some place where I could go and be quiet and satisfied," she told him. "I could not there, for there was all the setting of tables, and clearing up of tables, and dressing and washing of children, and everything else going on, and the constant falling of soot and coal dust on everything in the room was a constant annoyance to me, and I never felt comfortable there though I tried hard. Then if I came into the parlor where you were I felt as if I were interrupting you, and you know you sometimes thought so too." In her mind she had already "pitched on Mrs. Whipple's room. I can put the stove in it," she wrote. "I have furniture enough at home to furnish it comfortably, and I only beg in addition that you will let me change the glass door from the nursery into that room and keep my plants there, and then I shall be quite happy."

All this planning warmed the hearts of both of them. Calvin wrote romantically in answer.

"If only you could come home today, how happy should I be! I am daily finding out more and more (what I knew very well before) that you are the most intelligent and agreeable woman in the whole circle of my acquaintance."

Harriet wrote her own loving response to that.

"I was telling Belle yesterday that I did not know till I came away how much I depended on you for information. There are a thousand favorite subjects on which I could talk with you better than anyone else. If you were not already my dearly loved husband, I should certainly fall in love with you."

But she could not leave it there. The habit of melancholy, acquired during her adolescent years, was too strong. Cheerful as things might look, she had to remember that all was vanity, and she herself "a wisp of nerve." She thought of the times she went "owling about" when she should have had her mind on the children or housework or writing, and continued:

"The absence and wandering of mind and forgetfulness that so often vexes you is a physical infirmity with me. It is the failing of a mind not calculated to endure a great pressure of care, and so much do I feel the pressure I am under, so much is my mind often darkened and troubled by care, that life seriously holds out few allurements—only my children.

"In returning to my family, from whom I have been so long

separated, I am impressed with a new and solemn feeling of responsibility. It appears to me that I am not probably destined for a long life; at all events, the feeling is strongly impressed upon my mind that a work is put into my hands which I must be earnest to finish shortly. It is nothing great or brilliant in the world's eye; it lies in one small family circle, of which I am called to be the central point."

This pessimistic effusion written, she brightened again. Calvin was making plans to come east for her and accompany her home. He arrived, and then there was the protracted journey west, stopping at the homes of all the Beecher clan, now so spread out between Boston and Cincinnati that it was almost possible to reach a family roof every night. Brother George, married to a young lady from a well-to-do family, had a prosperous church in Rochester, New York. He had passed on to his older brother, William, his old post in Batavia, New York. From Albany to Batavia, Harriet and Calvin and small Hatty had the novel experience of riding for the first time on the new railway cars. They journeyed from one relative to another, hearing the news of the family, passing on the news that Harriet was really going to be a "literary woman" now, and drop the E. from her name.

Then they were home, and the plans could go into effect. Harriet could seize upon the room she had chosen for hers, move furniture into it, and arrange her plants to get the best light. Any kind of flowers or plants delighted her, and often enough, marveling at the shape of a flower's cup, the light and shadow on leaves, Harriet would wish she had time to paint and draw again, as she once had had. But there was no time. She must devote herself to writing. The *Souvenir* was waiting for more of her work even now. And, as Calvin had written to her while she was in the East, echoing a standard Beecher sentiment in regard to almost any project, "You have it in your power by means of this little magazine to form the mind of the West for the coming generation." Then Harriet realized she was pregnant again. The plans for so many hours of writing each day gradually began to go to pieces.

There was some pleasure in receiving the small book that the Harpers had made of her New England stories. *The Mayflower* was the title she had given the collection. There was nothing

about the Pilgrim ship in the book, or the wild flower either, but
she thought the title appropriate, since all the characters, with
their special brand of New England toughness and humor, could
trace their ancestry, and their very presence in New England,
to the original voyage of the ship.

She was pleased with the book. Calvin and everyone else
complimented her on it. And a very good little book it was, de-
serving of their praise, a collection of lively, shrewd, amusing
stories that were among the first to explore New England character with colloquial realism. "Uncle Tim" was one of the stories,
and then there was "Love versus Law," a tale she had woven out
of some of Calvin's humorous reminiscences of his childhood in
Natick, and there were others equally indigenous and nostalgic.

But she felt more and more wretched as her pregnancy advanced. The twins, seven now, Henry Ellis, five, and Freddie,
three, were excitable children, constantly demanding her time
and attention. Life was full of worries and alarms, slavery riots
down in the city, continual concern over the nearly moribund
Seminary. The plan of "forming the mind of the West" by her
writing was receding to an equal distance with her father's hopes
of "settling the complexion of the West forever."

Then, in a letter from Rochester, New York, came news that
almost shattered her. George, out in the garden of his new home,
shooting robins in his sweet-cherry tree, had accidentally shot
and killed himself.

The news, so sudden, so stunning, was beyond Harriet's powers
of acceptance. George, that lively, cheerful brother, who had so
enlivened the long-ago pilgrimage to the West with his hymn-
singing and tossing of tracts to natives, George, so quick and sure
in answering his examiners when he had applied for a license
to preach, so powerful and impressive in the pulpit of his new
Rochester church—how could he have met such an end?

The picture of her brother, lying dead in his garden, haunted
Harriet's mind, awake or asleep. Cincinnati's summer heat hung
down like a stifling blanket, day and night. In August, she went
to bed and was painfully delivered of her fifth child, another
daughter. She named her for the faithful friend whom she had
loved since her school days in Hartford—Georgiana May.

Then Harriet sank back into a weakness, a depression, a general physical collapse that made her brief collapse after Freddie's birth seem nothing. The baby was frail and cried weakly but constantly. Anna, so long the faithful nurse, had grown edgy, irritable and temperamental herself. Harriet lay in bed, slow tears seeping down her face, an "indistinct terror" in her soul, as though she knew not where "the ground might open next," and she reached out to take the baby from the scolding nurse with arms almost too weak to hold her.

She had "dropped the E. from her name." She signed her name, whenever she had to, for some mundane purpose, "fully and euphoniously, Harriet Beecher Stowe." But that was all that was left of the great plans of the summer before to "be a literary woman," just as it was "written in the book of fate."

Chapter 16

My dear Husband . . . I have been thinking of all your trials,
and I really pity you in having such a wife. I feel as if I had
been only a hindrance to you instead of a help, and most earnestly
and daily do I pray to God to restore my health that I may do
something for you and my family. I think if I were only at home
I could at least sweep and dust, and wash potatoes . . .

1843–1850

Three years after Georgiana's birth and George's death, Harriet
was far from Cincinnati, a patient of Dr. Wesselhoeft at his water-
cure sanitarium at Brattleboro, Vermont. She had already been
away from home six months, trying by this desperate, last-resort
measure to win back enough strength to raise her children
through their youngest, most critical years.

She had remained an invalid for months after Georgiana's birth.
Then she had revived briefly, and even managed to worry out
a few pieces of writing to sell to one of the New York religious
papers that had been so encouraging. After that she had slumped
again into illness, headaches, nagging pains, general weakness.
It was difficult to know what was wrong. Sometimes she thought
she was going blind—her eyes hurt and she could scarcely bear
light. Then those symptoms had abated and other complaints had
taken their place.

Poverty, endless, dragging, grinding poverty—that could be a
kind of bondage, as corrosive as any, especially when it seemed
unjust, not the condition commensurate with one's own or one's
husband's talents. "Our straits for money this year are unparal-
leled, even in our annals," Harriet wrote to Georgiana. Lyman
had gone east to try to stir up new endowments for Lane, but

even though he had met with some success, the benefits were
not forthcoming for Calvin at once. Calvin's salary was supposed
to be twelve hundred dollars a year. That year he had collected
only half of it. The next year had been a little better. All his
salary had been paid, and on time. But debts were piled up
from the year before, and Harriet was almost too tired, too despairing, to feel any relief.

Calvin was sent as a delegate to a church convention in Detroit,
and after that, on business for Lane, to the East, leaving Harriet
alone with her misery, her cares and her depression, in hot, damp
Cincinnati.

"My Dear Husband," she wrote him then, "It is a dark, sloppy,
rainy, muddy, disagreeable day, and I have been working hard
(for me) all day in the kitchen, washing dishes, looking into
closets, and seeing a great deal of that dark side of domestic
life which a housekeeper may who will investigate too curiously
into minutiae in warm, damp weather. . . .

"I am sick of the smell of sour milk, and sour meat, and sour
everything, and then the clothes *will* not dry, and no wet thing
does, and everything smells mouldy; and altogether I feel as if
I never wanted to eat again. . . . I feel no life, no energy, no
appetite, or rather a growing distaste for food. . . ."

Once embarked on describing how miserable she felt, it was
difficult to stop. "I suffer with sensible distress in the brain, as
I have done more or less since my sickness last winter, a distress
which some days takes from me all power of planning or exe-
cuting anything. . . ." She had a word or two of comment on
the children, who were "like other little sons and daughters of
Adam, full of all kinds of absurdity and folly." Then she was back
with her own unhappy self: "When the brain gives out, as mine
often does, and one cannot think or remember anything, then
what is to be done?"

Calvin was alarmed by the letter and wished there were some
way Hattie could join him in the East. Harriet wrote that she
wished there were too. "If God wills, I go," she wrote morosely.
"He can easily find means. Money, I suppose, is as plenty with
Him now as it always has been, and if He sees it is really best
He will doubtless help me." It was her father's old attitude all

over again. The Lord had sent the ravens to feed Elijah. One must simply wait on Him. And finally, as so often for her father, the Lord had provided for Harriet that summer. From somewhere the necessary funds were collected, and she set off for the East, to join Calvin and visit all the relatives there and along the way. But the holiday had not helped much. About the only thing it had done for Harriet was give her news about a wonderful new "water-cure" in Vermont, where, by means of sitz baths, douches, and various kinds of vigorous "hydro-therapy," many mysterious diseases had undergone miraculous cures. Sister Catherine was talking about going there. Mary Perkins was sure it would do her no harm.

Faced by the same old unending chores, when she returned to Cincinnati, the same old smells and dirty dishes and clothes that would not dry, Harriet drooped and pined and talked incessantly of Dr. Wesselhoeft's. If only she could go there, there might be some hope for her. But once again there was no money, and it was in the Lord's hands. If He willed, she would go. Enough such bravely resigned remarks dropped in the right places, and somehow friends, and even less than friends—mere acquaintances, who heard of poor little Mrs. Stowe's plight—found themselves acting as instruments of the Lord, and charitably contributing the donations that would make the cure a possibility for her.

Harriet brightened as those kind, unsought contributions came in. Soon there was enough money for her to spend a year at Dr. Wesselhoeft's—there was no use in going at all if one could not spend months. She wrote almost cheerfully to Georgiana: "My husband has developed wonderfully as a housefather and nurse. You would laugh to see him in his spectacles, gravely marching the little troop in their nightgowns up to bed, tagging after them, as he says, like an old hen after a flock of ducks. . . ."

The housefather and his charges were left in the general care of Anna, and to the friendly aid and assistance of family and neighbors, and she departed. The journey east was getting easier every year. It took only six days in 1846 to get to Boston by steamboat, stage and railroad. Harriet made the customary round of visits. Then, accompanied by both her sisters, Catherine and

Mary, she went to Brattleboro, and settled in for the long round
of treatment.

"The daily course I go through presupposes a degree of vigor
beyond anything I ever had before. For this week, I have gone
before breakfast to the wave-bath, and let all the waves and
billows roll over me till every limb ached with cold and my
hands would scarcely have feeling enough to dress me. After that
I have walked till I was warm and come home to breakfast with
such an appetite! Brown bread and milk are luxuries indeed,
and the only fear is that I may eat too much. . . . At eleven
comes my douche . . . and after it a walk. . . . After dinner I
roll ninepins or walk till four, then sitz-bath, and another walk till
six."

But in spite of the rigor, it was just the kind of escape Harriet had been craving from husband, children, and endless cares,
and she was improving with the treatment.

"My dear Husband, . . . I really pity you in having such a
wife," she wrote in September. "I think if I were only at home, I
could at least sweep and dust, and wash potatoes, and cook a
little, and talk some to my children, and should be doing something for my family. . . . I go through these tedious and wearisome baths and bear that terrible douche thinking of my children.
They never will know how much I love them. . . ."

But there was gaiety at the Brattleboro Sanitarium as well
as wearisome baths and terrible douches. Water-cures were
fashionable, and there were various well-to-do and social people
staying at Dr. Wesselhoeft's establishment. After the duties of
the day there was often dancing in the evening, or some other
form of pleasant recreation.

Calvin was growing more and more despondent at home in
Cincinnati, minding the children, perspiring through the summer, then, in the fall, drudging through the days at the Seminary.
Harriet, reading his letters, knew she should feel guilty, for laughing, for dancing, for throwing herself happily into the charades
and other entertainments, for sleeping so soundly in the cool
Vermont nights, and waking so cheerfully in the brisk, clean
mornings. "I really pity you in having such a wife," she wrote.
And, fretted by her guilt, she wrote him that he must take long

walks before breakfast, that he must not let his study stove
burn up all the vitality in the air, and above all he must *amuse*
himself. If only he, and some of the other good folk at Walnut
Hills would meet together for "dancing cotillons," how much
good it would do them! She could not admit how much pleasure
she was having from "dancing cotillons," that would be too
much, but the inference was clear.

The dazzling white Vermont winter came, and the patients
at the sanitarium were encouraged to enjoy outdoor activity,
sledding, skating, even snowball fights. Harriet wrote Calvin,
"I wish you could be with me in Brattleboro and coast down
hill on a sled, go sliding and snowballing by moonlight! I would
snowball every bit of the *hypo* out of you . . . !"

"There is no use my trying to get well, if you in the meantime
are going to run yourself down," she told him severely.

But she was having a good time. She could not help it. It was
flight and it was escape, and she wrote gaily of some nonsense
poems she and sister Kate had written for the Christmas jollifi-
cation at the sanitarium. (Gradually, almost without anyone
noticing it, Christmas had become a day to celebrate, even for
old-line Congregationalists, like the Beechers, once so disapprov-
ing of the holiday.) Then, after relating the nonsense, she reminded herself that she *must* think of how Calvin was burdened
with the cares she had fled and how difficult things were for him.

"Seriously, my dear husband, you must try and be patient,
for this cannot last forever. Be patient and bear it like the tooth-
ache, or a driving rain, or anything else that you cannot escape.
To see things through a glass darkly is your infirmity, you know.
. . ." She had almost forgotten it was often her infirmity too.

But her escape had to come to an end. After a year, it was
time to leave the sanitarium and start the long trek west. Harriet
prolonged the journey as much as she could, visiting with brothers
and sisters along the way. It was May 1847 before she arrived
in Cincinnati to greet her five children, grown fourteen months
taller, and a husband well-nigh worn down from fourteen months
of caring for them—a husband pathetically glad to see her. And
then, very soon, she was pregnant again.

It was as though she had never been away, never known release and freedom. The pains in her eyes came back and she
could scarcely see. With the other discomforts of pregnancy, it
was all she could do to creep through her days, much less do
any writing.

Miserable as Harriet was, Calvin was even more so, a round
bundle of aches and constant day-to-day exhaustion. He
brooded over the stories of sitz baths, walks and douches, which
Harriet had brought back from Brattleboro. Her health just now
hardly seemed much testimony to their curative powers, but they
beckoned him irresistibly all the same, appearing in their cool
distance to be the only things that could restore him. Harriet,
remembering his long vigil while she had been enjoying them,
could only agree.

As once they had referred the problem of Harriet's water-cure
to the Lord, now they talked about their hopes that Calvin might
have that vitally beneficial experience, and waited again for God
to provide.

Then a startling ray of sunshine pierced the gloom. All of a
sudden, Lane Seminary, after its years of bare, scratching existence, became financially solvent. It had nothing to do with any
increase in enrollment. It was simply the unexpected result of
rising real estate values in the hills, a boom that had come about
because of the discovery that these hills could be immensely
profitable when planted with wine-producing grapes. Lyman
Beecher, longtime advocate of temperance, wasted never a
thought on the irony of it, any more than he had troubled himself
about the paradox of thundering against liquor while standing
over a cellar full of rum. He learned with joy that Lane Seminary's farmlands were a far richer endowment than any Eastern
contributions could provide and looked forward to receiving all
the back salary owed him by the Institution.

The rich vineyards solved the problem in the aching, illness-
ridden Stowe house as well. Calvin was long overdue for a sab-
batical. The Seminary, with its new source of funds, could now
grant him a year. The Lord, in His mercy, had provided, just
as they had known He would. A year off, with salary, and a

long stay at Brattleboro water-cure for Calvin was entirely possible. They could begin planning for it.

With such a respite for Calvin promised, Harriet and he could
rejoice more wholeheartedly in good news from elsewhere in the
family. Henry Ward had known such success in Indianapolis,
that he had received a call to be the preacher of a brand-new
church in Brooklyn, New York. Seeing the possibility of far wider
challenges and rewards in this newly organized Plymouth
Church, Henry had accepted. He and his family would soon be
going east.

Harriet realized that with Henry's departure from the West,
all the Beechers except her father, herself and brother Charles,
would have left. Charles, returned from New Orleans, had finally
settled his religious doubts and delighted his father by joining
the ranks of Beecher sons in the ministry. He had a small church
in Fort Wayne, Indiana. But Edward's Abolitionist sentiments
had long since made life too difficult in Jacksonville, Illinois,
and he was back in Boston, preaching. Catherine, of course, was
peripatetic, but she was more in the East than elsewhere. Only
Hattie, Charley, and her father left in the West—it made Cincinnati seem more than ever a place of exile to Harriet, a big,
rough city that would be forever strange.

Exiled, "half-blind," cheered only by the fact that Calvin would
soon have his water-cure year, Harriet toiled through the last
months of her pregnancy. The baby was born in January 1848,
a boy, whom she and Calvin christened Samuel Charles.

It was something like a miracle. As she recovered from the
birth of Charley, all the lost health of the Brattleboro year seemed
to be recovered too. The pain in her eyes was gone. The awful
debility and lassitude disappeared. She moved, if not with the
energy of a Catherine, at least with an energy that made life
possible again.

It was well she did. Calvin's health was growing worse. There
were times when Harriet wondered how they would all endure
until June, when he was scheduled to leave for Vermont. But
somehow, in spite of his moans and sighs and retreats to bed,
they made it. She and the children saw him off at the Landing

for the first stage of the trip by steamboat, and then they returned to Walnut Hills, where Harriet must take command during long months ahead and keep the family afloat financially. Calvin was getting his salary from the Seminary, but Harriet knew how much of that would be needed for expenses at the sanitarium. She must help in any way she could.

Restored to health though she was, she did not think first of writing. With Calvin away, she thought of boarders, always such anchors to windward for financially troubled families. So she crowded the children into as few rooms as possible and rented the rooms she had freed. She also thought of the possibility of starting a small school for Walnut Hills children in the fall. Her twins were twelve (was it possible?), and Henry and Freddie were ten and eight. School provisions for the young had never been adequate up on the hill. Harriet was a teacher, trained in Catherine's fine, forward-looking ideas for forming the minds and the characters of children. Very well, she would run a school for her own children and a few others.

There were periodic letters from Calvin. He had hopes of help from the baths in time, but there was little improvement in his condition so far. Harriet read the letters, sighed, and hurried on about her activities. All the chores usually handled by the men of the family had to be done by her now. Making the trip down to town each day to shop in the market was one of these—an even bigger chore with boarders to feed and satisfy, as well as the family. She supervised the help in the kitchen, she ran the house and took care of the baby and sewed for the children, and the months sped along. In the fall, she started her school as she had planned. There was never a spare moment.

"Well, Georgy," she wrote that winter, "I am thirty seven years old! I am glad of it. I like to grow old and have six children and cares endless. I wish you could see me with my flock all around me. They sum up my cares, and were they gone I should ask myself, What now remains to be done? They are my work, over which I fear and tremble."

"Six children and cares endless," and then a new crisis. It was a good thing she had spent whatever months were necessary to

build up her health. It was a good thing, too, that in a crisis she
was apt to be much stronger and more indomitable than her
general nervousness and frailty would indicate possible. For
now, in the summer of 1849, an epidemic of cholera struck Cincinnati.

The first, faint warning that trouble might be on the way
was sounded in the spring when one of the city's doctors announced the presence in the city of Asiatic cholera. No one was
overly alarmed. Seventeen years before, the Beecher family had
ridden into the city to see, as part of its first impression of Cincinnati, all the evidences of a recent plague—smoke-blackened
buildings, hundreds of new graves in the cemeteries, and an unwonted number of stores and houses to rent. Ever since then
cholera had been more or less endemic in the city during the
summer months, with several people dying of it every year.
Surely this new warning presaged nothing more.

Then, in June, the death toll began to mount daily. In alarm,
the city authorities arranged for soft-coal fires to be lighted at
every street corner to try to neutralize the miasma in the air.
Soft-coal smoke drifted through the hot, windless atmosphere.
Soot settled on everyone and everything. And through the smoke
and soot and heat, hearse after hearse made its way to one
cemetery or another. Hearse after hearse rolled up the hill to the
graveyard near the Seminary, an ominous procession past the
Stowe house.

Calvin had been gone a year, and already it had been decided that for real improvement he should stay on in Brattleboro
through the summer. Now, with the news of the epidemic at
home, he wondered uneasily if he should return.

No, Harriet wrote him. "I am decidedly opposed to it. First,
because the chance of your being taken ill is just as great as
the chance of your being able to render us any help. To exchange
the salubrious air of Brattleboro for the pestilent atmosphere of
this place with your system rendered sensitive by water-cure
treatment would be extremely dangerous. It is a source of constant gratitude to me that neither you nor father are exposed to
the dangers here.

"Second, none of us are sick, and it is very uncertain whether

we shall be. Third, if we are sick, there are so many of us that
it is not at all likely we shall all be taken at once."

"None of us are sick," she wrote on June 29, beginning another of those diary-letters like the ones she had sent him years
ago, when he was in Europe. No one in her family was sick, but,
she felt a constant, all-pervasive anxiety, for the week had been
unusually fatal. "Hearse drivers have scarce been allowed to
unharness their horses," she wrote Calvin, "while furniture carts
and common vehicles are often employed for the removal of the
dead. . . . On Tuesday, one hundred and sixteen deaths from
cholera were reported, and that night the air was of that pecul-
iarly oppressive, deathly kind that seems to lie like lead on the
brain and soul. . . ."

An ever-darkening picture was recorded in the daily entries
that followed:

"July 1. Yesterday Mr. Stagg went to the city and found all
gloomy and discouraged, while a universal panic seemed to be
drawing nearer than ever before. . . .

"July 3. We are all in good health and try to maintain a calm
and cheerful frame of mind. The doctors are nearly used up.
Dr. Bowen and Dr. Peck are sick in bed. Dr. Potter and Dr.
Pulte ought, I suppose, to be there also. . . . Our own Dr. Brown
is likewise prostrated, but we are all resolute to stand by each
other. . . .

"July 4 . . . One hundred and twenty burials from cholera
alone yesterday, yet to-day we see parties bent on pleasure or
senseless carousing, while to-morrow and next day will witness
a fresh harvest of death from them. How we can become accustomed to anything! . . . Gentlemen make themselves agreeable to ladies by reciting the number of deaths in this house
or that. This together with talk of funerals, cholera medicines,
cholera dietetics, and chloride of lime form the ordinary staple
of conversation. Serious persons of course throw in moral reflections to their taste."

Then, on July 10, baby Charley did not seem so well and Harriet was at once in a panic. Symptoms that would seem trival
at any other time appeared like signs of a death sentence now.
She rushed the baby to a doctor, who was not encouraging, and

then hurried home with him to put him to bed again. The same night, one of her boarders woke her to tell her that Henry was vomiting.

Next day both the baby and Henry were recovering. The baby was "auspiciously cross. Never was crossness in a baby more admired," Harriet wrote to Calvin. "Anna and I have said to each other exultingly a score of times, 'How cross the little fellow is! How he does scold!'"

Perhaps they were going to be spared. All day Sunday an exhausted Harriet lay on her bed, listening to the fretful cries of the recuperating baby and reading her hymn book.

But death was everywhere. The next day their dog, Daisy, was suddenly seized by fits and ran out into the yard and died. News came that the old Negro woman who did their washing had died of cholera that morning. Harriet and the twins and Anna hurried to make her a shroud and then went to her funeral.

Another day went by and another, and still everyone in the Stowe house was well. Then baby Charley went into convulsions. This time there could be no doubt. This was no "summer upset." This was Asiatic cholera.

A hopeless but stoic Harriet began a new letter to Calvin. "We have been watching all day by the dying bed of little Charley, who is gradually sinking. . . . About four days ago he was taken with decided cholera, and now there is no hope of his surviving this night. . . .

"Every kindness is shown us by the neighbors. Do not return. All will be over before you could possibly get here, and the epidemic is now said by the physicians to prove fatal in every new case. Bear up. Let us not faint when we are rebuked of Him. I dare not trust myself to say more but shall write again soon."

She wrote again, three days later. She had watched her baby die. Then she had prepared him for his burial. Lyman Beecher was in the East and had been since before the start of the epidemic, so she did not even have her father to assist her with the funeral.

"At last it is over and our dear little one is gone from us," she wrote Calvin. "He is now among the blessed. My Charley—my beautiful, loving, gladsome baby, so loving, so sweet, so full of life and hope and strength. . . ." Her pen raced as it always did when she was pouring out emotion. Never had the baby been anything but a comfort. Yet she had just seen him in his death agony and could not help, or soothe, or do one thing. . . . But then her pen faltered. "I write as though there were no sorrow like my sorrow, yet there has been in this city, as in the land of Egypt, scarce a house without its dead. . . ." And her head fell forward onto her hands, suddenly spread out across the letter.

She moved around the house during the next days doing the chores that had to be done, grief or no grief; and caught in her own sorrow, she hardly noticed that with the end of July the epidemic in Cincinnati was dying out even more rapidly than it had begun. It would move on to other cities and areas of the nation, until finally, in August, President Zachary Taylor would proclaim a Day of National Fasting, Humiliation and Prayer. But in Cincinnati, the smudge fires were put out, steamboats began stopping at the wharves again, and business began to resume its normal course.

All through August, Harriet lived with little but her loss to occupy her mind. Then, at last, Calvin returned from his water-cure, having managed to prolong it a month longer than her own.

It was good to see him, good for a small, frail, grief-stricken woman to have some manly arm to lean upon, a husband against whose breast she could now weep out the tears she had been trying, as well as possible, to hold back. Sharing her sorrow did not lessen it, but the constriction of the pain was eased.

Finally she was able to lean back and look at him and see, with gratitude, that he did look much healthier than when he had left. And then, he gave her his news—probably the only kind of news that could have brought a sense of comfort and hope to her at this moment.

He had an offer from his alma mater, Bowdoin College, in Brunswick, Maine, to join the faculty there! They could leave the West, land of exile, and go back east to the New England that would always be their real home. It would only be necessary to stay in Cincinnati one more year—one school year, that is—

while the trustees of the Seminary found a replacement for Calvin, and then they could go.

Harriet looked at Calvin with eyes that were almost unbelieving. Then, as she began to realize that what he was saying was true, she gave him the first really happy smile she had smiled in a long time.

Then a series of unexpected snags began to make the prospect seem dubious. The Bowdoin offer, enticing simply because it was an offer from the East, was not especially attractive financially. The Professorship of Natural and Revealed Religion, which was the post Calvin had been offered, paid even less than his professorship at Lane, only one thousand dollars a year. He and Hattie were willing to accept it—the East being worth some sacrifice. But when Calvin went to tell the Lane trustees he wished to leave, they promptly raised his salary to fifteen hundred dollars.

They could not afford to disregard money altogether. From the Bowdoin salary, Calvin would have to provide his own house as well, at an "expense of between $75 and $100 a year." Lane's fifteen hundred dollars plus a good house, made it far more sensible economically.

Feeling something close to anger at Lane for shutting the trap on them just when they thought they were escaping, Harriet and Calvin discussed the problem. If there was some way a little more money could be coaxed from Bowdoin, then they would be justified in leaving Lane despite the financial temptations. Finally, Calvin wrote to the Bowdoin trustees, suggesting that if they gave him a bonus of five hundred dollars, free and clear above the salary, he would accept the post. Breathlessly they awaited the answer. And sighed with relief when it came. The bonus was granted.

Harriet began thinking about writing again for the first time in months. Any extra money that she could earn would make the move easier. She sent off notes to the New York editors to whom she had sold pieces before. She wrote to Dr. Gamaliel Bailey, the erstwhile Cincinnatian, who had once taken over James Birney's paper, but who was now in Washington, D.C.,

publishing a magazine called *The National Era*. Perhaps he remembered her from his Cincinnati days, and could use some
contributions from her.

Optimism began to fill the Stowe house in Walnut Hills. By
the next summer they would be gone from it, would have taken
the long trip east with the joyous satisfaction of knowing that
this time there would not have to be any long trip back again.

Harriet rushed through her chores, making the time to write.
She paid little attention to a vague nausea and other familiar
signs of discomfort. She was too eager about the future to feel
any of the suffering such a condition had brought her in the
past. She was pregnant again, but she was not going to let that
stop her for one moment.

She was pregnant, and the baby was due in July. How could
she move her family from Cincinnati in June, when the school
year ended, and find and settle into a new house in Brunswick,
so very close to her time? The answer to that problem was easy
to find, as all answers seemed to be now. She would simply leave
earlier in the spring, with two or three of the children. She would
leave when she could still travel easily, and while there would
still be time, after her arrival in Maine, to do all that needed to
be done.

She and one of the twins, young Freddie and even younger
Georgiana, stood at Cincinnati's Public Landing, saying good-bye
to Calvin and the other two children who would follow later. It
was good-bye for good to Anna, the faithful nurse Anna, whose
frequent irritableness could be forgotten now. It was good-bye to
her father, too, but only a brief one to him, for Lyman—seventy-
five this year, though who could believe it?—was retiring from
Lane Seminary in June, to come east himself. In June, the great
Beecher pilgrimage to the West would be over completely.

The breezes of spring blew down the river, a faint film of
green was beginning to show on either side of the water. Her
children clustered around her, Harriet stood at the landing, a
little bit of a thing in worn and out-of-style clothing, the very
picture of an underpaid professor's wife. Under her scrubby bonnet her face had new lines of sadness. But a new strength was

there too. And in spite of everything, she was looking beautiful, as she always could when happy. Her great eyes shone, her lips were soft and gentle as she said her good-byes. In her womb there was life, and in her heart there was hope. She was going back to the land she knew.

Chapter 17

1848–1850

"I came from Alabama wid my banjo on my knee,
  I'm g'wan to Lou'siana,
  My true love for to see. . . ."

It was a rollicking song to travel with, and Harriet could hardly
help hearing it on the steamboat that was bearing her east at
last. She could hardly have helped hearing it sometime in the
years just passed too, for it was an irresistible sort of song, and
it was in Cincinnati that it had first begun to spread. A young
man named Stephen Foster had brought it with him to that
city in 1846 and given it to a music publisher there to print.
He had been delighted to receive a hundred dollars for it, for
he was a bookkeeper by profession, drudging away his days in
one of the business houses by the Cincinnati waterfront, with
no thought of earning money from the songwriting he loved.

"Nelly was a lady,
  Last night she died,
  Toll de bell for lubly Nell,
  My dark Virginny bride."

Harriet had never met the young man with his head full of
rhythms and melody who also knew Cincinnati as a city of exile.
But she heard his songs, for there was a magic about them. The
young man gave them to minstrel troupes passing through the
city, pleased to hear them sung. And from the theaters down
in the city, where the minstrels sang them, they echoed out
to be sung in parlors all over Cincinnati, in the homes of people who would never have thought of attending a minstrel
show themselves. They echoed out beyond Cincinnati, leaping
from lip to lip, as the minstrels carried them here and there all

over the East, and as music publishers in New York and Baltimore and elsewhere hurried to print some version of these
amazingly popular items. Finally, early in 1850, a few months
before Harriet's departure from Cincinnati, young Foster had
left the city. Encouraged enough by the success of his songs to
think he might make some money from them himself, he was
turning his back on bookkeeping and going home to make songwriting his full-time profession.

"Oh! Susanna, oh don't you cry for me,
I come from Alabama wid my banjo on my knee."

It was that song especially that was sweeping the country,
it was that song that everyone was singing, that song that was
traveling in a way no song had traveled in America before—
from coast to coast.

Coast to coast! In one final surge the nation had reached its
full growth, expanded to its continental limits: by war, provoked if need be, as President Polk had prodded at Mexico to
stir up a conflict that might lead to the reannexation of Texas,
the cession of New Mexico, and perhaps even Upper California;
by business dealings, by diplomacy and treaty, by chicanery and
free interpretation. The means hardly mattered, the thing had
to be. Manifest Destiny, some might call it, and the march of
freedom, while others saw only a deep-laid conspiracy of slaveowners and the slave states to gain more land to fill with their
human chattels. It hardly mattered what people called it either.
The land was there, the nation overtook it.

A dozen lures beckoned men. In Iowa and Missouri, the pioneers who had lived to see that frontier settled and civilized
heard tales of the fertile valleys of Oregon and streamed out on
the Oregon Trail. Oregon must needs be part of the Union, and
the old boundary dispute with England settled somehow. The
Mormons, tired of wasting their strength in feuding with the
local population and each other in western Illinois, took to the
trail for the lands around the Great Salt Lake. Rich land in Texas
beckoned the southern planters always avid for more land for
cotton.

Then, in 1848, there was the wildfire tale of gold in California, gold free for the trifling effort of scooping it up from a stream bed and washing it free from the sand around it. Gold!

The news electrified the western world, and by 1849, men were hurrying toward California from every part of the hemisphere, by every possible route.

"Oh! Susanna, oh don't you cry for me,
I come from Alabama wid my banjo on my knee."

The men of the gold rush made the song their own, singing it as they walked beside their wagons, as they toiled on across deserts and mountains, as they sat by their campfires at night. A gay song, a foolish song:

"It rained all night de day I left,
De weather it was dry,
De sun so hot I froze to death,
Susanna, don't you cry. Oh! Susanna . . ."

But then, once arrived in California, gold or no gold, one problem beset them all. There was no government for these thousands of gold-seekers, come from so many and diverse areas to jostle and crowd back and forth across this one section so full of promise.

The war with Mexico was over now. California was a United States Territory, but Congress, for reasons of its own, was dallying about organizing territorial government. Finally, the men in California, exhausted by anarchy, desperate for some kind of law and order, organized California as a state themselves, drafting a state constitution, electing a governor and a legislature. With these already functioning, they applied for admission to the Union.

The Union! There it was, still a fact, still an entity—grown strong and huge as an entity. Rich and poor, commoners and those who liked to think of themselves as aristocrats, Whigs and Democrats, Free Soilers and "Barnburners," all these and more, might strain back and forth, seeking power or advancement or personal advantage—and somehow, through com-

promises here and adjustments there, the straining only made
the Union stronger, tougher, more tightly woven.

One strain alone resisted adjustment—slavery! The South had
become obsessed with the subject. No longer, for the South, was
it simply a matter of defending itself *from* burdensome measures that favored other sections, like the tariff. It had focused
its attention on its own "peculiar institution," to extol it as a positive good for all. Slavery had become a mania, a religion. Like
a man taken in liquor, who insists not only that he is harming
no one, but that a little drink would improve everyone, like a
religious convert, or a drug addict, the South could not be content
any longer to have its slaves, quietly and with no fuss. It had to
insist that slavery spread in every direction. Negroes, multiplying
by the thousands every year, could not all be contained in a few
Southern states. Slavery *must* expand. And why not? The right
to have slaves was an American right, protected by Constitutional
guarantees on private property. John C. Calhoun, very ill now,
his voice almost gone, but his mind and his heart as unyielding
as ever, spelled out the creed of his fellow Southerners. Slavery
followed the American flag, wherever it might be carried and
raised. At this point, California was applying for admission to the
Union as a free state!

It was unbearable to the South, compulsive on the subject.
Gone with the wind of panic was any lingering consistency on
the matter of states' rights, so long the keystone of its arguments
justifying slavery. It did not matter to the South that the Cali-
fornian delegates had themselves voted to prohibit slavery in
the constitution that had been ratified by an overwhelming vote.
Nothing mattered except that California should not be admitted
as a free state. Any state or territory admitted to the Union, with
a written-in prohibition of slavery, was simply the thin edge of
a wedge destined to overthrow slavery everywhere.

Union no longer meant anything to the South if it did not
mean protection for the principle of slavery everywhere. South
Carolina was ready to secede if California was admitted. Other
states were working themselves up to similar stands of defiance.

In the North, the uncompromising Abolitionists like Garrison
were ready for secession too. Long since committed to a stark

doctrine of primitive perfectionism, which warred with any
government that sanctioned any kind of injustice, Garrison had
been flaunting a secession slogan on the masthead of the *Liberator*
since 1843—"No Union with Slaveholders." But Garrison led
only a minority of the out-and-out Abolitionists. Most of them
still hoped that the slaves might be emancipated by political
action, and the Union preserved. James Birney, focal figure in
Cincinnati's troubles during the summer of 1836, was one of this
larger group, and in 1844, he had run for President, as candidate of the Free Soil party. Thousands of Abolitionists had
supported him, among them that gentle Quaker, John Greenleaf
Whittier.

But the Union! *Was* there any hope it could be preserved
with California asking to be admitted free? The Abolitionists
might quarrel among themselves as to the method and means of
abolishing slavery. The less extreme antislavery men might have
their varied ways of trying to solve the problem. But California,
in the last great surge of national growth, had, of its own will,
chosen to come into the Union as a free state. Could it be denied?
All over the North men united to say it could not be. And all
over the South, men of equally varying political positions united
to say it must be. Slavery advanced with the American banner.

A young giant of Union, sprawled across a whole continent
now, wrestled with a schizophrenic split that was threatening
to tear it in half. One young giant? Or two young giants, locked
together in a womb that still held them, the safe, secure womb
of Federal authority? Locked together, but struggling against
each other, each eager to be born with an individual life of its
own?

Harriet and Calvin Stowe were still in Cincinnati—working
and dreaming of the release they would know in just a few
months—when Congress convened in Washington, D.C., in December 1849, to try somehow, someway, to deal with the sickness
and torment of the Union.

President Taylor, old "Rough and Ready" Zachary, who had
led the army to win those new territories in the West, had his
own simple solution for the crisis. Admit California with her
free constitution, he recommended, organize the New Mexico

and Utah territories without any reference to slavery, and he himself, still a soldier, still a fighter, would deal with any threats of secession wherever they might arise.

It could not be so easy. Henry Clay, no longer the brave, bold "young Harry from the West," but an old man, tired of the years of fighting the hawk-faced man, Calhoun, who once, so long ago, had been his ally in "cementing" a nation together, was filled with fear at the thought of the South's secession. There must be compromise. Neither South nor North could live, two separate giants, stretched out beside each other, border to border. Clay was old enough to remember something from years ago—the days when first Spain, then France, had held the southern outlet to the Mississippi. There had been tempest enough then, in the sparse population along the northern banks of the Mississippi, when France had tried to close the river's outlet in the South. A great population filled that country now. What fury might there be if the mouth of the river were held by the power of a foreign state—the South?

The strategy was planned in the early months of 1850 by the men of the North who still hoped that the Union might remain one, not two. And in the Senate, the great debate began.

Clay spoke first, laying out the terms of compromise. Admit California, free, organize New Mexico and Utah with no mention of slavery. But, so that the South might see and know and believe that this *was* no threat to slavery there, there must be a new and far more stringent law to deal with those fugitive slaves forever seeping across the border to the North, and then being aided in their escapes by Northerners. There must be drastic penalties for those who aided them, there must be new machinery set up to seek out and return fugitives to their owners.

But to John C. Calhoun it was ridiculous, it was insulting, to imagine that such a sop could be considered a compromise. Strict laws about returning fugitives were no more than simple duty in the North. Glaring, his voice gone, he sat and listened while a colleague read his response. The South demanded justice, "an equal right in all the acquired territory," constitutional amendments that would restore a complete balance of power between

North and South in the Federal government, and the North must
"cease the agitation of the slave question."

Finally, it was Webster who was answering, Webster, an old
man now too. It was twenty years since he had cried out the
formula for holding America together during its awkward, growing age, "Liberty and Union, one and inseparable." His voice
had lost its resonance, his face was lined, but when he rose, the
Senate listened, as it always had.

"I speak today for the preservation of the Union. Hear me
for my cause."

Then he restated Clay's compromise.

Across the North, every variety of Abolitionist, every variety
of antislavery man, reacted with the shock of betrayal. Henry
Ward Beecher, grown more and more outspoken in his antislavery sentiments, since taking over his post in Brooklyn's Plymouth Church, cried that religion and humanity were too dear
a price to pay even for Union. Edward Beecher, an avowed
Abolitionist these fifteen years, was ready to denounce Webster
from his pulpit in Boston. In Washington, D.C., in the Senate,
William H. Seward of New York, rose to speak for the "conscience" Whigs, for all those who believed there was a higher
law than the Constitution, with its protection of property, human
or otherwise. There was the higher law of God. The Fugitive
Slave Bill, Seward cried, would endanger Union far more than
any antislavery measure that might ever be enacted.

In the North and the South both, there was fury at the terms
of the compromise. With the desperate will of the sick to get
sicker, the two faces of America's split personality screamed at
each other. The compromise could not be accepted.

Then, somehow, it was.

The country was not ready for the fatal, final split. In the
South, there were Southern Whigs, not ready for secession yet,
denying Calhoun's elaborate proof of a constitutional right of
secession. In the North, there were Democrats, able somehow
to accept the Fugitive Slave Bill. There were Whigs, convinced
by Webster's old and thrilling eloquence, "I speak for the
Union."

By September 1850, the essential bills were passed. As they were being passed, Calhoun lay dying. "The South, the poor South," he murmured. He had done all he could, devoted his life to weaving a net of logic that could hold the South he loved in the patterns of the past, leave it free to grow in those comfortable patterns. But the North was too strong, too selfish. The North found its profit in the new ways, and it would strangle the South if need be, to impose those new ways everywhere. So Calhoun died. And the bills were passed.

California was admitted as a free state. The Fugitive Slave Law was enacted. The Union, that great, sprawling new giant, was bound together awhile longer, in spite of the split that ran through its mind, its heart, its emotions.

Perhaps with good fortune, good business, good will, a thousand distractions in the way of new land to settle, new gold to spend, new ships to build, new factories to plan and build and run, new industries to start, new farms to plow, the split might grow less wide, less fatal in appearance. In the hum and clatter of everyday life, thousands of mutual concerns might weave a better net than one made of logic, to hold the two personalities of America together. In the North, in the South, those who had grown obsessive on the subject of slavery might gradually be induced to grow quieter, to see slavery as a joint problem that might, some way, be solved cooperatively.

It was the hope of many—of the majority really—in the North and the West, where men had no dreams of a gentlemen's empire for themselves, resting on slave labor, and sweetened with leisure and learning and good manners. In the North and the West, most men simply wanted to get on with their own businesses as sensibly as possible, while "great moral wrongs" worked themselves out in time.

But there was the Fugitive Slave Act, with which Federal judges must all need concern themselves now, which the Federal government itself must support—with troops if necessary—the Fugitive Slave Act, to create friction all along the borders between slave states and free, and in dozens of Northern towns and cities where escaped slaves might have taken refuge years before.

There was the Fugitive Slave Act, a far more immediate irritant to the North than any concept of a faraway free California could be to the South. There was the Fugitive Slave Act, dropping its barriers across the path of every unlucky Negro man or woman whose heart might have begun to lift at the prospect of freedom.

"Oh! Susanna, oh don't you cry for me,
I come from Alabama wid my banjo on my knee."

And there was Harriet Beecher Stowe, who all her life had been reacting to one kind of bondage or another, trying to escape in one sort of flight or another, come east out of exile, to be caught by the one theme that could touch her deepest passions and pick her up out of the role of quick, careless "literary woman," writing for "the pay," to ride on the wings of pure inspiration.

Chapter 18

I will write something—if I live!

1850–1851

There was no real reason for Harriet to add that last qualifying phrase. She was just one of the Beechers who never could resist dramatizing themselves.

Her health was quite good and she was happier than she had been in a long time. Brunswick, Maine, was not the New England she had known in her childhood in Litchfield, all pastoral and rolling and inland. It was the New England of the seacoast, rich with the sound and the smell of the ocean, overlaid with the pungency of pine and the spicy smells of the low-growing plants of the shore. The landscape was different, and the activities were different, for Brunswick, as well as being a college town, was a shipbuilding town and a town of men who went to sea. It presented Harriet with another aspect of New England altogether, but she loved it, rejoiced in breathing the quickening salty air, the look and sound of the sea, with its fretting inlets and bays, the look and sound and smell of the shipbuilding in the harbor, with the great white-pine masts towering over the unfinished hulls in the yards. And however different the environment, the New England characters, so familiar from her youth, were the same here as in Connecticut. There were the cranky, taciturn, edgewise souls; there were the drawling rustics; there were the stern, introspective souls, nurtured on Calvinism like herself; and all of these people she recognized and understood as she had never been able to recognize and understand the more variegated, flamboyant and yeasty population in Cincinnati.

There had been a few months of crowded activity after leaving

Cincinnati, in the spring. First there was the journey east with the three children, trying and tedious even though transportation had improved. The new railway cars were cindery and bumpy, and connections always seemed to be made in the middle of the night. Still, in spite of such discomforts, in spite of being six months pregnant, Harriet felt better with every stage of the journey. After leaving Pittsburgh, where they boarded a canal boat, the children were wild with delight at the mountain scenery, and Harriet felt well enough to walk a good deal between locks on the canal.

After more railway and boat travel, they arrived in New York City so late at night that it was two in the morning before they were finally safe at Henry Ward's house in Brooklyn. The next day, though, all the hazards of the trip were forgotten as Harriet began to enjoy the pleasures of visiting.

She was dazzled, first of all, by the evidences of Henry's success, his fine home, the splendid Plymouth Church, where he reigned like a king, the beautiful horse and carriage that his devoted congregation had given him, and all in addition to a raise in salary that had Henry making thirty-three hundred dollars a year. Every bit of it thrilled Harriet, and if she and her children looked like poor relations from the country in the midst of such riches, very well, she would play the role to the hilt. She was not pretending any of her admiration for her younger brother, who had become so handsome and self-assured.

Eunice, Harriet realized, had aged a good deal during the years in Indianapolis when she had known many cares as a mother. She had a firm, tight-lipped, managing way about her which contrasted with Henry's easy openness. But perhaps that was what Henry needed. Without such a wife, he might spend too much of himself and his income and exhaust both.

Aside from the family news, there was political talk to hear, troubled, angry talk about the California Compromise, expressions of dismay and almost disbelief at Webster's endorsement of the Fugitive Slave Act. For several years Henry Ward had been building up antislavery sentiment in his congregation by every means he could devise. Few ministers were taking such a course, but for Henry "the moment you tell me that a thing that should be done is unpopular, I am right there, every time." He preached against slavery in the pulpit, he helped collect funds to purchase slaves into freedom, he had gone further and himself had auctioned slaves off to freedom in the Tabernacle in New York City.

Now, Henry's face grew stern as he discussed with Harriet the ways in which he would preach disobedience of the Fugitive Slave Act to his congregation. There was a higher law than any made by man, God's law, which certainly forbade hunting down one's fellow man and sending him back to bondage. Henry talked and talked, and Harriet was still so close to the unending turmoil over fugitives and runaways in Cincinnati that she began envisioning the whole North as the same kind of uneasy hunting field. She remembered the handbills on buildings, the advertisements in the papers, the riots in the city, all the Negroes she had known, all those who had worked for her, the young ones she had taught in a Sunday School, those she and Calvin had helped when they could—and suddenly it seemed the whole country would know the same kind of tension she had known in Cincinnati, the whole country would become a land where there would never be any hope of anyone escaping bondage. Passionately she agreed with Henry that a law like the Fugitive Slave Act was a law that had to be broken by men and women who were true Christians.

After the emotional time with Henry in Brooklyn, she and the children traveled to Hartford to visit sister Mary Perkins and her family, and Georgiana, who could now have her first view of her namesake, small, lively Georgie Stowe. There was less excited talk about politics in Hartford than at Henry's, but the Hartford people, in their own quiet way, were also opposed to the Fugitive Slave Act.

Then Harriet's visiting took her to Boston and brother Edward's home. There the atmosphere was crackling as it had been in Brooklyn with rage and defiance. Harriet listened as Edward and his wife and their friends talked, and she was shocked to hear them describing how Boston had changed from its old, idealistic days into a city of commerce, callous to the plight of the downtrodden. Edward was one of the few ministers in Boston who was daring to speak out against this new threat to human freedom. Harriet listened and her heart flamed again.

But there had been dozens of mundane matters to concern Harriet in Boston. She had to shop and buy the furniture for the house they would be renting in Brunswick, and arrange for its transportation to Maine. It was already the middle of May, and her baby was due in July. Time was pressing, and there was little enough of it to spend thinking or talking of the troubles of the country. There were letters from Calvin, still in Cincinnati with the twin Eliza, and young Henry, and without Harriet to rally him, Calvin had fallen into one of his more severe depressions. He thought of Hattie, flying about the East enjoying herself while he stayed behind, concerned with the hard problems of the future, how they would make enough to live, how long he himself might expect to exist with his health so bad, and so on and on. It was familiar enough to Harriet. But she did remind him in one letter that it was not all fun and sociability for her. Traveling in her condition, with three children, shopping for furniture, arranging for its packing, pushing through crowds—none of this was exactly easy. Still, cheering him as always, she assured him that in spite of all this, she was making arrangements with editors in Boston "to raise money." He was not to worry, she would soon be back to writing again, and they would live somehow.

She and the children left for Brunswick, traveling by way of the steamboat as far as Bath. In Brunswick they were met by a kind Bowdoin professor and his wife who would be their hosts till their own home was ready. They were met also by one of Maine's most relentless and depressing northeasters, which de-layed all the luggage and furniture a week and more.

At last the furniture arrived, and Harriet made haste to inspect the house that had been rented for her and her family on Federal Street. It was a simple, gracious house, of a style that would one day be greatly admired for the purity of its New England lines. Henry Longfellow had boarded there, years before, when he was a student at Bowdoin, and so had his younger brother. But Harriet looked at the house and sighed. Her tastes had changed, along with those of most cultivated men and women in America. She admired the richness of fretted Gothic, or the elaboration of classic Italian architecture—anything that showed more imagina-tion, style, and cultivation, than this plain, staring nonentity.

But the house was solid, and as the sunny days of June came to Brunswick, there were hours of work, from morning till night, day after day, making the house habitable. Later, Harriet recalled, in a long letter to "sister" Sarah (brother George's widow), the racing against the time when the baby would be born:

"All day long, running from one thing to another, as for example, thus:—

Mrs. Stowe, how shall I make this lounge, and what shall I cover the back with first?

Mrs. Stowe. With the coarse cotton in the closet.

Woman. Mrs. Stowe, there isn't any more soap to clean the windows.

Mrs. Stowe. Where shall I get soap? Here H., run up to the store and get two bars.

There is a man below wants to see Mrs. Stowe about the cistern. Before you go down, Mrs. Stowe, just show me how to cover this round end of the lounge.

There's a man up from the depot, and he says that a box has come for Mrs. Stowe, and it's coming up to the house; will you come down and see about it?

Mrs. Stowe, don't go till you have shown the man how to nail that carpet in the corner. He's nailed it all crooked; what shall he do? The black thread is all used up, and what shall I do about putting gimp on the back of that sofa? Mrs. Stowe, there is a man come with a lot of pails and tinware from Furbish; will you settle the bill now?"

Recalling the frenzy, Harriet could not resist making a comic saga of it, as she had once a comic picture of her day in the nursery for Georgiana. She went on to relate the story of the hogsheads, bought to use as cisterns, and how, upon delivery, they had been found too large to go into the cellar, and how she had finally found a "real, honest Yankee cooper" to take them apart and put them together again in the cellar. One of the Bowdoin professors, stopping by, had had his own comment: "Well, nothing can beat a willful woman."

She had to tell the story of the sink, the sink that had been "in a precarious state" for so long, and the way she had enlisted a good handyman's sympathies into helping her, visiting his little shop over and over again.

"How many times I have been in and seated myself in one of the old rocking chairs, and talked first of the news of the day, the railroad, the last proceedings of Congress, the probabilities about the millennium, and thus brought the conversation by little and little round to my sink! . . . because till the sink was done, the pump could not be put up, and we couldn't have any rain-water. Sometimes my courage would quite fail me to introduce the subject, and I would talk of everything else, turn and get out of the shop, and then turn back as if a thought had just struck my mind, and say:—

"'Oh, Mr. Titcomb! about that sink?'"

The sink had been completed; two sofas, a barrel chair, divers bedspreads, pillow cases, pillows, bolsters, mattresses, and a host of other things had been completed. And one day, early in July, there were Calvin and twin Eliza and Henry, to be met at the Landing, and escorted to the house Harriet had prepared for them.

Then, Harriet went to bed and had her baby. It was another boy. With the memory still fresh in their hearts of a baby boy— gone just two years, in that cholera-ridden July in Cincinnati—she and Calvin decided to name this baby Charles too, although with one difference. The dead baby had been Samuel Charles. This one would be Charles Edward.

After that, there had been two weeks of rest in bed for Harriet, with a pile of Sir Walter Scott novels on the table beside her, and a nurse to care for her. Then, when she had to rise again and take over the household chores, and the care of the new baby along with the other children, she found she was still feeling competent and well. It was a good summer. There were expeditions down the shore to a fishing village, Harpswell, situated in an area that delighted Harriet and the children—all coves and bays and islands and jagged promontories of land. Everyone would swim and then picnic on the sand. While Calvin and the boys fished, Harriet could sit on the sand, or the rocks of one of the causeways, and look out over the bay and dream, weaving romances and fancies about the islands she saw.

She was thirty-nine and she had "six children, and cares endless," but she looked very well, prettier, perhaps, than she had ever looked. Her face had lost its childish roundness; it was slender, almost thin. Her skin was still soft and smooth, and the years that had put character there, had refined the beauty too. Her eyes were still great and lustrous, half-veiled by their heavy lids against the sun. Her mouth was still soft and full, though firmer than it had been, grown firmer through watching and helping Calvin through a hundred crises, grown sterner through watching over dozens of sick beds. But her smile was still girlish in moments like these.

Her brown curly hair blew away from her forehead, streamed and tangled in the breeze from the bay, and as she sat there on the rocks, hands hugging her knees, her long, full skirt tucked in around her ankles, she looked as charming a character as even she, in one of her fictional pieces, might have described.

She even found time that summer to do some writing. There were the editors she had spoken to in Boston and New York who had encouraged her to contribute to their papers. There was Dr. Bailey, in Washington, who was so very kind about accepting manuscripts from her.

She and Calvin needed the money even though that summer the future, which had looked bleak to Calvin for so long, was suddenly filled with new promise. He had just arrived in Brunswick when he received the offer of another post, this one at the leading theological seminary of the East, Andover Seminary, in Massachusetts. Calvin was fairly incoherent with pleasure. At last, after all the drudgery of the years at Lane, he was beginning to receive the kind of recognition in which he could take pride.

He rushed to the trustees of Bowdoin, to ask if he could be released from his appointment there, to accept the Andover post. But he had already asked the trustees for a couple of other favors. First he had asked for an increase in the five hundred dollar bonus they had granted him, because of the expense of the new baby. Secondly, and even more nervously, he had gone to confess that when he left Lane Seminary, no replacement had been found for him, and somehow the trustees had managed to extract a promise from him that he would return for the winter term, 1850–51. Would the trustees at Bowdoin allow him to go back to Cincinnati for that winter term? The trustees had agreed to increase the bonus. They had agreed that he might absent himself for the winter term. So naturally they were a little taken aback at this third request, when he simply asked to be relieved of his commitment altogether to take the Andover offer.

Secretly, Harriet must have thought it was the kind of muddle only Calvin could achieve. But the trustees at Bowdoin had been kinder and more sympathetic than might have been expected. Calvin Stowe *had* been one of Bowdoin's most brilliant graduates, twenty-five years and more before. One way or another, he had never had an opportunity to fulfill all his promise. In the end, they relented. He could go back to Cincinnati for the winter term this year. Then, after teaching one more full year at Bowdoin, he could consider his contract with them fulfilled. Two years more, and he would be at Andover Seminary, arrived in a position where he did not need to feel ashamed before young Henry Ward, his onetime pupil. In the meantime, there was just the thousand-dollar salary from Bowdoin, and what little extra he would receive from his brief time at Lane.

Harriet had to write. In the midst of her other activity, she turned out several pieces. "A Scholar's Adventures in the Country," related Calvin's gardening attempts in Cincinnati. Others were sober, moralizing essays, written out of the difficulties of her life. "Earthly Cares a Heavenly Discipline" was one of these, and widely popular among readers who had known earthly cares of their own.

But letters were coming from brother Edward's wife in Boston throughout the summer and the fall, letters that would not let Harriet forget there was one problem in the world that could not be rationalized as a heavenly discipline. The Fugitive Slave Act became law in September, and the letters from Boston became full of horrors. The wealthy and influential in Boston, thoughtful of their Southern investments, had taken their stand in favor of enforcement of the law, and the streets of Boston were open to anyone wishing to hunt down a slave, however long he might have been gone from his onetime master. The letters described heartrending incidents: long-established Negro families torn apart as the "man-hunters" broke in the doors of once-secure homes, Negroes fleeing to the wharves and stowing away on board ships for England and the continent, Negroes suddenly arrested as they pursued their innocent jobs.

Harriet could read in the papers of such incidents in other cities, in Syracuse, in New York City, and in Washington. The newspapers made a cause célèbre out of every incident, and "sister Katey," in Boston, was hardly trying to be temperate. And so, Harriet, in the piney coolness of Brunswick, began to imagine all the cities of the North turned into jungles, where men and dogs pursued hapless black men and women and children, who through desperate courage, had found their way to freedom.

Another letter came from "sister Katey," a letter full of outrage against the Federal troops who had been sent to Boston to quell the disturbances there, outrage against the mounting incidents, and finally frustration at her own and Edward's helplessness.

"Hattie," she wrote in this letter, "if I could use a pen as you can, I would write something that will make this whole nation feel what an accursed thing slavery is."

Hattie read the letter in her sitting room in the house on Federal Street. Then she looked up at the various children scattered about the room, busy with their books or other occupations. Suddenly she was telling them to listen, that she was going to read them their aunt's letter. The twins, and Henry and Freddie and even young Georgie, sensing a special urgency in their mother's voice, sat up and looked at her and listened as she read the letter aloud. They remembered all of their lives how their mother rose to her feet, clenching the letter in her hand, and looked at them with her great eyes glowing. She said:

"I will write something. I will—if I live!"

The thing was, she went on living, well enough, healthy enough, and no idea came to her about what she could write to waken and rouse people. The snows of winter began to pile on Brunswick, and it was time for Calvin to leave for Cincinnati, to put in his final three months of penance at Lane. Christmas came and passed, and Harriet was able to think of various pieces in her usual vein to send to the New York *Evangelist,* and to Dr. Bailey's *National Era.* But what, out of all she knew about its horrors, was she to write about slavery?

She tried one piece, "A Freeman's Dream," a sketch about a man to whom came a runaway slave, asking help. The man, remembering the law, turned the fugitive away. Later that night in a dream, the free man saw himself dead and cast into outer darkness for failing to recognize Christ Himself in a member of suffering humanity. But Harriet knew that she wanted to write something more powerful than that. "Sister Katey" had asked for something to make people "*feel*". Harriet wanted something to make people feel too.

The snows fell, the winds howled. She bought sleds for the children and went sliding and snowballing with them. She had liked doing that as a child, and had found new health in it during the long winter at Dr. Wesselhoeft's water-cure. But still no idea came.

One night in January she was filled with a new charge of determination. Henry Ward, who had given a guest lecture in Boston, took the railway cars to Brunswick and, late at night, battled his way in a blizzard from the station to the door of the Stowe house. Harriet pulled him in, filled the stove with wood, and for almost all the night they sat and talked.

It was Henry Ward who talked, chiefly, about what he had seen and heard of the Fugitive Slave Act, and of his schemes for rousing an even wider audience than his own congregation to its evils. For almost two years, he had been contributing regularly to a New York religious paper called the *Independent,* signing his contributions with an asterisk, so that people soon were calling them the "Star Papers." In these "Star Papers," Henry had already denounced the California Compromise. He had more plans for what he could write and preach and do, and Harriet was stirred, as she always was, by his drama and intensity. Finally she told him of her own decision to become a female agitator by writing something on the subject herself.

"Do it, Hattie, do it!" he cried. "Write something, and I myself will scatter it thick as the leaves of Vallombrosa."

But the next morning Henry Ward left, and life went on, and still Harriet saw no clear picture. A picture was what was needed, she knew. A series of pictures that would show what slavery was, vivid, real and immediate, would be more effective than any amount of explaining and theorizing.

Then, a strange thing happened one snowy, blowy Sunday in February, when she was at church with her family. It was a Communion Sunday, and such occasions had always affected her profoundly. She fell into one of her trances of abstraction, and sat dreaming as the service proceeded. At last, a picture flashed into her mind, sharp and intense. An old black man was being beaten and tortured by two other men, black like himself, but with cruel, brutish faces, while a white man, the master of them all, stood by, his face contorted with hate, urging the tormentors on. The whips cut at the old black man's flesh, but he refused to cry out, refused to beg mercy, refused to confess—what?—some falsehood the white man was demanding? Never mind. The black man was holding fast to some truth, even as the whips tore at him, and he sank bleeding to the ground. Even then, with death upon him, he looked up at his tormentors with pity in his face and forgave them. Harriet was transfixed sitting there in her pew, so real and near was the scene.

What was this vision? Simply a Negro version of the old, old story of Christ's sacrifice on the cross for all the sins of humanity, all the sins of those who "know not what they do?" It did not matter. The scene had played itself out for her, and she was so deeply in its spell she hardly noticed when the church service ended. Automatically, she stood, adjusted her bonnet, collected the children, and walked home with them.

With the spell still on her she sat down at the desk and began to write down what she had seen. She used up the paper in the desk and reached for some brown paper in which groceries had been wrapped. She wrote till the vision was written out, and the old man had escaped his torment in the surest, most triumphant way given to mortals, forgiving his enemies and going to glory.

Then she rose and went to see about dinner for the children, and supervised the meal. Dinner over, she herded the children into the sitting room, took up the sheets she had covered so densely with her writing, and still caught up in the emotion it had wrought in her, she read aloud the scene she had described. The more emotional of her children were in tears by the time she had finished.

"Oh, ma, slavery is the most cruel thing in the world," one of the boys sobbed. Harriet looked at him and nodded, and folded the sheets with a sense of power.

But the mood of exaltation did not last. The next day she looked at the sketch and it shocked her. It was too violent and too bloody. This could not be the "something" she had promised to write, not as it stood. The old man, "Uncle Tom"—his name had come to her as clearly and inevitably as the scene itself— had to be introduced somehow. There had to be some reason why his master had ordered him whipped, even to death. This was the picture of an escape from slavery, but it was not slavery itself.

Harriet refolded the written sheets and thrust them into a drawer in the bedroom. She had to let it rest for a while. Perhaps the events that led up to the awful scene would come to her later. She moved through her days after that brooding, "owling about," as she did the housekeeping and cooking, and washing of small faces. All sorts of pictures were coming into her mind, too many, really, pictures of the Negroes she had known in Cincinnati, pictures of what they had told her about their lives before they were free. Dozens of stories she had heard, hundreds of them, arranged themselves in pictures and flashed through her mind. But she had no thread, no clear line.

Calvin came home again, in March, and there was the renewed bustle that his presence always meant. Ever since the fall, she had again been running a school at home, as in Walnut Hills. It was, in many ways, the best and simplest way to make sure the children were educated as she and Calvin wanted them to be, but it was certainly not the easiest method for her. The twins had to be reminded daily of their hours for piano practice. There would be their thumping in the background, while the boys droned their lessons, and the baby slept or wailed.

One day, Calvin emerged from the bedroom where he had

been rummaging for some papers, his round face streaked with tears, the sheets of Hattie's "vision" clutched in his hand.

"Hattie," he said, "this is the climax of that story of slavery you promised Sister Katey you would write. Begin at the beginning and work up to this and you'll have your book."

She had known it in her heart all along. Seeing Calvin so moved and hearing him urge her on were just the spurs she needed. Somehow she would find the beginning, and the thread that would lead her to the final scene. Meantime, she decided to write to an editor she knew would be sympathetic to such a story, the editor whose right to print an Abolitionist paper she had helped Henry defend back in Cincinnati, fifteen years ago, Dr. Bailey of the *National Era*.

"Brunswick, March 9," she wrote, "Mr. Bailey, Dear Sir: I am at present occupied upon a story which will be a much longer one than any I have ever written, [already she knew it would have to be longer than any of the *Mayflower* stories, and she trembled a little as she contemplated the idea] embracing a series of sketches which give the lights and shadows of the 'patriarchal institution,' written either from observation, incidents which have occurred in the sphere of my personal knowledge, or in the knowledge of my friends. I shall show the *best side* of the thing, and something *faintly approaching the worst*. [Where had this idea come from—to show the *best side* of the thing? From all the debates in Cincinnati between her father and the unequivocating Theodore Weld, when her father had defended the long, slow solution of Colonization, pointing out the Christianizing, educating process that slavery could be in good homes? Or from debates even longer ago than that, debates around the supper table in Litchfield, when she had learned that the surest way to make a point was to present the opposing arguments and then demolish them? Wherever it had come from, there it was, the concept that would make the final, dreadful scene of Uncle Tom's triumph doubly powerful.]

"Up to this year," she went on, "I have always felt that I had no particular call to meddle with this subject, and I dreaded to expose even my own mind to the full force of its exciting power. But I feel now that the time is come when even a woman or a

child who can speak a word for freedom and humanity is bound
to speak. The Carthaginian women in the last peril of their state
cut off their hair for bowstrings to give to the defenders of their
country; and such peril and shame as now hangs over this country is worse than Roman slavery, and I hope every woman who
can write will not be silent. . . .

"My vocation is simply that of *painter,* and my object will be to
hold up in the most lifelike and graphic manner possible, Slavery,
its reverses, changes, and the negro character, which I have had
ample opportunities for studying. There is no arguing with *pictures,* and everybody is impressed by them, whether they mean
to be or not.

"I wrote beforehand, because I know that you have much matter to arrange, and thought it might not be amiss to give you a
hint. The thing may extend through three or four numbers. It will
be ready in two or three weeks.

Yours with sincere esteem,
H. Stowe."

Dr. Bailey, kind, obliging editor and old friend, answered
promptly, pleased to commission her slavery sketches, and offering her a generous payment, three hundred dollars for a work
that would only extend through "three or four numbers."

Harriet plunged into it, taking as her first "picture," the first
picture she herself had seen of the "patriarchal institution" on its
home grounds, the pleasant plantation in Kentucky she had
visited with Mary Dutton, eighteen years before. But that picture
alone would not do. She had to show the dark shadow that hung
over even the most sunshiny aspect of slavery. Even the best of
masters, the most loyal of slaves, lived in the knowledge that
any day some unforeseen event might force the master to sell
the slave. So the owner of her pleasant plantation would be a
well-meaning man who was unhappy because debt had just
forced him to such a pass. All his innate decency rebelled against
selling any of his slaves, and against the callous trader-in-men
with whom he had to deal. But it was give up one of his slaves
in payment against his debt, or bankruptcy, and the slaves were
his property. She set forth her first picture under the heading: "In
which the Reader is Introduced to a man of Humanity."

"Late in the afternoon of a chilly day in February, two gentlemen were sitting alone over their wine, in a well-furnished dining
parlor, in the town of P——, in Kentucky. There were no servants
present, and the gentlemen, with chairs closely approaching,
seemed to be discussing some subject with great earnestness.

"For convenience sake, we have said, hitherto, two *gentlemen*.
One of the parties, however, when critically examined, did not
seem, strictly speaking, to come under the species. He was a
short, thick-set man, with coarse, commonplace features, and that
swaggering air of pretension which marks a low man who is trying
to elbow his way upward in the world. He was much over-
dressed, in a gaudy vest of many colors, a blue neckerchief, be-
dropped gayly with yellow spots, and arranged with a flaunting
tie, quite in keeping with the general air of the man. . . ."

He was the trader—Haley, and Harriet let herself go in painting his portrait, the climbing, opportunistic go-between who did
so much to keep the system flourishing. Then she was sketching
in the rest of the scene, having the plantation owner speak of the
slave he was selling so reluctantly, "Tom . . . an uncommon fellow . . . steady, honest and capable . . ."

"You mean honest, as niggers go"—it was the trader, sneering,
and pouring himself another glass of brandy.

"No, I mean, really, Tom is a good, steady, sensible, pious fellow. He got religion at a camp-meeting four years ago; and I
believe he really *did* get it. I've trusted him, since then, with
everything I have—money, house, horses,—and let him come and
go round the country; and I always found him true and square
in everything."

Harriet was started. This was how a good, gentle old Negro
might be set on a course that would end under the whips of a
cruel master, far down in the cotton country. But the remembrance of the plantation that she had visited in Kentucky
brought another memory—of a beautiful young quadroon. She
intensified the lights and shadows of her picture. The trader was
insisting that more slaves than Tom were needed to cover the
plantation owner's debt. A small quadroon boy ran into the room,
and, just as Harriet had watched her host do years ago, Mr.

Shelby, her fictional plantation owner, encouraged the boy to
dance and perform. Then the door opened and the boy's mother
walked in. There she was—Eliza—the quadroon of long ago, the
"rich, full, dark eye, with its long lashes, the ripples of silky black
hair. The brown of her complexion gave way on the cheek to a
perceptible flush, which deepened as she saw the gaze of the
strange man fixed upon her in bold and undisguised admiration.
Her dress was of the neatest possible fit, and "set off to advantage
her finely molded shape. . . ." And how did Harriet know so
well to bring in by the very third or fourth page that nerve-racking suggestion of illicit sex, to catch and hold the most repressed
and moral reader? Was it because subconsciously, it was the
aspect of slavery that held Harriet in fearful fascination too?

The trader's lust aroused, he insisted that Eliza must be thrown
in to settle the debt. But against this, Mr. Shelby stood firm. It
was not to be considered. His wife thought the world and all of
Eliza. Balked, the trader began to dicker for Eliza's little boy,
the comely child who danced and mimed so cleverly. Mr. Shelby
did not want to sell him either.

"I am a humane man," he said, "and I hate to take the boy from
his mother, sir."

The trader was humane also, the very humane man of the
chapter's title. He knew there was no sense tearing a woman's
child out of her arms. He meant nothing like that. He had been
laughed at by some traders for his delicate feelings, but the fact
was, he thought it paid better in the long run, to take some care
in the "unpleasant parts like selling young uns and that—get the
gals out of the way—out of sight, out of mind, you know—and
when it's clean done, and can't be helped, they naturally gets
used to it. 'Tain't, you know, as if it was white folks, that's brought
up in the way of 'spectin' to keep their children and wives, and
all that. Niggers, you know, that's fetched up properly, ha'n't no
kind of 'spectations of no kind, so all these things come easier."

Mr. Shelby was willing to admit his Negroes might not have
been fetched up properly by the trader's standards. Still he did
not want to sell Harry. But the trader was inexorable, and he
held Mr. Shelby's notes. So Eliza, lingering by the door, learned
the worst. Her child might be sold. She ran, in anguish, to tell

her mistress, who would not believe it and told Eliza to calm her foolish fears.

But even as Harriet finished the first part of her first sketch, she was aware that she was introducing more threads to her plot than she had planned. She was introducing her readers to Eliza's husband, George Harris, a fine, intelligent Negro, owned by a neighbor of the Shelby's, and George was announcing to his wife his determination to run away from his cruel master to Canada, where he might be able to achieve a better life for himself, and her and their son. She was describing Eliza's reactions to *that*, and then Eliza's discovery that her master *did* mean to sell little Harry. After that, there were Eliza's desperate plans to make her own escape with her child. And she still had properly to introduce Tom himself, the Negro who would appear in the final scene of defeat and glory. Surely she felt a thrill of alarm. She was introducing so many threads. Would she be able to weave them all together to produce the pictures she wanted in three or four installments?

Never mind. She would write as she had always written, going as the story took her, and it would work itself out someway. She was getting around to Tom himself.

"The cabin of Uncle Tom was a small log building, close adjoining to "the house," as the negro par excellence designates his master's dwelling. In front it had a neat garden-patch, where, every summer, strawberries, raspberries, and a variety of fruits and vegetables, flourished under careful tending. The whole front of it was covered by a large scarlet bignonia and a native multiflora rose, which, entwisting and interlacing, left scarce a vestige of the rough logs to be seen. Here, also, in summer, various brilliant annuals, such as marigolds, petunias, and four o'clocks, found an indulgent corner in which to unfold their splendors, and were the delight and pride of Aunt Chloe's heart. . . ."

Harriet was writing almost without punctuation, using dashes in her haste—the printer could add commas and periods—rarely reading back over a sentence to change a word, or cross something out or make an insertion. The pictures were there in her mind. She had only to describe them. She had to describe how cheerful a Negro cabin could be, and how proud of her craft a cook like Aunt Chloe was. She must tell how the Shelby son, George, enjoyed visiting the cabin, and how he read the Bible to the young Negroes, Aunt Chloe's and Uncle Tom's children. Meantime, in the "big house," the deal to sell Tom and Harry was being consummated. There was Mrs. Shelby's shock to describe when she heard that Harry *was* to be sold. There was Eliza's flight from the "big house" at night, her boy in her arms. There was the scene Harriet saw in her mind of Eliza stopping in her flight at Uncle Tom's cabin:

". . . the light of the tallow candle, which Tom had hastily lighted, fell on the haggard face and dark, wild eyes of the fugitive.

"'Lord bless you! I'm skeered to look at ye, Lizy. Are ye tuck sick, or what's come over ye?'

"'I'm running away—Uncle Tom and Aunt Chloe—carrying off my child—master sold him!'

"'Sold him?' echoed both, lifting up their hands in dismay.

"'Yes, sold him!' said Eliza firmly; 'I crept into the closet by mistress' door tonight, and I heard master tell missis that he had sold my Harry, and you, Uncle Tom, both, to a trader; and that he was going off this morning on his horse, and that the man was to take possession today. . . .'"

She had only to write down the pictures she saw. But there were so many. They moved so quickly. She bundled up the first installment and wrapped it and sent it to Dr. Bailey. And she hurried through her housekeeping chores so she could sit down again and launch into the second. "The thing may run through three or four numbers," she had written him. "It will be ready in two or three weeks."

She did not know what she had begun, nor on what kind of an escape she had embarked, a flight that took her past all the pictures that had ever frozen her blood or caused strange sensations to frighten her. She did see that it was going to be much longer than she planned, much, much longer—possibly a work of real novel length. She already had a title for it—*Uncle Tom's Cabin*. Where had that come from? She did not know. Her memory and her imagination were full of Biblical analogies and metaphors about dwelling places—"this earthly house of his tabernacle," she had written in her first essay, and continued by saying man was not destined for that, but for "a house not made with hands, eternal in the heavens." The title had simply come to her, like the original vision of Uncle Tom's death.

But every full-length book had a subtitle. Harriet's first thought for a subtitle was, "The Man Who Was a Thing." Later, another subtitle came to her, "Life Among the Lowly." It was less specific than the first, but better, for it gave the story a universal quality. But this was hardly part of any conscious plan either. She was simply writing the story out of herself, out of what she had seen and heard, and what she had felt—a story of bondage, and all the ways one might fly from bondage into freedom.

The story would, ultimately, run many times the number of installments she had planned. She would be writing on it for a year. But as the third and then the fourth week passed after the time she had promised delivery of the whole to Dr. Bailey, she had no thought for how long it would take. She was blind and deaf to the noise and commotion around her, writing, writing, writing . . . *Uncle Tom's Cabin, or—Life Among the Lowly.*"

Chapter 19

In that dizzy moment her feet to her scarce seemed to touch the ground and a moment brought her to the water's edge. Right on behind they came; and, nerved with the strength such as God gives only to the desperate, with one wild cry and flying leap, she vaulted sheer over the turbid current by the shore on to the raft of ice beyond. It was a desperate leap—impossible to anything but madness and despair; and Haley, Sam and Andy, instinctively cried out, and lifted up their hands as she did it. . . .

1851–1852

Calvin had wept his ready tears when he read Harriet's first sketch of Uncle Tom in his final hour. The children had wept too. And they gathered around eagerly to hear more of the story whenever "Ma" had another chapter completed. But it never occurred to any of them to make allowances so that she might have more time to write on the story that was so interesting to them. Everyone had his needs, as various and clamorous as ever. Harriet had to snatch time for her writing when and where she could, had to fly from a thousand cares to join Eliza, the heroine who had captured her heart from the beginning, the heroine who, dark-skinned though she was, acted with the passion and vigor that had been locked up in Harriet for so long.

"That gal's got seven devils in her, I believe," said Haley, the trader, staring in amazement as Eliza leaped from the shore onto the river ice. "How like a wildcat she jumped!"

Seven devils were in Harriet too. Nothing could stop her, not meals to get, lessons to supervise, Calvin to soothe and get on his way each day. When he was home, Calvin needed the desk for his work, his papers and books and lectures, so Harriet took her

paper and pen to the kitchen table and wrote there. She got
Eliza safely to the home of an honest farmer in Ohio, very like
the farmer to whom Calvin and Henry Ward had driven the
fugitive from her own Walnut Hills kitchen one midnight. Then
she had to follow Tom's fortunes for a while. Tom was not the
sort to run away, to rebel, as Eliza was doing. It was not that
Tom was weak. Tom was strong, with a kind of strength Harriet
had yearned after for years, a strength that grew not out of resignation but of positive faith.

"I'm in the Lord's hands," said Tom to his wife, Aunt Chloe;
"nothin' can go no furder than he lets it—and thar's one thing I
can thank him for. It's me that's sold and going down, and not
you nur the chil'en. Here you're safe—what comes will come only
on me; and the Lord, he'll help me—I know he will."

It was the kind of strength that her father, Lyman Beecher,
had always preached. Rebellion against the Lord's will was worse
than useless, it was a sin. Strength came when one ceased resisting and aligned one's will with His.

Still, there were those who could not seek their strength that
way. There were those who insisted on their freedom here, in
this world. George Harris, Eliza's husband, was one of those, making his escape in an even bolder, more daring way than she. Assuming the pose of a Spanish gentleman, he was moving openly
across the country in his own one-horse buggy, with a colored
servant driving, entering openly into a Kentucky tavern to spend
the night, affecting an elegant nonchalance.

"Oh, George, but this is a dangerous game you are playing,"
whispered the nervous gentleman in the tavern who had recognized him and who was trying, in a moment of privacy, to dissuade him from his plans. Dangerous it was, but George, whose
"mother was one of those unfortunates of her race, marked out
by personal beauty to be the slave of the passions of her pos-
sessor," had inherited from his father, of "one of the proudest
families in Kentucky . . . a high, indomitable spirit." He was
not breaking any law of *his* country, he told the nervous gentleman. He had no country. He had said "mas'r" for the last time,
and was on his way to Canada, the land of hope. With good
fortune, he would one day be able to arrange for Eliza and the

boy to join him there. George had no idea that Eliza had already embarked with the boy on her own flight.

Summer came to Brunswick. So also did Lyman Beecher, with one of the daughters of the third Mrs. Beecher, to spend a month in the seashore air. Lyman, retired now, and beginning to show a little of the forgetfulness of age, nevertheless was full of a great project. He was going to collect all his sermons, preparatory to having them published in one grand and final work.

Naturally this project took precedence over any project that might be engaging Harriet or Calvin. Harriet agreed without a thought of protest. She might have laughed once, in print, over the way her father rejoiced in his own perfections, more constantly in his view than anyone else's, but he was still Pa, the man who could sweep all before him.

So she went out onto the back steps and thought of a dozen more ways that men and women in bondage could effect their escapes. Tom, in the custody of Haley now, was jogging along in the trader's wagon toward the river, where Haley was going to collect more human merchandise to load on a steamboat for the south. His legs fettered but his mind free, Tom "was thinking over some words of an unfashionable old book . . . 'We have here no continuing city, but we seek one to come; wherefore God himself is not ashamed to be called our God; for he hath prepared for us a city.'" Was this escape? Harriet did not call it that, but "a trumpet call" to "courage, energy, and enthusiasm." Still with that vision of a "city to come" in his mind, Tom would hardly notice the jail into which he was clapped while Haley went to a slave auction. "We have here no continuing city. . . ."

Then Harriet was picturing "La Belle Riviere, as brave and beautiful a boat as ever walked the waters of her namesake river . . . the stars and stripes of free America waving and fluttering overhead." On deck was a crowd of well-dressed ladies and gentlemen, and below, with the freight, was Haley's gang, including Tom, and including also, a comely Negro woman with a baby in her arms, whom Haley had bought while Tom was in jail. The boat was stopping at various towns along the river on the way south, and at one of these stops Haley was arranging for the sale of the baby. In another moment when the mother had, all unawares, left the baby alone, he was spiriting the child away and off the boat with the new owner, showing in action that he was indeed the "humane man" he boasted of being. The mother, when she discovered her dreadful loss, did not scream. "The shot had passed too straight and direct through the heart, for cry or tear." That night, though, Tom woke with a start. Something had brushed past him in the dark, moving toward the side of the boat. Then he heard a splash. "He raised his head—the woman's place was vacant!" And that *was* escape, the only escape one desperate soul could find from a torment too great to be borne.

Trembling with the reality of the scene she had just described, Harriet remembered something she had read only a month or so before. An eminent American clergyman, a friend of both Calvin and her father, had made some remarks about slavery in a sermon and had been quoted in the papers as saying it was an institution that "had no evils but such as are inseparable from any other relations in social and domestic life." She had been horrified when she read the pious remark. Now, as the bereaved mother's suicide was discovered, she put an unctuous clergyman aboard the boat and had him utter the same remark as a dismissal of what had happened. Then Harriet could not resist adding a footnote naming the real-life minister who had first voiced the sentiment—Dr. Joel Parker. In this story she was writing, everything was pouring itself out, there were no more frustrations. It never crossed her mind there might be repercussions.

The children wanted to picnic again and fish from the rocks at Harpswell. Harriet made time for them, and was as gay as anyone, even though her steamboat, *La Belle Riviere*, which was carrying Tom ever farther into the southland, was also carrying her into country she did not know. Home from the picnic, she wrote letters to such men as Frederick Douglass, the well-known Negro Abolitionist, and others, who might know something about the details and workings of a big cotton plantation in the deep South. But even if answers from them were slow in coming, or did not come at all, she had a few documents on hand that would help her. She had a paper written by a Southern planter, and other items she had picked up in the spring during a quick trip to Boston, to read in the Anti-Slavery reading-rooms. Besides, she already knew who was going to be Tom's first master in the Deep South.

Harriet saw the man as vividly as she had once seen Byron in her imagination—"graceful, elegantly formed." He had a gaze "clear, bold, and bright, but with a light wholly of this world; the beautifully cut mouth had a proud and somewhat sarcastic expression, while an air of free-and-easy superiority sat not ungracefully in every turn and movement of his fine form. . . ." There he was, the man who had moved through her dreams as a figure of romance ever since she was ten, the man who had appeared briefly, in toga and laurel wreath, as the Greek noble, Cleon, when she was thirteen. Now she was paying homage to the South's picture of itself as the outpost of aristocracy and chivalry by giving to the South the best she had—her own more mature and sophisticated version of Byron—Augustine St. Clare.

St. Clare was the father of a beautiful little girl named Eva, who combined a singular dreamy earnestness with "an airy and innocent playfulness," a playfulness that led to the misadventure of her falling overboard from the deck of *La Belle Riviere*. Tom plunged into the water to her rescue, and it was in gratitude for this, as well as to humor Eva's whim, that Augustine St. Clare decided to buy Tom.

Harriet was excited as she contemplated where the story might take her now. Family events churned around her. Calvin was being honored. Natick, Massachusetts, the town of his birth, had invited him to be the principal speaker at its two-hundredth anniversary. Harriet helped him gather the materials from which he could compose his address. Still the story spun itself on in her mind. St. Clare would take Tom to his fine town mansion in New Orleans. The reader would again be introduced to "the best side of the thing," as Harriet pictured the indolent life of the Negroes owned by St. Clare. And just to show that some Southerners did indeed understand the Negro better than many of the Negro's far-off Northern champions, as they were always maintaining, there would be St. Clare's spinster aunt from New England, Aunt Ophelia—a little like long-dead Aunt Harriet in Nutplains, a little like a hundred New England spinsters Harriet had known.

In real life, sister Catherine was again making news. An opinionated New England spinster herself, Catherine had taken umbrage at the efforts of various groups of women who were agitating for the vote. It was outrageous to Catherine. Woman's great spheres of influence were in the home, the school, the nursery. Women would only weaken and ultimately destroy their strength in those areas by concerning themselves with the callous world of politics. Never one to be hampered for a moment by the nineteenth-century view of woman's place, she was annoyed when any other woman claimed an equal privilege to crusade for a cause. Accordingly she had decided to answer the manifesto of the Woman's Suffrage Convention of 1848 with a blast. *The True Remedy for the Wrongs of Women* had just been published.

Meantime, Henry Ward, for reasons of his own, was adopting the woman's suffrage cause as another of his crusades. After reading Catherine's manifesto, he wrote his father that he thought Catherine not only unsound in her views but mentally unstable as well. Catherine appeared in Brunswick to complain to Hattie, and in the midst of everything else, Harriet did her best to mediate. She wrote to Henry, urging him to be more charitable to his older sister. Lyman and his stepdaughter having finally taken themselves back to Boston, where Lyman was making his home, she wrote to her father too, defending Catherine.

But the story kept growing. She had a splendid time introducing Aunt Ophelia to the carelessness of St. Clare's Southern opulence. Many firm Yankee notions of thrift and order were expounded. Perhaps Aunt Ophelia might try to do some teaching of the young Negroes in St. Clare's establishment. Harriet had taught small Negroes in Cincinnati Sunday School classes, and knew there would be plenty of opportunity for comedy in such scenes. She had been balancing comedy with tragedy all the way so far, instinctively, not in accordance with any conscious plan. Topsy appeared, Topsy who "spected" she "just grow'd."

Twice now, Dr. Bailey had done something unusual for the *National Era*. Soon after the first installments of *Uncle Tom's Cabin* had appeared in his magazine, he had begun to receive letters from readers, praising the story. He had printed one prim

and polite note, all the more telling for its Quaker phrasing.
"Sir: 'Uncle Tom's Cabin' increases in interest and pathos
with each successive number. None of thy various contributions,
rich and varied as they have been, have so deeply interested
thy female readers of this vicinity as this story of Mrs. Stowe
has so far done and promises to do." In September, he again
noted that letters were coming in "by every mail," many asking
if the story were to be printed as a book when the magazine
publication was completed. He commented that "a note from
the author" touching that point "might be of service."

Catherine had discussed the matter of book publication with
Harriet when she was in Brunswick to relate her troubles with
Henry. Cheered by the idea of managing something, she had
offered to arrange the matter. When she went back to New York,
she visited the publishers of her book, *The True Remedy*, and
spoke to them about Harriet's serial, which seemed to be attract-
ing a good deal of attention. Catherine's publishers considered
the story as she outlined it, and frowned. Except in a few centers
like Boston and New York where zealots were insisting on keeping the problem alive, most of the people of the North were eager
to forget slavery and let the California Compromise settle the
quarrel. Or so it seemed to these gentlemen. And was not Webster forever thundering, "Agitation must cease"? So was this the
time to publish an antislavery novel first serialized in an ob-
scure antislavery magazine? The answer, they decided, was no.

Harriet hardly had time to feel disappointment. In Boston,
a certain Mrs. Jewett had been following the story in the *National
Era* with interest, and her husband ran a small publishing house.
He rarely handled fiction, but even so, Mrs. Jewett induced her
husband to read the back installments of *Uncle Tom's Cabin*.
He did so, and was impressed enough to write to Harriet. By
the middle of September 1851 the *National Era* was announcing
that the Messrs. Jewett and Company of Boston would publish
Mrs. H. E. Stowe's story, "immediately after its close in the *Era*."

"Immediately after its close—" The tone suggested that the
story was nearly completed. Harriet herself, when she stopped to
think about it, could hardly help but feel that it must be. But the
pictures kept flowing on in her mind, one after the other, and

more and more story kept unfolding without her having any real decision in the matter. She wrote and wrote and bundled up the papers to send them to Dr. Bailey, and then sat down to write again on the next installment.

School was in session. Calvin was trotting each day to his classes at Bowdoin, and, again, Harriet set up a school at home for the children. This fall she arranged to have some help with it, and she also discovered that Calvin's office at the college was a haven to which she could escape and write undisturbed for an hour or so every day.

Mr. Jewett, in Boston, began to feel some alarm at the story's ever increasing length. He had envisioned a slender volume that would bring him no great loss even if it did not sell well. Now it was beginning to look as though the story would not fit in one volume. He wrote to Harriet, asking if she could not hurry it to a conclusion. Dr. Bailey was also feeling uneasiness, and he suggested in the magazine that since the story had already run to such lengths, Mrs. Stowe might conclude the whole thing in a few paragraphs. A storm of letters from readers answered him. "Please signify to Mrs. Stowe that it will be quite agreeable to the wishes of very many of the readers of the Era for her *not to hurry through* Uncle Tom."

Harriet would have been glad enough to oblige both Mr. Jewett and Dr. Bailey, but the story had her in its grip as thoroughly as it held her readers.

Calvin left home for a while. He had gained a special dispensation from the Bowdoin trustees, who were allowing him to teach for the winter term at Andover in the school to which he had already committed his heart and his future. Harriet helped him prepare for departure, and then hurried back to her writing.

But now the story as it unfolded was filling Harriet with a kind of horror. Little Evangeline, that child of airy, otherworldly innocence, was fading, her hands growing thinner, her skin more transparent. She sat with Uncle Tom in the garden of her father's house, and instead of romping and playing, she remained quietly by him and looked up at the heavens with a strange and earnest air. Eva was going to *die*!

Harriet could hardly bear it. It was like living through that

July week in Cincinnati all over again, when baby Charley had
been so suddenly torn away from her. She did not want Eva to
die, but the pictures in her mind were inexorable. Eva, Evangeline, "the little evangelist," had done her angel's work on earth,
and now the sojourn was over. It was time for her to return to
heaven, bearing with her those wayward hearts to which she
had given a new vision of love and Christian kindness.

"O, God, this is dreadful!" St. Clare said, turning in agony from
her bed, and wringing Tom's hand scarce conscious of what he
was doing. "O, Tom, my boy it is killing me!"

"Pray that this may be cut short," he said—"this wrings my
heart."

And finally, indeed, it was over:

"A bright, a glorious smile" passed over Eva's face. "O! love—
joy—peace!" she murmured and "passed from death into life."

Yes, "into life." For Eva too, it was escape. But at this point,
Harriet, exhausted and heartbroken, put down her pen, and
took to her bed for forty-eight hours, in the collapse she had
not been allowed two and a half years before when the first little
Charley died.

Her collapse meant that one issue of the *National Era* appeared
without an installment of *Uncle Tom*, and thousands of readers,
more thousands than had ever looked at the *Era* before, felt
a shock of disappointment.

The story stretched ahead of her interminably. Tom had *still*
to be sold to the cruel Southern master who would take him into
the heart of the cotton country where "something faintly approaching the worst" of the system could be portrayed. But after
the respite she wrote with a new and driving energy that carried
her on, week after week.

Snows fell on Brunswick and sea winds whistled around the
house. "I will write something—if I live!" How long ago was it
that she had said that? A year? More than a year—almost a year
and a half.

But the end was in sight. Simon Legree had been introduced.
He was a hardfisted master modeled on the character whom
brother Charles had met during his months in New Orleans and
later described to Harriet. Harriet had given him a name that

was pure inspiration, and now Legree had begun his relentless persecution of Tom, a persecution based on little but a hatred of Tom's mysterious strength of character. His final attack on Tom and Tom's triumphant escape from earthly torment were surely not far away.

Mr. Jewett wrote about the terms of the book's publication. This being a matter of business, Calvin took time from his Andover classes and bustled down to Boston. Mr. Jewett, not sure of any profit in the offing, suggested that if the Stowes would put up half the cost of publication, they could have a half share of the profits. However, if this was unacceptable, they might settle for a straight ten percent royalty on all sales.

Calvin pondered, requested time to think it over, and then went asking advice from various acquaintances, among them a friend named Philip Greeley, a Congressman from Massachusetts. But this pondering and advice-seeking was merely a matter of form. Where on earth could he and Harriet get the money to pay for half the publication costs? This long tale, for all the interest it might have aroused in *National Era* readers, for all the power he himself might find in it, had been a bad blow for the Stowes financially. Harriet had contracted for a series of three or four sketches and Dr. Bailey had paid her three hundred dollars. The three or four sketches had become fifty or more, and during the course of writing them Harriet had not had a moment or a thought for any other kind of financially rewarding writing. As a result, she had made far less than she was accustomed to make in a normally successful year of writing. Obviously they could not dream of sharing publication costs on *Uncle Tom*.

Congressman Greeley gave Calvin sage advice that reaffirmed this necessary conclusion. Since it was hardly likely that the book would have a large enough sale to compensate for sharing its production costs, he urged Calvin to take the royalty by all means. "There may be enough in it for Mrs. Stowe to buy a silk dress," he said.

Harriet was winding things up. All the characters who had wandered into the story unbidden would find their places finally. Cassy, another beautiful mulatto, not young, but with a face that conveyed "a wild, painful, and romantic history," had suddenly appeared as the victim of the lusts of Simon Legree. Cassy could be encouraged to escape from Legree by the quiet strength and faith of Tom. And Harriet already knew how she would take her place in the final tableau. Eliza, her son, Harry, and her husband, George, were already free in Canada. There would be one more view of them there.

But before that, Uncle Tom must suffer his martyrdom. It was time to fit into place the vision that had come to her a year ago. She had the motive now for Tom's quiet defiance of Legree. What was it that Legree was insisting Tom tell, or die? What else but where and how the escaping Cassy had fled, of course. But Tom would die before he would betray the helpless. The stage was set.

Under the fury of Legree, who had made up his mind to conquer Tom or kill him, the obedient brutes, Sambo and Quimbo, laid on their whips. Until—"I b'lieve, my soul, he's done for, finally," said Legree, stepping forward to look at Tom. "Yes, he is! Well, his mouth's shut up, at last—that's one comfort!"

But Tom was not quite gone. "His wondrous words and pious prayers had struck upon the hearts of the inbruted blacks" who had worked Legree's vengeance on him, and then Tom spoke faintly, once more, to forgive them for what they had done. Awed and wondering, Sambo and Quimbo felt their souls awakening. It must have been God who sustained Tom through his torment, a God who might sustain and comfort them too. They fell on their knees by Tom. In his last agony, Tom had converted them. Then he was gone.

There remained only a few threads, young Master George Shelby's discovery of what had happened to Tom, his vow never to own slaves again. There was the escape of Cassy, to Canada, where she was united with Eliza and George Harris, and—yes, the ways of fate are strange—Cassy was Eliza's mother! There must be George Harris' bold resolve to work for the future of his race in Africa, where that race had its one hope of developing into a nation among nations. And Harriet was almost at the end of her story. George Shelby had only to return to the Shelby plantation in Kentucky, where the story had begun, and free his slaves and then remind them of Uncle Tom himself.

"It was on his grave, my friends, that I resolved, before God, that I would never own another slave, while it was possible to free him; . . . so when you rejoice in your freedom, think that you owe it to that good old soul, and pay it back in kindness to his wife and children. Think of your freedom every time you see *Uncle Tom's Cabin;* and let it be a memorial to put you all in mind to follow in his steps, and be as honest and faithful and Christian as he was."

And she was finished.

No—not quite. Perhaps it was the impetus of the writing still driving her on, or perhaps she found it hard to sever the tie that had held so long. At any rate, she was writing an epilogue. Speaking of herself in the third person, she wrote: "The thought of the pleasant family circles that she has been meeting in spirit, week after week, has been a constant refreshment to her, and she cannot leave them without a farewell.

"In particular, the dear children who have followed her story have her warmest love. Dear children, you will soon be men and women, and I hope that you will learn from this story to remember and pity the poor and oppressed. When you grow up, show your pity by doing all you can for them. Never, if you can help it, let a colored child be shut out from school or treated with neglect and contempt on account of his color. Remember the sweet example of little Eva. . . .

"Farewell, dear children, until we meet again."

"Farewell, dear children . . ." Did she really think that in this saga of bloodshed, violence, cruelty, illicit passion and tragedy, she had been writing for children? Perhaps, in that moment, she did, forgetting all the dark aspects of the story, and remembering the scenes of tender sentiment or the many scenes of rollicking comedy. And perhaps, in the same instinctive way she had written the whole story, she was right, for the story would ultimately come to have the same enduring, universal appeal as folklore—also full of violence and laughter intertwined—the force of a legend that could not be forgotten or shaken off, then or later.

"Farewell, dear children . . ." Looking back on what she had done, it did not seem to her that what she had written would accomplish what she had vowed to do—awaken people, North and South, to the horrors of slavery and the cruelty of the Fugitive Slave Act. She had presented so many of the South's arguments in defense of slavery. Had that been wise? Of Uncle Tom's three masters, the two kindly ones had both been Southerners. Her villain, the brutal Simon Legree, had not even been a Southerner at all, but a renegade Yankee. The Abolitionists, dedicated to the proposition that every slaveowner was by definition an unprincipled monster, were not going to like that. There were other matters the Abolitionists were not going to like, comments that had flowed from her pen as the story rolled along, reflections she knew from her own observations in Cincinnati were true, but which were not comments or reflections that pleased the zealots. She had seen how, as a general rule, the Southerner did understand and *like* the Negro better than the Northerner, for all the Northerner's intellectual sympathies. She had described in her story, how the New Englander, Aunt Ophelia, though righteously determined to educate the young Negro, Topsy, could not bear to touch her. But little Eva, the Southerner, nestled happily in Uncle Tom's arms. It was all true, as she described it. But Northerners might not like hearing it.

Then she comforted herself. Even if it did not please the North, her story might do some good in the South, awakening kindhearted Southerners to evils that were inherent in the system they had inherited and accepted. Perhaps there might be some, like George Shelby in her story, who would see the light and free their slaves.

She knew she had offered no solution to the total problem of slavery. It was all very well for the mulatto, George Harris, to sail with his family for Liberia, and work there to build a nation for his race, but the very word Liberia set off cries of outrage among the Abolitionists. And certainly a far-off Liberia, however disputed even as a future possibility, was of small help to millions enslaved in the South. She could see a hundred things that might weaken the effect of the book or make enemies for it among the people she had hoped to convince. Then even her dissatisfaction began to fade and become remote. She had done what she could, the only way she had been able.

"Farewell, dear children . . ."

What she felt most was release. Years later, remembering the sense of freedom that had come to her after finishing *Uncle Tom's Cabin*, she would try to explain it by saying that "the indignation, the pity, the distress, that had long weighed upon her soul seemed to pass off from her, and into the readers of the book." It was part of the explanation, certainly. She had felt indignation, pity and distress for the slave, and it had passed from her, in some mysterious fashion, in her writing. But some more personal indignation and distress, some more personal form of bondage had been lifted from her, too. She did not know how or why she had been able to make her own escape as she wrote of dozens of other escapes in the story. But there it was—she was free.

She stood in the backyard of the house in Brunswick and watched the railway train make its daily approach on the tracks only two blocks away. And the chuffing and clacking and plumes of steam no longer filled her with the sense of yearning that once they had. She felt free just standing there, with no need to travel or search. Down near the wharves and the shipbuilding yards, she could stand for a moment, and look at the masts of the unfinished ships, and feel the wind whipping her hair, and the same feeling of release and happiness would sweep through her.

"Who can speak the blessedness of that first day of freedom?" she had soliloquized in her book when George and Eliza Harris stepped onto the soil of Canada. "Is not the *sense* of liberty a higher and a finer one than any of the five? To move, speak and breathe—to go out and come in unwatched, and free from danger! . . . They had nothing more than the birds of the air, or the flowers of the field—yet they could not sleep for joy. 'O, ye who take freedom from man, with what words shall ye answer it to God?'"

It seemed very remote and unimportant that on March 13, Calvin was in Boston, signing the contract with Mr. Jewett. She had already sent the publisher a list of corrections to be made

in the book version of the story—not many, just some changes
in the names of characters and so on. She knew the book must
be in the process of being printed even as Calvin met with
Mr. Jewett, for it was scheduled for publication March 20. But
the date was hardly of much significance. She knew that Mr.
Jewett planned to print five thousand copies of the book. She
wondered if he would sell enough so that she would be able
to buy a silk dress, and she hoped he would. She speculated on
what it might mean to Calvin and her in actual dollars if all the
printing were sold—ten percent of $1.50, which was the price of
the edition in cloth binding, multiplied by five thousand. But
then she quit thinking along those lines. No one had any hope
of its selling that many copies.

Calvin was home in a week or so, bringing with him the first
copies of the book, actually bound between hard covers. It was
very satisfying to look at the two neat, thick, black cloth-covered
volumes, a solid, finished manifestation of the long year of writing. And it was really thrilling to look at the deluxe edition,
"in gilt," two volumes in lavender cloth, richly stamped with
gold all over the cover, and the edges of the pages gilded too.
Calvin was pleased and excited by the unusual fact that various
bookstores in Boston were announcing the forthcoming publication of *Uncle Tom's Cabin*, even before the book was out, something he had never seen done before. He thought this augured
well for the book's chances. But he was also perturbed about
something. Harriet's footnote attributing a certain quotation to
Dr. Joel Parker had been retained in the book version just as
it was in the magazine. He wondered if it was wise to single
out one real-life character for such mention especially when a
great many other eminent clergymen had often uttered similar
sentiments.

Harriet did not dare be as hopeful about the book's sales as
he, but she did agree that the footnote about Dr. Parker should
be deleted. She had planned to add that instruction to her list
of corrections, but had forgotten. So she wrote to Mr. Jewett,
asking for the deletion.

But by that time the unbelievable was happening. Mr. Jewett
was distracted with something completely outside his previous

experience. The first edition of *Uncle Tom's Cabin* had sold out in less than two days! Three thousand had gone the first day, the rest in a flash on the second, and the orders were piling up as he went about rushing a second printing through the press.

Harriet and Calvin were not aware of what was happening, at first. By the time Mr. Jewett could get around to writing them, and the letter could reach them, still another printing had been rushed through. And then, within another week—another printing!

Gradually, the news came through, and they took it in as well as they could. Twenty thousand copies had been sold in less than three weeks. So many more copies were being sold than either of them had dreamed of that there was an air of unreality about it all.

The book's amazing popularity was being reported by the press. The Boston *Traveller* noted that in Mr. Jewett's publishing house, "three power presses were running twenty four hours a day." Other papers were making similar references to the stir.

The New York *Independent* published a review on April 15, that ran a column and a half, winding up a paean of praise with the cry, "Let *all men* read it!" Other reviews, equally extravagant, were appearing.

Suddenly mail began to flood in upon Harriet in Brunswick. Mail that came from all over the North and East, mail from the South, mail from the lowly, mail from the great.

She was not only free, she was rich. There *was* "enough in it for Mrs. Stowe to buy a silk dress."

Part Two

FREEDOM

Still, still with Thee, when purple morning breaketh,
When the bird waketh and the shadows flee;
Fairer than morning, lovelier than the daylight,
Dawns the sweet consciousness, I am with Thee!

Hymn by Harriet Beecher Stowe

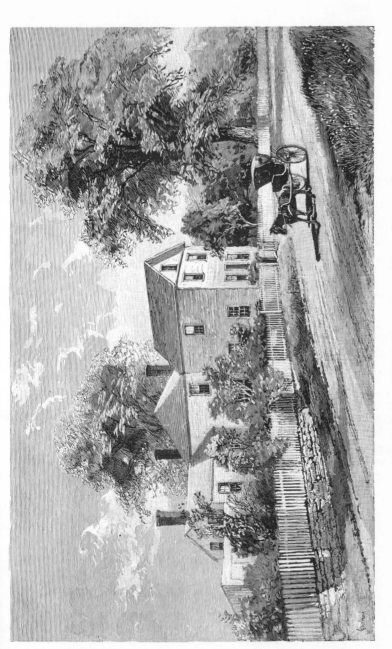

1. Birthplace at Litchfield, Connecticut   From photographs and from views in the AUTOBIOGRAPHY of Lyman Beecher, published by Messrs. Harper & Brothers

2. Harriet's father, Lyman Beecher   From a painting owned
by the Boston Congregational Club

3. Lane Theological Seminary, 1841   Drawn by C. Foster
Engraved by Doolittle & Munson

THE
CHRISTIAN SOUVENIR:

AN OFFERING

FOR CHRISTMAS AND THE NEW YEAR.

EDITED BY
ISAAC F. SHEPARD.

BOSTON:
PUBLISHED BY HENRY B. WILLIAMS.

Philadelphia: Perkins & Purves. New-York: Collins, Brother & Co.. Baltimore: Guessling & Brothers. Cincinnati: U. P. James. St. Louis: Dinnies & Raulford. London: Wiley & Putnam.

1843.

THE CORAL RING.

BY MRS. H. E. B. STOWE.

"THERE is no time of life in which young girls are so thoroughly selfish as from fifteen to twenty," said Edward Ashton, deliberately, as he laid down a book he had been reading, and leaned over the centre table.

"You insulting fellow!" replied a tall, brilliant-looking creature, who was lounging on an ottoman hard by, over one of Dickens's last works.

"Truth, coz,—for all that," said the gentleman, with the air of one who means to provoke a discussion.

"Now, Edward, this is just one of your wholesale declarations—for nothing only to get me into a dispute with you, you know," replied the lady.

"On your conscience, now, (if you have one,) is it not so?"

"My conscience feels quite easy, cousin, in subscribing to that very sentiment as my confession of faith," replied the gentleman, with provoking sang froid.

18

4.   Pages from THE CHRISTIAN SOUVENIR

5. House at Brunswick, Maine, where UNCLE TOM'S CABIN
was written

Uncle Tom

The cabin of Uncle Tom was a small log building close
adjoining to "the house" — as the negro always par excellence
designates the masters dwelling. In front it had a neat
garden patch where strawberries raspberries & a variety of
fruits flourished ~~& vegetables~~ under careful tending — ~~down~~ The whole
front of the dwelling was covered with a large big scarlet
nonia & a native multiflora rose which entwisting
& interlacing left scarce a vistage of the building
to be seen & ~~in the spring was redundant with~~
~~its clusters of roses & in summer so was bedecked~~
~~with the scarlet tubes of the honey some~~ Various
~~you~~ brilliant annuals such as marigolds four
o'clocks & petunias found here and there a thriffty
corner to ~~vegetate~~ unfold their glories & were the delight
& pride of aunt Chloe's heart

Let us enter the dwelling — The evening meal
at "the house" is over & Aunt Chloe who presides
over its preparation as head cook has left to inferior
officers in the ~~kitchen~~ the business of clearing away
& washing dishes & come out into her own snug
territory to "get her old man's supper" & therefore
doubt not that it is her you see by the
fire place presiding with anxious interest

6.   Facsimile page of UNCLE TOM'S CABIN

7.   Harriet Beecher Stowe in 1853   From a crayon by
Richmond, made in England

8. Calvin Stowe   *Courtesy of the Bowdoin College Library,*
Brunswick, Maine

Chapter 20

It is not fame nor praise that contents me. I seem never to have needed love so much as now. I long to hear you say how much you love me. . . .

1852

Harriet was in New York, breathless with fame and praise such as she had never imagined. It was impossible to say she was not enjoying them, and the magical way she had stepped from obscurity into success and acclaim. The rest of the letter to Calvin was an excited account of the things that had been happening to her. Other letters home had been equally breathless recitals of events and honors that seemed so improbable she could only relate them without comment or elaboration.

But fame had descended on her so suddenly and swooped her up to be the center of everyone's attention. A reaction was beginning, so that she felt the need to restore some contact with the Harriet she had always been, a Hattie she could recognize.

She had decided on the trip to New York early in May. Reports from Boston on the continuing success of *Uncle Tom's Cabin,* seemed to justify a jaunt. Also, there was a letter from the editors of the New York *Independent,* eager to know if Mrs. Stowe was interested in doing some writing for them. The *Independent* being one of the country's more influential religious papers, Harriet had been pleased and flattered. It had seemed stimulating to go to New York for a conference. She could make the trip a slow, rambling journey with stopovers to visit family and friends.

At the station in Brunswick, saying good-bye to Calvin and the children, she was just as she had been for years. Plainly dressed, she was the countrified professor's wife surrounded by the family which was her chief "work," her reason for living, over which she "feared and trembled." A busy and careworn house-wife, a loving and anxious mother, it was only for reasons of necessity that she was also a "literary woman" on the side. And only an accident that just now she could afford a little vacation. It was exciting. Her eyes shone. But climbing up into the rail-way car after the train had pulled in, she had no idea she was stepping into a world where just being the same wife, mother and literary woman she had always been, would not be enough —where the sheer pressure of her fame would mold her into an image for the public.

The first stop had been Boston. From there she wrote home that she was "all in a whirl" and "Mr. Jewett very animated"— as well he might be, with her book's sales spiraling upward daily and the demand showing no signs of slackening. She visited brother Edward and his wife, and they were full of congratula-tions. "If I could wield a pen as you can," sister Katey had written Harriet a year and a half before, but she had never dreamed that even Hattie, the family's literary genius, could wield a pen to such effect. *Uncle Tom's Cabin* was a sensation in Boston. Every-one was reading it and talking about it. She saw her father in Boston too, and it was good to have him congratulate her on her achievement. The final volume of his collection of sermons was soon to be published. Jokingly, Lyman wondered if her suc-cess might eclipse his, and Harriet laughed too, at such an idea.

Then Harriet had "touched on" Hartford to visit sister Mary and her family. While there she was struck with a flash of busi-ness insight, and decided to ask Mary's husband, Thomas Perkins, to manage her affairs for her. Calvin could handle things when the sums in question were only three or four hundred dollars. But Mr. Jewett had told her that when her first royalties were paid her in July, she might expect a check in the thousands. The *thousands!* Calvin would only grow dizzy trying to cope with such amounts. Brother Thomas, a shrewd businessman as well as a good lawyer, agreed to handle financial matters for her. Re-lieved on that score, Harriet went on to visit with Georgiana May Sykes. How dreamlike it was to talk with Georgiana and remem-ber when they had walked by the Park River and Hattie had

vowed to become a great writer. Georgiana gazed at her with
the same admiration as always, awed to think how the prophecy
had come true.

After a stop in New Haven with Mary Dutton and her father,
Harriet had traveled on to New York and Henry Ward's house
in Brooklyn. And, praised and congratulated though she had
been along the way, it was only when she arrived in New York
that she began to realize the immensity of what was happening.

The May Anniversaries were in progress when she arrived—
those annual nineteenth-century events that stirred all areas of
the Protestant faith, churches, missionary societies, temperance
groups, antislavery workers, women's suffrage groups, into a
storm of gatherings, assemblages, mass meetings and congresses.
Henry, the great man of the great Plymouth Church, was in the
thick of it, due to preside, to speak, or appear, everywhere.

Henry was quick with his congratulations to Hattie. Her book
was doing wonderfully. He had not read it, and he seemed to
have forgotten his promise to scatter it "thick as the leaves of
Vallombrosa." But Harriet could see how busy Henry was, and
the book was scattering itself, thicker, wider, farther, faster than
Henry Ward could have hoped.

And wherever Harriet went with him, to whatever gatherings,
receptions or soirees, suddenly and amazingly, it was *she* who
was the center of attention, not he. Whispers, running through a
room, that Mrs. Stowe was there, were enough to disrupt the
meeting as people hurried toward her, pushing through those
already surrounding her, to speak just a word to her. Almost
buried in the crush, Harriet would smile and nod and turn from
side to side, as hands reached toward her and voices clamored
at her.

Two of Henry's most devoted and wealthy parishioners, Mr.
and Mrs. John Howard, were so impressed with their minister's
sister that they appointed themselves her guardians. Mr. Howard
interposed his bulk between her and her admirers when the crush
became too threatening. Mrs. Howard hovered nearby, eager to
be of service in any way she could, bringing her water, urging
her to sit down for a while, even speaking for her when Harriet
was confused by importunities.

In the strange daze of success, everything began to seem possible. Catherine was in New York for the Anniversaries, and Catherine's current project was the raising of funds for a new educational organization for women. She was also interested in trying to launch a new school for girls in Milwaukee. Harriet was delighted to be able to tell Catherine that of course she would contribute to the fund, and yes, if Catherine wished, she could use her name on the list of sponsors of the new school. How strange and rewarding to have her oldest sister coming to *her* with such requests!

Then there was the surprise of the Jenny Lind Concert. The Swedish Nightingale was making a final appearance in New York after her triumphant American tour, and seats in the Castle Garden had been sold out for months. But Harriet had only casually voiced her regret that she would not have the opportunity to hear Jenny Lind when the magic took over.

"We had first-rate seats," she wrote Calvin, "and how do you think we got them? When Mr. Howard went early in the morning for tickets, Mr. Goldschmidt (Jenny Lind's pianist and recent bridegroom) told him it was impossible to get any good ones, as they were all sold. Mr. Howard said he regretted that, on Mrs. Stowe's account, as she was very desirous of hearing Jenny Lind. 'Mrs. Stowe!' exclaimed Mr. Goldschmidt, 'the author of "Uncle Tom's Cabin"? Indeed, she shall have a seat whatever happens!'

"Thereupon he took his hat and went out, returning shortly with tickets for two of the best seats in the house, inclosed in an envelope directed to me in his wife's handwriting. Mr. Howard said he could have sold those tickets at any time during the day for ten dollars each."

Harriet reported to Calvin that the concert "was a bewildering dream of sweetness and beauty." She wrote of Jenny Lind, "Her face and movements are full of poetry and feeling. . . . Today I sent a note of acknowledgement with a copy of my book. I am most happy to have seen her, for she is a noble creature."

And what was the result of thanking Jenny Lind and sending her a book? A long letter from Jenny Lind in return, thanking Harriet for the great joy she had had in her book.

The whole thing was a figment of romance far stranger than

anything she might have imagined for one of her stories. Harriet folded the letter, written to her by the greatest singer of the age, and put it away with the other letters of praise and gratitude she was receiving, to save for her children, and one day, her grandchildren.

She had also become involved in redeeming some slaves, just as Henry had been doing for several years. This was an unexpected and splendid opportunity to do something in keeping with her new role as spokesman for the slave. Four years before, Henry had worked his congregation to a pitch of enthusiasm for redeeming two young Negro girls, named Edmundson, being held in the slave warehouses of Washington for shipment to New Orleans. During the last year, Harriet had been contributing a little something now and then, to help with the education of the girls. Now the old mother of these two girls was again in New York, hoping that the freedom-loving parishioners of the Reverend Beecher's church could help her. She had two more children who were slaves whom she wanted to rescue from the traders. Henry Ward was doubtful about appealing to his congregation again in behalf of the Edmundson family. Then he thought of Harriet's eminence and turned Milly Edmundson over to her.

Harriet was tremendously moved by her meeting with the slave mother.

"I never knew before what I could feel till, with her sorrowful, patient eyes upon me, she told me her history and begged my aid," she wrote Calvin. "The expression of her face as she spoke, and the depth of patient sorrow in her eyes, was beyond anything I ever saw.

"Well," said I, when she had finished, "set your heart at rest; you and your children shall be redeemed. If I can't raise the money otherwise, I will pay it myself."

Imagine being able to say such words and mean them, "I will pay it myself!" But first Harriet wanted to try raising the money, and so she had hurried about, organizing meetings of ladies to whom Milly might tell her story, asking for contributions from new friends and old in New York. She even decided to write Jenny Lind.

"Well, I have received a sweet note from Jenny Lind, with her name and her husband's with which to head my subscription list." It was another note to add to the previous letter from Jenny Lind, another letter to treasure.

Excited and stimulated, Harriet found just one letter to stop her for a moment. Calvin had forwarded the letter from Brunswick, to which address it had been sent by its writer, Dr. Joel Parker, whose name still lingered in the footnote in *Uncle Tom's Cabin*. Mr. Jewett had been too busy rushing through new editions to make any corrections in the plates. Just as Calvin had predicted, Dr. Parker had not been pleased to find the footnote in Mrs. Stowe's "widely-extended book." He felt it an "aspersion" to his "professional reputation and usefulness" and demanded a "full and public retraction of the calumny."

Harriet was dismayed to read such harsh words in the midst of a whirl where everything she did was right. Then she felt a surge of anger. Why should she retract something that was true? She was sure she had not misquoted Dr. Parker. She had read exactly the statement she attributed to him in a report on one of his sermons—slavery was an institution that had "no evils but such as are inseparable from any other relations in social and domestic life." She decided to ignore the whole matter.

There were a thousand other things more important. There were the meetings with the editors of the New York *Independent*, which resulted in a big, bold-type announcement in the newspaper:

NEW CONTRIBUTOR

MRS. HARRIET BEECHER STOWE.

"The proprietors of The Independent have effected an arrangement with Mrs. Harriet Beecher Stowe by which the columns of this journal will receive from her pen frequent and perhaps weekly contributions. These contributions will be of a miscellaneous description, embracing every variety of incident, of subject, and of character, from 'The Mayflower' to 'Uncle Tom's Cabin'. . . ."

This new commitment meant that somehow, snatching moments from meetings, teas, dinners and receptions, Harriet had to prepare a column for the *Independent*. She did not try to be too original in her first contribution. Henry Ward, in the course of his "Star Papers" for the same newspaper, had covered dozens of topics. Pressed for time, her head whirling, she chose one that had concerned him recently and elaborated on it, spiritedly attacking a rival newspaper to the *Independent*, a religious paper called the *Observer*, which was supported by the "Old-School" Presbyterian forces and was proslavery in policy.

Another letter came from Dr. Joel Parker, stiffer than the first, threatening a libel suit if Mrs. Stowe did not make a public retraction of the calumny offered him by the footnote in her book. Reading this threat, Harriet became cross. She answered Dr. Parker, telling him that if the sentiments she had quoted in her book were *not* his, as he had once publicly expressed them to be, then it was up to him, not to her, to make a public denial and retraction. Full of satisfaction, she folded the letter, put it in an envelope, addressed it loosely to Dr. Joel Parker, New York, and gave it to her new and ever helpful friend, Mr. Howard, to mail.

It was hardly her fault that, due to a variety of circumstances, the letter was a week getting to Dr. Parker, and that during the course of the week, Dr. Parker worked himself into further extremities of outrage. The delay was not her fault. The extremes of Dr. Parker's outrage were not either, but just a less attractive aspect of the varied reactions to sudden fame. And so when Dr. Parker's third letter arrived at the Beecher house in Brooklyn, Harriet answered it by messenger, but withdrew not an inch from her previous stand. It was Dr. Parker who needed to redeem himself with the public, not she. And she added that from now on, "Any further communications must be addressed to my brother, H. W. Beecher, who is in full possession of the subject."

She was washing her hands of the business, running away from it altogether. Henry Ward would find some way to quiet Dr. Parker, she was sure. Very soon it seemed that he had. He was meeting with Dr. Parker's lawyer, and though adamant about Harriet's good faith, he was granting that perhaps Harriet had misrepresented Dr. Parker's feelings about slavery by quoting one sentence out of context. He was suggesting that Harriet write

a public letter to that effect, and that Dr. Parker write a public
letter in response, accepting that admission as an apology and
so ending the controversy.

Reluctantly Harriet agreed to even that much of a retraction.
But letters from Calvin, alone in Brunswick, showed he was working himself up to a state of panic over these difficulties with
a fellow minister. He was ready to rush to Boston to get Lyman's
advice on the matter. So Harriet wrote a stiff note, admitting she
might have misunderstood the whole of Dr. Parker's meaning,
and gave it to Henry. Then she went back to happier, more
praise-filled activities.

But by now, her head was spinning. There had been too much
of everything all at once. She thought of Calvin, jittering about
in his agitation, and right now his alarmist tendencies only caused
her to smile. He was her own dear husband, however exaggerated his responses at times, and one thing was true and sure however bewildering her life became—he loved her with a steadfast
love through ups and downs, and she loved and needed him.

Suddenly she shut herself away from everything that was happening to write to him.

"It is not fame nor praise that contents me. I seem never to
have needed love so much as now," she wrote, when it seemed
that, except for the acrimonious Dr. Parker, there was love all
around her. "I long to hear you say you love me. . . ."

It was a relief to be planning her trip home. She decided to
travel by easy stages, stopping off again with Mary Dutton in
New Haven, and with the Perkinses in Hartford. On this return
trip, her new friend, Mrs. Howard, was traveling with her as
far as Hartford, to help spare her any inconveniences or fatigue.

Only six weeks had elapsed since she left Brunswick. Only six
weeks, but so much had happened! She had heard throngs clapping at her entrance into a room. She had heard her name cried
at her again and again, in admiration, in love, and simply in a
sort of senseless attempt to claim some connection with her celebrity. She—Harriet Beecher Stowe—was a celebrity. Everyone in
New York knew her name. Wherever she went, when her identity became known, heads craned to stare, people became eager
and anxious to please her.

The characters she had created, or the characters who had *seemed* to be hers during the year she had lived with them— Uncle Tom, little Eva, Eliza and Topsy and Aunt Ophelia—were the greatest celebrities of all. They seemed to belong to everyone now, and to have a life of their own. She had heard half a dozen new songs in New York, inspired by one or another of them. Every day there were poems in the papers or magazines about them. Whittier had written a poem about the little evangelist, Eva.

"Dry the tears for holy Eva,
    With the blessed angels leave her; . . ."

It was not such a fine poem perhaps but it reflected the passionate response to Eva's innocence and goodness that seemed to well in every heart.

Who were those characters who had once lived with her alone, and then with her family, but who had stepped out on the stage of the world to make people laugh and cry and grow fierce with sympathy and indignation?

Who was she herself? The "Mrs. Stowe" whom everyone rushed to meet? The "Mrs. Stowe" whose name alone could send the fabled Jenny Lind scurrying for tickets for her concert? The "Mrs. Stowe" whose book was in everyone's hands? Could she possibly be the same little Mrs. Stowe who had stepped onto the railway cars six weeks ago in Brunswick, waving good-bye to her round, rumpled husband, and tall, weedy children?

The questions went with her as she and Mrs. Howard rode the cars and made their visits. In Hartford they were staying overnight with Mary. Harriet and Mrs. Howard shared the guest bedroom. And all her life Mrs. Howard remembered what happened that evening, after she and Harriet had retired to their room, when Harriet finally answered the questions that had been haunting her.

Mrs. Howard remembered how she had undressed and gotten into bed, but how Harriet had been much slower. Harriet was in one of her fits of abstraction. Nothing would end those, neither her new freedom, nor her new fame, nor anything. "Owling about" the room, from bureau to wardrobe to chair, she dropped her many petticoats, took down her hair and picked up a hairbrush. Then, clad only in her shift, she suddenly dropped down on the floor, tucked her feet under her and began to brush her hair. To Mrs. Howard, she looked like a girl as she did so, so small, so slight, her brown, curly hair floating out under the strokes of the brush. Mrs. Howard was awed. Such a tiny, girlish creature to have written such a tremendous book. Perhaps even now she was plotting and planning another story that would be equally powerful. Mrs. Howard almost held her breath, so close to the workings of genius, and so fearful of disturbing it in any way.

Suddenly Harriet broke the silence. She was not thinking of a new book at all. She was thinking, she said, of a letter she had recently received from brother Edward. Edward had been reading the New York newspapers and had learned something about the immensity of the acclaim she had known there. Edward was pleased and proud, but, her counselor ever since the days of her adolescence, he was writing to ask if all the praise she heard might not lead to pride and vanity.

"He is afraid it will work harm to my Christian character," Harriet said soberly. Then, with a quick movement she put down her hairbrush and spoke with great earnestness. "Dear soul, he need not be troubled. He doesn't know that I did not write the book."

"What?" said Mrs. Howard, amazed. "You did not write 'Uncle Tom'?"

"No," Harriet said. "I only put down what I saw."

"But you have never been in the South, have you?" asked Mrs. Howard.

"No," said Harriet, "but it all came before me in visions, one after another, and I put them down in words."

So she answered the questions that had been tormenting her, answered them in a way that satisfied every doubt and still left her free to be just what she was and had always been. It was not really she who had written *Uncle Tom's Cabin*, not she who had created the characters who stepped forth to live their own lives so amazingly. She had only been the instrument, writing down the visions she saw, which had been given her, she now realized, by God.

The Lord had written the book.

It was the answer that would sustain her through everything, through even wilder adulation and far fiercer attacks than she had already known, relieving her of responsibility forever.

She did not worry herself by going on to ask *why*, of all the people in the world, the Lord had chosen her as His instrument. The Lord's ways had always been His own, passing man's understanding. He had arranged strange and miraculous things for her before—sending her the means wherewith she could take the water-cure, rescuing her and Calvin again and again from insolvency. This time He had simply chosen that she should "write something," as she had vowed, and had chosen to dictate what it would be Himself.

She shook off her bemusement and contemplated the future with new assurance. The Lord had written the book, but she, His handmaiden, was the one who would reap the earthly benefits. And thanks to the money she would soon be receiving, a great many things were going to be different and much easier. She thought about those things happily and began making various decisions. There was nothing unusual about her doing this before she saw Calvin again. When it came to practical, everyday matters, it had always been she and not Calvin who not only made the decisions but put them into action.

She thought that they must soon be leaving Brunswick. Calvin was scheduled to take up his new post in Andover in September. This meant that once again, as two years before, she must superintend at the upheaval of moving and settling her family and household into a new home. Harriet was sorry to be leaving Brunswick. She had loved it from the beginning, but Andover was also in New England. And with money available, not only would the move be easier than any move she had made before, but the new home could be more tastefully decorated and furnished than any home so far. She wondered what sort of house the Andover trustees had assigned to the Stowes, realized with a lift that if she did not like the assigned house, she had money to seek out one she did like, and she resolved to take a trip to Andover to look over the situation as soon as possible.

While still in Hartford, she also took thought of the enormous correspondence in which she was now involved, with more letters coming in daily. Half sister Isabella, a handsome, commanding young matron of thirty, was living near Hartford. Her husband, John Hooker, was a lawyer whom she had met in Thomas Perkins' law offices. Visiting with sister Belle, Harriet suggested that she return with her to Brunswick for a visit and help with all the letters. Isabella thought it would be very interesting.

Harriet said good-bye to Mary and Thomas and to Mrs. Howard, who was returning to New York, and in company with Isabella, journeyed home to Brunswick.

It was good to see Calvin again, and good to hear him say, "I love you," just as she had longed to. She was also glad to find him relieved of anxiety about the Joel Parker fuss. Henry had settled the matter, as promised, by publishing Harriet's letter of qualified retraction in the *Independent,* along with Dr. Parker's acceptance of the implicit apology.

It was good to see the children again, but above all, to Harriet, it was delightful to make her first real use of the magic wand that success had given her. With money, she could hire a cook for the kitchen, a housekeeper for the rest of the house, a governess to take care of the children. With money, all the cares that had burdened her so long were gone in a twinkling, the house transformed into a model of neatness and regularity, and she could settle down in the sitting room with Isabella and begin tackling the vast collection of letters, papers and reviews that had piled up in her absence.

Her book had been out just three months, and except for the high, outraged complaint by Dr. Parker, it seemed to be going "by acclamation" everywhere. Everyone responded to it, even those whom she had thought might be displeased. The arch-Abolitionist William Garrison had written her a letter of gratitude, and still the book that pleased such an extremist of the North as he, was selling almost as well in the South as the North, according to Mr. Jewett. Harriet was happy with that news.

Then suddenly, reading the mail as it came in, Harriet began to sense a change. Everybody did not love the book after all. Its very power, the very vitality of the characters who had such an uncanny ability to make everyone laugh and cry and rage, held a threat. And here and there, people were beginning to recognize it and realize, with alarm, what the consequences of such power and vitality might be.

Harriet knew, as all antislavery people did, that a great deal of Northern money was invested in the institution of slavery. Bankers, cotton manufacturers and brokers, shipping interests, manufacturers who sold to the South the many products that its one-track economy could not provide for it—all these were willing enough to allow the South its "peculiar institution," even gladly to support the Fugitive Slave Act. In Boston, in New York, and other big Northern cities, these quietly influential members of society were the ones who were glad to keep the South happy by allowing "man-hunters" to raid Negro communities at will.

Knowing all this, Harriet should not have been too surprised when one of the country's most important financial papers, the New York *Journal of Commerce* published an angry attack on *Uncle Tom's Cabin*, declaring that it was a completely untrue picture of slavery. This attack, it turned out, was the opening gun for a debate that began to rage in papers across the country, as those who felt threatened financially by the book began to deny its validity, and those who had had their human sympathies aroused, fought back.

Almost as suddenly as the financial powers of the North realized they might be threatened by the book, the South awoke to its danger. At first, it had simply seemed an exciting work of fiction to Southern readers, just as it had to Northern ones, with characters that gripped one's emotions. But now the South saw, with a shock of revulsion, that under the lure of story and melodramatic enticement, the book was a violent and powerful work of propaganda—more powerful, more terrible because of all its enticements than the most outrageous harangues of William Garrison or any other missionary Abolitionist.

Sitting in her parlor, Harriet could not know that all at once it was becoming dangerous in the South to own or even acknowledge having read *Uncle Tom's Cabin*. She could not know that her name, uttered so admiringly by the crowds she had met in New York, was being hissed at in the South, and she herself en-

visioned as some spiteful, hate-ridden witch. But she did begin
to hear echoes of the South's mounting fear and rejection.

Mrs. Jewett sent her a review of *Uncle Tom's Cabin* that had
appeared in the *Alabama Planter*.

"The plan for assaulting the best institutions in the world may
be made just as rational as it is by the wicked (perhaps unconsciously so) authoress of this book. The woman who wrote it must
be either a very bad or a very fanatical person. For her own domestic peace we trust no enemy will ever penetrate into her
household to pervert the scenes he may find there with as little
logic or kindness as she has used in her 'Uncle Tom's Cabin.'"

It was hardly the worst of the reviews that were appearing in
the South, but it shocked and troubled Harriet. How could anyone call her "a very bad or a very fanatical person," when she
had been at such pains to show "something of the best" of the
system?

Anonymous letters from the South began to find their way to
her, and the abuse, the fury, the outright obscenity of the worst
of these were like nothing she had seen before. One day, Calvin
opened a small parcel from the South, addressed to her, and
found therein a human ear, cut from the head of some disobedi-
ent slave and sent to Harriet to show how the South could respond to Northerners who tried to incite insurrection among its
Negroes.

As these horrors began to pile up, Harriet could think of only
one course to avoid distraction. She would not look at them,
would not think about them. They were mutterings of a dragon
in the pits of hell.

She turned her back on them to read through more letters of
praise and congratulation. They did not feed her pride, for, after
all, the Lord had written the book, but they gave her a sense of
awed satisfaction. And, mindful that the Lord was her collabora-
tor, she could answer these in a quiet, dignified manner, wrap-
ping His mantle around her and signing herself "Yours in Christ."
It gave a rather lofty, pontifical sound to her letters, which would
last for quite a while, but her success was still new, and her realization that it had been God's doing was new too.

After just a few weeks at home, long enough to see that the new domestic arrangements were functioning well, long enough to take care of the most pressing correspondence, she went to Andover to examine the house that would be their new home.

Andover was lovely in the summer, its great trees green and dark against the blue sky. The various professors and their families whom she met were helpful and charming. They knew Professor Stowe's wife had recently written an amazing book. They were impressed with it and told her so, but being restrained and quiet men and women of learning and culture, they made no undue fuss.

Harriet was not displeased to discover that the house assigned by the Seminary to the Stowes did not meet her idea of what she wanted. Now she had an opportunity to drive or walk about Andover looking for something more suitable, a house large enough to accommodate the family and gracious enough to entertain the guests and visitors she knew would be coming in greater numbers.

She noticed a large, rather plain stone building on the edge of the campus. The Seminary had used it for some years as a carpenter shop, where its theological students could engage in that popular panacea for many ills, "manual labor," and at the same time earn something toward their support by their craftsmanship. Their product had been coffins, an article well suited for inducing theological meditation during its construction, and Andover coffins had been famous. Lately, the building had been converted to a gymnasium, as athletics began to crowd out "manual labor" in Eastern schools.

Neither the building's past use or its present one bothered Harriet. She gazed at it with a speculative eye, and saw how it could be transformed into just the kind of home she wanted. With all sorts of visions leaping to her mind, she hurried to the authorities and proposed that they remodel the old coffin factory according to her plans, as a residence for Professor Stowe and his family.

She was not daunted when they replied that they had no money for such a project. Her first check had come from Mr. Jewett in Boston. It was for $10,300! Could anything daunt her with such a check in hand?

She would advance the money for the alterations, she told them grandly, and would take the Seminary's note for the sum, to be paid back at some future date. The authorities were not especially pleased with that scheme either, since it still left them responsible for unneeded, unwanted remodeling. But Harriet's success had already given her more authority than she had ever shown before, except with Calvin. Moreover, she was operating within woman's traditional sphere in this case, arranging for a proper home for her husband and her family. And she was an author, she reminded them, an author who would undoubtedly be receiving various guests of note, and an author who needed a fitting place in which to work. Small, speaking as softly as ever, but with a new note of command in her voice, she asked them again if they could not see their way to agreeing with her proposal. This time they did.

And so began the happiest of summers. She had fame, she had assurance, she had new friends, and she had leisure. Rising with the dawn, she was free of any demands from husband or children and could wander out on the dew-wet grass of the campus, breathing in the fresh morning air, marveling at the clean, cool perfection of everything around, composing hymns in her mind, hymns that seemed to sing themselves to her with no conscious effort on her part.

She began thinking about what she would write next. Long accustomed to the role of "literary woman" who wrote when she could find the time, it did not occur to her to rest on the laurels she had won with *Uncle Tom*.

Neither did it occur to her to write anything more in the same vein. She was not a crusader, like Catherine, who could continue to write and talk and preach on one subject endlessly, trying to pound home a point. She had written out everything there was in her to write on the subject of bondage, spent all her passion and emotion on the theme. Released and free, her imagination rose like a cork to play on more familiar waters, with scenes and characters and themes that had always been dearest to her, the scenes and characters of New England.

She had been half-dreaming a story during many of the hours when she sat on the shore at Harpswell, in Maine, gazing off at the islands in the bay. Now she began to think about her "Maine story" again, a story that would have one of those islands as its setting. "I am composing it every day," she wrote Calvin, "only I greatly need living studies for the filling in of my sketches. There is 'old Jonas,' my 'fish father,' a sturdy, independent fisherman farmer, who in his youth sailed all over the world and made up his mind about everything . . ."

But she was also writing her columns for the *Independent*, and sending contributions to the *National Era*. And at Andover, with no housekeeping chores to burden her, she wanted to do some sketching too. "Yesterday I was out all the forenoon sketching elms," she wrote Calvin. "There is no end to the beauty of these trees. I shall fill my book with them before I get through . . ."

There were various festivities given by faculty members to attend. "We had a levee at Professor Park's last week,—quite a brilliant affair. Today there is to be a fishing party to go to Salem beach and have a chowder. . . ."

And so though she planned and "composed every day," nothing actually got written on the "Maine story." Because along with the sketching, the dreaming, the levees and fishing parties, she had one overwhelming preoccupation during these weeks. She was plotting the transformation of the old stone "coffin shop" and supervising the workmen as they went about carrying out her plans, and every bit of this was pure delight.

She had lived in a great many homes by now—in the crowded ramshackle house in Litchfield, in various plain, serviceable houses in Cincinnati, and in the big, plain, New England house in Brunswick. None of them had been what she thought a house should be. None of them was any reflection of her taste, nor of the tastes of the cultivated men and women she met in Boston and New York. Now she could have the kind of house she wanted, indulging, not her wildest dreams perhaps, but all her dreams of comfort and warmth and beauty.

She had built the cabin for Uncle Tom and his family. Now she dreamed a home for herself and hers. And she had the money to make the dream come true.

Chapter 21

1852

There were a great many more things to spend money on in America than there had ever been before. The new process that Eli Whitney had introduced to the country in the early nineteenth century was chiefly responsible. Interchangeable parts, assembly-line methods, mass production, for an ever increasing, ever more eager-to-buy mass market.

In 1799, when Roxana Beecher had been a bride in the little fishing village of East Hampton, Long Island, there had not been a carpet from one end of the town to the other. "All had sanded floors." Then, a small legacy had enabled Lyman to buy a bale of cotton for Roxana. She spun it, wove it, laid it down, and painted it all over with roses—a homemade floor covering that was the sensation of the village.

By 1836, when Roxana's daughter Harriet was a bride in Cincinnati, things had not changed so very much. The wealthy (like Uncle Samuel before the panic), who could afford to buy imported rugs and carpets, might have Turkish or French floor coverings. But anyone in only moderate circumstances continued perforce with druggets of wool or cotton or hemp, and rugs braided, or woven or hooked at home from old scraps of material. Furniture was plain and solid, pegged together by local carpenters, joiners or cabinetmakers, and families cherished those few heirloom pieces that might have filtered down to them from more affluent ancestors. Harriet cherished a desk that had belonged to Great-grandfather Ward, years before, in Nutplains.

But it was just then, in the 1830s, that things were beginning to change. New inventions like "fancy weaving looms," as well as new assembly-line methods, were being tried in small factories and mills all over the North and East. People were discovering machines could produce cheaply all kinds of fabrics that once were obtainable only at great cost from abroad, fabrics for dresses and cloaks, for draperies, hangings and upholsteries. A machine was invented to weave an ingrain carpet, and then another that could actually produce an astonishing and flamboyant facsimile of Brussels carpeting. Wallpaper was being printed domestically; no longer was it a luxury that had to be imported from France. Machines were invented to turn and carve chair rungs, bedposts, table legs.

At first all these wonders, so reasonable compared to the former imports, so marvelously precise and identical compared to rude handicraft products, came forth in a mere trickle. But soon the original stream had swelled into an overwhelming tide, pouring across the country, carrying on its crest a welter of factory-made tables and chairs and sofas and beds, carpets and curtains and knickknacks.

By 1850, when Harriet was buying furniture for the Brunswick house, she could wander through a rich profusion of such items in Boston shops. She could gaze at intricately carved sofas and chairs, covered in horsehair, at bolts of colorful chintzes, rolls of wallpaper, and she could yearn after elaborately worked metal hanging baskets for ferns or flowers, and marvelous conceits for birdcages. But the Stowes had no money then. When Harriet went with her few basic purchases to Brunswick, she and the woman who "helped" had to cover the sofas and lounges themselves and make the bolsters and pillows and mattresses.

Then, suddenly, in 1852, she had money. There was ten thousand dollars in the Stowe exchequer, and more would soon be coming in! Even if she used only a fraction of it in fixing up the "coffin factory" in Andover, she had money to spend to a degree she had never imagined, and the wealth of goods from which she could choose was like nothing America had ever known before.

The miraculous tide of machine-made goods had created a lust for elegance and splendor across America. Harriet had ridden on the Ohio River steamboats, which, like the Mississippi River boats, were considered floating palaces. Like most of their passengers, she had been impressed by their acres of wooden filigree, their gilding and stained glass and mirrors. Calvin, on his trip to Germany in 1836, had stayed at the new Astor House in New York and had been awed by that land palace "lighted entirely by gas!" and packed with incredible luxuries. Harriet had visited that brilliant edifice during the course of her *Uncle Tom* triumph in New York and had been in various other hotels and homes where lavish tastes were indulged almost as freely.

Still, what she wanted for herself and her family had little to do with this kind of display. What she wanted to create, from the profusion of goods available, was something else—a home rich chiefly in a sense of comfort. It was as though she had been starved for comfort. She wanted no more of the austerity of the rough, bare New England houses she had known as a child, and again in Brunswick. She wanted no more of the crowded, inconvenient, makeshift kinds of houses she had known in Cincinnati. She wanted space and sunshine, plants, and a clutter of cushions and comfortable chairs. And she wanted pictures, lots of pictures. There had been only a few miniatures on ivory in her childhood, not much more in Cincinnati. Now she could have lithographs and rich engravings, pictures that would give her imagination all sorts of landscapes and figures on which to feed.

It was 1852. Reading the papers at the end of July, Harriet was shocked, as were Americans everywhere, by news of a disaster on the Hudson River. Two steamboats, the *Henry Clay* and the *Armenia,* making the trip down the river from Albany to New York City, had been pitted against each other by their captains and crews in a race to prove which was the faster. Sparks flying up the smokestacks from the overheated boilers had set the *Henry Clay* afire. Dozens of passengers had perished in the ensuing inferno of flame and panic. But as she read over the casualty list, did Harriet realize that one of the victims, Andrew Jackson Downing, was the man to whom she owed many of the ideas she was putting into action as she transformed the "coffin factory"?

She may have, for during the forties Mr. Downing had published two highly popular books on landscape gardening and cottage architecture, books that had done much to shape culti-

vated tastes all over America. Mr. Downing had preached a doctrine of "smiling lawns and tasteful cottages," and had awakened
many Americans to the "dishonesty" of living in a little Greek
temple. It was he who had started the trend to "soft, quiet
shades" for houses, dark rose, brown or lilac, to blend with the
surroundings. He, too, had approved of comfort. "Verandas, piazzas, bay-windows, balconies, etc. are the most valuable truths
in Domestic Architecture," he had written.

And even as he went to a watery grave, these were the "truths"
Harriet was pursuing as she bustled around the dismantled interior of the building she had decided to call the Stone Cabin.
Window seats were a comfortable "truth," and she was arranging
for as many of these as possible. The house being stone, there
was no need to dim any harsh white exterior paint. But she
planned to have all the trim painted in soft, muted colors. Then,
these "truths" taken care of, she was ordering bolts of chintz to
be made into curtains, and yards of carpeting, and all the hanging baskets she wanted for plants and flowers.

In only one feature of the house was she looking back to the
houses she had known as a child. She hated the airtight stoves
she had known in Brunswick and Cincinnati, which "burned up
all the vitality in the atmosphere." She wanted big, open fireplaces everywhere, where fires could glow and leap with welcoming warmth all winter long. The cost of firewood would be
no obstacle anymore. She could even afford to buy herself and
her family their own woodlot.

1852 . . . Fashions in women's clothing had changed as much
as home furnishings in the years since Harriet was a bride. Machines had not yet taken over any part of the cutting and sewing
of clothes. Machines were simply providing fabric in greater
abundance than ever before. And as though to take advantage
of this abundance, skirts in the forties had gradually begun to
bell out slightly over petticoats. Then suddenly they were mush-
rooming into great, swinging circles, held out by seven, eight,
nine or ten petticoats. The wiry strength of crinoline was absolutely required to hold out such a weight of skirt, and with ten
yards and more of fabric suspended from a small waist, some

women were wearing the wire cages that had been invented to hold out this tentlike immensity.

Harriet would hardly have been human if she had not used some of her riches for new clothes. "There may be enough in it for Mrs. Stowe to buy a new silk dress," Congressman Greeley had said. There was enough in it for more than one. And though Harriet was not vain enough to lavish money on clothes, she had bought material for several new dresses in New York and had some of them "made up" in New York and in Brunswick. So she had the consciousness of being well dressed as she wandered about the Stone Cabin, making decisions and urging haste on the workmen. Her great skirts dipped and lifted about her small figure as she roamed the house or left it to go out and stand in the sunshine for a while, so full of a sense of her blessings that she could not help smiling as she gazed across the campus.

1852 . . . And there was a new richness and sense of promise everywhere.

While Harriet was peacefully enjoying the first fruits of success, the mood of the whole country was oddly peaceful too. Except for the extremists North and South, people were not finding the California Compromise of two years ago so unbearable after all. The Fugitive Slave Act was causing trouble chiefly in the cities. Elsewhere people could almost forget it, except when a new incident was reported in the papers. Harriet's book, designed to awaken them to its evils, had indeed struck everyone with tremendous emotional force. But the emotions the book had aroused were still simmering privately. No untoward event or crisis had yet given them a general rallying point. Almost everyone was eager that nothing should, and that the nation should have a time of peace.

In this election year, the Democratic party had nominated a bland and charming fellow with almost no political experience as its Presidential candidate. He was Calvin's old schoolmate from Bowdoin days, the agreeable Franklin Pierce, a man with no very firm opinions on any issue. In West Newton, Massachusetts, Nathaniel Hawthorne, another Bowdoin graduate, was writing a campaign biography of his old school friend, and the more radical members of Hawthorne's family were saying, "If he makes out Pierce to be a great man or a brave man, it will be the greatest work of fiction he ever wrote."

But few people wanted a brave man or a great man in 1852. They wanted someone to keep the peace, and Franklin Pierce seemed like just the man. He was what Northern antislavery men would soon be calling a "dough-face," meaning a Northerner with proslavery leanings and Southern sympathies.

In this interlude of quiet, the old, great political figures were leaving the scene. Daniel Webster would die, disappointed, discredited, no longer a hero to the Whigs since his fight for the California Compromise. Henry Clay, his partner in that cause, would also die. The old order was passing, in 1852, and a new one readying itself.

Abraham Lincoln was busy with his lawyer's career again, in Springfield, Illinois, having turned his back on politics after one term in Congress. He was riding the circuit of county courts, taking cases as they came. His drawling humor delighted those with whom he worked and relaxed, but his sloppiness and his periodic bouts of melancholy exasperated his wife. She was a woman far more eager than Harriet Beecher Stowe for fine clothes, elegant furniture, all the material riches the new country was producing in such a tempting tide. She wondered if she would ever have the opportunity to live and dress as she deserved, winning the admiration and respect she craved.

Down South, the price of cotton was rising, and crops were increasing, but the demand kept pace with whatever rise in production there was. For a little while, it seemed that the economy of the South was strong enough to resist the pressures brought on it by other sections, unfair though these were.

Out in the Great Plains of the Middle West, there was a new richness. Once, the land there had seemed too fertile. But now thousands of acres were golden with wheat, and more thousands of acres were being plowed every year. Cyrus McCormick's reaper, invented in the thirties, was the first machine to help the western pioneer control and make use of the land's abundance. After that, there had come other mechanical aids, the harvester, a self-knotting binder, a steel-toothed cultivator, an improved

plow with a steel moldboard that made it easier to break the
tough prairie sod. By 1852, Cyrus McCormick's plant in Chicago
was turning out a thousand reapers a year. Mass production,
Eli Whitney's gift to the North, was making it possible to build
those machines, and dozen of others, in a quantity that could
actually keep pace with the ever rising number of immigrants
from the East and from Europe. The immigrants were coming
to the Great Plains by railroad cars now, instead of in their
own wagons. More and more produce was being shipped East
and South by railroad, faster and more cheaply than the waterway routes could possibly handle it.

Railroads! They were the great dream, as canals had been
thirty years before. Everywhere, railroad tracks were being
laid. Everywhere, men were planning and scheming for new
routes to open new areas to settlement and commerce. And the
biggest dream was for a railway to span the continent, ocean
to ocean.

But which route should such a transcontinental railway follow? It could take a northern route, following Meriwether
Lewis and William Clark's trail to the West. Or it could cut
across the center of the continent, following the path of the California and Oregon pioneers. Or it might take a southern course,
through states and territories already more settled than the land
of the northern or central routes. Which should it be? North and
South, men plotted and planned for the route that seemed most
advantageous to them. A northern route would bind California
and Oregon more firmly to the Union than before. A southern
route might win for the South all it felt it had lost in the California Compromise.

The transcontinental railway would be one of the first concerns of Franklin Pierce's administration. He would not be in
office six months before a survey would be ordered to investigate
and compare the three routes most frequently suggested. Jefferson Davis, Pierce's Secretary of War, and his closest adviser as
well, would be in charge of the surveys. And Davis, a Southerner,
devoted to the principle of states' rights, would be so caught
by the dream of what a transcontinental railway going through

9. Lord Byron *Courtesy of Culver Pictures*

10.　Lady Byron　*Courtesy of Culver Pictures*

11.   The House with eight gables in Hartford

12.   H.B.S.   *Courtesy of Culver Pictures*

13.   Henry Ward Beecher   From a photograph by Rockwood, in 1884

THE ADVANCED WOMAN OF THE PERIOD.

"'You go for the emancipation of woman; but bless you, boy, you
haven't the least idea what it means—not a bit of it, sonny, have you now?
Confess!' she said, stroking my shoulder caressingly.

14.   Illustration of the "new woman" from MY WIFE AND I
by Harriet Beecher Stowe, J. B. Ford & Co., N. Y. 1872

15. H.B.S. in later years   From a photograph by Ritz and
Hastings, in 1884

16. The home at Mandarin, Florida

the South could mean to that area, he would gladly advocate its construction by funds from the Federal government.

Many other men, North and South, would also be temporarily ignoring or junking long-held principles as they contemplated the benefits of the transcontinental line going through *their* sections. The wrangle over that ribbon of rails to the West would be, in its own way, as fateful as any other kind of western expansion, in driving another wedge between the North and the South. It would be a wrangle to help create a new political party, destroy one political figure, and bring Abraham Lincoln out of Springfield, Illinois, into politics again—this time to stay.

But now it was 1852. Three routes were under consideration. Everyone had hope. The machinations, the deals, the wholesale jettisoning of principle had not started yet. Lincoln still rode from one circuit court to another. Northern and southern Democrats were still able to agree on a candidate for President, agree so wholeheartedly that they could sweep Franklin Pierce into office. And the Union could continue a while longer.

And in Andover, Massachusetts, Harriet Stowe, flushed with her first success, rich with a sense of money to spend, could plot her next novel and plan it as a Maine story. And meantime, pick and choose among all the things that money could buy.

Chapter 22

I am utterly incredulous of all that is said; it passes by me like a dream. . . .

1852–1853

The real wonder was that Harriet was incredulous so rarely, and that she moved through the mounting uproar of the fall of 1852 and the winter of 1853, a busy, self-contained little figure, still given to fits of abstraction, still muttering now and then in gloomy tones, "—if I live," and still chiefly picturing herself in the role she had played so long, that of a devoted wife and mother who was only a literary lady on the side. Perhaps that role was even more important to her now, a safe retreat from which she could look out, unstaggered, on ever wilder improbabilities.

The family joined her in Andover by the end of August. It was time for Calvin to begin preparing for his first classes in the fall. The renovations in the Stone Cabin were still far from completed, so Harriet settled Calvin, the children, and the family dog, in a pleasant Andover boardinghouse, went back to Brunswick to close the house there, then returned to begin making arrangements about the children's schools.

Such responsibilities and activities were reassuring. Life went on. The children's needs and Calvin's frets and worries went on, and it was good that they did. Because by the end of August, it was becoming plain that what had seemed like dazzling success to Harriet when she was in New York in May had been only the beginning. Mr. Jewett was reporting one hundred thousand copies of *Uncle Tom's Cabin* sold at the end of six months and still no slack in the demand. The songs, the poems, the lithographs, the paintings, inspired by the characters and scenes of the book, were continuing to pour forth. Now there came new evidence of the way the book seemed to exist as a force completely independent of her. Two dramatic adaptations of *Uncle Tom's Cabin* had been made during the summer. One was playing in Boston, one in New York, and both were doing a tremendous business.

Harriet had had nothing to do with these adaptations, and had not even granted permission for them to be made. Author's copyrights did not protect dramatic rights, and would not, for eighteen more years. Anyone who wanted to make a play of her book could do so, and put it on the stage whenever, however and wherever he liked, with no financial obligation to the author. So Harriet had no thought of complaining about these dramatic versions of *Uncle Tom;* they were simply proof that the popularity of her book was increasing all the time instead of diminishing.

Naturally, in 1852, Harriet could have no idea of how many, many more dramatic versions of *Uncle Tom's Cabin* there would be, nor of how dozens of companies would be presenting one version or another, night after night for years, nor of how at least one version would be on the boards somewhere across the incredible span of seventy-five years and more. In 1852, hearing about two companies presenting *Uncle Tom* dramas, she could have no idea of the fantastic profits the dramatization of her book would ultimately yield.

But even when some realization of how profitable those dramas were did come to her, years later, she would never be heard to complain because she had not shared in the riches from them. It was just another one of the ironies studding the annals of the Beechers, that instinctively and completely dramatic as they all were, they disapproved of the theater. Lyman Beecher had used his pulpit as a stage all his life, weeping and laughing and half-hypnotizing his congregations. Henry Ward was even more theatrical, acting out whole scenes on the pulpit platform of Plymouth Church, pretending to wrestle with a big fish on the end of a line, pretending to chop wood, or to wrestle, or to rock a baby—as bravura an actor as ever lived. Harriet was a mime and a clown who could hold family and friends spellbound when the mood was on her, and she wrote in scenes like a born dramatist. But to her, and to all the Beechers, the stage itself, with professional actors on it, was vaguely disreputable in the 1850s, tolerable only when it was used for some highly moral purpose. And so, while *Uncle Tom* dramas ground on, year after year, Harriet could comfort herself with the thought that those did preach against the evils of slavery, and she would neither protest their success, nor bewail her own lack of profit.

And she had no idea of something that would ultimately be even more unfortunate than any financial loss. As various adapters wrenched the story line from the book to make a drama of it, every subtlety was soon to be lost in the process. The plot was reduced to its barest, most melodramatic essentials. The characters, already close to prototypes, were reduced to simple caricatures of good and evil. All the arguments by which Harriet had led up to her melodrama in the book, all the shadings of character and refinements of motive by which she had given a semblance of individuality to the figures who moved through it, were thrown to the winds. Above all, the emotional honesty and unity of her central theme—the need of mankind to be *free*, his endless urge to escape bondage—were swept away in the lurid excitement of the chase, and the bathos of deathbed sentimentality.

One day Harriet would see a stage version of *Uncle Tom*, and sit through it laughing and crying with the rest of the audience. But when it was over, she would shake her head in bewilderment. It would seem to have nothing to do with her or what she had written.

Simplified in plot, the focus on the chase, instead of the escape, heightened by the addition of "live bloodhounds" ("count them— five, ten, or twenty!"), the sentimentality of Eva's death wrung out to new extremes by having the child ascend bodily, by means of wires, to "heaven," the stage versions would have an immense theatrical effect. And through such stage versions, thousands and thousands who might never have been reached by the printed word, would receive the bare bones of Harriet's message—slavery was bad.

But with time, distortion, following its own laws, would increase. Ultimately, as tastes in sentiment and melodrama changed (partly in a surfeit of so much *Uncle Tom's Cabin*), the characters who had loomed as folk-heroes, would be distorted once again, into catch names and phrases.

In Harriet's book, Uncle Tom had been ideally saintly, but he was still a man of strength and dignity, attempting man's greatest achievement on earth, an alignment of his will with God's. Ultimately, as the stage Uncle Toms droned their pious speeches of resignation, night after night, year after year, Uncle Tom would come to be a synonym for any servile, bootlicking Negro who seemed to love his chains. Little Eva would become the synonym for any sickly sweet child heroine, and "Eliza crossing the ice" would be a catchphrase to describe any kind of lurid and utterly unbelievable melodrama.

It was just as well for Harriet that she could not prevision such a reversal of all she had meant in the original portrayal of her characters. Just as well that she would never know that what she had written as a passionate plea for the dignity of the Negro and the overwhelming need of every human to be free, would one day be angrily, or contemptuously, denounced as contributing to the Negro's degradation. Of all the ironies in the Beecher annals, this one would be the bitterest.

She had seen her Negro characters remarkably honestly, neither wallowing in an unreal love for them, as many of their Northern defenders did, not seeing them each and every one capable of every perfection once their bonds were released, nor condescending to them in any way, but writing about them as human beings entirely. Some were handsome, intelligent and daring, like Eliza and George Harris, some clowning but good-hearted like the Shelby slaves, Sam and Andy, some imps of precocious instinct, like Topsy, some grieving, and some saintly, but all—all, were human beings craving to be free.

It was as well she would never know what would happen one day. She, who ran like quicksilver from any hint of bondage, trapped one day, and labeled an apologist for submission and servility? Little Harriet—the runaway—the mother of the *Uncle*

Tom despised by the twentieth century? It was as well she could
not know.

There were other, more immediate effects her book was producing that she did not know yet. She knew that the book's
influence and popularity seemed to be steadily increasing in
America. But she did not know that *Uncle Tom*, in a leap as
dizzying as Eliza's from the shore to the ice, had crossed the
ocean, and by the end of August was meeting with vast success in
England. Harriet would have no financial return from that either.
The book had been pirated, in the same offhand fashion that
American publishers had long been practicing themselves, no-
tably with the novels of Charles Dickens. The very week *Uncle
Tom's Cabin* was published, a young man leaving the United
States for England had taken a copy with him and offered it to
several publishers in London. Finally, a group of three men had
formed a small company and brought out the first British edition
in July. For a while, they wondered why they had bothered.
The book languished in the bookstalls.

Then, oddly enough, considering the book's initial lack of success, two more pirated editions were published. And suddenly,
for no reason anyone could name or explain, *Uncle Tom's Cabin*
became an instant and wild success. Books melted away from the
bookstalls, and the startled publishers began the same kind of
furious reprinting that had had Mr. Jewett so "animated." The
first publishers to issue the book hastily bound up their remaining printed sheets and rushed them to the market, but no matter how many publishers climbed aboard the bandwagon, it
seemed they could not overload it. The book was sweeping England, even more dramatically than it had swept America. One
publisher who put it out in penny parts was selling *Uncle Tom's
Cabin* at the rate of thirty thousand a week, and a cheap "railway" edition was doing almost as well.

Immediately after the book's publication, Harriet had thought
of England and hoped that the book might be read there. She
had wrapped up and sent copies, along with letters, to various
important figures, well known for their philanthropic activities
and antislavery sentiments. Such titled philanthropists as the

Duke of Argyll and the Earls of Carlisle and Shaftesbury had received copies from Brunswick. Harriet had also written to Charles Dickens, Thomas Macaulay and Charles Kingsley, liberals all, and known for their sympathy with the oppressed. She had even sent a copy to Queen Victoria's Prince Consort. She had been moved, she said later, by talk she had heard that England might one day close Canada to the fugitive slaves escaping from the states. She hoped her book might strengthen antislavery sentiment in England, where millowners and workers both were inclined to sympathy with the South because of their dependence on its cotton.

It was fall of 1852 before Harriet began to hear of her book's wildfire success with English readers. Then, in November and December, she began receiving responses from the great and titled to whom she had sent copies.

The Duke of Argyll, the Earl of Carlisle, the Earl of Shaftesbury, were writing her, and awesome as it was to find mail from such personages in the Andover post, the lavish nature of the letters' contents was even more overwhelming. A small, nervous New England lady could only cling more firmly to her role as housewife and mother and her conviction that God had written the book, and her husband, reading the letters with her, could only hem and haw and beam with bewildered pride.

"I return my deep and solemn thanks to Almighty God who has led and enabled you to write such a book," Lord Carlisle wrote, and continued with much more in the same vein.

"I cannot refrain from expressing to you the deep gratitude that I feel to Almighty God who has inspired both your heart and your head in the composition of 'Uncle Tom's Cabin,'" wrote the Earl of Shaftesbury and he too went on in further praise of "such a book as yours, which has absolutely startled the whole world. . . ."

By December, when his Lordship wrote that, he was not exaggerating too much in speaking of "the whole world," for, by then, *Uncle Tom* had made an Eliza-like leap across the English Channel and was sweeping the continent.

Soon after the book's success in England it had jumped to France. Almost at once, six different pirated versions were in translation and on sale in the bookstores and bookstalls of Paris. Three Parisian newspapers began serializing *La Cabine de l'oncle Tom*. French interest in the book was so fevered that many readers bought all three papers to make sure some vital passage had not been omitted in one or the other, and so profound was the impact of the religious elements in the story that Parisian booksellers were suddenly surprised by a run on Bibles, "la Bible veritable de l'oncle Tom!"—the same Bible Uncle Tom read.

No longer just a book, but a natural force, a hurricane or a tidal wave, it swept on to Germany, Italy, Portugal, in more swarms of pirated translations, running serially in the newspapers, or published in cheap paper editions. It swooped up through the Scandinavian countries, through Sweden and Finland, and finally into Russia.

Everywhere, it met with a response that was almost uncanny, from the sophisticated, the literary and the powerful, as well as from the impoverished or downtrodden, who might, in their various ways, identify with "Life Among the Lowly."

Heinrich Heine, in Paris, read a German translation and was so profoundly affected by it the religious doubts that had tormented him for years seemed to disappear. He reached for his Bible saying, "With all my sense I have come no farther than the poor ignorant Negro who has just learned to spell. Poor Tom indeed seems to have seen deeper things in the Holy Book than I."

George Sand reviewed the book for a Paris paper. Notorious in America because of her amatory adventures, her writing frowned upon by the respectable, George Sand felt no need to even scores with anyone across the sea, and was both lavish and penetrating in her comments. "Mrs. Stowe is all instinct; it is the very reason she appears to some not to have talent. Has she not talent? What is talent? Nothing, doubtless, compared to genius; but has she genius? She has genius as humanity feels the need of genius,—the genius of goodness, not that of the man of letters, but that of the saint."

And in Russia, when Count Lev Tolstoi came to read a copy

at last, he declared it was among the great achievements of the human mind.

All these hosannas did not reach Harriet at once. The first, and unsuccessful transatlantic cable would not be completed for six more years. News came by boat. The total impact of her book broke on Harriet gradually, far more gradually than the book itself broke upon the world. In fact, in the early part of the fall, when "Tom-mania" was beginning to reach feverish heights in England and France, a good part of Harriet's concern was focused on a tempest in a teapot, another tempest brewed by the disgruntled Dr. Joel Parker, he of Harriet's careless footnote in *Uncle Tom's Cabin*.

What was wrong with Dr. Parker? Did he really feel his reputation so endangered because Harriet had attributed to him sentiments about slavery that were not quite altogether his? Or did he and his advisers actually have some hope of weakening the effectiveness of the book by making trouble for her? And aside from all that, had he not been pacified by the retraction that Henry Ward had caused to be published in the *Independent*? Had he himself not written and signed a letter accepting the apology?

The answer to the last two questions, at least, was "No." In the latter part of September, the *Independent's* rival, the *Observer*, suddenly came forth with a sensational charge. Both the retraction and Dr. Parker's acceptance of the same were forgeries by Henry Ward Beecher, it declared, and then it went on to decry Harriet Beecher Stowe as coarse, mercenary, unladylike and a liar.

Calvin was aghast when he read such words and Harriet was amazed and troubled herself. And it was not very comforting to find, upon investigation, that there was a small grain of truth in the forgery charge. Harriet knew her brother had rewritten her retraction to suit himself. Now she and Calvin discovered he had written Dr. Parker's letter of acceptance as well. Relying on the word of Dr. Parker's lawyer that he was sure Henry knew how to phrase their agreement, he had then sent the letter to the *Independent*, without showing it to either Dr. Parker or his lawyer first. That Henry had been careless could not be denied.

Easy, quick and trusting, eager to take people at their word, he had been anxious to have the matter settled and to turn his attention to more important affairs.

Now, as Harriet's book roared across Europe, as it plowed ever deeper, wider furrows across America, she, Calvin and Henry had to concern themselves with this.

After the first dismay, and then the scurry to gather together necessary papers, and the efforts to keep Calvin calm, Harriet was able to treat the whole matter rather lightly. But Henry Ward worked himself up into towering rage as he prepared his answer. "For myself," he began, in his rebuttal in the *Independent*, "I profess no event of my life, not the loss of my children, nor bereavement . . . nor sickness . . . have ever filled me with so deep a sorrow. . . ." And he went on, column after column, explaining how it could not have been a forgery, and how it was really Dr. Parker who was speaking falsely, and so on and so on.

For a while, readers of both the *Observer* and the *Independent* bought papers avidly, chiefly because they were intrigued by any news about the famous preacher, Henry Ward Beecher, and his equally famous sister, Harriet Beecher Stowe. But the idea that anything Dr. Parker charged them with could really damage either of their reputations was unthinkable all along. In due time, the whole fuss died down. Defeated by popular opinion even more than by Henry's trumpeting, Dr. Parker sank back into quiet for good. Henry recovered from his most profound sorrow. And somehow, the footnote attributing a certain opinion of slavery to Dr. Parker continued in every edition of *Uncle Tom's Cabin* from then on, in spite of all the apologies, recriminations and promises that had been made.

What really was beginning to alarm Harriet in the fall of 1852, while in Europe Heinrich Heine was being moved to reach for his Bible, and George Sand was praising her genius, was the mounting criticism of her book in America. A well-known physical law was beginning to operate—for every action there must be an equal and opposite reaction. With the book and its characters becoming a staple of conversation in the North, and with its effects being felt in Congress, where antislavery senators like

Charles Sumner of Massachusetts, were using it as a textbook, the opposite reaction was building irresistibly. The abusive letters, the articles denying the book's validity, which had shocked her in June, and which she had tried to ignore, had been only a trickle compared to the flood of fury and denial the book was evoking now.

"Go, go, go,
Ol' Harriet Beecher Stowe!
We don't want you here in Virginny—
Go, go, go!"

Harriet could not hear the children of Richmond chanting their newest sidewalk song, but letters from the South were reaching fresh heights of vituperation, and she had plenty of other sources for learning about the violence of feeling in the South. It both shocked and grieved her. She had thought she was speaking to the South even more than the North, and picturing so much of the "best side" of slavery, that it could not help but listen. Now the South was denying that *any* aspect of slavery as depicted by her was true. Everything she had written was false and pernicious. A spate of "anti-Tom" literature was beginning to appear in the magazines and bookstores of the North as well as the South. There were books called *Uncle Tom's Cabin As It is; or Incidents in the Real Life Among the Lowly;* or *Life in the South, A Companion to Uncle Tom's Cabin;* and, perhaps most popular of all, *Aunt Phillis' Cabin, or Southern Life as It Is,* by Mary H. Eastman.

It did not comfort Harriet to know that her book had a veritable army of defenders, ready to meet any criticism with a clamorous counterattack. A reader of the *National Era,* scandalized by the attacks on that magazine's most famous and popular serial, wrote to Dr. Bailey, begging him to answer Mrs. Stowe's critics. Dr. Bailey did not think it necessary. "We should as soon think of coming out in defense of Shakespeare," he replied loftily. But other editors did not hold themselves so much above the battle and flayed any attackers of *Uncle Tom.* Still, to Harriet the shock came from realizing how many people denied the book utterly.

It was true—all true, she kept wanting to cry out to them. She had written the book as fiction, yes, but it was all based on fact. That was what was important. Did even her champions and defenders, swept up by their emotional attachment to the characters in the story, realize how very true everything that happened to them was?

Uncle Tom's defenders were as incensed by literary criticism of the book as by attacks on its validity. Harriet could not have cared less about that. She had not been concerned about the literary merits of her story when she wrote it, and she never would be. When, in the general chorus of praise from overseas, the London *Times* was heard to voice a slight dissenting note, suggesting that the novel was faulty in construction, this was reported in many American papers almost as though it were a slur against the Gospels. The *Times* had also urged that there be "no more Uncle Tom's Cabins, engendering ill-will, keeping up bad blood. . . ." Charles Dickens was another English reviewer who was able to temper his enthusiasm for the book, calling it "noble but defective." And the book's defenders had fumed at that.

Harriet brushed aside any such complaints. The only criticisms that bothered her attacked the book's validity. What was wrong with the people of the South? Did they not know what went on in their own land? Were they unaware of the laws on their own statute books? With the South howling such rejection, perhaps doubts about the book would spread in the North. Perhaps the effectiveness of the book would be weakened as doubts grew about the *facts*.

Gone, finally, was any hope of working on the "Maine story" that she had begun to dream during the summer months. While the Joel Parker quarrel was in progress, Harriet was serene enough to compose a hymn and its first lines could run:

"When winds are raging o'er the upper ocean,
    And billows wild contend with angry roar,
    'Tis said, far down beneath the wild commotion,
    That peaceful stillness reigneth evermore."

But she could not summon any "peaceful stillness" to reign beneath this wild commotion, not while people were saying and writing that there never could have been a man like Simon Legree, never could have been a daring escape like Eliza's, above all, that there never had been and never could be such abuses of slavery as those of which she had written. Somehow she had to silence this commotion herself and prove to people that every incident they criticized and denied, not only could have happened, but sometime, somewhere, *had* happened.

She had had few documents beside her when she wrote the book. Scenes, events, and characters had simply flashed before her mind, living out the story for her. But that did not worry her. She remembered when she had met or heard about the original models for many of her characters, and when she had experienced or heard about some of the events. What was more, by now she did have a great many documents.

The documents had come to her, unbidden. Ever since the publication of *Uncle Tom's Cabin,* her mail had contained, along with the praise and the abuse, a great deal of evidence that what she had written was not imagined. In wonder or in gratitude, people wrote telling her of stories almost identical with episodes in her book, enclosing clippings, handbills, and other items that corroborated the story. Since she had been in Andover, some readers had made their way to her in person, so they might ask how she had known or heard or guessed about some incident in their own lives that tallied exactly with something in her book.

It did not matter that writing *Uncle Tom* had been as impetuous and uncalculated an act as her conversion long ago, or her feast on the tulip bulbs, long before that. She had the facts she needed to defend every word she had written. It never occurred to her that the book really needed no defense, that even as it had scattered itself "thick as the leaves of Vallombrosa," even as it had leaped almost of itself across oceans and channels and languages, so it would hold its own against any kind of attack. Just as she had forced herself once to spend months and years examining her sins in penance for her easy conversion, so she would force herself now to examine pile on pile of documents. If she still did not have proof for every instance in her book, she would find it. She would read Southern laws and statutes and look up court proceedings. With the results of this labor, she would present to the world incontrovertible proof that no matter how instinctive the original act had been, it was all right. The Lord had written the book. Now it was his handmaiden's task to make that clear.

She made up her mind in November that writing a *Key to Uncle Tom's Cabin* was the first writing task that lay before her. The Stone Cabin was ready for occupancy at last. By the first of December the Stowes were moving out of the cramped quarters at the boardinghouse and settling into the comfort of their new home. There was snow outside, but inside, pots of ivy and other plants framed the deep windows of the long parlor, making a green bower of every brightly cushioned window seat. In the wide, open fireplace, a great fire burned, just as Harriet had dreamed of it, sending a glow around the room and filling it with the fragrance of woodsmoke.

Only a year before, she and hers had been in the bleak, cluttered house at Brunswick, where airtight stoves fought the chill air that leaked in at every crack. She had still been living with all the characters of her book, writing the last chapters of *Uncle Tom's Cabin* on the desk, on the kitchen table, or wherever she could find a spot, while family life eddied around her and money worries lurked just beyond her concentration, ready to fret at her whenever her story let her go.

Now she could go into her own retreat in the Stone Cabin and close the door behind her and write for hours without interruption, if she chose. Someone else would mind the children, fix the dinner, mend and make the clothes. There were no more money worries. She had only to retire to her study and begin on her documents and memories.

It was easy enough in the beginning. She had only to take up one character after another from her book and explain his origin. The Shelbys, those good-hearted plantation owners, were modeled on a family she had visited in Kentucky. It was on that same visit that she had seen the beautiful mulatto girl, who served as a model for Eliza. She would admit that some of the characters were syntheses. Augustine St. Clare was a prototype of all that was fine, sensitive and gentlemanly in the Southern character. Aunt Ophelia symbolized many of the faults of Northerners in their relationship to Negroes, faults that Southerners justifiably deplored. And so it could go, for character after character. Simon Legree was modeled on a personage her brother Charles had described to her on his return from New Orleans. Harriet could remember the very words he had used, telling her of the slaveowner he had met who boasted that his great, gnarled fist, like an oak burl, had grown strong "knocking down niggers."

All her time was not devoted to the *Key*. The letters attesting her book's success in England were streaming in. She and Calvin had to read them together, marveling at the people whom she, as an instrument of the Lord, had been able to reach. There was a letter from the private secretary of the Prince Consort, thanking her, in the name of Prince Albert, for the book, and passing on his promise to read it. There were elaborate resolutions of gratitude from the Congregational Union of England and Wales, and there was a magnificent Bible paid for by a collection taken up at a mass meeting of laborers in London. There was news that at least two artists of the Royal Academy were at work on pictures based on *Uncle Tom's Cabin*. Uncle Tom and little Eva were inspiring British songwriters, just as they had inspired American, and *Uncle Tom's Cabin* had been dramatized in England, and was playing to crowds in London.

An even more exciting communication came from the British Isles. An eminent pastor of Glasgow, Scotland, Dr. Wardlaw, was writing to say that Glasgow's two antislavery societies wished to extend an invitation to "Mrs. and Professor Stowe" to visit the British Isles. The visit could be at any time that met their convenience, and every other arrangement could be made in conformity with their desires as well.

A visit to the British Isles—all expenses paid!

"I am utterly incredulous of all that is said; it passes by me like a dream. . . ."

She was referring to the mingled roar of praise and criticism in which she lived when she penned that one bewildered line

in a letter, but this invitation was part of the general incredi-
bility of everything. Sixteen years and more before, Calvin had
taken his one, never-to-be-forgotten European trip, and she had
wished that she could go too, but the wish had seemed absurd.
Now, through her own efforts, she had won this dream for herself
and Calvin both.

It seemed proper that she and Calvin should talk gravely of
how it was her duty to accept the invitation. She was now considered one of the spokesmen of the American antislavery forces.
She could, just by her presence in Great Britain, help influence
British opinion toward the cause. But however she and Calvin
justified their acceptance, neither could help a thrill of anticipation as they discussed just when they should go and what arrangements should be made about Calvin's classes, the children
and the house.

They decided on a departure in early April. That would
allow them time for a proper visit with their hosts in Scotland
before going on to attend the famous May Anniversaries in London, an event they did not want to miss if they were going
abroad.

Then, just because the prospect did please her so much, perhaps, Harriet was lapsing into her melancholic strain as she wrote
her acceptance: "Should God spare my life till April, I trust
to mingle prayers and Christian affections with the Christians
of Scotland."

She had thought, in the beginning, that her *Key to Uncle Tom's
Cabin* would be a preface to all new editions of the work, and
that she could complete it in a few weeks. Gradually it became
clear that the *Key* must be much longer than that, a book in
itself, and that she had been wildly optimistic in estimating the
time it would take. There were mountains of documents to
read, piles of fine-printed law books to pore through, stacks of
letters, each of which might contain some vital bit of evidence.
Doggedly, Harriet pursued the task, though the work was a
strain to the eyes, the mind and the heart. In this *Key*, everything
she read or wrote reflected the most savage aspects of slavery.
Never could she turn, as she had in writing *Uncle Tom*, to
some scene of comedy or sentiment for relief.

Every now and then she lifted her head from these labors to cope with her correspondence. She must answer the letter from the Earl of Shaftesbury.

"My Lord," she wrote, "The few lines I have received from you are a comfort and encouragement to me, feeble as I now am in health, pressed oftentimes with sorrowful thoughts. . . ."

"Feeble" was an exaggeration, but she was very tired, and pressed not only with "sorrowful thoughts" but with the need to work without slackening if she and Calvin were to meet that star-crossed April sailing date.

There were signs that her labor was worthwhile. Senator Sumner, once again using *Uncle Tom's Cabin* as his text in a speech to Congress, had been challenged by a Southern senator as to the validity of a certain "Wanted: Dead or Alive" poster in the book. No such "Dead or Alive" posters had ever existed, the Southerner declared. Senator Sumner wrote to Mr. Jewett, asking if Mrs. Stowe had any proof that such posters were used in the South. Mr. Jewett forwarded the letter to Harriet, and it was very satisfying to answer it. She had indeed invented the wording of the poster as she wrote the book, but confirmation that such posters were used in the South had just recently been received. She gave Senator Sumner the circumstances, and with this letter to him began what would ultimately be a long friendship.

Plans for the trip abroad were stirring up a cheerful family commotion around her. Realizing that she might need someone to act as a secretary while she was in the British Isles, her first thought was of someone in the family. Her choice was Charles, currently pastor of a church in Newark, New Jersey. Surely his congregation would allow him leave of absence for a few months. Charles, handsome, gay, and thinking of the church music he could hear abroad, was delighted with the idea. So it was arranged that Charles would accompany them. Then the news of the contemplated journey reached brother George's widow in Rochester, New York, and Sarah Beecher decided to join the group too. Money had never been a problem to her. She would come along and bring her son and her brother. Thinking about the trip, Harriet could now envision a family group of six, just

the sort of party she liked. Her own children would be staying
with various families in Andover, or with members of the
Beecher clan elsewhere in New England.

Still the work on the *Key* ground on. And still letters kept
pouring in, letters that she must somehow find time to answer.
There was one letter from London that she took pains to answer
at conversational length. It was from Mrs. Eliza Follen, formerly
of Boston, a lady whose name was well-known to Harriet as the
author of a juvenile classic, *The Well-Spent Hour*. Harriet had
read the book as a schoolgirl, and later read it to her own children. Mrs. Follen had also been engaged in the Abolitionist
activities in Boston before leaving the United States, so now
she was writing Harriet, the new prophet of the movement, to
ask something about her. As flattered by the inquiry as by
any letter from the great, Harriet pushed the manuscript of the
Key to one side for a while.

"My dear Madam," she wrote, "I hasten to reply to your letter,
the more interesting that I have long been acquainted with
you, and during all the nursery part of my life made daily use
of your poems for children. . . .

"So you want to know something about what sort of woman
I am! Well, if this is any object, you shall have statistics free
of charge. To begin, then, I am a little bit of a woman,—somewhat
more than forty, about as thin and dry as a pinch of snuff;
never very much to look at in my best days, and looking like a
used up article now. . . ."

Disparaging the way she looked was a habit with Harriet.
The daguerreotype of herself that she had at last been persuaded
to have made in the fall did not show any "used up article," but
a woman with great eyes, a mouth both sad and humorous, and
a look of character and strength. But Harriet saw in it, and in
the mirror, only what she had been acustomed to see all her
life—"a wisp of nerve," a frail reed shaken by the wind.

After the disclaiming introduction, she settled down for a long
epistolary chat with Mrs. Follen, suddenly reveling in this opportunity to review her life. She began with her marriage "to a
man rich in Greek and Hebrew, Latin and Arabic, and alas!
rich in nothing else," and rambled on to write of her children,

and the tragedy of the first Charley's death. She told of how she
had become a "literary woman," forced by the pressure of accounts that "wouldn't add up," to turn out pieces that would get
her family "out of the scrape." She wrote of her life in Cincinnati, and the Negroes she had known there, and her experiences
with fugitives. Till finally she wound up, of course, with the *Key*.

"I suffer exquisitely in writing these things. It may be truly
said that I write with my heart's blood."

In closing the letter, she was back at her old theme, ". . . if
I live."

"If I live till spring, I shall hope to see Shakespeare's grave,
and Milton's mulberry tree, and the good land of my fathers,—
old, old England! May that day come!"

Then, after that respite, it was back to work on the *Key*.

Further evidence that she was regarded in England as the
foremost figure in America's antislavery movement came in
March. A group of philanthropic ladies in London, roused to new
heights of antislavery sentiments by reading *Uncle Tom's Cabin*,
decided to send an appeal to the women of America to "raise
your voices to your fellow-citizens, and your prayers to God,
for the removal of this affliction" of slavery. Secure in the fact
that Great Britain had ended the slave trade and slavery in all
its territories in the 1830s, the ladies saw nothing meddlesome
in their concern with the American problem and circulating their
appeal through the British Isles they obtained the signatures of
half a million women to their "Affectionate and Christian Address . . . To their Sisters, the Women of the United States of
America." It was to Harriet Beecher Stowe that they wanted
to send this bulky document.

The Duchess of Sutherland headed the project. The Duchess
wrote to Harriet, informing her of the appeal, and asking her to
accept it in the name of her countrywomen.

Harriet responded, accepting the honor in all humility. And
obviously this letter could not omit mention of that all-engrossing
subject, the *Key*.

"I write it in the anguish of my soul, with tears and prayer,
with sleepless nights and weary days. I bear testimony with a

heavy heart, as one who in court is forced by an awful oath to disclose the sins of those dearest. . . ."

But the sailing date was fixed. They were to leave from Boston on March 30, sailing on the *Niagara* to Liverpool. Heavy heart or no, Harriet was writing frantically fast and then rushing from her desk to oversee the packing that was being done and make the last-minute decisions about the house and the children.

"I am utterly incredulous of all that is said. . . ."

There was no time even to be incredulous anymore. She was a wife and mother, and with Calvin as helpless as always in any domestic emergency, the head of the house as well. At the same time, she was a literary woman, famous on two continents, trying desperately to complete a unique and staggering task—an over-powering collection of evidence no critics could deny.

"If I live till spring . . ." More and more, she wondered if she would.

But then, somehow, the *Key* was finished. She packed it carefully so she could deliver it in person to Mr. Jewett in Boston. The trunks and portmanteaus were packed. They closed the doors of the Stone Cabin and were on their way.

"A little bit of a thing," "used-up" perhaps, but scarcely showing it, she was walking with Calvin and brother Charles, and the contingent of three from Rochester, down the Boston pier toward the gangplank of the *Niagara*. Ahead lay "Shakespeare's grave, and Milton's mulberry tree," the good land of her fathers—and such triumphs, acclaim, ovations, demonstrations, that it was well indeed she firmly believed by now the Lord had written *Uncle Tom's Cabin*. And even better, that under her moods she was still the merry, mischievous girl she had always been—ready, when things became *too* much, to escape into laughter at the world, and sometimes even at herself.

Chapter 23

Wife bears it all very well. She is gaining in health. She is meek,
humble, pious, and loving, the same that she ever was. The Lord
preserve her!
    If the Dutch beat the D——l, she beats the Dutch. But it makes
me feel inexpressibly blue. The Lord keep our wits and save our
souls! . . .

1853

A month of triumphs in Scotland, another round of even
greater triumphs in London, and Calvin Stowe had run through
every emotion in his repertoire, to wind up where he so often
took refuge, in depression and the "blues."

To him and Harriet both, it had simply been unbelievable at
first. They had expected some lionizing of Harriet, but had
thought that it would be confined to the meetings, receptions
and other functions of the antislavery societies of which she was
the guest. Instead, from the moment they landed in Liverpool,
there had been great crowds lining the streets, just to see Harriet.
There had been hosts of people besieging whatever house shel-
tered her, eager for a look, a word, a handclasp. There had been
floral tributes, one presentation after another of "penny offerings"
collected to help the poor American slave. Every meal, breakfast
not excepted, had been a thronged gala. At every stop their train
made, night or day, on the way from Liverpool to Glasgow, Glasgow to Edinburgh, there had been crowds collected at the station, waiting for just a glimpse of Harriet.

Mrs. "Beecher-Stowe," they called her in England and Scotland, and all over Europe as well, as she would gradually discover. And Mrs. "Beecher-Stowe" was everyone's idol, it seemed,

from Archbishops and Lord Mayors to farmers and chimney
sweeps. There were pictures of her everywhere, terrible pictures,
copies of copies that grew more unrecognizable with every new
reproduction. "Useful," as Harriet said cheerfully, "like the Irish-
man's guideboard, which showed where the road did not go."

She had borne it all "very well," too, just as Calvin wrote home
to report. Now and then, simple fatigue and exhaustion had
forced her to keep to her room for a morning or a day, canceling
all engagements. She had collapsed so in Glasgow, the city that
was their original host, but after a day's rest she had rallied and
resumed the overpowering schedule of receptions, teas, break-
fasts, and other huge, municipal functions.

"Wife" was actually "gaining in health," Calvin wrote home.
It was a mystery to him. For himself, "I am tired to death of the
life I lead here. All that was anticipated by the newspapers, &
ten times more, has befallen us. From the lowest peasant to the
highest noble, wife is constantly beset, & I for her sake, so that
we have not a moment's quiet."

They had managed to find some time for sight-seeing in Scotland and that had been a relief for Calvin, a time of whole-
hearted enjoyment for the whole Stowe party. The railway had
taken them through some of the Sir Walter Scott country, and
Harriet was thrilled each time she saw in reality some landmark
or scene that had printed itself on her imagination years ago,
when she had first read Scott's novels as a girl in Litchfield. "Carlisle," "Lockerbie," seeing the names on stations brought the
stories in which they had figured surging back to people the landscape with romance.

In Edinburgh, where Harriet's reception had been even more
dramatic than in Glasgow, they had been driven past Scott's monument. The sight of it had filled Harriet with sudden melancholy.
Incredible homage surrounded her, as it had once surrounded
Scott. The ghosts of all her Puritan ancestors rustled about her
briefly, reminding her that even triumphs like these were fleeting
and meaningless: "Vanity, vanity, all is vanity."

Still, she grew day by day more humorous, more inclined to
see the funny side of many things that happened. At a tea attended by no less than two thousand people, she speculated pri-

vately about the teapot required for such an army, and wondered
if "Mrs. Scotland had put in another spoonful for the pot." In her
first face-to-face encounters with men and women of title, she
made "rather an odd piece of work of it, generally saying Mrs.
first, and 'Lady' afterwards, and then begging pardon." When
her hand was wrung by a huge and admiring farmer, she saw
herself "as a grasshopper in my own eyes." And often she had to
laugh privately, in amazement, at some of the extravagant things
people said to her.

She also tried to keep it firmly in mind that it was not she herself who was being so honored and acclaimed. She was simply
a symbol around which antislavery emotion could rally, a spokesman for those sentiments, who had become so almost accidentally, through a book "written by the Lord." She could always
retreat into this role of being merely an instrument, and temper
the lavishness of the conversation and talk around her by raising it to the dignity of labor for a common cause, in which all
good Christians were as one.

But Calvin had no such roles to which he could resort for comfort. And as the fanfare went on, it grew more and more wearing.
From Edinburgh they had gone to Aberdeen and more acclaim,
and still another purse collected for Harriet to use to help the
cause of the American slave. Since no lady, even such a famous
one as Mrs. "Beecher-Stowe" could properly speak in public, it
was always Calvin who had to respond to the addresses of welcome, the presentations of money and of gifts. It seemed to him,
as they finally left Scotland, that for days he had been doing little
but give one speech after another, "in behalf of my wife." For his
own sanity, he began to see Harriet as even more "meek, humble,
and pious" than she was, clinging to a familiar picture of a dowdy
little New England housewife, who had been his companion so
long.

Every sight-seeing interlude became precious to Calvin. A day
and a half at Stratford-on-Avon was another relief, with Harriet
bubbling about, soaking up atmosphere, plucking a sprig from
what she hoped was Shakespeare's own mulberry tree, and speculating eagerly about Shakespeare's life as a family man and good
churchgoer.

After that, there was the tumultuous welcome of London sweeping down on them and engulfing them. It did not matter that they were staying in London—as everywhere during their tour of the British Isles—with a Protestant clergyman, a "dissenter" in most British eyes. The "dissenter's" house with Harriet inside it became a mecca to the fashionable and powerful. The Duchess of Sutherland, who had written to Harriet in America a month before, in connection with the "Affectionate and Christian Address of the British Women . . ." to their American sisters, was Harriet's patroness in London. Stafford House, the beautiful London residence of the Duke and Duchess, was the scene of various fetes, large and small, public and private, in Harriet's honor. There was a Lord Mayor's dinner, with hosts of dignitaries present.

". . . the speeches that are constantly poured into poor wife's ears from all quarters, are enough to turn the strongest head. Lord Palmerston, the judges, the bishops, the literati, all speak the same language; and every distinguished man of every grade makes it a point to see her. J. P. Morley, Milman, Moncton Milnes, Tribler, Dickens, have all called upon her with great apparent rapture; and old archbp. Whately seized her hand and said, 'Now, I'll have this engraved on my tombstone.' Even the archbp. of Canterbury has sent for us to Lambeth Palace; and this week and next are entirely occupied with visits of this kind. It . . . distresses me, for it is too mad."

". . . too mad." Was it possible that Calvin was a little jealous of "wife's" triumphs? It hardly seemed likely. Years before, in Cincinnati, he had told her that it was "written in the book of fate" that she become a literary woman, "then, my word for it, your husband will lift up his head in the gate. . . ." Later, it was he who had urged her on with the writing of *Uncle Tom*, after she had laid aside her first hastily scribbled vision. And he had been as thrilled and surprised as she by the book's success.

True, he was often able to turn from that larger picture and become agitated out of all measure by some trivial difficulties, such as Dr. Joel Parker's outbursts. But such minor aberrations aside, the roly-poly man who had been a "visionary boy" haunted by a strange kind of second sight, had his moments of worldly shrewdness, moments when his second sight, instead of producing gnomes or dancing fairies, or images of his first, dead wife, could penetrate close to the heart of things.

That particular kind of insight was beginning to operate for Calvin now, in London.

Why, he asked himself, were first Scotland, then England, so outdoing themselves in their furor over "wife"? Her book was a sensation, true enough. Thousands and thousands had known real and profound emotion in reading it. A certain amount of grateful lionizing could be expected, as Charles Kingsley had warned Harriet in a letter. But Calvin had sat on dozens of platforms by now, and noticed something else as well. Speech after speech that began as praise of Harriet, seemed to turn, almost automatically, into a long diatribe of abuse of the United States, where such a sin as slavery was still allowed to flourish, and then a paean of self-righteous enthusiasm for Great Britain, where no child was "born a little slave, To labor in the sun. . . ."

"It distresses me . . . it is too mad."

In America, the press that was following Harriet's triumphant progress through the British Isles, had early caught a hint of what was beginning to distress Calvin. The British were finding in Harriet's visit a wonderful opportunity to vent anti-American feeling. When Harriet heard about the editorial comment being made in the United States in connection with this British attitude, she was hurt and outraged. It cast a shadow over all the glorious sympathy she seemed to see roused for the slave. She wrote home to deny that the British were showing any anti-American sentiments.

But Calvin was not so threatened by the truth. Walking at Harriet's side, standing on platforms to speak for her, he saw more and more that what appeared to be fantastic homage for "wife" was actually a great national orgy of self-love for the British. While adoring Harriet, the little American who had herself pointed the finger at her country's great sin, they could pour out all their longtime envy and resentment of those states that had once been their colonies, and in doing so, build themselves into pillars of blameless humanity.

Calvin chose a dramatic moment to erupt. The May Anniversaries in London had reached their climax with the Anti-Slavery anniversary on May 20, and since Mrs. "Beecher-Stowe" was scheduled to attend the great meeting celebrating the anniversary, more than four thousand people had packed themselves into Exeter Hall. Harriet sat in a private gallery with the beautiful and gracious Duchess of Sutherland. It was Calvin, her spokesman, who had to sit down on the platform and listen as speech after speech rang out in self-gratified praise of Great Britain for freeing her slaves, and holy outrage against America, which would not do so. (In America, the "anti-Beecher" religious paper, the *Observer*, would later report those speeches as "nothing but downright, fanatical, unreasoning, blind, stupid, insane, unmitigated vituperation.")

For Calvin, right there on the spot, they were, whatever else they might have been, suddenly too much. It came his time to respond for "wife," and he rose, rumpled, moonfaced and sidewhiskered. But for once, he dispensed with his usual platitudes and folksy good humor.

Looking sternly out over the packed auditorium, he began to say what was on his mind. It was all very well for England to congratulate herself on freeing her slaves, he said, but only a few slaves had been involved, and they on the very fringes of the empire. It was an act that had no real repercussions for the people of the British Isles. The startled four thousand listened with their mouths open as he went on. American slavery was something different, he said. A three-billion-dollar economy was involved, and to suddenly abolish slavery might send the entire economy of the country into ruin. Consider furthermore, he told them, who was chiefly responsible for maintaining the health of that slave economy. England herself! England depended on slave-grown American cotton for her mills and consumed four-fifths of the American crop. If England were to insist on free-grown cotton, American slavery *could* be ended, almost at once.

"But are you willing to sacrifice one penny of your own profits for the sake of doing away with this cursed business?" he asked the audience.

There was silence, and then some scattered booing as he wound up his attack. If he had not been Mrs. "Beecher-Stowe's" husband, there might have been worse. The newspapers next morning made that quite clear. Some shrieked that the speech was "an insult to the head and heart of the country, an outrage on Christianity itself," and some merely muttered that the Professor had been impractical to say the least.

But Calvin had put his finger on the real pulse that beat under the British triumph. And whether Harriet was willing or not to accept all of Calvin's insights and deductions, she was not displeased by her husband's sudden and heroic stand. Warming and intoxicating as the praise for herself was, wonderful as it was to see such British sympathy for the slave, she *had* heard the anti-American sentiments she tried to deny and she did not like them either.

There were other political implications in the London visit. Harriet was surrounded by distinguished figures, and the Duchess of Sutherland, her chief sponsor, was a favorite of Queen Victoria. But while everyone else in London fought to do Harriet honor, the Queen made no move to receive her, nor had Harriet been greeted by a word from the Prime Minister. Harriet could understand and accept the motivations behind this seeming rebuff more easily, and she and Calvin could discuss it with each other quietly and privately.

Harriet had become the very symbol of Abolitionism in England. If the Queen or the Prime Minister took any official notice of her, it would be almost the same as giving the endorsement of the British government to the Abolition movement in the United States. However much the country at large might enjoy telling the United States what it must do to be saved, English industry did depend on American cotton, as Calvin had pointed out. There were wheels within wheels in England's attitude to Harriet, as would all come clear later, when Harriet's book had played its role in bringing on war in the United States. Then England would *have* to take a stand—for or against the cotton it needed—or for or against the slavery it deplored—and it would take it a long, long time to make up its mind.

"It . . . distresses me, for it is too mad. . . . I would rather be at Andover about my business than anywhere else in the world," Calvin wrote lugubriously.

But soon now, he would be on his way back to Andover. Harriet was going on without him to Paris, accompanied by brother Charles, sister Sarah, and the rest of the entourage. From there, they planned a tour of Switzerland and Germany. But none of the plans woke any envy in Calvin. He was going back to the world he knew, a world of books and students and lectures and his own private visions, unvexed by all the tangled motives that caused such bizarre behavior in the world beyond the study and the classroom.

He kissed Harriet good-bye at the station and gave her some last-minute advice, including the advice to leave London as soon as possible. But the Duchess of Sutherland was waiting for Harriet, even as he spoke. The Duchess was going to take her to Parliament to meet some of its members and observe its operation. So Harriet had only half an ear for Calvin's warnings. She was blooming, and looked very well in her new London clothes, and she laughed as she hushed away his worries.

Calvin got into the railway carriage and sighed. "Wife" did indeed "beat the Dutch."

Harriet scarcely knew which was the dream by now, the new life she was leading, or the one to which Calvin was returning. She was finding wholehearted pleasure in hobnobbing with lords and ladies, and seeing that many of them were simple, affectionate, family-loving Christians, very like the people she had known all her life. She could meet anybody (except for the Queen) on an equal footing, and be accepted just as she was, modest, a little shy, given to periodic outbursts of Yankee humor or New England piety, even "owling about" now and then. But she wrote to Catherine that sometimes it gave her a "strange, mythological feeling" to meet, face-to-face, some personage who had long seemed legendary. It was like a fairy tale to become almost one of the family in Stafford House, and she wrote Catherine long descriptions of that splendid residence, with its stately drawing rooms, its brocade walls, its crystal chandeliers, its periwigged flunkies, and the meal in the middle of the day that was called "lunch." The Duchess was fair, stately and handsome. It was delightful to be her friend, and to be almost as close a friend of several other ladies of nobility.

The days after Calvin's departure were a continuance of the whirl, with teas, concerts, and other functions. The *Key to Uncle Tom's Cabin*, on which she had worked so frantically nearly to the day of sailing, had been published by now, the English publication coming out simultaneously with the United States edition. Harriet saw the *Key* in all the bookstores, and it was pleasant to learn that it was starting off with a tremendous sale both in England and in America. There would be another small fortune in royalties waiting for her when she returned home.

Meanwhile, it was even more gratifying to hear her new friends praising this latest book, saying it did indeed reinforce the message of *Uncle Tom*. Harriet went to tea at Stafford House, and the Duchess took her into a private room and embraced her and cried, "Oh, Mrs. Stowe, I have been reading that last chapter in the 'Key.' Argyll read it aloud to us. Oh, surely, surely you will succeed,—God surely will bless you."

In many ways, it was difficult to tear herself away from all this, despite Calvin's advice and even with the unknown wonders of the continent awaiting her. But Charles had already written to Paris, making arrangements for Harriet and her party to stay in a private home there, and enlisting friends who promised there would be no more pomp and publicity. And Harriet was, after all, a little tired.

Then, just the day before she was to leave England, the thing happened that was calculated to give her the "strangest, most mythological feeling" of all.

She met Lady Byron!

Harriet had heard mention, now and then, of Lord Byron's widow ever since her arrival in London. One morning Harriet visited with Mrs. Follen from Boston, the lady who had inspired her long, chatty letter a few months before. During the course of their conversation Mrs. Follen spoke of Lady Byron, so active in all good works, so pious, but unfortunately confined to her home much of the time because of frail health. It had been almost "strange and mythological" enough to hear her spoken of so familiarly and to realize she was living in the same city. The years had rolled back suddenly for Harriet, and she was a girl in Litch-

field, Connecticut, first in love with Byron and his poetry, and
envisioning the cold and marble-hearted lady who rejected the
poet's pleas for forgiveness. She spoke of those early emotions
to Mrs. Follen, and went on to wonder at the somewhat different
picture she was getting of Lady Byron now. Mrs. Follen shook
her head slightly. It was understandable that a small girl might
have thought that Lady Byron was hardhearted. Many people
thought so still. Too many. But it had not been Lady Byron's cruelty that brought about the rupture between her and the poet.
Not for a moment. There had been certain unbearable circumstances. Mrs. Follen did not go on to enlarge just then. She simply told Harriet that Lady Byron was a wonderful woman who
had been much misunderstood, and she hoped Harriet might
have an opportunity to meet her.

And then, Harriet did. She was invited to a luncheon at Ox-
ford Terrace, where, "among a number of distinguished guests,
was Lady Byron. . . ." Harriet only spoke to her briefly at that
first meeting, only saw her for two hours or so, but it was enough
for a tide of feeling to well up in Harriet so strongly that it instantly drowned an impression she had had for years, and oblit-
erated her old image of Lady Byron forever.

That night Harriet wrote about Lady Byron in another entry
to one of her journal-letters to Calvin.

"No engravings that ever have been circulated in America do
any justice to her appearance. She is of slight figure, formed with
exceeding delicacy, and her whole form, face, dress, and air
united to make an impression of a character singularly dignified,
gentle, pure, and yet strong. No words addressed to me in any
conversation hitherto have made their way to my inner soul with
such force as a few remarks dropped by her on the present religious aspect of England,—remarks of such quality as one seldom
hears."

That was all. A brief luncheon meeting, and a few comments
about the "present religious aspect of England"—but the second
of the two fateful legends of Hattie's girlhood was on its way to
developing into its own strange reality. The Aunt Mary legend
had been the first prophetic note, the first of the seeds that had
ultimately flowered in *Uncle Tom's Cabin*. *Uncle Tom's Cabin*

had led to fame, and to England, and in England her fame had
led her to Lady Byron.

"No words addressed to me . . . hitherto have made their way
to my inner soul with such force. . . ." They were not the words
that would one day lead Harriet into the scandal that would almost destroy her fame. Those would not come for two years and
more. These simply fixed in Harriet's heart a new and dazzling
image to admire, as she had once instantly admired and loved
Eliza Stowe, and before her, Mary Dutton, and even before her,
Catharine Cogswell.

So Harriet's two months in the British Isles came to a climax
in a quiet meeting far more meaningful than all the triumphs
had been.

"Tomorrow we go," she continued, in her letter to Calvin, "go
to quiet, to obscurity, to peace—to Paris, to Switzerland. There
we shall find the loveliest glen, and, as the Bible says, 'fall on
sleep.'"

Chapter 24

Yours for the cause . . .

1854–1856

On the one hand, she was Hattie, free at last to be all the things she had always had the potentiality for being, gay, grave or sad, eager to report to the world her conclusions on every subject that caught her attention.

On the other hand, she was suddenly someone she had never planned to be at all—the leader of a cause.

As a result, for the next few years her life would be a bewildering mélange of Hattie doing what she wanted to do, and then of Harriet being the Mrs. Stowe the world expected and wanted, Mrs. Stowe, the crusader, who signed herself "Yours for the cause." Herself she had freed ten years and more before the Emancipation Proclamation would spell out freedom for the slaves in whose name she had spoken. But since she had spoken as she had, she was now a leader of the antislavery forces, and must remain one until all the slaves were free.

The Scotch and the English had been the first to proclaim her new role. After that, there had been three months on the continent, where it had been almost forgotten, for there had been no more of the national hysteria of homage that she had known in the British Isles. No other nation, it seemed, had such a need as Great Britain to humble the United States by elevating Harriet Beecher Stowe. What there had been was just enough of that special attention and recognition due to a famous writer to make her trip extraordinarily pleasant. And she came home bubbling over with it, as eager as any returned tourist to tell everyone about her travels, all she had seen and heard and done.

She had loved Paris. Its flowers, its gaiety, the kind, cultured people she met there, delighted her. After Paris, she and Charles and the rest of the party had traveled on, by boat and diligence, to Switzerland. They stopped in Geneva first, Geneva, the city where, three hundred years before, John Calvin had originally preached the doctrine that had darkened so many years of Harriet's youth. Did she make a pilgrimage to the cathedral there where he had stood, severe and implacable, forging the chains that would bind so many, and ponder on how they had held her so long, but how at last she was free?

There was no mention of any such pilgrimage in her letters home, no indication that she even remembered Calvin's long association with the city. Her eyes were all for the scenery, the glorious Mont Blanc, and the other lofty, snow-capped Alps. She did reflect that there were phases in nature to "correspond to every phase of human thought and emotion," and that the "stern and cloudy scenery" of the Alps answered "to the melancholy fatalism of Greek tragedy or the kindred mournfulness of Job." But that was all. Her chief concern was the beauty, the awesome grandeur of everything, and steadily "gaining in health," she had skipped up the prescribed trails to marvel at breathtaking vistas. Or traveling on through the mountain country by diligence, she had become enraptured by the delicate wild flowers of the region, wanting continually to stop the coach so she could gather more, feeling almost a wild frustration as to how one could really *express* one's love for such beauty.

Byron's image haunted parts of Switzerland, and this ghost she did acknowledge. She and Charles went out on Lake Leman, dipping their oars into the same waters on which Byron had rowed. They visited the Castle of Chillon, which he had celebrated in poetry, and when the guide discovered Harriet's identity, he insisted she put her name on the wall, already inscribed with many famous names, including Byron's. Was there a "strange, mythological feeling" in that—seeing her own name, scratched in the freestone by Charles, just above Lord Byron's, for all the world to see? She looked at the scrawled inscriptions inscrutably and did not say. But as they traveled on, through the Wengen Alps, she and Charles and Sarah quoted lines from

Byron's *Manfred* to each other, and when at last they came to
the Rhine they read *Childe Harold*. For Harriet, there was still
no shiver of premonition in *Manfred*, with its defense of illicit
love. There was just the drama of the poetry.

Germany brought reflections on religion at last. Visiting the
cathedrals that were required objects for sight-seeing, a Puritan
from New England, accustomed all her life to bleak, bare Meeting Houses, she finally admitted the lure that the beauty of
Gothic architecture had for her, and even more traitorous to the
teachings of her youth, the lure of Roman Catholic ritual. "Surely
there is some part in man that calls for such a service," she wrote
home, "for such visible images of grandeur and beauty. Wealth
spent on these churches is a sublime and beautiful protest against
materialism." It was one sort of justification for the response her
beauty-loving heart could not repress.

Returned to Paris, where the Sabbath was a day for festivities,
visiting and dancing, Harriet found she could not really disap-
prove of that either. But at last, in France, the one country where
almost no traces of Calvinism lingered, she managed to find a
defense for the faith in which she had been nurtured. Hard and
stern and rejecting of beauty as that creed was, was it not a fact
that "wherever John Calvin's system of theology has gone, civil
liberty has gone with it"? She considered the endless political
troubles of France. Perhaps they were the direct result of France
having expelled all her "Calvinist and Puritan stock." "The great
difficulty has been that the destruction of the reformed church
in France took out of the country entirely that element of religious rationalism which is at once conservative and progressive."
Pleased by the theory she was evolving, she decided that three
elements made for a stable society, blind faith, a reasonable religious freedom, and skepticism. Take away the reasonable, religious freedom and the society would oscillate like a pendulum
between the extremes of superstition and skepticism—as France
did.

Comforted by finding this positive good in the faith of her
fathers, a faith already so modified in her own mind, she was
able to enjoy without guilt the positive good that other faiths
offered to humanity—the beauty, the sense of richness that had

been so lacking in Calvinism. And she could sympathize with the cheerful disregard of the French for the Sabbath, while still reminding herself that the Puritan habit of setting one day out of seven aside for meditation on things not of this world, inculcated an individual strength of character and fixity of purpose that the French could never know.

Like every observant traveler, she had found a new perspective in foreign lands, as well as undreamed-of pleasures in strange scenes and experiences—incredible natural wonders and man-made beauty. And the first thing she wanted to do when she got back home was tell and tell and tell. A travel book! That was what she wanted to write. She had written many of her letters home with just such a goal in mind.

But she also came back to the United States in September of 1853 with twenty thousand dollars given her in the British Isles for use in the antislavery cause in America. She came back laden with gifts and testimonials to herself as leader of the cause; caskets, gold pens, silver inkstands, a gold slave bracelet, and twenty-six volumes filled with the signatures of British women who had endorsed the "Affectionate and Christian Address . . . to the Women of the United States." She also came back to discover that however famous she had been when she left, she was even more famous now, and regarded in the United States as a leader of the antislavery movement in a way that Garrison and Weld and the other intransigent Abolitionists could never be. Where they had repelled thousands with their extreme pronouncements and programs, she had won millions through her drama, so real, so vivid, of one slave figure after another, fleeing, fleeing, to a life where one could breathe in freedom. Millions who had been only neutral before, felt their emotions choking them, as they resolved that something must be done about slavery soon.

So the role of crusader and focal figure in "the cause" was thrust upon her, and, feeling as she did about slavery, it never occurred to her to refuse it. Being a true Beecher, dramatic to the heart, she even felt a fine satisfaction in playing the role as she thought it should be played. A leader in "the cause," Harriet was grave, dedicated, burdened but uncomplaining. Buried in an avalanche of correspondence, constantly sought out with appeals, requests, suggestions, she was patient and thoughtful as a woman with a mission should be. And earnestly, impulsively, happily, she contributed sums from the "offerings" she had brought back in dozens of random directions, helping to found a Negro Normal School with one donation, pressing a few dollars into the hand of an itinerant Negro at the back door with another.

But she would not be cheated of her travel book. That fall she set about gathering up the letters she had written to Catherine and Edward and the other members of the family, and the friends like Georgiana and Mary Dutton. Charles had kept a journal through the course of the trip. She would use sections of that, alternating with the letters, to describe experiences the letters might have omitted. It was more like play than work, to read the letters and the journal and sort them and fill in whatever details were necessary, living again as she did so, the magical weeks on the continent. She could close her eyes and see the Alps or the beauties of the delicate Alpine flowers or the dim arches of a Gothic cathedral. She could see again, in her mind's eye, some of the paintings that had enthralled her in one museum or another, for she had discovered art, real art, in Europe, and she was eager to share her delight with everyone in America. She must speak of the genius of Rubens who painted with such intensity, such "internal sympathy" far removed from "chalky second hand tradition," that one could overlook the grossness of his women. She had not liked the early Italian painters, they had seemed tediously trivial, but there had been a sublime statue of Venus in the Louvre that she must describe more fully. And reading the letters and the journal again, she had to laugh again at some of the humorous incidents that had occurred—the same kind of misunderstandings, foolish frights and misadventures every traveler has known, and laughed at later, since the first sightseer took to the road.

Sunny Memories of Foreign Lands, she was calling the book, a title as wholesome and obvious as her pleasure in the trip. Any real discussion of the antislavery missionary work in the British

Isles she would leave for Calvin to report on in a preface. For
herself, she wanted just the sunshine a while longer.

With her travel book, with her efforts as a crusader, and her
activities as the wife and mother she had always been, she was
very busy. The twins, Hatty and Eliza, were seventeen now,
very pretty, and looking so much alike that one of them wore a
red ribbon around her neck and one a blue, so their schoolmates
and teachers could tell them apart. Then there was the quicksilver little girl, Georgiana, already ten years old, and generally
in some sort of mischief, and there were the three boys, her handsome oldest, Henry, the middle boy, Freddie, taking after her in
his slight stature, and the baby Charley, just two, and a perfect
example of the kind of infant rambunctiousness that Harriet enjoyed describing.

Life was full, and it was curious how easily Harriet managed
it all, Harriet who had been forever collapsing and expecting
imminent death. Success and self-confidence seemed to have released vast unsuspected stores of energy in her. She had "gained
in health" through the European trip. Back home, the strange,
new health persisted, even though Harriet might not admit it,
so she was able to pursue all her careers, and once again start
writing columns periodically for the *Independent* as well.

The art she had enjoyed in Europe gave her the inspiration for
a present for Calvin that fall—an oil portrait of his first wife, Eliza
Stowe. It was a portrait that had to be pieced together by the
chosen artist from such memories and sketches as Calvin and
Harriet together could provide, for Eliza had died before the day
of daguerreotypes. But Calvin and Harriet both considered the
painting a lovely thing when it was completed, and they hung it
in the parlor of the Stone Cabin, and spent many an hour sitting
before it, talking of Eliza's unique charms and virtues, just as
they had talked of those when they were courting, almost twenty
years earlier.

The year 1853, which had been almost as dramatic for Harriet
as 1852, came to a close, with Harriet and her family happy and
busy in the Stone Cabin in Andover. And then, in the first weeks
of 1854, came the thunderclap that startled the nation.

National events, so far as they concerned slavery, were no longer merely a background to Harriet's life. She was a leader in the antislavery cause. Whatever happened to affect the status of the slave, affected her. When Stephen A. Douglas, the senior Senator from Illinois, rose in the Senate to propose his Kansas-Nebraska Bill, with all its shocking implications, it was as though he spoke directly to her, proposing to *her*, with incredible effrontery, that the Missouri Compromise of 1820 be repealed.

That was what it amounted to, even though Douglas tried not to word it quite so bluntly, and even though he himself cared little whether or not slavery advanced northward past the barrier that the Compromise had erected at 36° 30'. What Douglas cared about was the railroad to the Pacific, which had been agitating so many people since 1852.

Jefferson Davis, Pierce's Secretary of War, had progressed so well in his campaign for the southern route for the railroad that he had induced the President to buy, for ten million dollars, a bit of Mexico through which the southern route would have to pass.

But Stephen A. Douglas, "the little giant," who had so much energy and bounce that people also called him "a steam engine in britches," had steam engines on his mind as well, and his own reasons for wanting the transcontinental railway to take the central route. He was speculating heavily in western lands, including land in Chicago, the city proposed as the eastern terminus for a railway following the central route. However, to make the central route practical, United States law and government had to be extended over the vast plains west of Iowa and Missouri, and this was where the difficulty arose. All previous plans to organize that huge area into a Territory of Nebraska had failed. All of it was north of the 36° 30' line, and Southern congressmen wanted no part of a territory where slavery would automatically be precluded.

Avid for the railroad that would make him wealthy, Douglas dreamed up the only possible solution for winning Southern support for a Territory of Nebraska, a principle that he was pleased to call "popular sovereignty," and which provided that the settlers in the territory could themselves determine whether or not

they would have slavery. Not entirely out of his mind, and aware
that this scheme would raise "a hell of a storm" in Northern quarters, he further proposed that the area be divided into *two* territories, not just one, a Nebraska Territory more or less contiguous
with Iowa, and a Kansas Territory equally contiguous with Missouri. In this fashion, he fondly dreamed that antislavery Iowans
might take over the Nebraska Territory, and proslavery Missourians the Kansas Territory, thereby, in effect, keeping a certain
balance as before.

It was an extremely tempting idea to the Southerners with
whom he discussed it. In fact, the prospect of extending the slave
realm was so pleasing to Jefferson Davis that he gladly gave up
his own dream of a southern route to the Pacific, and began urging President Pierce, the doughface so easily molded by him, to
make the Douglas proposal an Administration measure.

The thunderclap exploded and the North reeled, and Harriet
with it. For most people, the law Douglas wished to repeal had
seemed as fixed and eternal as the right of habeas corpus—there
would be no slavery north of the 36° 30' limit. More than that,
the Douglas proposal made such a suggestion at a time when
the minds and emotions of the people of the North had been
heated on the subject of slavery as they never had been before,
by the impact of *Uncle Tom's Cabin*. One slave after another,
fleeing, fleeing, fleeing . . . the cruel bondage.

With no thought for any of this, Stephen Douglas was asking
to open territory long expressly prohibitive of slavery to the slave
power.

In Congress, the Abolitionist Senators, Sumner and Chase, and
the Abolitionist Representatives, a scant three in number, rallied
themselves to "resist it by speech and vote and with all the abilities God has given us."

In all the states of the North, Abolitionists and antislavery men
forgot their differences for a while, and met in wide-eyed horror,
wondering what they could do. Out in Illinois, Abraham Lincoln,
the lawyer who had foresworn politics, reacted to the proposal
as he had never reacted to any political news before. He was
stirred in some profound and total way just as Harriet had been
struck in some vital part by the news of the Fugitive Slave Bill,

and convictions, opinions, and feelings that had been scattered and vague before, began to merge and harden and form themselves into something more than a new point of view—a new philosophy.

Harriet Beecher Stowe, in Andover, spokeswoman for the slave, steadied herself after the initial shock and rushed into action as a crusader.

The course of action she chose reflected one constant concern of hers. Ever since the years in Cincinnati, it had agitated her that clergymen would not, could not, unite on a stand against slavery. She could understand, if not excuse, by now, the Southern ministers who were anxious to align themselves with the interests of their congregations, and so were actually able to find Scriptural support for the "peculiar institution." But why were Northern clergymen as a whole so reluctant to take a public stand against slavery as a moral evil? All through *Uncle Tom's Cabin*, though the Reverend Joel Parker was the only minister to be named by name, Harriet was continually making sharp, satirical comments on the ostrichlike or equivocating attitudes of the so-called Christian clergy. (But being Harriet, when William Garrison attacked the church for its lethargy, she wrote him reams in the church's defense.) This was her opportunity to prove her contention that *if* all the power of the clergy were united in protest, the forces of slavery would be vanquished in a moment.

Her plan was a petition, to be signed by all the clergy of New England. Surely now, with the gauntlet down, they would rally and unite. With brother Edward's help, she instigated the meeting of a group of preachers in Boston who would write the petition. This achieved, she and Edward rushed everyone who was available into action to canvas for signatures. Edward went out through Massachusetts and New York with a copy of the petition. Calvin carried one wherever he went. Even seventy-eight-year-old Lyman Beecher went calling on ministerial friends with a petition. And sympathetic ministers all over New England joined in the effort.

Stimulated and optimistic, Harriet wrote to Senator Sumner predicting such an "uprising of the country as never has been heard of since the days of the Revolution," and suggesting that a committee chosen from the clergy of all denominations, travel to Washington bearing the united clerical protest. By the first of March, the canvassers were so successful that the petition had been signed by more than three thousand ministers. Harriet drew a deep breath of vindication and waited for results as the committee duly departed to inform Congress of the church's will.

There were almost no results at all. The South had its ministers also, to whose voices the Southern Senators far preferred to listen. The petition gave Senator Sumner and the other Abolitionists ammunition to continue and prolong the debate over the Kansas-Nebraska Bill in Congress, and that was about it.

Harriet swallowed her disappointment and went on to address another group whom she always believed could work miracles, if united—women. These she exhorted from her column in the *Independent*.

"Women of the free states! The question is not, shall we remonstrate with slavery on its own soil? but are we willing to receive slavery into the free states and territory of the Union? . . . O women of the free states! what did your brave mothers do in the time of our revolutionary struggle? Did not *liberty* in those days feel the strong impulse of a woman's heart?"

But it was all of no avail. President Pierce whipped his Northern Democrats into line. On May 25, 1854, the Kansas-Nebraska Bill was passed, and the stage was set for the struggles that would follow so inevitably. Soon now, the proslavery Missourians must rush into Kansas Territory so they would have the majority when it came time for the elections to determine the territory's slaveholding status; Northerners must send Northern immigrants into the territory in even greater numbers to hold the line for freedom; the Missourians must put up a blockade at the Missouri River to halt the Northerners; there must be conflicts, bloodshed, finally massacres. It was all inevitable now.

Having done her best in the crisis and failed, Harriet gave up on crusading for a while. Of course she continued her correspondence with antislavery people, and went on disbursing random sums to help the cause. But chiefly, she was turning her attention

to other things, and being, for a time, the Harriet she was by nature and by instinct.

Elsewhere, the Kansas-Nebraska Bill was having a variety of
repercussions. In Michigan, a group of antislavery men were
meeting to form a new antislavery party, "opposed to the extension of slavery, and to be known as 'Republicans' until the
contest be terminated."

In Illinois, Abraham Lincoln, his new convictions firmly shaped
and deeply felt, was stepping out of political retirement to stump
for an old friend who was running for Congress. Incidentally,
this stumping was giving him his first opportunity to challenge
Stephen Douglas, also doing some speechmaking in Illinois, trying to justify the Kansas-Nebraska Bill to his constituents. Soberly and earnestly, Lincoln was voicing the conclusions he had
reached, conclusions that would be sustaining him for the years
to come. He felt no malice or hatred toward slaveowners. "I
surely will not blame them for not doing what I should not know
how to do myself. If all earthly power were given me, I should
not know what to do as to the existing institution . . . But all
this, to my judgment, furnishes no more excuse for permitting
slavery to go into our own free territory than it would for reviving
the African slave-trade by law."

"Slavery," Lincoln was saying, that summer of 1854, "is
founded on the selfishness of man's nature—opposition to it in
his love of justice. These principles are in eternal antagonism,
and when brought into collision so fiercely as slavery extension
brings them, shocks and throes and convulsions must ceaselessly
follow."

But in Andover, it was turning into a family summer for Harriet, a summer full of memories and nostalgia.

Lyman Beecher was visiting at the Stone Cabin. Sister Catherine was spending a great deal of time there, and brother Charles
also came frequently. Together, Harriet, Catherine and Charles
were working on a project that they hoped had not been delayed
too long—an autobiography of their father. Lyman was now
seventy-nine. Physically, he still had an amazing amount of his
customary energy and enthusiasm, but mentally he had begun

to retreat into long periods of forgetfulness, and his conversation
was often vague and incoherent.

Somehow, though, they were determined to put together a
record of his long and tumultuous life. Charles had collected the
tumbled, disorganized letters and papers saved through the years
and was working at the mammoth task of sorting and editing
them. Singly and together, Harriet, Catherine and Charles were
talking with their father, trying to prompt his memory with names
and events from the past.

It was helpful that Lyman had always been a legend-maker,
and the stories that his children had heard so often long ago were
revived now as they sought to remind him of the days of his
youth. Already, in 1854, those days seemed to belong to a time
almost unimaginable. He was born when the United States were
still colonies, just daringly declaring their independence. But
Catherine and Hattie and Charles reminded him of the bucolic
tales he had told about the Revolution, prompted him to remember his first little church on Long Island, and his first stirring
crusade—against dueling.

Their own memories of their father through the years came
flooding to their minds, and they wrote to all the other brothers
and sisters, asking them each to contribute a chapter of reminiscences. And so there was the recollection of the way Lyman had
kept a gun in the study of the Walnut Hills house in Cincinnati,
to be ready whenever a flight of passenger pigeons went over.
Though deep in concentration, he would always hear the whirr of
their wings, leap from his desk, grab his gun, and run out to bag
enough pigeons for dinner before going back to his sermon. Someone else remembered the way their father had used to push his
spectacles back up onto his head when he became excited in the
course of a sermon. A little later, needing spectacles again, he
would reach for another pair in his pocket, put them on, in turn
push them back and forget them, until sometimes he would wind
up a sermon with three pairs of spectacles glittering across the
top of his head. According to a colleague, this habit helped him
"see all around a situation."

So the summer was filled with a sense of the past for Harriet
and a tenderness for her father that would well up suddenly,

bringing tears to her eyes. He lay resting on a sofa one afternoon, and Harriet, brushing back his crest of white hair, told him fondly what a handsome man he was. And he opened his eyes, and smiled the old Lyman smile, as he answered with all the old Lyman spirit, "Oh, tell me something new, Hattie!"

Other personal projects engaged her. Her travel book of "sunny memories" had been published in July and the reports came that it was doing very well. She had a new publisher. Mr. Jewett, the publisher of *Uncle Tom's Cabin* and the *Key* had gotten himself into financial difficulties. It was puzzling, considering the profits that had rolled in from both those books, but there it was. He had sold out to a firm called Phillips, Sampson and Company, which was now Harriet's publisher. Catherine suggested that Hattie get out the Geography she had written for children in Cincinnati, revise it, and put it on the market again. So Harriet busied herself with that. September came, and the opening of school, and she flung herself into plans for a bazaar to raise money for the academy her girls attended.

In Kansas Territory, the tension was mounting, as bands of armed men crossed the border from Missouri to seize the polls for the November election. Border Ruffians they were calling them in the papers.

But Harriet was feeling pleased that her father's autobiography was completed, and a Beecher family reunion was being held in the Stone Cabin to celebrate the occasion. Henry Ward rode all night from a preaching engagement to join them. With his arrival the urgency of the situation in Kansas came closer. Henry knew how to make the plight of the antislavery men, trying to hold Kansas for freedom, seem as near and desperate as a struggle right outside the door. He had been filling his sermons with that drama for weeks. And his congregation at Plymouth Church, tempered to respond to its emotional and passionate preacher like a well-trained orchestra, had already collected funds to buy rifles for the free-soilers in Kansas, and were shipping off barrels of those rifles, labeling them "Bibles."

Harriet's crusading consisted of little more than contributing some engravings of a portrait of herself to William Garrison for use in an auction to raise funds for redeeming another slave.

Late in November, news came that the Border Ruffians had captured the election in Kansas, and were sending a proslavery delegate to Congress. It was not total defeat for the free-soil men, for a more important election in Kansas would come in the spring, when the Territory would elect the legislature to draw up the constitution of the future state. But still, in the columns she was writing regularly for the *Independent*, Harriet wrote not a word on these matters. Little sermons, parables, light pieces in the same vein as the fugitive essays she had written for the ladies' annuals were her only contributions.

She thought often of the friends she had made in England, of Lady Sutherland, and the beautiful, frail Lady Byron. For a while, the news of the British fighting in the Crimea was even more shocking to Harriet than any news from Kansas. Someone's blundering had sent a cavalry brigade into an ambushed valley and the slaughter had been terrible. Among those who had fallen was Lady Sutherland's second son. Harriet hurried to write Lady Sutherland a letter of condolence. And she was suddenly seized with a new love for her own sons, a new need to appreciate them, especially Henry, so sunny-haired, good-tempered and bright.

The winter took on elements of gaiety as Harriet arranged evening diversions for her family and Andover faculty friends. She became the Harriet who loved laughter and parties as she planned charades, little concerts and tableaux vivants. Perhaps, in a fashion, she was running away again, as she had once run away from Cincinnati to the Vermont water-cure, running away this time from the crusader's role that really, in her heart, baffled her.

In May the election in Kansas to choose a legislature was held. Once again the Border Ruffians won the day. But this time, the antislavery men replied by holding an election of their own, and creating their own legislature. Kansas had two governments, ready at any moment for armed conflict with each other. A civil war in miniature was in the making in the territory of Kansas.

Harriet, the crusader, was still silent. She revised her first book, *The Mayflower*, for Phillips, Sampson and Company. She wrote her columns for the *Independent*, and she still found plenty of topics that had nothing to do with the trouble in Kansas. One week she devoted the column to a review of Henry's new hymn

book, *The Plymouth Collection of Hymns and Tunes.* Charles had
helped in the selection of the music, and Harriet's own hymn,
"When winds are raging o'er the upper ocean," was included.

Peripheral activities, such as editing hymn books, did not slow
Henry Ward's engagement in the antislavery struggle. The
Sharp's Rifles were still being shipped to Kansas, and the whole
country was calling the rifles "Beecher's Bibles," by now. This
year, Henry Ward was no longer confining his dramatic auctions
to redeem slaves to the platforms of public meeting houses. He
was bringing beautiful young female slaves up onto the platform
of Plymouth Church, and auctioning them off to freedom from
there, often working the women of his congregation into such a
state that they tore off their jewelry and dropped it into the
collection plates.

And Harriet was still silent.

It was not until the fall, not until after another reunion of the
Beecher clan in the old Stone Cabin to celebrate Lyman Beecher's eightieth birthday, that she at last began to think of speaking
out.

Phillips, Sampson and Company had been pressing her for several months to write another antislavery novel. Perhaps, she
thought, that was the one way she could help in the struggle.
Getting up petitions, writing letters, doling out sums from the
British funds to help the cause—none of those efforts seemed to
have any important results. But a novel—a novel that dramatized
a problem in unforgettable pictures, as *Uncle Tom's Cabin* had
done—that did leave its mark. Perhaps she should try again to
speak to the people of the South. This time, though, instead of
trying to picture slavery, perhaps she could dramatize for them
the unwholesome effects of slavery on the slaveowners themselves. Warming up to the thought that novel-writing was her
unique contribution to the cause, she reviewed several antislavery
novels in one of her columns, and declared, "the use of the novel
in the great questions of moral life is coming to be one of the
features of the age. A novel now is understood to be a parable—
a story told in illustration of a truth or fact."

So she began to think of a parable, to wait for the pictures to come flashing into her mind as they had done when she was first composing *Uncle Tom.*

The pictures came. Pictures would always come to Harriet's mind when she thought about a theme. What was the gentlest impeachment she could make of slavery's unwholesome effects on slaveowners? A sense of irresponsibility. Instantly she saw a gay, coquettish young girl, an orphan, who, through the death of her parents, had become the mistress of a great plantation. She could dance through the story, thoughtless but lovable, leaving every tedious aspect of life to others, the management of the plantation to the overseer, the cooking, the sewing to slaves. In the end, she must be reformed, her generous woman's heart awakened. Who would accomplish that awakening? Another Southern slaveowner, a noble, thoughtful young man, convinced of the evil of slavery and working for some means to press the cause of emancipation in the South. Once again, Harriet, in her anxiety to have the South *listen* to her, was going to do all she could to admit something of "the best" of the thing.

As for "something approaching the worst," there would be her heroine's brother, a young man good looking and intelligent, but depraved and debauched by having had, since babyhood, his lightest whim indulged by the slaves around him. And as a focus for his viciousness? Who but the overseer, managing the plantation for his sister and himself, a handsome, earnest young mulatto, very like the clever, thoughtful George Harris of *Uncle Tom's Cabin.* He too would be the product of illicit passion, as George had been, but now, to *really* come to something approaching the worst of it, this young mulatto would actually be the half brother of both the heroine and her brother—son of their own father. As always, it was the dark thread of lust and its consequences that drew Harriet irresistibly when she thought of the evils of slavery. The Aunt Mary legend still echoed and re-echoed in her mind, stirring the buried fears and hated fascination. Unaware of the relationship, the brutish brother would goad and torment the loyal overseer and lust after his pretty Cajun wife, until—until— Harriet foresaw all kinds of dramatic confrontations, electric revelations, and finally, of course, unforgettable moral lessons.

"Vivid lights, gloomy shadows, grotesque groupings . . ." Looking back on *Uncle Tom's Cabin* and its amazing success, it seemed to Harriet that those were the qualities that had given it such force. Those were the elements that offered a novelist the widest "scope for the exercise of his powers." With the scene of her new book a plantation in the Deep South, very near the Great Dismal Swamp, it seemed to Harriet there would be opportunities for even more "vivid lights, gloomy shadows, grotesque groupings . . ." and so even more power in the book that resulted.

She had all she needed with which to begin—or so she thought. She was altogether unaware of the one thing that was missing that had been present when she began to write *Uncle Tom's Cabin*, a terrible, inner need to write it, so that the story burst all bonds as it poured forth, and she herself had been passionately at one with every one of her fleeing characters. It was this that had made it so compelling to millions of readers. Caught by Harriet's own tension, her readers too had felt themselves fettered, and then known the eager terror of the escape. Because of the sense of flight that ran through the book, long passages of sermonizing and moralizing asides, could be swept by in a flash, and the book had moved like light.

But Harriet had released that urgency in herself in *Uncle Tom's Cabin*. There was no more of it. She still felt strongly about the evils of slavery, but she was making a conscious and intellectual decision to write about them now. What the real burden of owning slaves was she could only surmise. The very decision to focus it chiefly on slaveowners deprived her of the sense of movement that was so strong in *Uncle Tom*.

She was oblivious of that. She looked forward to the way the story would unfold.

She began to write on the new book in February of 1856. Ultimately its title would be *Dred; A Tale of the Great Dismal Swamp*, but the title character was no part of her original plan. He would suddenly appear, halfway through the book, a visionary Negro, modeled somewhat on the insurrectionist, Nat Turner, whose slave rebellion in 1832 had so shocked the South. The real-life case of the Negro, Dred Scott, who was suing for his freedom on the grounds that his master had taken him twice into free states, had already begun its climb through the courts to the Supreme Court. There was some public interest to be gained by using his name for her title character, though the book had nothing to do with his case. And it was the haunting, fearsome sound of the name in itself that had the real appeal for Harriet. To start with, she simply called the book *Canema,* after the name of her heroine's plantation.

Off in Kansas, free-soil men and proslavery men were skirmishing and rioting, as their respective leaders drew up opposing constitutions for the State, and in Andover, Massachusetts, Harriet Beecher Stowe was at last engaged in the kind of crusading she understood and doing the best she could for "the cause."

Family activities were always there to concern her whenever she laid down her pen. Brother William, poor, unlucky William, had lost another church because of some quarrel with his congregation. Harriet and Calvin did what they could to find him another pulpit. The twins, almost twenty, were young ladies, full of frivolities, all of which amused and delighted their mother. Henry and Freddie were both away at boarding schools, Henry in his last year, preparing for Dartmouth the next fall. But that still left the spirited Georgie, and the endlessly active and inventive young Charley to keep family life from being dull. And Harriet's story progressed, easily, day after day, through March and April and May.

Then the troubles that had been simmering in Kansas erupted all over the place. In May, Harriet's friend, Senator Sumner, reacting to a Senate rejection of the Free-State Constitution for Kansas, rose to make a long, impassioned speech on "The Crime of Kansas." In the course of it, he allowed himself some intemperate remarks about a certain Southern senator named Butler, who, Sumner felt, was chiefly responsible for the Kansas difficulties. Those remarks would have fearsome consequences in the next few days. But in the next few days, there was terror in Kansas itself, as a force of Missourians rode in to plunder and destroy the Free-State capital of Lawrence. Four days later, on May 26, a band of free-soil fighters led by a Northern immigrant

to the territory named John Brown, retaliated by breaking into
the cabins of five proslavery settlers on Pottawatomie Creek and
killing them all. By that time, in Washington, Sumner would be
lying unconscious, near to death.

A young nephew of the Southern senator, whom Sumner had
attacked, had retaliated for the insults against his uncle in a fashion as appalling as the Kansan revenge. Walking into the Senate
Chamber where Sumner sat at his desk, the nephew had stepped
quietly behind Sumner and beat him into insensibility with his
gutta-percha cane.

All of the news was terrible, all of it roused Harriet, but the
attack on her friend Sumner filled her with the most violent reaction and the most furious need to retaliate in her turn, in the
only way she could.

Overnight, the mood of her book changed. A conversational
approach to the "best of the thing" was no longer possible. The
visionary Negro, Dred, appeared, the leader of a band of fugitives
hidden in the Dismal Swamp. Dred spoke in the phrases of the
old Hebrew prophets, predicting doom and destruction on a people so blind to God's laws as to own human lives. The depraved
Tom Gordon, brother of her lighthearted heroine, Nina, became a
brutish sadist, whipping an old minister who preached emancipation, and falling upon Edward Clayton, the hero, to beat him
with his cane, exactly after the fashion of "Bully" Brooks, Butler's nephew.

Writing in righteous anger, Harriet became convinced that once
again, as in the case of *Uncle Tom*, pure inspiration was impelling
her, and this book would be even more powerful than the other.

As the story began to race, as the sonorous speeches of Dred
rolled from her pen, other reminders of the days when she had
been writing *Uncle Tom's Cabin* came to Harriet. She remembered how that book had been pirated, and how she had learned
that the only way to secure a British copyright was for the author
to be standing on British soil when the book was published in
England. With this book looming in her mind as even more tremendous in impact than *Uncle Tom*, she had no wish to lose her
British royalties again. Thinking of England and her friends

there, the idea of sailing overseas in time to secure the copyright became very attractive. England beckoned her like an island of ease and comfort, reward for all her efforts. She wrote to her publishers in Boston, asking them to make sailing arrangements for her.

Calvin was going, for at least a short stay. Harriet looked at the twins and decided they would benefit from some finishing touches to their education in Paris. Young Henry, she thought, should have a few weeks of sight-seeing in England and possibly on the continent, before entering college. She asked sister Mary Perkins to go with them.

The plans were made, the sailing date fixed for the end of July, and the dressmaking and packing began. And again Harriet knew the same rush to meet a deadline that she had experienced with the *Key to Uncle Tom's Cabin*. She set herself a schedule of twenty pages a day, except for the Sabbath. Sometimes it meant writing far into the evening, and even then not quite completing her stint. To speed matters, she tried something new, dictating portions of the story to the twins.

But write as fast as she could, the sailing date loomed nearer and nearer, and the end of the story was not yet in sight. There were always other matters to attend to, letters she must write, columns for the *Independent*. She snatched a few moments to follow the news of national politics. The new Republican party had held its first Presidential convention in June and had nominated the swashbuckling explorer of the West, John C. Frémont, as its candidate. Seeing in him some shade of her old Byronic hero, his sins washed away in the nobility of his purpose, Harriet was at once a passionate supporter of "Free Speech, Free Soil, Free Men and Frémont!"

By the last week in July it was clear that the pattern she had followed in completing the *Key* would not be the pattern this time. She wrote her publishers that she could not finish before sailing, but would try to write something on shipboard, and would surely send the remaining pages soon after arriving in London. She saw Freddie, Georgie and young Charley settled with relatives. Then she and Calvin, Henry, the twins and Mary Perkins, were off for Boston and the ship.

They had a smooth voyage this time, and Harriet was able to do a little writing. In London, she let Calvin and Mary shepherd Hatty and Eliza and Henry in their first sight-seeing tours while she stayed at a desk. And finally:

"*Io triumphe*—it's done!—& I send it. You may have it published as soon as you please. We shall have Dred out (in England) within ten days from this 13th of August. Congratulate me! . . . I am worn to a rag but shall mend now rapidly. Write us *all* the news, do—and how *our* President's cause comes on. For the credit of our country, I hope he will succeed. . . ."

"Io triumphe. . . ." It was done. It was not quite the last crusading Harriet would do, but it was the last long and sustained effort, and certainly the last novel she would write on the subject of slavery, though dozens of novels would come from her pen in the years to come.

Nor was "Dred" in any way as powerful as she had dreamed it would be as she sped through its writing. There was none of the universal, hysterical acclaim for it that had followed the publication of *Uncle Tom's Cabin*. Many of the reviews in England were carping, and not all the reviews in the United States were favorable. But in England, and in the northern United States, thousands of people bought it and read it. In Great Britain, 165,000 copies were sold the first year of its publication. In America, 150,000. It was, for its time, a great popular success.

Harriet was pleased. "God," she wrote in one of the curiously ambiguous statements she made from time to time, "to whom I prayed night and day while I was writing the book, has heard me and given us of worldly goods *more* than I asked."

But now, the book written, in a frenzy of concentration, she was ready to run away from all such activity for a long time, and enjoy again the beauties and wonders of the Old World, which had left such "sunny memories" before.

Chapter 25

*I left you with a strange sort of yearning, throbbing feeling—
you make me feel quite as I did years ago—a sort of girlishness
quite odd for me . . .*

1856–1859

Harriet was writing a good-bye letter to Lady Byron before
boarding a ship to sail back to America. She had been in Europe
almost a year, and it had been even more rewarding than her
first visit abroad.

She had met Queen Victoria, and it had been "just the very
pleasantest little interview with the Queen that ever was," according to Calvin, who always seemed to lapse into extremes of
folksiness when referring to Harriet's triumphs. "An accidental,
done-on-purpose meeting at a railway station, while on our way
to Scotland," was the way Calvin described it, and naturally Harriet had been pleased by this supreme token of British recognition.

There had been dozens and dozens of other stimulating experiences, a visit at Inverary Castle in Scotland, with the Duke
and Duchess of Argyll, a visit at Dunrobin Castle with her
friends, the Duke and Duchess of Sutherland. Once again, as
three years before, Harriet had been pleased by the simple, un-
ostentatious lives of these grand Lords and Ladies, once one got
to know them. And it had been pleasant, too, that her own unaf-
fected American ways seemed to inspire them with such affection for her.

Calvin had sailed back to America to be there for the first
autumn classes at Andover. Seventeen-year-old Henry, whose
freshman classes were beginning at Dartmouth, had stayed on

with Harriet for another month because his mother did not want him to miss the experience of visiting Scotland. Then, after the Scotland visits, Harriet, sister Mary and the twins all came back to England to see Henry off to America, and had stayed on in London for a while.

Paris was next and there Harriet became part of a group of charming, cultured people. A talented sculptress had begged to do a likeness of her in marble, and daily sittings in the Montmartre studio had been combined with French lessons. Harriet was even more at home in Paris than on her first visit, and so much did she understand and enjoy French ways, she briefly considered writing a book about French society and manners, and did write several columns on the subject to send back to the *Independent*. Then, in January, she had enrolled the twins, Hatty and Eliza, in a Protestant boarding school in Paris, and she and Mary had taken off for the warmer latitudes of the South.

For three months they had toured Italy, jaunting from Marseille to Rome, Naples, Pompeii, Leghorn, Florence. Every place that one *ought* to go, they went, and everything that one ought to see, they saw, and Harriet reacted to all of it with the same unselfconscious enthusiasm she had brought to her first European tour. They climbed Vesuvius, and visited Venice, where one could really "catch romance," and they gazed at da Vinci's "Last Supper" in Milan. They went back again to Rome for Holy Week and once again Harriet's religious horizons, already broadened enough for her to respond to the incense and stained glass of German cathedrals, expanded. "Rome is a world! Rome is an astonishment! Papal Rome is an enchantress," she wrote Calvin. The crowds, the color, the pageantry, the spectacle of an entire city devoting itself to such a great commemorative display for Holy Week, affected her so profoundly that any of the old-time hostility to Roman Catholicism she might have imbibed from her father was swept away utterly. Her heart responded to its majesty and history.

There had been new friends in Italy and dozens of well-known Americans to meet and greet in Rome. In Florence, she and Mary had met the Brownings, Elizabeth Barrett Browning, already a celebrated poet, and her husband, Robert, not so famous yet as

she. They had returned to Paris in May, to pick up the twins.
But the twins were having such a good time, and doing so well
in their studies, Harriet agreed they might stay on through the
summer and return to America with a group that would be sailing
for the states in the fall.

So Harriet and Mary went on to London alone for the last
visits there before sailing.

A wonderful year was ending—a year of escape from all cares.
But quite the most wonderful part of it for Harriet had
nothing to do with what she had seen and learned. The special
glory of this year was something else—the swift and intense rip-
ening of her friendship with Anne Isabella, Lady Byron, and an
awareness of that new relationship had run like an electric current under everything else she thought and did.

"You make me feel quite as I did years ago—a sort of girlishness quite odd for me. . . ."

The intimacy had started very soon after the Stowes had first
arrived in London in August 1856. With *Dred* finished and dispatched to America, Harriet was ready to start seeing people and
enjoying herself. Among the first people she saw was Mrs. Follen,
with whom she had talked about Lady Byron three years before.
Mrs. Follen had told her that Lady Byron was still in town, kept
there by poor health, although August was hardly the season for
London. Accordingly Harriet had sent off a note to Lady Byron
by messenger, wondering if they might have a meeting. The
same messenger had returned with Lady Byron's reply:

"My dear Friend,—I *will* be indebted to you for our meeting,
as I am barely able to leave my room. It is not a time for small
personalities, if they could ever exist with *you;* and dressed or
undressed, I shall hope to see you after two o'clock. . . ."

Plainly, at their one meeting three years before, Lady Byron
had felt the same instant affinity for Harriet as Harriet had felt
for her. There had been a note or two, exchanged across the sea,
in the interval between. Meeting again, they met as friends. Lady
Byron had received Harriet in her boudoir, feeling too ill to rise
and dress. But to Harriet, even Lady Byron's sickroom had been

filled with glamour, seeming only "a telegraphic station whence her vivid mind was flashing out all over the world."

Harriet was very flattered to hear that Lady Byron had been enough interested in her to ask for particulars about her from Mrs. Follen, who had been the original source of Harriet's information about Lady Byron. Mrs. Follen had told Lady Byron about Harriet's early love for Byron and his poetry.

"It was one of the things that made me wish to *know* you," Lady Byron confided in her gentle voice with its meaningful stresses. So the friendship began to deepen. In the warm August days that followed there were more meetings. Lady Byron's health had improved somewhat, and she gave a luncheon for the whole Stowe party. Later, there had been an evening party for them all.

Then it was time for Harriet and the family to leave for Scotland. But there was a note from Lady Byron waiting for Harriet at Dunrobin Castle, thanking her for the copy of *Dred* that she had left as a gift before departing. Lady Byron had read the book and admired it greatly.

"I feel that one perusal is not enough," she wrote. And also, "I know now, more than before, how to value communion with you."

Later, after Harriet had returned to London, there was another note. Lady Byron wished to contribute something for the "sufferers in Kansas." By this time, Lady Byron was at her country place, at Ham Common, but Harriet had been eager to arrange another meeting even so.

"I do so long to see you," Harriet wrote in answer. "I have so much to say—so much to ask; and need to be refreshed with a sense of a congenial and sympathetic soul."

It was not difficult to arrange. Harriet and Mary had been invited to visit with Charles Kingsley who lived out in the country, even farther from London. On their way to see him, they stopped off for a luncheon with Lady Byron at Ham Common. At this meeting, Lady Byron had urged that they both stop for a longer stay on their way back. She had, she added mysteriously, something of special importance that she wished to discuss with Harriet privately, and at length.

Of course Harriet and Mary arranged to make the second visit. And that was the visit when the most unexpected confidence of all had been made, the confidence that made Harriet feel bound to Lady Byron with the most intimate and unbreakable of ties.

After luncheon, on this visit, Lady Byron had left Mary with two other luncheon guests and taken Harriet with her into a room where they could converse privately. There they had remained for a space of several hours. And there, during those hours, Harriet had heard from Lady Byron's own lips, the true story of *why* she had left Lord Byron.

Incest!

The word should not have taken Harriet wholly by surprise. Mrs. Follen had recently been somewhat more specific about the trouble between Lord and Lady Byron. Still, sitting face to face with Lady Byron, listening as she slowly and painstakingly led up to the revelation, hearing her voice grow fainter and fainter, seeing her wince, gasp and almost collapse when she did finally pronounce it, gave the word fresh horror. Her husband, Lady Byron at last whispered, had been guilty of *incest* with his half sister, Augusta Leigh. Not only had he confessed it to her himself, but by a variety of actions toward his half sister, with Lady Byron as a witness, he had made the existence of such a monstrous relationship devastatingly clear.

Three years before, Lady Byron had made a few remarks on religion to Harriet, and no words ever addressed to Harriet had "made their way to her inner soul with such force." These words went farther yet, penetrating the locked depths of Harriet's mind.

There they sat, in the quiet, dignified room, filling with November shadows, Harriet, a small, taut figure, her curls brown and glossy, her eyes wide. Across from her was Lady Byron, as small as Harriet herself, but her hair a silver aureole around her head, and her pale gown gleaming in the fading light. In the silence, the room echoed with the words Lady Byron had spoken, evoking terrible images.

Pictures flashed into Harriet's mind and she was powerless to stop them. Pictures from all the dark stories she had ever heard of slavery had erupted into her mind to fill *Uncle Tom's Cabin* and *Dred* with awful confrontations and unnerving flowerings of lust. Pictures came now, of the handsome, tormented poet whose image she had loved all through her youth, with his face contorted into a mask of lechery. She saw him reaching out to some shadowy woman who looked strangely like him—a half sister would, would she not? He pressed the woman to him . . . The pictures flashed giddily across Harriet's mind, and as they did so, she looked across at the gentle creature who had seen such sights in reality, suffering under them as under the lash of a whip.

She did not ask why Lady Byron had been impelled to share this story with her. It had all happened forty years ago and more, in spite of the way she made it sound as immediate and shocking as yesterday. Harriet was a new friend, of a dozen meetings at the most, from another country, and another background altogether.

But it was just because Harriet *was* a stranger and came from another country that she was telling her, Lady Byron explained. She wanted Harriet's advice. She was wondering, for a variety of reasons, if the time had come at last to tell the story publicly, and Harriet's advice could be more valuable than that of any of the friends who had long known the facts.

In her quiet voice, Lady Byron told Harriet of the long, silent martyrdom she had suffered at Byron's hands. She did not call it martyrdom, exactly. With a gesture of her small, white hand she disclaimed any desire for sympathy or pity. But the fact was that once she and Lord Byron had parted, her husband had begun to use all of his arts to conceal from the world the true reason for that parting. In poems, in letters, in conversation, he had done everything he could to convince the world that the parting was her fault. He had depicted her as cold and mercenary, shown her as the tool of an unscrupulous maid, held her up to ribald ridicule—anything, anything to keep the world from even suspecting his own monstrous secret. And he had been successful. The belief that his wife was as cold and cruel as he said had spread. Only think how far! Had not young Hattie Beecher, far across the sea in America, received just the image of Lady Byron that Lord Byron, in his guilt, had been determined everyone should have?

Harriet was appalled by the enormity of the subtle net Lord Byron had woven to trap this wronged and lovely lady. And all the while Lady Byron talked, her heart had been swelling within her. It made no difference that Lady Byron waved away sympathy. Harriet often thought in terms of "crucifixion." She had thought of herself as well-nigh "crucified" when she was compiling the *Key to Uncle Tom's Cabin* forced to bear, as Jesus once had, the sins and crimes of erring humanity. Now she could not help seeing Lady Byron in the same crucified role, bearing Byron's abuse and contumely in silence.

But *why* had she kept silent, when a word from her would have shown the world what a devil he was, Harriet cried.

"My dear, there was the angel in him too," Lady Byron answered.

She had not parried any of her husband's attacks against her with a revelation of the true story of their parting. She had let him go on and on, building her up into the monster—because she had to spare their little daughter, had she not?—had to protect his unfortunate accomplice, Augusta, but above all, she had to protect *him*, and leave him an avenue of return to repentance. She had to give the angel in him a chance to triumph. To the very day she heard of his death she had hoped for the triumph of that angel.

She still hoped for it, she said. She believed the process of redemption went on after death. She believed that the angel and devil in her husband had been wrestling all these years for supremacy. And now—and it seemed to Harriet that Lady Byron's eyes shone with an almost heavenly light as she said it—now, somehow, she felt a perfect conviction that her husband was a redeemed spirit.

It was a long, long way from any of the theology of Harriet's youth, which claimed all souls were saved or damned before creation, and simply moved, chained to a predetermined fate, through life to Heaven or Hell. It was a long way from even the modified form of that doctrine, which Harriet herself had finally accepted, that man could strive through goodness and love, during the course of his life, to win a place in Paradise. But now, in this shadowy room, spellbound by Lady Byron as she was, Harriet found a curious appeal in the new vision. Death did not end man's opportunity to redeem himself. The struggle could go on and on—in the light of eternity—as long as was necessary.

Lady Byron went on. Recently she had learned that a new and cheap edition of her husband's work was contemplated. In the preface and introductory remarks, the old stories about her parting from him would be revived, emphasizing the poems that painted the picture of her he wanted the world to have. Various of her friends had been insisting to her that it was time the falsehood and the slander were ended. Was it right or just, they asked, that a new generation of readers should fall victim to Lord Byron's lies? Was it right that one so steeped in corruption as Byron should again shine before the world as an innocent martyred by her? It was the matter of this new edition that had brought up the question.

It did not seem like an anticlimax to Harriet. "I can scarcely think," she had written to brother Edward, long ago, "without tears and indignation that all that is beautiful and lovely and poetical has been laid on other altars. . . ." Now, her mind reeling with the confidences and pictures and visions of the last hours, it seemed infamy that thousands and thousands of new readers, many of them young as she had been, should be lured and corrupted by the blandishments of one whose heart had not been "enlarged and purified," but was black with sin.

"For myself," Lady Byron was saying, "it can only be a new torture to tell the truth publicly." But it was more than the insistence of her friends that was troubling her. There was her conviction that her husband was now a redeemed spirit. Redeemed and repentant, might it not be the one thing that would set him free in Paradise, if the falsehoods he had left on earth were swept away? Was this, perhaps, the final sacrifice required of her, if her husband's soul were to be truly saved? And she looked at Harriet intensely. This, then, was the advice she wanted from her. Should she tell the truth, or still remain silent?

Harriet's mind was a turmoil. It could only bring pain to this refined gentlewoman to reveal such facts about her husband. But then she thought of the picture the world had of her, the picture she herself had once believed true. She thought of the long, long years of misrepresentation walling Lady Byron away from a world that should have admired and loved her. She thought of Lady Byron imprisoned in her husband's lies.

"I think you should tell," Harriet whispered. And then her voice grew stronger. Yes, in spite of the pain it would cause her, it was time to tell all, to save the youth of this generation from laying its heart on a false altar, to save Lord Byron's soul, and, yes, to let the world know Lady Byron's own essential goodness and what she had suffered so long for her husband's sake.

So they gazed at each other for a while, and perhaps it was not so unlikely that Harriet should have felt such a passion of love and protective adoration for the older woman. Lady Byron had a mind of cool, almost mathematical precision. Long ago, Mary Dutton, who had somewhat the same kind of mind, had laid a spell of her own on Harriet. Harriet's mind was all emotion, her responses were quick and instinctive, and she found the other type irresistible. Lady Byron was patient, as the impetuous, runaway Harriet had never been patient in her life. And it never occurred to Harriet for a moment that this endlessly patient forbearance might have been the one thing in Lady Byron's nature that drove her husband into ever wilder excesses. Not for an instant could Harriet even dream that the saintly lady opposite her might have used patience and forgiveness as weapons. For in both Harriet and Lady Byron there was the same need to see everything in terms of salvation. In both of them there was the same need to dramatize themselves in a focal role whatever the situation. And inside both of them, the ghosts of old passions still lingered, strong and compelling, dictating their actions beyond any hold of reason.

Again Harriet whispered, "Tell." And again Lady Byron sighed and smiled faintly, and lifted a restraining hand. Let Harriet think about it awhile, as she herself had thought about it so many years.

The room was dark, so long had they been closeted there together. Lady Byron rose. It was time they joined the others. They went out of the shadowed room into the lighted sitting room where Mary and the other ladies had been entertaining themselves all those hours. And to Harriet, emerging into the

light, everything looked foreign and dreamlike, as it had long
ago, when she emerged from the church in Hartford, Connecticut, her impetuous conversion toppling around her ears.

Think about it awhile, Lady Byron had said. As if she could
think of anything else! She and Mary were spending the night
with Lady Byron. Alone with Mary in their room that evening,
Harriet poured out the whole story Lady Byron had told her.
Mary was shocked, incredulous, shaken, even more obviously
than Harriet had been. But then Harriet asked if Mary did not
agree that it was time the truth were told. And Harriet was very
startled when Mary cried out, "No!" But Mary persisted, so firm
in her belief that any airing of the story of incest could only
bring trouble and disaster, that Harriet began to waver.

The next day, as they parted from Lady Byron, Harriet whispered that she would write her later, when she had considered
the whole matter more fully.

Think about it. It had been close to uppermost in Harriet's
mind for a few weeks, as she and Mary and the twins took off
for their stay in Paris. Then, in Paris, she had finally written Lady
Byron her considered judgment, obviously influenced by Mary.
The truth now might bring Lady Byron too much pain, stirring
up scandalous talk. Perhaps the time was not ripe, after all. Must
it even be told while Lady Byron lived?

"I would say, then, leave all with some discreet friends, who,
after *both* have passed from earth, shall say what was due to
justice."

After that, there was no need to think about the matter constantly. But in spite of the distractions of the winter, in spite of
the friends and gaiety in Paris, and the sights of Italy and Rome,
the "Papal Enchantress," in Holy Week, the story was somewhere
in the back of Harriet's mind, endlessly agitating when she
brooded on the story itself, endlessly warming when she thought
of how it was to herself that Lady Byron had chosen to tell it,
asking her advice.

Then she and Mary were in London again, in May, preparing
to sail for home, and there were still more new friends and new

experiences. Harriet met the young art critic, John Ruskin, just beginning to make a name for himself with his theories about blending ethics and aesthetics. His view that art should have a moral purpose matched very well with Harriet's own views, so he and she enjoyed each other, and he took her out to his home in the country to show her his collection of paintings by Turner.

But the chief joy in returning to London was seeing Lady Byron again, pressing her hands in token of understanding, and exchanging glances that spoke of the secret they shared without any need for words.

Then Harriet and Mary departed for Liverpool, to board the *Europa* and sail for home. But Harriet could not leave without another note to Lady Byron, a note full of an almost bewildered intensity of unexamined feelings.

"I left you with a strange sort of yearning, throbbing feeling—you make me feel quite as I did years ago—a sort of girlishness quite odd for me. I have felt a strange longing to send you something. Don't smile when you see what it turns out to be. I have a weakness for your pretty Parian things; and it is one of my own home peculiarities to have strong passions for pretty teacups and other little matters for my own quiet meals, when, as often happens, I am too unwell to join the family. So I send you a cup made of primroses, a funny little pitcher quite large enough for cream, and a little vase for violets and primroses—which will be lovely together—and when you use it think of me and that I love you more than I can say.

"I often think how strange it is that I should *know* you—you who were a sort of legend in my early days. That I should love you is only a natural result. You seem to me to stand on the confines of that land where the poor formalities which separate hearts here pass like mist before the sun, and therefore it is that I feel the language of love must not startle you as strange or unfamiliar. You are so nearly there in spirit that I fear with every adieu that it may be the last; yet did you pass within the veil I should not feel you lost.

"I have got past the time when I feel that my heavenly friends are *lost* by going there. I feel them *nearer*, rather than farther off.

"So goodbye, dear, dear friend, and if you see morning in our Father's house before I do, carry my love to those that wait for me, and if I pass first, you will find me there, and we shall love each other *forever*.

Ever yours,
H.B. Stowe."

So she gave all the romantic passion of a heart that had never been really satisfied to Lady Byron, and crossed the ocean with Lady Byron's story locked in her memory, to be examined again and again in moments of solitude.

"I have got past the time when I feel that my heavenly friends are *lost* by going there," Harriet had written. And then not two months later came the blow that wiped out her serenity in an instant. A dear one *was* lost "by going there," and the doors of Heaven seemed to clang in her face.

She did not see her oldest son, Henry, on her return. With the end of the term examinations soon to begin at Dartmouth, Henry had written that he would not be home to greet her until his summer vacation. So Harriet was welcomed at the Stone Cabin by Calvin and the three children who were there, Freddie, Georgie and young Charley. Since Freddie looked somewhat pale, Harriet took him off to a water-cure establishment, always her favorite resort for any lapse in health. Leaving him there, she traveled to New York City for a brief visit with her old Brooklyn friends, the Howards, before returning to Andover. It was at the Howards' home that the telegram reached her. Henry Stowe had been drowned while swimming in the Connecticut River. His body was being sent to the Stone Cabin in Andover.

The shock was staggering. Henry, strong, tall and fair, snatched away when he had still not begun to test any of the promise of his young manhood.

In a daze, Harriet traveled to Andover, where she found Calvin prostrate, the house filled with Henry's weeping classmates, who had accompanied the coffin, and in the coffin, Henry, looking "so calm, so placid, so peaceful," that she could not believe he would not wake and smile upon her, and that her "voice which always had such power over him could not recall him."

Hardly knowing what they were doing, Harriet and Calvin made the arrangements for the funeral service and for the coffin to be placed in a vault, till a grave plot could be chosen. They went to Hanover, to collect Henry's things from his dormitory room, and to talk to his classmates, and hear, over and over, in painful but necessary desperation, every detail of how the tragedy had occurred. Henry had been a fine swimmer, but in swimming back across the river there had been some miscalculation. He had not reached the sandbar in the middle, which gave a needed respite, and had been caught in the swift current beyond it, and whirled down and under.

They returned to see the coffin interred in the Andover Seminary graveyard and to plant the grave with pansies and immortelles and white petunias.

All the while, it was as though the God of love in Whom Harriet had finally put her faith had vanished, and in His place was the terrible God of wrath of her childhood, implacable and mysterious, the God who had dashed Catherine's beloved Professor Fisher to his death in the wreck of the *Albion* in 1822. The terrors, the fears, imbedded in her mind the year she was eleven, and witnessing her sister's grief, came rushing back.

"Gone, gone, and his spiritual state unknown? Oh, God, I cannot bear it!"

The grief she had known when the first little Charley died of cholera in Cincinnati, almost ten years before, was easy compared to this. He had been an infant. She had been able to cling to the thought that Jesus had taken him to Himself in all his innocence and purity.

But now, it was as though life had come full-circle, and any ideas of advance or improvement or progress were illusion. Nothing changed, after all. Lady Byron's friendship had revived in Harriet the "strange, throbbing, yearning feelings" of her lost girlhood. Henry's death brought back its terrors.

She lay on her bed whenever there was not something that demanded to be done, and her mind was a torment of questions.

"You trusted in God, did you?" she asked herself. "You believed that He loved you! You had perfect confidence that He would never take your child till the work of grace was mature! Now He has hurried him into eternity without a moment's warning, without preparation, and where is he?"

Still, she was not the child she had been. It was 1857, not 1822. Catherine had triumphed over a vision of God, crueler than any earthly parent could be. Henry Ward preached of a God of love, so did Edward, and Charles, and the other brothers too, Thomas and James.

Harriet wrote to Catherine, because Catherine, of all people, would understand.

"I saw at last that these thoughts were irrational, and contradicted the calm, settled belief of my better moments, and that they were dishonorable to God, and that it was my duty to resist them, and to assume and steadily maintain that Jesus in love had taken my dear one to his bosom. Since then the Enemy has left me in peace. . . .

"It is our duty to assume that a thing which would in its very nature be unkind, ungenerous and unfair has not been done. . . . No! No such slander as this shall the Devil ever fix in my mind against my Lord and my God! . . . He certainly did not make me capable of more love, more disinterestedness than He has himself. He invented mothers' hearts, and he certainly has the pattern in His own, and my poor, weak rush-light of love is enough to show me that some things can and some things cannot be done. . . ."

So she fought away the Devil. And she sat at her desk in her study and never noticed the silver inkstand before her, the inkstand she had brought back from England four years ago as a leader of "the cause." Her mind did not register it or remember why it was there, even as she dipped her pen into it over and over again. She was writing out an answer to her pain, an allegorical sketch to prove that a terrible loss could ultimately offer a spiritual gain to the bereaved. She did not really believe it as she wrote it. She was trying to force herself to believe it. There had to be an answer to the question of *why* a loving God could do this to her and to her son.

The world at large, though, had not forgotten why the silver inkstand was on Harriet's desk. In her private grief, she might have forgotten all about "the cause," but to the world, she was still Mrs. Stowe, the crusader, Mrs. Stowe who had leaped to fame as the writer of *Uncle Tom's Cabin* and *Dred*, and who was still the leading antislavery writer in America.

In Boston, a young man named Francis Underwood, who had plans for an antislavery magazine that would combine articles of high literary quality with sympathy for the cause, was discovering that without Mrs. Stowe as a contributor, such a magazine might never be launched. He had already talked with Longfellow, with Whittier, with Dr. Oliver Wendell Holmes and James Russell Lowell, and all of them were eager to contribute to such a venture. Then he talked with Mr. Phillips, head of Harriet's publishing firm, Phillips, Sampson and Company, but even though he offered such a galaxy of talent as that, Mr. Phillips was reluctant to support any antislavery magazine unless Mrs. Stowe was connected with it. Mrs. Stowe, after all, had been the first to disprove the old belief that there was no money in antislavery writing.

Accordingly, Mr. Underwood and Mr. Lowell—who had been chosen as editor of the prospective magazine—traveled to Andover to try to interest Harriet in their project. Roused from her preoccupation, she was glad to join them. She gave them the sketch she had just finished, "The Mourning Veil," for publication in the first issue of the new magazine, and promised a serial story for the future.

Thus began the magazine venture that would become the *Atlantic Monthly*. And, as Harriet attended various contributors' meetings in Boston after that, so also would begin her friendship with Dr. Holmes, which would last the rest of her life. But even though the new magazine was dedicated to furthering the antislavery cause, somehow Harriet was not inspired to new literary crusading efforts.

From the beginning, when she liked to say she was writing for "the pay," her pen had followed her spirit. She had written on a thousand subjects by now, tragic and trivial, moral and humorous, but however widely her subjects ranged, she always wrote of what concerned *her*, out of instinct, and never by plan.

Now, as the family in the Stone Cabin settled down around its bereavement, and Harriet made her daily visit to Henry's grave, and Calvin visited it twice and sometimes three times a day, the serial Harriet had promised for the new magazine began to "compose" itself in her mind. And it had nothing to do with slavery—at any rate, not the kind of slavery that the new magazine was dedicated to opposing.

The struggle against the fears that Henry's soul had been lost, and the memories it had brought back of Catherine's similar struggle years ago, had also brought back a flood of memories of the religious teachings of her childhood, and with them, an overwhelming question. How was it that men as good and kind and abundantly loving of life as her father, could have been committed to a doctrine so fiercely based on death, torment and wrath?

She was concerned now, though she never phrased it so to herself, with the kind of bondage she herself had known, not a bondage physical and immediate, such as the Negroes knew, and with which she had identified so easily, but a bondage more difficult to escape, since it was a thing of the spirit. How had all the mothers of New England, raised as she had been, managed *not* to go completely insane when death had taken one of their brightest hopes, as Henry had been taken?

The daughter of a clergyman, the wife of a clergyman, sister of six brothers in the ministry, Harriet knew a good deal about New England's theological history. Now she began to study it more thoroughly. She wrote a short piece on famous New England ministers as her second contribution to the new *Atlantic Monthly*.

The plot of the serial that she would call *The Minister's Wooing* began to take shape in her mind. A minister would be one focal character in the story. He would be no portrait of her father. Instead, she would write about a real clergyman of the generation preceding her father's, Samuel Hopkins, of Newport, Rhode Island. A grave, good man, so educated in the convolutions of Calvinist logic that he lived in a world apart from reality, he would offer Harriet a chance to show how a basically generous nature became so trapped by theology that it was unable to offer others the love or comfort they craved.

Remote and austere as this Reverend Hopkins might be, he would still be the choice of a pious widow, Mrs. Katy Scudder, as an ideal husband for her only daughter, Mary. But the daughter, a gentle, obedient soul, with a "winged spirit" that caught at all religion's truths without being trapped by its dogma, would already have given her heart to a gay, gallant "unconverted" sailor lad. And yes, the sailor would go to sea, and be reported lost in a shipwreck, and there would be the "form gliding like a spirit," "the eyes wide with calm horror," when Mary heard the news. The sailor boy's mother, Mrs. Marvyn, caught by the chains of Calvinism would go nearly mad with grief, knowing that her son had died "unconverted." ("Gone, gone, and his spiritual state unknown?") There would be no comfort or even hope for the mother in the minister's sorrowful but rigid exhortations to be resigned just as there had been no comfort for Catherine years ago, when Lyman had counseled the same. What comfort there would be, would come from the "winged spirit" Mary, and from one other source, the great, warm heart of the black slave, Candace, who, in her humility, had, like Mary, caught at the truth that Jesus was love.

Harriet was writing a book out of her own life at last, not as she had done with *Uncle Tom*, simply projecting her own emotions into another pattern of life altogether. She was writing on a subject that had obsessed her since childhood, and as she wrote, she could release her speculations about *why* such a cruel and stern God had held New England in thrall so long, and justify her own escape to the God of love.

When she actually began writing *The Minister's Wooing*, a year had passed since she had parted from Lady Byron with that "strange, yearning, throbbing feeling." She wondered why she had not had any word of sympathy from Lady Byron, to whom she had written very soon after Henry's death, with news of her loss. It was a small, secret hurt, fretting at Harriet along with the greater, more overwhelming pain. She wrote her another letter, even as she was starting work on the novel.

"My Dear Friend,—I did long to hear from you at a time when few knew how to speak, because I knew that you did know everything that sorrow can teach,—you whose whole life has been a crucifixion, a long ordeal. But I believe that the 'Lamb,' who stands forever in the midst of the throne 'as it had been slain,' has everywhere his followers, those who are sent into the world, as he was, to suffer for the redemption of others . . ." And she went on, in the same apocalyptic vein, telling her strangely silent friend that she was sure her reward would come one day in Heaven, when she saw the angel, once chained and defiled within Lord Byron, set free from sin at last. . . .

Then she turned to her story. The scene was Newport, in the late eighteenth century. And for all her rodomontades of mysticism when writing of religion to Lady Byron, no one in America knew as well as Harriet how to evoke the homely charms and comforts of the New England locale, the big, spotless kitchens, with their floors of snowy boards sanded with whitest sand, the ancient fireplaces, the solemn old clocks tick-tacking in the corner. No one else had even begun to write as easily, as conversationally as she about the "old, staring, rattle-windowed meeting house," where the choir was "faw-sol-laing or singing fuguing tunes." No one else had thought to write about the various characters of such an old New England town (characters like Uncle Lot, of her very first story), the gossips, the respected widows, the sharp men of business, the venerated minister. This was Harriet looking back into her memory of Litchfield when so much was peaceful and sunshiny. And it was Harriet going to the heart of the shadow that could blot out the sunshine.

"It is impossible to write a story of New England life and manners for a thoughtless, shallow-minded person. If we represent things as they are, their intensity, their depth, their unworldly gravity and earnestness must inevitably repel lighter spirits . . ." she wrote. "In no other country were the soul and the spiritual life ever such intense realities, and everything contemplated so much (to use a current New England phrase) 'in reference to eternity.'"

But the sophistication Harriet had learned since those days was giving objectivity to her story, and adding an extra dimension to it. The months in Europe, and above all, her friendship with Lady Byron, were subtly there also.

Mary, her gentle heroine with the "winged spirit," was surely, without Harriet being conscious that it was so, a very young Lady Byron, translated to New England, and suffering for the redemption of her sailor sweetheart, lost at sea "unconverted." More than that, a subplot gradually became a more and more important part of the story, and this involved a gay, beautiful and bewitching young Frenchwoman, in love with, and having an affair with— Aaron Burr, of all people. The delightful French girl, Virginie, gave Harriet an opportunity to bring a discussion of Roman Catholicism into her story, and to make understanding and tolerant comparisons between it and the "protesting" faith of the Calvinists. Aaron Burr, fascinating, worldly, already committed to his dreams of empire, was still another Byron in Harriet's long line of Byronic heroes, not as depraved as she now knew the real-life Byron to have been, but bearing some of the same scars. As Harriet re-created him in her imagination, Burr would show, as Byron had, the cynicism that was sometimes the result of being raised in the shadow of Calvinist fatalism. Burr had been, after all, a grandson of the redoubtable Jonathan Edwards, that same Edwards who had renewed the grip of the old religion on New England when it had seemed failing in the mid-eighteenth century. And Burr could be half-converted by Mary's purity and saintliness.

So Harriet began writing out old conflicts, old memories, and many newer emotions too. And so easily did this story come to her, spinning itself along almost as *Uncle Tom* had done, there was time for all sorts of other activity. She wrote her columns for the *Independent*, now and then remembering her role as crusader with an editorial against slavery. Poems sprang to her mind. And, her need for gaiety and laughter asserting itself, she organized a Picnic Club for the twins and Freddie and their friends, a club that met regularly at the Stone Cabin for games and music and charades.

The Minister's Wooing began to appear in installments in the
Atlantic Monthly, and Mr. Lowell, the editor, wrote her a long
letter. "What especially charmed me in the new story was, that
you had taken your stand on New England ground. You are one
of the few persons lucky enough to be born with eyes in your
head,—that is, with something behind the eyes which makes them
of value."

Spring came, and the story neared its conclusion. Young Freddie was talking about signing on as a crew member on a wind-
jammer during the summer, a ship due to dock, after several
months of voyaging, at Liverpool. The twins, Hatty and Eliza,
nostalgic for Paris, had talked of it so much through the winter,
that Harriet sent them off to the continent in March with their
cousin, Henry Ward's daughter. Now, with the book coming to
an end, Harriet began to think of Europe for herself, just as she
had done after finishing *Dred*. Georgie was sixteen, gay and
lively, and old enough to benefit from the experiences of a trip
abroad, just as her sisters had before her.

The book was near enough completion by the middle of May,
for Harriet to write once again to her friends in England, advising them of her forthcoming visit. She wrote the Duchess of
Sutherland, the Duchess of Argyll, and most eagerly of all, she
wrote Lady Byron.

"I am at present writing something that interests me greatly,
and may interest you, as an attempt to portray the heart and
life of New England, its religion, theology, and manners. Sampson Low & Son (in England) are issuing it in numbers, and I
should be glad to know how they strike you. It is to publish this
work complete that I intend to visit England this summer."

This time there was a response from Lady Byron, and one
warm enough to make up for the long silence. "I have an intense
interest in your new novel," Lady Byron answered. "More power
in these few numbers than in any of your former writings, relatively, at least to my own mind." Then, after further interested
comment on the book, and a few reflections on life and faith and
the need for more spirituality everywhere, there were the words
Harriet wanted most of all.

"I shall hope to be visited by you here. The best flowers sent me have been placed in your little vases, giving life, as it were, to the remembrance of you, though not to pass away like them.

Ever yours,

A. T. Noel Byron."

She was going to see her again, the one woman who, more than any other she had known, seemed to embody all the things a woman might be ("in intelligence equalling the male, in piety excelling . . ."). If she had ever really known Roxana, the mother who died when she was so young, even perhaps if Catherine had not developed into such an opinionated, domineering figure, she might not have had this need to make an ideal of a remote and glamorous figure across the sea. But life had gone as it had. There had only been a legend of a saintlike mother. So now, in her heart, it was Lady Byron to whom Harriet turned when she wanted comfort in her grief, when she wanted praise for her writing, Lady Byron who was mother, friend and guardian angel all at once.

She and Calvin and Georgie set sail for England, and once again, Harriet would be gone from America, gone from "the cause" and remote from the ever growing tension and bitterness, for almost a year.

Chapter 26

"Have you heard of the wonderful one-hoss shay,
    That was built in such a logical way
    It ran a hundred years to a day,
    And then, of a sudden, it—ah, but stay,
    I'll tell you what happened without delay. . . ."

It was Dr. Oliver Wendell Holmes, pride of the Harvard Medical School, but even more celebrated as a punster, poet, and irreverent commentator on the affairs of the day, writing his own cheerful and satiric obituary of the harsh old doctrines of Calvinism.

"Seventeen hundred and fifty-five,
    Georgius Secundus was then alive, . . .
    That was the year when Lisbon-town
    Saw the earth open and gulp her down. . . ."

And it was approximately then, according to the rhyming Doctor, (when Jonathan Edwards was tightening the last link of logic in the old Calvinist creed) that "the Deacon finished the one-hoss shay."

"Now in building of chaises, I tell you what,
    There is always *somewhere* a weakest spot, . . .
    But the Deacon swore, (as Deacons do,
    With an 'I dew vum,' or an 'I tell *yeou*,')
    He would build one shay to beat the taown
    'N' the keounty 'n' all the kentry raoun';
    It should be so built that it couldn't break daown;
    'Fur,' said the Deacon, 't's mighty plain

That the weakes' place mus' stan' the strain:
'N' the way t' fix it, uz I maintain,
  Is only jist
'T' make that place uz strong uz the rest.' "

So the Doctor romped on in his rollicking rhyme to tell how
the Deacon built a chaise with *no* weakest spot.

"Do! I tell you, I rather guess
She was a wonder, and nothing less!
Colts grew horses, beards turned gray,
Deacon and deaconess dropped away,
Children and grandchildren—where were they?
But there stood the stout old one-hoss shay
As fresh as on Lisbon-earthquake day!"

Eighteen hundred, eighteen ten, eighteen hundred and twenty
came, "Running as usual; much the same."

"Thirty and forty at last arrive,
And then came fifty, and *fifty-five*. . . ."

The chaise was a hundred years old, and each part was still
as strong as every other part.

"And yet, *as a whole*, it is past a doubt,
In another hour it will be worn out! . . ."

"First of November, 'Fifty-five!
This morning the parson takes a drive.
Now, small boys, get out of the way!
Here comes the wonderful one-hoss shay. . . ."

But . . . !

"All at once the horse stood still,
Close by the meet'n' house on the hill. . . .
—First a shiver, and then a thrill,
Then something decidedly like a spill,—
And the parson was sitting upon a rock,
At half past nine by the meet'n' house clock, . . .

—What do you think the parson found,
When he got up and stared around?
The poor old chaise in a heap or mound,
As if it had been to the mill and ground!
You see, of course, if you're not a dunce,
How it went to pieces all at once,—
All at once, and nothing first,—
Just as bubbles do when they burst.

End of the wonderful one-hoss shay.
Logic is logic. That's all I say."

The readers of the *Atlantic Monthly* laughed at this sally of
the "Autocrat of the Breakfast Table." Even Harriet had to smile.
It was true. The tight, unanswerable logic that had once seemed
to bind man in an inexorable, unchanging path from birth to
death to eternity, seemed to have simply evaporated without
any need for refuting logic, burst like a bubble, "all at once."
Men *could* change, improve their own characters, work to change
the world around them, lift up the less fortunate. Everything was
not predetermined. Man was a force in the universe in his own
right.

1857, 1858, 1859. . . .
It was as well that people could laugh at the lighthearted picture of some old, worn-out chains falling away. For with the new
freedom, there were new problems. Freedom meant—what? The
right of everybody to be and do just exactly what he wanted?
One more doughface President, Buchanan, was still holding
the two restless, muttering giants of North and South in uneasy
union. But how long could that frail structure of Union hold
when every movement of one giant seemed like insolent provocation to the other?
1857. . . . The Northern giant, rough, powerful, committed
since Jackson's day to the idea that one man was as good as another, stiffened with shock when the Supreme Court's Dred Scott
decision was announced. The Southern-born, slaveowning Chief
Justice had elaborated on the decision so there could be no doubt

about the kind of edict it was and the defiance it hurled at the North.

A Negro was not a citizen. A Negro had no legal rights to sue. A Negro owned as a slave could be taken by his owner anywhere, into free states or territories, and it changed his status not at all. Once a piece of property, always a piece of property. The Missouri Compromise of 1820, weakened by the Kansas-Nebraska Bill, was practically struck from the books by this decision.

Poised and arrogant, the Southern giant, committed since Calhoun's day to the idea that men built the only kind of civilized, cultured society worth having on the base of a slave economy, waited to see what the North would do, and fingered the weapons of nullification and secession that Calhoun had forged for it. The North, in its despair at the Supreme Court decision, realized it had the same weapons, and so the Northern states began doing some nullifying of their own, declaring the Fugitive Slave Act unconstitutional and penalizing citizens who helped Federal officers enforce it. And a great religious revival was suddenly under way—not the old-style revival beloved of Lyman Beecher, but a new kind of revival of need for a God who would encourage and support in times of trouble. Harriet Beecher Stowe, in Andover, working away at the novel that ultimately turned to just this God, was reflecting as always the emotions of her time with uncanny precision. There would be a wide and eager audience for *The Minister's Wooing*, with its message that God is love.

1858 . . . And what the North was going to do next was further tested as two men debated back and forth under the August sun, in one little Illinois prairie town after another. The immediate stake was one senatorial seat. Abraham Lincoln had come out of political retirement completely, a candidate of the new Republican party for Senator from Illinois, and was directly challenging the little "steam engine in britches," Stephen A. Douglas. In "joint discussions," they were clarifying two Northern points of view. And so, though the stake at the moment was small, North and South listened.

"A house divided against itself cannot stand," Lincoln had said when he accepted the senatorial nomination of the Republicans. "I believe this government cannot endure permanently half *slave* and half *free*. . . . It will become *all* one thing, or *all* the other. . . ."

He retreated somewhat from the intransigence of that position when Douglas accused him of inciting a war of sections. He had not meant, Lincoln explained, that the house should be made free by any interference with slavery where it already existed. He had simply meant to make the moral issue clear. There was and would always be controversy between the sentiments "of one class that looks upon the institution of slavery *as a wrong*, and of another class that *does not* look upon it as a wrong." The South listened and muttered "Black Republican," and looked again at its weapons, which could break the bonds of union.

Douglas, the Democrat, spoke in more mollifying tones. The rights and wrongs of slavery were nobody's business outside the slave states, he said, and the Southern giant agreed. But Douglas was a man trying to hold too many positions at once. To please the South and please the North at the same time was growing more impossible by the moment. To please the North, Douglas had broken with Buchanan when Buchanan tried to force the proslavery constitution on Kansas. Defending his own principle of "popular sovereignty," Douglas had insisted the people of the territory had a right to vote on it. The majority of the settlers in Kansas territory were antislavery now. The South had *not* liked that.

And now Lincoln was pushing Douglas into an even more perilous position so far as the South was concerned. Was there any legal way, he asked, that the people of a territory could exclude slavery, if that was their wish? Douglas was damned whichever way he answered. If he said there was no legal way that slavery could be excluded from a territory (even at the territory's *wish*), he would lose the Illinois vote for the Senate. If he said there was a legal way to exclude it (despite Federal rulings), he lost whatever grudging tolerance the South still had for him.

He answered honestly. There was a way slavery could be excluded from a territory. Slavery could not exist anywhere without local police regulations. If a territorial legislature refused to pass a black code, they could effectually keep slavery out.

So Douglas kept his senatorial seat in the 1858 elections, won in Illinois, but lost any real hope of winning the Democratic nomination for President in 1860. The South had heard his "Freeport Doctrine," and the South would not forget.

Two giants, growing more aware every day, every hour, of the differences between them, were insisting on the differences now, and taking pride in them. One was a gentleman, one a commoner. One took pride in his strength, the power of his factories, the might of his own self-reliance. One took pride in his heritage, his honor, the graces of life he knew so well how to cherish and enjoy. And North and South, there were the radicals, eager to push those differences to their uttermost extremes.

In the South, in 1857, 1858, 1859, the radicals no longer felt it was enough to insist that slavery followed the flag. What use was it to open territories to slavery if there were not enough first-class slaves to be transported there to build a real slave economy? Slaves were growing more and more expensive. Prime field hands cost so much that only the wealthiest planters could afford them. The obvious next step was repealing the Federal law that prohibited slave trading. Already Negroes from the west coast of Africa were being smuggled into the South through the sea islands of Georgia, where customs supervision was lax. "If it is right to buy slaves in Virginia, and carry them to New Orleans, why is it not right to buy them in Cuba, Brazil, or Africa and carry them there?" cried the voice of extreme Southern logic.

The North had its own extremes. The pale-eyed Abolitionist, John Brown, who had traveled from Pennsylvania to join in the Kansas fight for free soil, had a new scheme. If it was right for slaves to be freed, what was to be gained by waiting? He would himself invade one of the Southern slave states, rally its slaves to rebellion, and establish a free Negro state in the stronghold of the Appalachians, with himself as its chief.

It was 1859, and Harriet Beecher Stowe, who had once roused the South to fury, and whose name was still anathema there, was jaunting around Europe. She had delivered her one great stroke against the institution the South held so dear. She was still committed to the cause, but a dozen other matters concerned her now.

But John Brown was ready for *his* stroke. He had come down out of the North with a tiny band of zealots, and established headquarters in a Maryland farmhouse. The night of October 16 he and his men crept into Harpers Ferry, Virginia, where a government arsenal was located, seized the arsenal, took a stand at the bridge that led to it, and waited for the slaves to rally.

Not a slave rallied. In his blind belief that a fiery desire for freedom raged in every slave heart, John Brown had overlooked the fact that the fire might be tempered by custom, duty, fear, even love. He thought he was acting as an instrument of the Lord. Harriet Beecher Stowe also had thought she was an instrument, and still did, the *new* Lord who encouraged men to work out their own destinies. But somehow it never crossed John Brown's mind that a wild-eyed, bearded stranger like himself, standing with a rifle at the head of a bridge, was a curious rallying figure, more likely to frighten than attract.

But he accomplished more than he planned. In his hopeless, hapless foray, he roused the southern giant to a terror it had not known since the days of Nat Turner's insurrection. The North was sending its mad Abolitionists to the South's own territory, to incite the slaves to insurrection! The militia rallied, and a company of Marines bore down, to subdue and capture and punish John Brown and whatever was left of his pitiful band. Within ten days he was sentenced. In less than two months he was hanged.

The North had a martyr, the South had a symbol. Forgotten, in the North, was the irresponsibility of his raid, though public leaders made a show of deploring it. Forgotten, his bloodthirsty behavior in Kansas. In the dignity of his death, he united the North. Ralph Waldo Emerson called him "that new saint, than whom nothing purer or more brave was ever led by love of men into conflict and death."

In Europe, Harriet Beecher Stowe read at last of the raid and its consequences and spoke out like a crusader once more for the *Independent*: "We hear here in Italy of a brave, good man who calmly gave his life up to a noble effort for human freedom and died in a way that is better than the most successful selfish life. We read of troops of soldiers to guard that one calm man— a whole country under martial law and yet not able to subdue the tremor caused by his great quiet spirit."

Yes, "the tremor" was beyond subduing. The South was shuddering uncontrollably at this evidence of what it might expect from the North. The North could not be trusted in any way.

April 1860 . . . The raid was only six months past when the Democratic party met in Charleston, South Carolina, to nominate a candidate for President. Stephen A. Douglas of Illinois was the logical choice, and if Southern and Northern Democrats could have united he would undoubtedly have won the election. But the Southern delegates remembered what he had said at Freeport, and the delegates from the Deep South cotton states wanted more than any Northern Democrat could allow—a platform that stated explicitly that slavery was *right*. North and South glared at each other through the eyes of Democrats, and then the delegates from the Deep South states walked out to name their own candidate on a platform of slavery extension. The delegates who were left had to adjourn and arrange for a new convention, with fresh delegates, before they were able to nominate Douglas, on a platform that left the matter of slavery in the territories to the Supreme Court.

May 1860 . . . The Republican party convened in Chicago and, after a great deal of maneuvering and the usual amount of political chicanery, nominated a man whose humble birth, homely wit, and fairly blank political record made him seem the surest candidate—Abraham Lincoln.

In the Deep South, there was not the slightest doubt in men's minds—if Lincoln were elected, South Carolina and the other cotton states would secede. Nor was this prospect viewed with any grief by the men who had split the Democratic ticket and given the Republicans their almost inevitable victory. Rather, there was a heady air of jubilation at the thought of it—the gentlemen of the cotton kingdom would come into their own at last.

The Southern giant had had enough of lecturing on its morals in regard to slavery, enough of grudging toleration of its constitutional rights, enough of prohibitions against taking those rights wherever it went, enough of vicious sneak attacks, enough of false portraits of itself—like the one Harriet Beecher Stowe had painted—held up for all the world to see. The Southern giant itself wanted to be free!

Chapter 27

What think you? Have you had any more manifestations, any truths from the spirit world?

1860–1863

It was like Harriet that she should come back to America in June 1860 and pay almost no attention to politics.

She heard Lincoln was the candidate of the Republican party, and she was disappointed more than anything else. She knew nothing much about him. She and Calvin had hoped that their old friend from Cincinnati, Salmon P. Chase, would get the nomination. Henry Ward, she discovered, had become a fervent Lincoln man, and was campaigning for him as vigorously as he had campaigned for Frémont in 1856, in the pulpit as well as out of it. For Henry Ward, it was "a fault, a sin, for any man to be unconcerned in political duties."

But Harriet was far more concerned with spiritualism, home decoration, a romantic novel she had begun to compose in Italy as part of a rainy-day game, and half a dozen other things.

It was the shock of her son Henry's death that had roused her interest in spiritualism. She could not bear to have him so utterly *gone*, and was unable to resist the possibility that some special kind of awareness might pierce the veil that hid him from her. She was dismayed and disgusted by table-rappings, which were forever making the news these days, and repelled by squeaks and tricks with tables and chairs. But aside from these spurious manifestations, there were some supernatural phenomena, she felt sure. After all, there was faithful Calvin, as far removed as any man could be from charlatanism, who was quite honestly visited intermittently by visions of the beloved dead Eliza and other figures, dead, living and wholly imaginary. Were these visions just the result of some kind of morbid pathology, as Calvin sometimes suggested, or was there a "real scriptural spiritualism," fallen into disuse, to which a few people, "from some constitutional formation," were more readily receptive than others?

Harriet found some encouragement for her hopes in Europe. Her faultless Lady Byron had not scoffed at the mention of spiritualism. On the contrary, she was eager to "pierce the materialism" of the age, and it gave Harriet new confidence to talk to her. Then, in Italy, in Florence, meeting again with the Brownings, the acquaintanceship she had formed with Elizabeth Barrett Browning suddenly became a warm friendship when she discovered that Mrs. Browning was earnestly considering the possibility of spirit communion, and desperately "wishing it might be so." In Florence, Harriet also had met a woman, a "very earnest Christian," who had kept "carefully aloof from all circles and things like that," but who had a long history of visions, very like Calvin's. When she was with this woman, Harriet felt the spiritual presence of her lost son so strongly, it had seemed there could be no doubt but he was near. A guitar, hanging on the wall, had suddenly sounded a chord, though no one stood close enough to strike it. How could one explain it? Calvin, long since returned to Andover, had recently written that the guitar in the parlor of the Stone Cabin had sounded mysteriously. He too thought it might be Henry. But Harriet—brooding over the matter in Florence, talking about it with Mrs. Browning, and the new friend of the mysterious visions—had concluded that it must have been Eliza, since "her spirit has ever seemed to cling to that mode of manifestation," and, she suggested, "if you would keep it in your sleeping-room, no doubt you would hear from it oftener."

She went on to tell him of a work about spirit-writing that she was reading, and again insisted, "We ought to enter fully, at least, into the spiritualism of the Bible. . . . What think you? Have you had any more manifestations, any truths from the spirit world?"

After the manifestations she had had in Florence, Harriet came back to America more willing and eager to believe than ever be-

fore. It was an eagerness that she would keep out of her public
writings, rarely as she allowed any notion of what was expected
of her to still her voice. But an uneasiness went hand in hand
with her anxious interest in this matter. So she kept silent publicly,
but she began a correspondence with Robert Dale Owen, one
of the foremost prophets of spiritualism, and letters would go back
and forth between them for years.

Harriet had brought back other mementos from the year in
Europe. She sat in her bedroom in the Stone Cabin and carefully,
sadly, folded a pair of pale kid gloves into tissue paper, and
with them, a pressed rose, souvenirs of Lady Byron whom she
would never see again on this earth. Harriet treasured the memory of their final meeting—a long, quiet, sunstruck afternoon that
they had spent together in a garden. Lady Byron had looked
so very frail, Harriet had known she could not live much longer.
The rose was from the garden where they had sat. And the gloves
were Lady Byron's own, impulsively thrust upon Harriet when
she discovered on getting into her carriage for the station that
she had forgotten hers. A pair of gloves, a rose, and wrapped
up with them, a secret. Harriet sighed. Lady Byron, who spoke
so confidently of the "angel" in Lord Byron, had been herself
the angel. Would her brightness at last be revealed by someone
who had known it, now that "both were gone"?

Harriet had other memories of her latest year abroad that she
kept to herself, her own secret. The renewal of her friendship
with John Ruskin, for instance. How much had that meant? What
depths had it begun to stir, what possibilities of shared interests
and laughter?

She had met the art critic again in Geneva, while Calvin and
Georgie were still with her in Europe. She had felt the same immediate friendliness as three years before, and the Stowes and
Ruskin were often together. There was a pleasure in the lunch-
eons and excursions undertaken with Mr. Ruskin that was new
to Harriet. She and he seemed to have so much to talk about and
understood each other so easily. She found herself laughing with

him, too, in a free and merry way, quite different from the comfortable, familiar laughter she shared with Calvin.

After those shared weeks, plans had been made for the spring,
when Mr. Ruskin was going to be in Geneva again. Surely Mrs.
Stowe could arrange her schedule to be there too? It had sounded
delightful to Harriet and she had agreed that of course she could
arrange it.

But then, when spring had come, she suddenly canceled the
plans for Geneva, writing a note to Mr. Ruskin to tell him she
was hurrying on from Paris to London, and then home. And she
wrote to Calvin, in Andover, at the same time, telling him, "I
long for home, for my husband and children, for my room, my
yard and garden, for the beautiful trees of Andover. We will
make a very happy home, and our children will help us."

What had happened? Deep in her heart, still the heart of a
young girl in so many ways, had she suddenly grown frightened
of the way she felt when she was with Mr. Ruskin? Why was she
insisting to Calvin on something she had never felt the need to
insist on before—that they could make a happy home, and their
children would help them? Had she herself, a long-married
woman, with grown children, actually been allowing herself to
flirt with another man?

At any rate, she did not see John Ruskin again. But when she
finally returned to Andover, there was a letter from him, forwarded from London, where he had addressed it, hoping to reach
her before she sailed:

"Dear Mrs. Stowe, — It takes a great deal, when I am at Geneva, to make me wish myself anywhere else, and, of all places
else, in London; nevertheless, I very heartily wish at this moment that I were looking out on the Norwood Hills, and were
expecting you and the children to breakfast tomorrow.

"I had very serious thoughts, when I received your note, of
running home; but I expected that very day an American friend,
Mr. S., who I thought would miss me more here than you would
in London, so I stayed.

"What a dreadful thing it is," he went on, "that people should
have to go to America again, after coming to Europe!" And it

was even worse, he wrote, for people to do so after having been "cruelly pleasant" to friends there.

"I've no heart to write about anything in Europe to you now. When are you coming back again? Please send me a line as soon as you get safe over, to say you are all—wrong, but not lost in the Atlantic."

It meant nothing, of course. He was only teasing when he spoke of her being "cruelly pleasant," and the regret, expressed again and again, "I really am very sorry you are going. . . . It was a shame of you not to give me warning before. I could have stopped at Paris so easily for you!" was just the normal, friendly regret of any gentleman at having some plans canceled.

Still, Harriet carefully kept John Ruskin's letter. And what it really meant to her no one would ever know.

Other European experiences were having a more obvious influence on her activities. She had met her dear friends, the Howards, in Europe and it was when she and the twins were jaunting about Italy with them that rain kept them all inside one day. To while away the time, Harriet suggested they all collaborate on a story. However, it was she who began the tale, and everyone was so pleased and excited by the way it started off, that she determined to turn it into a book when she came back to America. It was an historical romance about a beautiful Italian girl named Agnes, who sold oranges at one of the city gates of Sorrento, and it was full of the things Harriet had enjoyed in Italy, its color and sunshine, the emotionalism of its people, the drama of its religious life.

She found more in Italy than the inspiration for a new story. In Florence, she had met James T. Fields, the junior partner in the Boston publishing firm of Ticknor and Fields, and the man soon to succeed James Russell Lowell as editor of the *Atlantic Monthly*. Harriet's old publishers, Phillips, Sampson and Company, had failed just as she was finishing *The Minister's Wooing*, so that book had been published jointly by two firms, one in Boston and one in New York. She was ready to think about some new and better arrangements, and the idea of having Ticknor and Fields as her publishers in the future became even more appealing to Harriet as she grew better acquainted with Mr. Fields and his young, beautiful and clever wife, Annie. They had sailed back to America together, along with Nathaniel Hawthorne and his wife. Hawthorne's book, *The House of Seven Gables*, had been a "discovery" of Mr. Fields. Altogether they were so congenial that even the shy and retiring Hawthorne had wished the voyage could be prolonged endlessly.

Now, back in America, thinking about her new story, *Agnes of Sorrento*, it seemed quite logical to Harriet that she should suggest it to Mr. Fields, in his new role as editor of the *Atlantic Monthly*, as a serial for that magazine, before having it published later, as a book, by Ticknor and Fields.

She had brought back other writing projects from Europe. The different types of homes she had seen in England, in Paris, in Italy, the varying manners of home decoration she had admired, had inspired her with the idea of writing a series of home beautification columns for the *Independent*. In New York, after her return, she had visited the *Independent's* offices, and met a young and brilliant protégé of Henry Ward's, Theodore Tilton, who was the new assistant editor. Mr. Tilton had been pleased with the idea, but he was even more eager to stimulate the circulation of the paper with a serial story by Mrs. Stowe. Already committed in her own mind to doing *Agnes of Sorrento* for the *Atlantic Monthly*, Harriet allowed herself to be persuaded by the volatile young man into writing another serial for the *Independent*.

And so, as North and South eyed each other, waiting on the event of the election in the fall of 1860, as Lincoln stayed silent in Springfield, Illinois, refusing to campaign lest any unconsidered utterance add new fuel to fires barely under control, and as the great division *Uncle Tom's Cabin* had done so much to provoke loomed closer—what was Harriet doing? She was following her own star.

She remembered the "Maine story," which she had started to "compose" after *Uncle Tom's* success, and decided that it would do very nicely as a serial for the *Independent*. She titled it *The Pearl of Orr's Island*, and planned to return, in its plot and theme, to the Puritan days and religious issues that had concerned her in *The Minister's Wooing*. She would begin on it first, and then when it was nicely underway, turn to *Agnes of Sorrento*, set in the days of Savonarola, and also carrying its share of religious conflict as it showed in the struggle between faith and dogma in the Roman Catholic Church. Two novels, to work on alternately, and a series of home beautification columns—these were Harriet's literary concerns, as the slavery issue that had once released all her passions hung like a sword over the union of the United States.

The results of the election were definite by November 7. Lincoln had carried the North and been elected. Harriet put aside her work on *Pearl* long enough to write a column of gratitude for the result, and then went back to her "Maine story."

The machinery for declaring formal secession was being set in motion by South Carolina. In all the cotton states of the Deep South there was a joyful hysteria prevailing, since the North had finally done the insufferable. Alexander H. Stephens, of Georgia, soon to have an important place in the new Southern government, wrote, ". . . the people are run mad. They are wild with passion and frenzy, doing they know not what." Stephens was trying to counsel Georgia, and the other cotton states, that secession was an act of total folly, which would achieve them none of the dazzling freedom they envisioned. Jefferson Davis, one-time Secretary of War for the United States, was another Southerner who was aware that Lincoln was not quite the brutish baboon most Southerners thought. He was also advising that Lincoln's administration be given a chance. After all, Lincoln had never pledged himself to abolish slavery. But no one in the South was listening to counsels of moderation anymore. "The people are run mad. . . ."

In Washington, D.C., always a city of Southern sympathy and temperament, joy and panic were intermingled. It was almost four months till March, when Lincoln would be inaugurated and the new regime would officially take over. So President Buchanan was praying and trembling and wondering to whom he could turn for advice, and Southern government officials made the most of the interlude, issuing orders to transfer Federal cash to the New Orleans mint, emptying Northern arsenals and ship-

ping arms to the South. Rumors flew about that the Governor of
Virginia was planning to seize the capital and prevent Lincoln's
inauguration.

"There will be no war!" Henry Ward Beecher was assuring his
congregation in Plymouth Church. Henry felt that Lincoln's election had ended the threat that had hung over the country so long.
Staring into the future, he predicted the states of the upper South
—Virginia, Maryland, Delaware, Kentucky and Missouri—would
align themselves with the free Northern states and slavery would
retreat to the Deep South. Everything was going to be better as
soon as Lincoln was inaugurated. As for seceding South Carolina, and the other Deep South states that might go with her,
let them go. "We can stand it, if they can."

As snows began to pile up around the Stone Cabin, Harriet
wrote along on *Pearl*, and pursued her domestic concerns.
Freddie was away at school. After his one trial voyage at sea,
Freddie had decided he wanted to be a doctor. Accordingly Harriet had sent him, right after her return from Europe, to her new
friend and fellow contributor to the *Atlantic*, Dr. Oliver Wendell
Holmes. So Freddie was attending Harvard Medical School, and
Harriet and Calvin both contemplated his future with satisfaction. The medical profession would be a new one for any Beecher
or Stowe male, but certainly a doctor of medicine served humanity almost as vitally as a doctor of divinity.

Christmas came, and Freddie was home for the holidays, with
cheerful reports on his studies and plenty of anecdotes about the
legendary Dr. Holmes. Christmas was a festive time as a matter
of course now, for Harriet and her family, and the Stone Cabin
was hung with holly wreaths and pine boughs, and night after
night there were musical gatherings and parties to fill it with
laughter. The twins and their friends, Freddie and his, Georgie
and hers, and young Charley's noisy group kept it pulsing with
activity.

The first installment of *The Pearl of Orr's Island* ran in the
Independent after Christmas. And by this time Harriet was far
enough ahead with the story to turn her attention to *Agnes of
Sorrento*. "I have reread my little darling, for whom I have a
peculiar love," she wrote to Mr. Fields. "Authors are apt, I sup-

pose, like parents, to have their unreasonable partialities. Everybody has—and I have a pleasure in writing 'Agnes of Sorrento' that gilds this icy winter weather. I write my Maine story with a shiver, and come back to this as to a flowery home where I love to rest."

It was a shock to get a very restrained reply from her friend, Mr. Fields. He would like, he wrote, to see more of the story before scheduling it for publication.

Harriet was not used to criticism by now, even such mild and implied criticism as this. She gathered Calvin and the twins around her in the parlor and read aloud the opening chapters of *Agnes*. And she was gratified and reassured when they told her it was as good as anything she had ever written.

"Their advice decides me it is better to go on," she wrote to Mr. Fields. And as for his suggestion that she might be better represented in the *Atlantic Monthly* with one of the New England stories she did so well, she was firm about that too. She was already writing one New England story as a serial for the *Independent*. The public did not need two from her at the same time. There was also the possibility that she might unconsciously borrow back and forth between the two stories, if she were to start another New England tale. In other words, it was *Agnes* she wanted to do.

Naturally Mr. Fields capitulated. Mrs. Stowe's name was still one of the most celebrated on the *Atlantic's* roster. And so Harriet engrossed herself in *Agnes*, feeling an exaggerated enthusiasm for it to make up for the snub from Mr. Fields. She left it reluctantly to hurry through another installment of *Pearl*, whenever one was required, and considered it the least of her efforts.

Since so much in Harriet's life went by contraries, it is not too surprising that general critical judgment would one day completely reverse her own judgment of the two stories. *Agnes*, on which she lavished such care and affection, would seem one of the dullest, most unreal books she ever wrote, a romantic hodgepodge, while *Pearl*, the neglected orphan, would seem fresh and perceptive, full of the insights Harriet had when she wrote about the kind of people she really knew. John Greenleaf Whittier ultimately preferred *Pearl* to all her other books. Sarah Orne Jewett, a young writer looking for a model to follow, found in it an approach to the kind of setting and characters she also knew, and was inspired to further explorations of the same world. "It is a little classic," she would say. But Harriet, juggling two books at once, writing her columns, and looking after her family in her spare time, was simply writing *Pearl* as fast as she could, and the idea of such a judgment would have amazed her.

Delegates from the seven Deep South states met in South Carolina in February, and formally seceded from the Union. A provisional government was set up for the Confederate States of America, with Jefferson Davis as Provisional President, and Alexander H. Stephens, Vice-President. President Buchanan, in Washington, was turning the capital into an armed camp in preparation for Lincoln's inauguration and listening desperately to anyone who might have some compromise to suggest that would lure the seceding states back into the Union. Lincoln was anxious for compromise too, and advised of Buchanan's efforts, was willing to go along with many of the suggestions proposed by his advisers. Against only one proposal he stood firm, and that was the suggestion to reestablish the 36° 30′ line as a boundary for slavery. Reestablishing this old Missouri Compromise line would throw Kansas, at last voted a free state by its settlers, back among the slave states. "Let there be no compromise on the question of *extending* slavery," Lincoln wrote. "Have none of it. Stand firm. The tug has to come, & better now, than any time hereafter."

Rumors of assassination plots filled the air as Lincoln slipped into Washington for his inauguration. The dome on the Capitol was still uncompleted. A ramshackle scaffolding around the unfinished dome looked desolate against a sky that was alternately bright and dark.

Lincoln stood in the portico to read his inaugural, and fumbled with his high hat. His longtime rival, the "little steam engine," stepped to his side to hold the hat for him, old hostilities forgotten, as Lincoln pleaded again for the ideal so many men had spoken for—union: ". . . if destruction of the Union, by one, or by part only, of the states, be lawfully possible, the Union is *less* perfect than before, which contradicts the Constitution, and therefore is absurd."

He was striking the theme to which he would hold above all others in the months and years to come, the theme that would first annoy and then infuriate the Northerners who, like Harriet, were concerned first of all with slavery and their conviction it must be ended. For Lincoln it was "the more perfect Union," envisioned in the Constitution, that came first. "I have no purpose, directly or indirectly," he said, "to interfere with the institution of slavery in the states where it exists. I believe I have no lawful right to do so, and I have no inclination to do so."

"Physically speaking, we cannot separate," he said, and he urged the country to consider the subject calmly. "Nothing valuable can be lost by taking time."

So he made one last attempt to hold the two giants together in the embrace of his own long arms. "I have no purpose . . . to interfere with the institution of slavery," he said.

But the South did not believe him and did not care what he said anyway. The North would interminably breed new John Browns, new Harriet Beecher Stowes, to incite and harass it, whatever Lincoln said. So there was laughter, jubilant, excited laughter at his declaration, "Physically speaking, we cannot separate. . . ." The South *had* separated—seven of its states had, at any rate, and the rest would surely join the others soon.

"Nothing valuable can be lost by taking time," he said. And in the South they scoffed at this also. The South was spoiling for a fight to test the hot-tempered mettle of its chivalry. So in the South, men watched the Federal forts and arsenals. These could carry the issue. The Southern states claimed these Federal outposts for their own, now they had seceded. Any attempt on the part of the Federal government to supply them or reinforce them would be all that was needed as an excuse to start firing. The South watched Fort Sumter, off the city of Charleston, South Carolina, where supplies were running low. Confederate guns on the shore were trained on the fort—ready.

Lincoln was taking his time, weighing the problem. A hostile act, which would certainly drive Virginia and the states of the upper South into the Confederacy? Or a tame yielding, which would compromise the whole principle of union? Early in April, his mind was made up. A small expedition with supplies for the fort set out for the South. The commander in charge at Fort Sumter was parleying with a delegation of Southern officers. Eager to avoid any incident, Fort Sumter's commander asked only to be allowed to surrender with honor before the expedition arrived. His conditions were refused. The ships of the relief expedition from the North were sighted from the Charleston embankment in the dawn of April 12 and Confederate guns fired on the fort.

It was done. The war had begun. In the North the vision of Southern guns firing on the flag was doing what nothing else had been able to do—uniting every shade of opinion, wiping out every casual hope that the "Southern sisters could depart in peace." For Henry Ward Beecher it was no longer "We can stand it if they can." From his pulpit in Brooklyn he was crying, "I hold that it is ten thousand times better to have war than to have slavery."

Young Frederick William Stowe, in Boston, closed his medical books. He knew there was only one thing for a son of Harriet Beecher Stowe to do in such a crisis. Anticipating any Presidential call for volunteers, he was so prompt at the recruiting offices that his name went down on the roster of Company A of the 1st Massachusetts Volunteer Infantry.

In Andover, his mother, tiny, great-eyed, was roused at last from the romantic adventures of *Agnes,* and the New England scenes of *Pearl.* She wasted no time in soul-searching or assessing her own responsibility for the event. She who had brooded all through her girlhood over every tiny evidence of sinfulness in herself, had no thought for the interlocking consequences of an impetuous act by which she had hoped to do good, no sense of burden for the young men, including her own son, whom she had helped to send flocking to the colors. It was no part of her nature to brood in that way. Guilt because of the tangled consequences of an act did not oppress nineteenth-century thinking. One reflected on what was right or wrong, good or evil, in terms of God's laws, and one *acted* on those terms, under God's eye, and what came, came.

Harriet was so far from any kind of self-consciousness that she wrote for the *Independent* after Lincoln's war proclamation: ". . . this is a cause to die for and—thanks be to God!—our young men embrace it as a bride and are ready to die. . . . If war be an evil, it is a less evil than many others and one attended by many and high forms of good."

It would not be a long war. Along with everyone else in the North, Harriet was sure of that, unaware of or untroubled by the fact that the South was equally sure of a quick victory. Men there were rallying to protect their own homes, their own fields, their very way of life. Did not this give them a unique advantage over the unthreatened North, defending some vague principle?

But Harriet was sure that the principle, allied with the North's greater strength, was more than enough. And so, full of a contained, but nonetheless high sense of jubilation, Harriet watched as the Andover students, formed into their own company of "Havelock Grays," drilled on the campus in front of the Stone Cabin. How could she help feeling a thrill at the brave sound of drums and fifes, the brave sight of the boys advancing and wheeling and halting and advancing again?

With the other faculty wives, she sewed red braid on blue shirts to transform them into uniforms. When plans were made to present a flag to the "Grays," she organized a gala at the Stone Cabin to follow the presentation. And on the day of the presentation, how could she avoid an overwhelming surge of emotion, as the brand-new soldiers came marching across the campus, singing a brand-new marching song that seemed to have come from nowhere with a rhythm of doom and triumph.

"John Brown's body lies a-mould'ring in the grave,
John Brown's body lies a-mould'ring in the grave,
John Brown's body lies a-mould'ring in the grave,
As we go marching on."

Every week, she traveled to Boston to visit Freddie, quartered in the Armory, and it filled her with emotion to see him, so slight and boylike in her eyes, but now assuming the stand and dignity of a soldier.

What else should she feel but jubilation, contain it though she might, when at last the slaves were going to be freed? Freedom! It was the one issue, the only issue, to Harriet Beecher Stowe.

As a result, the months that followed were full of shocks and disappointments to her, blows that filled her first with bewilderment, and then with a raging desire to fight, in whatever way she could.

England's stand was the first shock. She could hardly believe it when the news came that Queen Victoria had proclaimed British neutrality, thereby virtually recognizing the belligerency of the Confederate States and the right of those states to rebel. England! where she had been a national heroine presumably because of that country's sympathy with the slave; England, where so many humane people had heaped her arms with gifts and showered her with contributions to help the slave—that England was now predicting in its public press that the Southern cause would soon be successful!

It had been all very well for Calvin to point out, in 1852, to the vast audience in Exeter Hall, that England bore a great deal of the guilt for American slavery through its dependence on slave-grown cotton. Still, Harriet could not believe that now, just because such cotton was being held back from England by blockades, and just because English cotton mills were shutting down as a result, all the high moral principles against slavery that she had heard expressed so constantly were being jettisoned without a moment's hesitation.

She thought of her friends in England, the Duke and Duchess of Sutherland, the Earl of Argyll. Surely they had not been making a dupe of her, as the American newspapers had charged in 1852. It was not possible. But there in the newspapers before her were the reports of the statements Lord Shaftesbury had made, sympathetic to the South—that same Lord Shaftesbury who had drafted the "Affectionate and Christian Address" to the American women.

Harriet refused to believe they were betraying the cause. Her column in the *Independent* reasoned out what must have happened. The South had been planning rebellion for a long time, and had agents in England, spreading propaganda that the differences between the North and the South were political. England thought this was merely a war of politics, a war to impose majority will on a minority. It did not realize it was a war to end slavery.

But still no word of understanding came from the Duchess of Sutherland. No word came from anyone. "O England, England!" she wrote in her column, "What, could ye not watch with us one hour?" And her heart, which had once been so warm and full of love for England and all her friends there, grew hard.

She had given up on *Pearl* in the spring, after the war was declared, promising Mr. Tilton that she would resume writing the serial sometime in the fall. It was too much to work on two novels with this crisis at hand. All through the summer, however, she continued to write *Agnes of Sorrento*, though it seemed to her "nobody in these stormy times will ever stop to read it." But her first concern was England. Would a letter to Lord Shaftesbury, explaining the true facts, convince him that it was a war to end slavery and not a political war that the North was fighting?

In New York for a brief visit with the Howards, she had an opportunity to see Freddie. Word came that the troopship from Boston with the 1st Massachusetts on board, had tied up at Jersey City. Excitedly, Harriet and Eunice, Henry Ward's wife, took the ferry across the East River, hurried across Manhattan to board another ferry, and then there they were, at the gates of the great depot, a depot barred to civilians. But the name "Stowe" proved magic enough to open the doors, and soon they were inside, among throngs of soldiers, looking for Freddie. Then a "blue-overcoated figure bristling with knapsack and haversack, and looking like an assortment of packages," came rushing toward them. Harriet had time to hug and kiss her soldier Freddie, time to stuff his knapsack with oranges, and give him her blessing, and he was off to battle.

Harriet was home, writing her letter to Lord Shaftesbury, marshaling every argument she could think of to prove it was not a war of politics, on the very day Freddie and the Northern forces were having their first taste of real fighting near the little creek of Bull Run, fifteen miles from Washington. The next day, she and all the North were shaken when they heard of the debacle, with untrained Union troops flying in panic from a Confederate counterattack.

Later dispatches showed the results not quite so disastrous as had been thought. Union losses were less, and a little later, Freddie was home on furlough, to tell his mother that Bull Run had been just an accident. As soon as the troops were better trained and welded into a fighting army, the story would be different. He had done well enough at Bull Run to win a promotion. Soon he was gone again, full of optimism, to Washington, and still another promotion—lieutenant in the cavalry.

Had the North needed this shock to wake it up to the fact that a host of farmboys, factory hands, office workers and college students needed more than a patriotic devotion to the Union to make a fighting army? Perhaps so.

A far greater worry to Harriet than the defeat at Bull Run was the fact that the weeks were dragging on and Lincoln had still done nothing to justify her impassioned letter to Lord Shaftesbury about the cause of the war. Why was Lincoln doing nothing at all to prove this was a war to end slavery, not a war of politics?

One man, General John Frémont, her hero since the days of the 1856 Presidential campaign, was taking a stand. Placed in command in Missouri, Frémont was freeing slaves by proclamation throughout all the territory under his command. Another general, Butler, was accomplishing almost the same end, in another area, by declaring captured slaves "contraband of war," and so no longer the property of their former owners. But it was Frémont's unequivocating stand that pleased Harriet:

"At last, a blow has been struck which finds an echo in the heart of a whole nation. The hour has come, and the man! Frémont does not call the slave contraband of war. That position, advantageous and ingenious in its day, is now abandoned for higher vantage ground. Frémont does not even speak of the slave as property. He makes the just distinction: the *property* of the traitors he declares confiscated, their slaves, if they have any—free. There we have it, fair and square. Out goes his banner! down goes his glove! and, if anyone does not like it, let him try conclusions sword with sword,—that is all!"

There, in the *Independent*, Harriet had it, fair and square, but Lincoln did not see it so. First he announced that Frémont had exceeded his authority, and then, on further thought, he relieved Frémont of his command. Harriet and Calvin looked at each other, as Abolitionists everywhere were looking at each other, wondering what sort of man they had elected in their folly. Not a war of politics? Then what was it, in the face of this? With Harriet beside him, urging him on, Calvin wrote his old friend, Salmon Chase, now Lincoln's Secretary of the Treasury:

"I do not know that you have either time or inclination to listen to a word from the common people, but I wish you could hear the cries of surprise, indignation, disgust and contempt, which now everywhere find utterance at the removal of Frémont. The feeling is frightfully earnest. . . .

"Stringham and Butler took Hatteras, the only success we have had in the East; and Stringham is immediately dismissed and Butler sent to New England. Frémont was driving the enemy before him, his officers and soldiers were enthusiastic in his behalf; and in the face of the enemy and on the eve of victory, he is superseded, as if he were a Benedict Arnold.

"Our Government gives rewards to defeat and shame, and punishes success and honor. Imbecility and treachery are sure of favor; fidelity and energy are equally sure of hostility and disgrace. . . ."

Perhaps, even so, he was modifying some of the phrases that Harriet was muttering by his ear as he wrote. Why had their son, and thousands of other sons of the North, gone out to battle, even to die, if not to free the slave?

It was beyond Harriet's understanding that Lincoln had rebuked Frémont as he did just so that no one *could* label the war a war of politics. "Genl. Frémont's proclamation," Lincoln wrote in answer to another cry of protest, "as to confiscation of property and the liberation of slaves, is *purely political*, and not within the range of *military* law, or necessity. If a commanding general finds a necessity to seize the farm of a private owner, for a pasture, an encampment, or a fortification, he has the right to do so, and to so hold it, as long as the necessity lasts; and this is within military law, because within military necessity. But to say the farm shall no longer belong to the owner, or his heirs forever; and this as well when the farm is not needed for military purposes as when it is, is purely political, without the savor of military law about it. And the same is true of slaves. If the General needs them, he can seize them, and use them; but when the need is past, it is not for him to fix their permanent future condition. That must be settled according to laws made by law-makers, and not by military proclamation. . . ." Patiently, carefully, Lincoln went on to explain that Frémont's course denied the government of the United States, by making rules of property by proclamation. Patiently, carefully, he went on to explain how that course could lead to disaster, alienating all the border states.

A small and emotional literary woman who had made the cause of the slave her own a decade and more ago, was not interested in a lawyer's careful distinction between acts of political policy, and true military law, nor in a President's unwavering determination that the concept and theory of a *Union*, governed by a constitution, came first, before the freedom of any slave. Raging in the cause of what she thought was right, Harriet used her column in the *Independent* to tell Lincoln what he ought to do:

"Now is the time—the accepted time. Now emancipation can be given as a gift; by-and-bye it will seem to be wrung out as a cowardly expedient. Let the people petition the Government! Let them demand that this mighty weight be cast in our scales now!

"Let the President of the United States proclaim that all men shall hereafter be declared free and equal, and that the services of all shall be accepted, without regard to color. . . ."

She kept up her attack all through the winter of 1861–62. Gone completely was the "withered and exhausted" Hattie of the days of her youth, gone the self-pitying, periodically collapsing Harriet of the early days of her marriage. Now she was a woman inexhaustible, finishing her novel *Agnes of Sorrento* in the last months of 1861, starting the second part of *The Pearl of Orr's Island*, running her house, worrying about Fred, stationed near Washington, and also trying, with every stratagem at her command to prod a reluctant President into action she wanted.

When *The Pearl of Orr's Island* was completed, in the spring, Harriet could turn all her attention to Lincoln and the war. Lincoln had removed the slow-moving George B. McClellan and replaced him with Henry W. Halleck, as General in Chief, and reinstated Frémont, putting him in charge of the newly formed state of West Virginia. A decisive battle was expected very soon in the East. But still no word from Lincoln about the fate of the slaves!

Lincoln said nothing, even though in the West, at Fort Donelson, and then at Shiloh, a tough and doughty general named Grant had been giving the North some battles it could claim as victories.

The advance the North had been waiting for came at the end of June. McClellan, still in command of the Army of the Potomac, began to move on Richmond—the move that could "crush the rebellion." But General Robert E. Lee, of the Confederacy, and his lieutenant, Stonewall Jackson, had been waiting too, and so instead of the victory for which the North was so eager, there were seven days of desperate fighting and McClellan's forces were back again almost where they had started. It was not really a retreat. McClellan had brought his army safely out of what might have been a disastrous trap and had inflicted far greater loss on the Confederates than that sustained by his own men. But it looked like retreat to the North. It looked like one more defeat and disaster.

Henry Ward Beecher, the erstwhile supporter of Lincoln, joined Harriet now in outraged admonitions to the President through the columns of the *Independent*. The President should call for a draft of a million men, Henry wrote, and also for immediate "military emancipation of the slaves." The future was dark indeed so long as the President was "more interested in politics than in prosecuting the war." And Harriet wrote, "How long must this people wait . . . with this great arrear of crime and injustice still unrighted?"

In August there was still another disaster, the second Union rout at Bull Run. "The voice, *Let this people go,* has been as evident to us as to the old Egyptians;" Harriet wrote, "and every refusal has been followed by defeat and plague. . . ."

Lincoln did try to explain what he was doing. He was not goaded into a statement of policy by either Harriet or Henry. He gave the statement in an answer to a letter from Horace Greeley, the liberal editor of the New York *Tribune.*

"My paramount object in this struggle is to save the Union and is not to save or destroy Slavery," Lincoln wrote Mr. Greeley, who blazoned the newsbeat across the front page of his paper. "If I could save the Union without freeing any slave, I would do it; and if I could save it by freeing all the slaves, I would do it; and if I could do it by freeing some and leaving others alone, I would also do that. What I do about Slavery and the colored race, I do because I believe it helps to save this Union; and what I forbear, I forbear because I do not believe it would help to save the Union."

Harriet had begun to tremble as she read the statement in the *Tribune,* feeling that it negated every belief she had about why the North was fighting. In a passion, she paraphrased the statement for the *Independent,* writing it as she thought it would have been written if Christ were in the White House.

"My paramount object in this struggle is to set at liberty them that are *bruised* and *not* either to save or destroy the Union. What I do in favor of the Union, I do because it helps free the oppressed; what I forbear, I forbear because it does not help to free the oppressed. I shall do less for the Union whenever it would hurt the cause of the slave, and more when I believe it would help the cause of the slave."

When two causes are interlocked, for which does one fight first? Is it possible to defend both at the same time? It had been a profound rejection of the spread of slavery, as allowed by the Kansas-Nebraska Bill, that had roused Lincoln out of political retirement. He was a man completely convinced that slavery was wrong when he won the Republican nomination for President. And then he had become President, and the South, revolting against the idea he embodied, was trying to destroy the one framework within which freedom might really mean anything—for white or Negro—the Union. "Liberty and Union, One and Inseparable," Daniel Webster had cried long ago, putting liberty first. For Lincoln, when the fearful choice had come, it was Union that had to come first. But the two causes were interlocked as inexorably in him as thought and action, reason and emotion, all the other dichotomies that make life an agony to those who crave the absolute. From the beginning, Lincoln had his plans and hopes for compensated emancipation, legal, constitutional, within the frame of union. But those who sought the absolute, in both North and South, would have none of that. So Lincoln had waited, choosing the Union first, striking for the Union, fixing the concept of union in men's hearts.

But even as Harriet bitterly paraphrased his statement, haranguing for her absolute, Lincoln was readying his blow for the interlocking cause with the cause of union. He was only waiting for some victory for the Union that would make the stroke one of strength, not weakness. Would a victory never come?

After the disaster of the second battle of Bull Run, the North was beginning to feel despair. Lee's army was romping through Maryland, and the goal was Washington. General Halleck was in his offices in the War Department, staring at the dispatches as they came in. In England and in France too, prospects looked so promising for the Southern cause, it seemed only the matter of another battle before their governments would recognize the Confederate States as independent, and the Union in America dissolved. Then Lincoln summoned McClellan back again.

On the seventeenth of September, McClellan managed to catch Lee and Jackson, between Antietam Creek and the Potomac River, and after a fierce battle, it was Lee who retreated across the Potomac, with the Army of Northern Virginia.

At last there was a Union victory that justified Lincoln's second stroke—the stroke for freedom.

Five days after Antietam, Lincoln announced to his cabinet that he had decided on a "fit and necessary war measure for suppressing" the rebellion, the text of an Emancipation Proclamation which he proposed to sign and put into effect on the first of January 1863. The three-month interlude was to give all rebelling states an opportunity to surrender and rejoin the Union. For the President, by virtue of his power as commander in chief of the army and navy, would, upon that day declare that all slaves within any state or district in rebellion against the United States, should "be then, thenceforward, and forever free."

Henry Ward Beecher was ecstatic when the news came through. For the last year and more he had been serving as editor in chief of the *Independent*, and now he had his managing editor, Theodore Tilton, run the full text of the Proclamation under the headline, "The Most Important Paper Ever Published in the Independent."

Harriet, like many other Northerners who had made slavery the focal issue of the war, was afraid to be pleased. Lincoln had waited so long for this move. She had worked herself into such a state about his motives while he waited, that now she wondered about his motives in this. Did he really mean it, or was it another political move?

Gradually she allowed herself to hope. As she did, the attitude of England began to agitate her more and more. Confederate gunboats were being built in British shipyards. British papers were arguing that the Southern states had as much right to rebel as the thirteen colonies had.

Harriet looked at the oak cabinet that held the twenty-six volumes filled with signatures of British women who had sent the "Affectionate and Christian Address" to the women of America, urging them to help wipe out the sin of slavery. She had received that Address in the name of the women of America, but she had never officially replied to it. Now she realized in a flash of inspiration that *this* was the moment for the reply, asking for British support as the United States tried to do just what so many British women had urged.

She wrote to James Fields in Boston and suggested that her "Reply to the Affectionate and Christian Address" be published in the *Atlantic Monthly*. But a little doubt still lingered. She wanted to be very sure Lincoln did plan to sign the Proclamation on January 1. "I am going to Washington to see the heads of Department myself," she wrote, "and to satisfy myself that I may refer to the Emancipation Proclamation as a reality and a substance not to fizzle out of the little end of the horn."

She took one of the twins with her, and also Charley, twelve years old now, old enough to benefit from the experience of seeing Washington in wartime, and perhaps meeting the President. Arrived in Washington, Harriet's first thought was of Fred, stationed in a neighboring camp. One way and another, she obtained a pass for him to stay with her and the rest of the family for forty-eight hours at their Washington hotel. The next day Massachusetts Senator Henry Wilson made arrangements for Harriet to have her interview with Lincoln. Charley was by her side as she entered the White House and was escorted to one of the small rooms that Lincoln used as a study. Small, neat, composed, her great eyes intent, she watched as an immensely tall figure unfolded itself from a chair, and stood and came toward her, the movements slow and a little awkward. The rest would be legend, forever after, to Harriet and all her family. Towering over her, Lincoln put out his great hand and took her small one in it.

"So this is the little lady who made this big war?" he said.

And looking into his eyes, did Harriet see at last some of the endless, ever-widening vistas of suffering and decision and un-exulting achievement, which were partly the consequences of her own impetuous blow for freedom?

Legend was made of a few homely comments—Lincoln rubbing his hands before an open fire and saying, "I do love a fire in a room. I suppose it's because we always had one to home," and Lincoln responding to a question of Harriet's about how he found time to dine when he had so many cares, problems and visitors to meet by saying, "Well, I don't exactly, as you say, *dine.* I just browse around a little, now and then."

Legend said nothing about any serious talk concerning the proposed Proclamation and Lincoln's intentions. It was simply implicit in what Harriet said later that Lincoln told her enough about the various pressures and difficulties besetting him so that she understood his delay and was instilled with a complete belief in his good faith. Implicit too was the fact that Harriet came away from this meeting not only with the belief that the Proclamation was a "glorious expectancy," but with a changed attitude toward Lincoln himself.

Young Charley was full of questions as soon as they left the

White House. Why, he asked, did the President say "to home" instead of "at home"?

Harriet's changed feelings about the man she had just met were reflected in her answer as she quoted St. Paul: "Though I be rude in speech yet not in knowledge; but we have been thoroughly made manifest among you in all things."

Convinced that there would be no humiliation in putting her trust in Lincoln, Harriet went back to the hotel and finished her "Reply to the Affectionate and Christian Address of British Women," and sent it off to James Fields at the *Atlantic*, who would in turn see to its British publication. As she finally wrote her "Reply," she made it a temperate and eloquent document. The sarcasm and satire that she sometimes used so recklessly in her columns were put by, and she closed with a paragraph from the original "Address" that had been presented to her:

"We appeal to you as sisters, as wives, and as mothers, to raise your voices to your fellow citizens, and your prayers to God, for the removal of this affliction and disgrace from the Christian world."

In the end, her "Reply" had little effect in the British Isles, either for good or ill. People there were not making up their minds on the basis of reason, any more than they were in the United States. But Harriet had made her answer at last to the tempestuous ovation of 1852, and England would no longer beckon her as a bright land of promises fulfilled and fairy tales come true. She would never return there again.

January 1, 1863. That had been the date Lincoln promised, if nothing went wrong. Harriet was in Boston on that New Year's Day, and Boston, like many other cities in the North, had been preparing an Emancipation Jubilee, trusting that Lincoln would not fail them. Harriet decided to attend the Jubilee in the Boston Music Hall.

She was sitting in the balcony, and had listened through the musical items on the first part of the program. At intermission the news came. The telegraph was reporting the news from Washington that the President had just signed the Emancipation Proclamation.

The hall broke into an uproar, with everyone cheering, waving, weeping, tossing handkerchiefs and hats in the air and kissing each other. Lost in the throngs of the balcony, Harriet was cheering and weeping too. Then someone passed along the word that Mrs. Stowe was in the hall.

"Mrs. Stowe?" "Mrs. Stowe!" "Mrs. Stowe!" People were pointing toward her, and those nearest her were pushing her to the balcony rail. She went to it and looked down on the packed host of faces turned toward her, a hall full of people shouting their acclaim. At this moment of jubilee it had not been forgotten who had done the most to rouse the North to the plight of the slave.

A compound of passions—deep feeling and sentimentality, laughter and moodiness, self-righteousness and humility, dark fears, unsounded emotions and clear insights—all these, fused by a hatred of bondage, had produced a book that had shaken the world. Now the woman who was that compound had her reward. The slaves were free.

This was an ovation that could never sound hollow in her memory as those abroad finally did. She had her sense of achievement. And so far as Harriet was concerned, the war was almost over at this moment. Her involvement with it as a public figure was ended.

She could go back to Andover and turn to all the things that had concerned her when the war began, other stories stirring in her mind and waiting to be written, the making of a home for her husband and her family, and always, underneath the other preoccupation, the wistful, secret yearning, that somehow, the veil could be pierced, and she would hear her dead son Henry's voice again.

Chapter 28

"My house with eight gables is growing wonderfully. I go over every day to see it. I am busy with drains, sewers, sinks, digging, trenching, and above all with manure! You should see the joy with which I gaze on manure-heaps, in which the eye of faith sees Delaware grapes and d'Angoulême pears, and all sorts of roses and posies."

1863–1865

Harriet was building her dream house in Hartford in a grove by the Park River, the very same grove in which she and Georgiana May, had talked of building houses, years ago when they were schoolgirls.

Five months before, Calvin Stowe had taught his last class at Andover Theological Seminary and retired from teaching. He was sixty, hard as it was to believe, and with Harriet making enough money from her writing to support the family, there seemed no reason for him to continue in work he had never enjoyed. He was going to devote himself to the scholarly pursuits that had always been his chief interest, and perhaps write a definitive treatise on the subject that had been his main concern for so long—the origin of the books of the Bible. The decision for retirement had been made a year before and they had agreed on Hartford as the city where they would like to live when they were free. Sister Isabella lived there with her family, and so did Mary Perkins and hers. Aside from the family ties, Harriet had been fond of Hartford since her school days, and there *was* a small, secret satisfaction in making a childhood dream come true. So she went to Hartford, surveyed the situation, and bought four acres on the river.

She looked forward to planning the first house that would be built entirely to her specifications, and all through 1863, it was well she had such a distraction, for the year that had begun with the Emancipation Proclamation and her ovation in the Boston Music Hall took on a gray and somber cast by spring.

Ten days after the New Year, word came that her father was dead. But that was not what darkened the year. Lyman Beecher was eighty-eight. For the last few years he had been living near Henry Ward in Brooklyn, and, his mind almost gone, had wandered about the neighborhood, a thin shell of a man, lost in the loneliness of old age. None of his children could grieve at his leaving. He had gone at last to join Roxana, remembered and beloved to the end in spite of the mists that had blotted out everyone else. The tears his children shed were only gentle tears as they remembered the glories of his life, and they felt fond pride as the newspapers of the North recalled all the achievements and the wit of Lyman Beecher.

Other deaths that had occurred much further in the past still brought more pain to Harriet—Henry's death, Lady Byron's death. More than a year before she had heard of the death of Elizabeth Barrett Browning and she still sorrowed for that lost friend too, who had understood her craving for the solace of spiritualism.

And her mood so far as the war was concerned was hopeful as the year began. Now that the Emancipation Proclamation had wiped the stain of slavery from the Union banners, surely there would be no more sickening defeats. When spring came and the armies marched again, surely there would be victory after victory until quickly the final victory would bring Freddie home again.

So in the early winter she ran away from her impatience for those victories into plans for the new house in Hartford. The three trips that she had made abroad were her inspiration. All the beauty she had absorbed there would guide her as she designed a house that would be a symbol of the distance she had come from the beauty-starved days of her childhood. She planned for gables and turrets, reminiscent of the medieval castles and ruined abbeys of England and Scotland, and for verandas and piazzas like those she had admired in Italy. Inside the house there must be warmth and richness. She wanted walls paneled in oak, and the oak must be cut from the trees in the grove where the house would stand. She wanted carved balustrades and railings and richly carved mantelpieces. And her heart was set on one feature—a great two-story-high conservatory at the rear of the house. An Italian fountain would play in its center, and the fountain and the plants and blossoms around it would be visible from the wide entrance hall. She planned for her study to look out over the conservatory, so that she would always have green things to look at when she lifted her eyes from her writing.

This cheerful occupation filled every spare moment in the winter. The aesthetic aspects decided on, she had to think about the practical ones, closets, pantries, cellars. Calvin was little help in the speculations. Whatever Harriet referred to him, he was apt to reject as too costly. The whole project was beginning to frighten him financially. So Harriet turned most often to the twins for advice and suggestions.

Hatty and Eliza were also steeped in the arts of the past from their sojourns in Paris and travels on the continent. They were interested in the plans for the new house and their suggestions were often helpful. As a result, Harriet and her two daughters spent many hours together, huddled over sketches, scribbling new plans, considering and rejecting.

Attractive as Hatty and Eliza were, it was curious that there had been no hint of romance for either of them. Had their foreign experiences cultivated them beyond any interest in the young men they met in isolated Andover? Did their mother's fame stand like a barrier between them and any young men they met elsewhere, as they glided, tall, handsome and contained, in her wake? Harriet, who had contemplated spinsterhood at twenty-two, never seemed to give a thought to the fact that they were still unmarried at twenty-seven. And Hatty and Eliza appeared perfectly content to hover around her, taking her dictation, helping her with her correspondence, lavishing their affection on the cats, dogs and birds that were always part of the family. They appeared perfectly content now, caught up with their mother in the project of the new house.

Then the first general conscription bill was passed in March. And in Andover it was necessary to realize how many people were not primarily concerned with the winning of the war, and did not find "the cause" one they were willing to embrace and die for. Business was booming in the North, contrary to Southern expectations that the loss of Southern markets and the withholding of cotton would cause it to collapse. With lavish government orders to fill, many Northern businessmen were getting rich quickly, and spending their new wealth recklessly for clothes, carriages and entertainment—the realities of the war miles away. With the means of exemption from conscription so easy—only three hundred dollars to buy a substitute—it was simple to keep those realities at a distance. Young men were not everywhere eager to flock to the colors, many were continuing placidly with their schooling or with the jobs that the war economy made possible.

And so, in the cities of the North, where the burden of conscription fell on those too poor to buy substitutes, there was a sudden outbreak of rioting, as the poor rebelled against fighting for a cause that could never help them—the freeing of millions of Negroes who would then come North and take their jobs. All over the North there was a louder and louder muttering from the men who were beginning to feel that the South never could be defeated anyway, and it was time to make a peace, any kind of peace. In May, when only a Northern victory could have helped to quiet the unrest, there was news of the terrible destruction Lee and Jackson had inflicted on Hooker and his army in the Wilderness in Virginia. Where *was* the victory that should have followed the Emancipation Proclamation?

Harriet turned to her house plans in desperation, running away from her bewilderment and the constant nagging anxiety about Freddie, attached now to the forces of Major General George Gordon Meade.

Finally the long time of gloom and waiting was broken. In

July there was glorious news of a Union victory at Gettysburg. Once again the Southern forces had been repulsed in their attempt to invade the North, seeming, like Antaeus, to lose strength when their feet no longer touched native soil. At almost the same time, there was more enspiriting news from the West, where the determined Grant was showing his mettle. Vicksburg on the Mississippi had fallen on the last day of the Gettysburg battle.

The rejoicing in the Stone Cabin did not last long. A week after the Gettysburg victory, a letter written in a strange hand came to that house, just as similar letters were going to many others. Fred, who had been fighting in the Gettysburg battle, had been wounded. Wounded only! He was not dead. "It may cheer your heart to know that he is in the house of good, kind friends," the chaplain wrote. "He was struck by a fragment of a shell, which entered his right ear. He is quiet and cheerful, longs to see some member of his family, and is, above all, anxious that they should hear from him as soon as possible."

Wounded, but not too seriously. It was nowhere near as bad as the news that was going to brother Charles, who now had a church in Georgetown, Massachusetts. His oldest son had received a wound so desperate it was feared it might prove fatal. To make the news doubly distracting in that home, Charles was facing, as Beechers so often seemed to be doing, a heresy trial brought by members of his congregation who thought him too liberal. His wife had to insist that he stay and not let the trial go by default, while she traveled by herself, through the simmering heat, to find and nurse their son.

Calvin Stowe hurried off, round and panting, to take the first train toward Gettysburg. But he fell into the clutches of a pickpocket when he had progressed no farther than Springfield and had to return home. By then it was decided that it might be wiser for him not to join the confused crowds of soldiers and family and wounded near Gettysburg. A letter from Fred himself reassured Harriet and Calvin. He was in an army hospital and there was no need for them to come or to worry. So neither of them went to him, but not to worry was impossible.

A letter came from England, shortly after that, from one

friend who, it seemed, had remained true to Harriet's cause—the Duchess of Argyll.

"My Dear Friend," Harriet hastened to answer her, "Your lovely, generous letter was a real comfort to me, and reminded me that a year—and, alas! a whole year—had passed since I wrote to your dear mother, of whom I think so often as one of God's noblest creatures, and one whom it comforts me to think is still in our world.

"*So many*, good and noble, have passed away whose friendship was such a pride, such a comfort to me! Your noble father, Lady Byron, Mrs. Browning,—their spirits are as perfect as ever passed to the world of light."

Memories of Lady Byron and of Mrs. Browning led Harriet to reflection: "I think how suffering is, and must be, the portion of noble spirits, and no lot so brilliant that must not first or last dip into the shadow of that eclipse."

She went on to tell of her own life. "This year has been one long sigh, one smothering sob to me," she told the Duchess. The prevailing anti-Northern feeling in England was still a bitter thought. "I saw *your* Duke's speech to his tenants! That was grand! If *he* can see these things, they are to be seen, and why cannot Exeter Hall see them? It is simply the want of an honest heart.

"Why do the horrible barbarities of *Southern* soldiers cause no comment? Why is the sympathy of the British Parliament reserved for the poor women of New Orleans, deprived of their elegant amusement of throwing vitriol into soldier's faces, and practicing indecencies inconceivable in any other state of society? Why is *all* expression of sympathy on the *Southern* side?" The long months of waiting and despair had left Harriet as ready as anyone to believe the atrocity stories that were circulating. "You see I am bitter. I am."

So Harriet used the new house in Hartford as an escape from such unwonted feelings too. Actual construction had begun. She could travel to Hartford and watch trees being felled, ground broken and a foundation being laid. With the plans for the house so elaborate, Harriet and Calvin realized it could not be ready by fall and made arrangements to stay on at the Stone

Cabin through the fall and winter. Meantime, she was in Hartford as often as possible, sometimes staying with Mary, sometimes with Isabella, but spending her days at the grove by the
river, where the house was slowly beginning to rise.

She had done no real writing for a long time, not since her
"Reply to the Affectionate and Christian Address." Now, her
head full of houses, their planning and construction, she wrote
to James Fields to ask if he would be interested in a series of
"house and home" papers for the *Atlantic Monthly*. She envisioned a series of ten or twelve sketches that would draw the
distinction, in various lively ways, between a house and a home.
She sent him one sketch she had already written, "The Ravages
of a Carpet," an amusing piece tracing the ways in which the
purchase of a new carpet gradually led to the transformation of
a comfortable living room into an elegant but forbidding parlor.
She had already planned a second on "Homekeeping *versus*
Housekeeping," another humorous essay, describing the near destruction of a marriage due to the wife's insistence on keeping
everything spotless, the carpet unfaded, the best dishes un-
chipped.

These were fresh themes in 1863, not yet banal, just as her
New England characters and themes were not stereotypes either,
at the time she first wrote about them. Nor was the *Atlantic
Monthly* an unlikely magazine to publish such "homemaking"
papers. Writing under a masculine pseudonym, pretending to
be a mild, amused, but observant male, Harriet gave her "house
and home" studies some of the same flavor that Dr. Holmes
gave to his comments as the "Autocrat of the Breakfast Table."

The Union forces were struggling with the forces of the Confederacy in the hollows and on the mountain slopes of Chatta-
nooga, Tennessee. The armies in the East watched each other.
And Harriet wrote of homemaking and supervised the building
of her house. When she wrote again to Mr. Fields, she told him
cheerily, "Tell Mrs. Fields, my house with *eight* gables is growing
wonderfully. I go over every day to see it. I am busy with
drains, sewers, sinks, digging, trenching, and above all with
manure! . . ." To keep an eye of faith on Delaware grapes and
d'Angoulême pears in the future, was surely as good a way as
any to live through an anxious time.

Fred's wound was proving more of a problem than anticipated. He had been three months in army hospitals, and the
wound still was not healing properly. There were letters between
Harriet and Fred, then a letter from Harriet to Secretary of War
Edwin M. Stanton. Then Harriet was traveling to New York to
get Freddie and bring him home, honorably discharged from the
army due to physical disability.

She was happy to see Freddie again, and it was a relief to
forgo that particular kind of anxiety and suspense a mother knows
when her son is continually facing death on the battlefield.
Freddie was pale, and his unhealing wound troubled her, but
she was sure that once he was home and nursed with her own
loving care, it would mend.

Henry Ward had just returned from England, where he had
given a grueling series of speeches in behalf of the Northern
cause. Audience after audience, he told Harriet, had been either
vaguely or forthrightly hostile when he began to speak. In Man-
chester, the hall had been filled with rough characters present
for the express purpose of preventing the speech with shouts,
groans, stamping, catcalls, anything that would keep him from
being heard. But he had persisted. He had talked above the
uproar, and insisted until the clamor died down, and at last he
had spoken for an hour and been rewarded with thunderous
applause.

He met another demonstration by proslavery elements in
Liverpool, and it had been an hour and a half before he could
be heard above the pandemonium.

Presenting fine shades of meaning in such circumstances had
been a good deal like "driving a team of run-away horses and
making love to a lady at the same time," Henry said. But now
he could tell Harriet that the sympathy of the British working-
man was swinging completely to the cause of the North, in spite
of the hardships the Northern blockade was causing him. Because
of this, the efforts of proslavery forces in England to get Parliament to recognize the Confederacy had finally been dropped.

Harriet was very proud of her brother. How well he deserved
the ovation the people of Brooklyn and New York had given him
on his return! She would be even prouder of another honor still

to come. A few months later, Lincoln, after reading the speeches, would tell his Cabinet that if the war were ever fought to a successful conclusion, there would be but one man—Beecher—to raise the flag at Fort Sumter, for without Beecher in England there might have been no flag to raise! And she would never give a thought to how much she herself might have contributed to Henry's success in Great Britain, never pause to remember that it was her own *Uncle Tom's Cabin* that had first roused the British working class to sympathy with the slave. The emotions that book had awakened in the hearts of the poor had not been forgotten by them, as they seemed to have been by the statesmen there. It was Mrs. "Beecher-Stowe" who had paved the way for Henry Ward Beecher. But how could she have cared for that? She and Henry and antislavery people everywhere were all one, fighting for the same cause.

Henry told her another bit of news quite casually. He was giving up the editorship of the *Independent*. It seemed perfectly reasonable to her that he should, burdened with commitments as he was. Henry gave the impression that it was some disagreement about advertising policies between him and Henry G. Bowen, who owned the paper, that had led to the parting of the ways. Henry would certainly never tell his sister Hattie, and there was no one else to tell her either, that there might be a deeper, more tangled reason for his sudden departure from the paper to which he had contributed, and which he had influenced for so long. It would be ten years and more before a story about a deathbed confession Henry Bowen's young and beautiful wife had made would become public, ten years and more before that story and other evidences of Henry's passionate nature manifesting itself privately, as well as publicly, would erupt into a national scandal. And even when that story and a dozen others clamored in Harriet's ears, she would not believe them, not of Henry, her incomparable younger brother. Just now she simply accepted the fact that he was no longer connected with the *Independent* and that Theodore Tilton was editor in chief in his place. With things changed in that fashion, she decided she might as well sever her connection with the paper. She had as many markets as she wanted for her work.

She collected Freddie's belongings, and she and Freddie boarded the train for Andover and the family celebration that was being planned for the return of "their soldier boy."

Had she had any hints in New York as to something more than a head wound that was troubling her soldiering son as a result of his services in behalf of her cause? Had there been any smell of liquor on his breath, any vague incoherence of speech to momentarily bewilder her? If there had been, she pushed them away from her. He was still in New York, seeing army friends, close in spirit to his wartime experiences. Once he was home, everything would be all right. If he had, once or twice, in the days they were in New York together, been drinking alcoholic stimulants to excess, there were all sorts of excuses for it, and all sorts of equally valid reasons why it was only a temporary and most uncharacteristic kind of behavior. Then they came home to the happy greetings of Calvin, the twins and Georgie and young Charley, and there was the festive dinner as planned, and various neighborhood celebrations in honor of Freddie's return.

The scene Harriet could never bear to remember occurred at one of these—a happy company of family and neighbors all together. Suddenly there was Freddie—unmistakably and beyond the hope of anyone's overlooking it—so intoxicated he could scarcely stand or speak.

Stunned, Harriet tried to believe it was the effect of liquor on a system still weakened by the wound he had received. It would not happen again, it could not, not to a son of hers, not to a grandson of Lyman Beecher, one of the founders of the Temperance movement, not to a member of a family that had always been abstemious.

But it did happen, again and again. It made no difference that the family's supply of wine and liquor, even the medicinal brandy, was quietly banished by Harriet. It made no difference that no liquor was served or available at the homes of neighbors or friends. There were other places in Andover for Frederick Stowe to get the stimulant for which he seemed to have a desperate craving. There were stores that sold spirits. There were

saloons and taverns to which the lowest riffraff went, and Freddie
Stowe went there too.

He was not happy in the grip of this need. There were times
when he seemed to suffer more than Harriet or Calvin or the
rest of his bewildered family. There were private scenes with
Harriet, and with Calvin, scenes of terrible remorse and earnest
resolution, so earnest that Harriet and Calvin were bound to
believe that things would indeed be different.

Fred would remain sober for a few days, or a week or so, and
Harriet would fuss over the head wound that was slowly healing.
They would talk of his returning to medical studies, and he
would get out the papers and books he had from the few months
at Harvard Medical School. And then, just when it seemed all
was well, off he would go again, to come home lurching, vague
and unfocused.

"The more of manliness there yet is left in man in these circumstances, the more torture. The more sense of honor, love of
reputation, love of friends, conscience in duty, the more anguish.
. . ." So Harriet wrote, years later, when she was finally able
to put a character who suffered from alcoholism into one of her
books. And she would write also of "the fear, and terror, and
lingering agony" of those who watched the "slow fulfilment of
doom." And by then she had a surprising amount of insight into
the kind of sickness alcoholism is.

But it was new and terrible and bewildering in the first months
Fred was home. Harriet wrote her lively, affectionate "House
and Home Papers" for the *Atlantic Monthly,* and she journeyed
to Hartford to see if any progress was being made on the house
there, in spite of the winter weather. She took on another writing
assignment, for a religious magazine, a series of biographical
sketches called "Men of Our Times." But whatever concerned
her, underneath there was always the worry about Fred.

Full-time work on the house in Hartford was resumed in the
spring. Harriet went in April to stay and do what she could to
hurry the completion. Enough of the house was finished to justify
sending on the household goods from Andover by the first of May.
A thousand things remained to be done to make it the house of

Harriet's dreams, and everything was costing a great deal more than she had expected, confirming Calvin's gloomy predictions. She realized she would have to write furiously to keep up with the ever-mounting bills.

Then there were the ambitions of her youngest son, Charley, to cope with. At fourteen, Charley was suddenly seized with the desire to go to sea. There was a war going on; gunboats and blockade-runners filled the coastal waters. Still, Harriet allowed herself to be persuaded by her eager, sturdy adolescent, and found a berth for him in the crew of a Boston sailing vessel bound for the Mediterranean.

The war seemed to be going on in another world for Harriet by now. In March 1864, Lincoln saluted the tough and persistent general who kept winning battles in the West, and made him General in Chief of the armies of the United States. Then Ulysses S. Grant came east and began his long and costly efforts to bludgeon Lee and his army into submission, habitually wearing, as he did so, "an expression as if he had determined to drive his head through a brick wall." There was something very close to a brick wall when the Virginia Wilderness was again the scene of battle, and the North lost more than seventeen thousand men as Grant and Lee struggled. Only a few days later, Grant slammed his head against the wall again at Spotsylvania, and lost thirty-one thousand more men. Grim and unshaken, he said, "I . . . propose to fight it out on this line if it takes all summer."

Harriet read the war dispatches in the papers and sighed. There was news in July from the South, where Sherman was besieging Atlanta. But dreadful as all the news was, it was not her war anymore. It had finally and completely stopped being her war when Freddie was discharged and she had brought him home and discovered that wound more grievous than any wound from a shell.

She packed young Charley off for his voyage at sea, and she and Calvin went to the coast for some quickening ocean breezes. Harriet wrote Mr. Fields she hoped they would refresh her and help her in her plan to "write and write, write and forward these chats as fast as possible, and then keep right on till *all* are done."

An idea for another book came to her. In the past she had taken her inspiration from many things that affected her personally—slavery, sister Catherine's tragedy, the conflicts of the old harsh religion, sunny days in Italy. Now, for the first time she was taking her inspiration from Calvin, the anxious, kindhearted, erudite visionary who had been her companion so long. Calvin had always been a mine of odd New England legends, tales of witchcraft and haunted houses and all the curiosa that ran like counterpoint to the forthright daylight of the New England scene. It was like Harriet to be seized just at this time with the idea of tying all those legends together within a loose framework of story and making a book. The mystic melancholy that tinged the legends was very much in keeping with the kind that was beginning to pervade a country saddened by three years of war.

Then she put the idea aside for a while. "I do not feel the public mind is just now in a state for a story," she wrote James Fields. "It is troubled, unsettled, burdened with war. . . . Home is the thing we must strike for now, for it is here we must strengthen the things that remain." So instead of beginning a new book, she continued her "House and Home Papers" and the biographical sketches of "Men of Our Times," and she took on an assignment to write for a new juvenile magazine, *Our Young Folks,* which would ultimately be absorbed by *St. Nicholas Magazine.*

Now that she had moved into the new house, full of richness and elaboration, she was able at last to make another move, one that once would have seemed unthinkable—from the church she had known all her life to a new kind of house of worship. One way and another, she had been preparing for the move for a long time. The European cathedrals had enchanted her with their soaring arches and spires. The rituals full of sonorous poetry had moved her. All had been preparing her. "There is some part of man that calls for such a service," she had written home from Europe in 1852. Certainly there was some part of her that called for a service to help her feel the beauty in religion, rather than one to knot the brain with logic. Something that would help her know the beauty of faith was what she had needed and wept for through the tormented years of her adolescence.

So she joined the Protestant Episcopal Church in Hartford, which the twins had already joined. Calvin was no longer connected with any Presbyterian or Congregational school. Her father, stout defender of the old faith, was gone. There were no considerations to prevent her, no apologies she needed to make. She picked up her prayer book, made the sign of the cross and knelt to worship in a house of God where the strength of ritual sustained her. She was back in the faith of her mother. The catechism of that faith was the first one she had learned, as a girl of five, long ago in Nutplains.

A grace note to the move was the fact that her daughter Georgie, twenty-one this year, was entertaining her first real beau, an engaging and intelligent young man who was an Episcopal clergyman. Seeing that in spite of her "ballet of the cat with the mouse," Georgiana did seem to be truly impressed by the young Reverend Allen, Harriet could not help feeling that *some* things worked themselves out in a satisfying way.

"Burdened with the war" that seemed as though it would never end, the North was approaching the Presidential elections of 1864. Defeatists were charging Lincoln with prolonging the war for his own purposes, and they were agitating for any kind of peace. Lincoln was pondering what he could do to save the Union between the time of his defeat in the election and the inauguration of his successor, because he was convinced that any successor would have "secured his election on such ground that he cannot possibly save it afterward."

Then Sherman captured Atlanta and began his march to the sea. The mood in the North changed. Lincoln was elected. Late in December, Sherman wired Lincoln that he had captured Savannah for him, as a Christmas present.

Harriet wrote her children's stories and "struck for the home" with her "House and Home Papers," and was delighted when Georgie and the Reverend Allen announced their engagement. She caught her breath in dread every time Freddie left the house, and only felt the dread leave her when he came home again, sober. The war might seem remote, but it had left its mark on her and hers. And suddenly, another cheerful "House and Home Paper" planned, she would find herself writing instead an article that was "an offering of sympathy to the suffering and agonized whose homes have been forever darkened." At least hers had not been *forever* darkened, she told herself. Fred *would* conquer his terrible craving. He wanted to. With a will, there would be a way.

Charley was home from his sea voyaging at Thanksgiving, "with the same boy's face, but with hands so spread with hard work that they looked twice too big for him." He had had a hard voyage, doing a full man's work, but Harriet could not see that "the radical passion for the sea" had much abated. "Unfortunate is the hen who hatches a duck," she said cheerfully.

The chief diversion of the winter was planning and preparing for Georgie's wedding next August. When Harriet was not writing, or tending the plants in her new conservatory, or in some other way engaged, there was the trousseau to be considered, and long lengths of silk and velvet, muslin or brocade to admire and discuss.

General Grant suddenly emerged from his long winter quiet in the spring and began beating his head and his army against Lee. And all at once the Confederate forces were no longer a brick wall. Despair and defeatism were riddling the Southern giant, as they had shaken the Northern giant the summer before. No country abroad was supporting the Southern cause. The army was starving and exhausted. The will to victory was dying. On April 9, with Grant and his army pursuing Lee and the Southerners, Sheridan brought up his army to cut off any escape to the South. On April 9, with an abruptness that made the fact difficult to grasp, it was all over. Lee was signing the terms of surrender in Appomattox Court House.

It was over. The Southern giant, defeated, had given up the dream of independence. There were not two giants, but one, who had suffered some hideous emotional schism. One giant so weakened by the struggle that recovery would take a long time.

It was not a moment for rejoicing. It was a time for relief and gratitude that the slaughter had ended, and a time to listen to

Lincoln as he reiterated what he had been saying since 1861, that he was President of the United States and as such he could have no thought of conqueror and conquered. The rebellion must be forgotten as quickly as possible, and each Southern state would be readmitted to full privileges of Union as soon as ten percent of her white citizens had taken the oath of allegiance.

The Beecher family knew a time of pride as Henry Ward Beecher journeyed South on a gunboat to make the address at the raising of the United States flag over Fort Sumter, just as Lincoln had declared he must do in the event of a successful issue of the war.

Then on April 15 there came the news that Lincoln had been assassinated. The war was over, the day of the jubilee had come, but where in all the land was there anyone who could feel jubilation now?

For the living, life went on.

Preparations for a wedding filled the big house in Hartford, which Harriet liked to call Oakholm. Carpenters, upholsterers and dressmakers were all about. Georgie and her clergyman, Henry Allen, had impetuously decided to be married in June instead of August, and Harriet was obsessed with a need to have everything in the new home perfect for the wedding. Everything that was still unfinished must be completed at once. Oakholm was a symbol to her, of her victory over poverty and all that was bleak, unimaginative and bare. Panelings and draperies, carpeting and paintings and bits of statuary, must be hurried into their proper places. She wanted the conservatory to be a mass of foliage and bloom, and the fountain playing as brightly as any in Italy. She wanted the grounds to be beautiful with roses and blossoming trees and green lawns creating vistas wherever one looked.

So the wedding was "an absorbing whirlpool" to Harriet for a month and more. And when the event took place, all the time she had snatched from her writing seemed justified. The wedding day was perfect. The house, rich and splendid, was filled with flowers and guests. The bride in her wide and billowing hoops of white satin was as beautiful as a bride could be, and her husband a handsome and modest bridegroom.

It was a day, an occasion, to bring a flush to Harriet's cheeks, and make her eyes as wide and lustrous as Georgie's. It was a day that, in a very special way, crowned her successes both as a writer and a mother, and she swooped through the crowded rooms in her wide crinolines, as gay as such a day of jubilee decreed.

But when the bride and bridegroom had finally driven away, when all the guests were gone, and only the family remained, there was something less than perfect peace even at Oakholm.

There were, on the most mundane of levels, sheafs of bills that would keep Harriet at her writing desk for months, as she sought to keep pace with the cost of her mansion. When she looked beyond her domestic circle of home and family and writing, she was wrestling with a kind of vindictiveness quite new to her. She felt a vengefulness against the conspirators who had killed Lincoln, a rage against the whole South, implicated somehow, she felt, in Lincoln's assassination. And far beyond that, or so it seemed to her just now, the South was responsible for all the long agony of killing and maiming in the war.

And the beautiful house itself was haunted by a ghost who filled Harriet with sadness whenever she looked at him—the ghost of a slight, excited young lieutenant who had ridden into battle at Gettysburg, but who was now a bewildered, frightened man, caught in the grip of a sickness Harriet had no notion how to cure. By heroic efforts, Freddie had managed to stay sober for Georgiana's wedding. But in no time afterward, he was drunk again.

Chapter 29

They were the years that should have been years of convalescence for the whole country, years when the so nearly severed
half should have been knit back with the whole, every shock
that would aggravate the open wound avoided. A certain number of states had declared themselves outside of the Union. In
a dreadful war, they had been defeated. Had it not been a war
to prove they could not disengage themselves from the Union?

According to Lincoln, it had. According to Lincoln, "Finding
themselves safely at home, it would be utterly immaterial
whether they had ever been abroad." The whole thing was to
"get them into their proper practical relation" with the Union
again. Let the nerves and bones that had been broken be placed
in their proper places, let healthy, healing impulses start flowing
back and forth, let the blood start circulating, North and South,
until there was at last one whole and mended body.

But Lincoln was gone.

Andrew Johnson, stubborn, lonely, with few friends and less
prestige, did his best and failed. Then there was the war hero,
Grant, for President, and he did not even try. He knew how to
"beat his head against a stone wall," until he battered the wall
down, but when the South was no longer an enemy to conquer
on the field, he had no notion what to do with it, and only wanted
to forget it.

Instead of the wound being eased and coaxed into healing,
it was exacerbated and irritated and made so much deeper, it
was a wonder the Southern giant did not wither and die, an
atrophied, useless portion of the body.

1865 . . . 1866 . . . 1867 . . . In any struggle, the will to sur-
vive must release and even benefit from the most extreme and

basic passions. The extreme passions of the Radical Republicans
had served a purpose during the war, stiffening the Northern will
to fight. But the war over, those passions were running wild.

Ironies abounded. Radical Republicans, who, ten years before,
had been crying that secession was illegal and that the South
could not secede, now screamed that the South was a conquered
province that had forfeited all rights in the Union. Southerners,
on the other hand, who ten years before had shrieked to heaven
of their right to leave the Union, now clamored for their privileges in a Union they had "irrevocably dissolved."

But the power, of course, was with the side that had won the
war. And the taste of power was intoxicating. Let there be more
and more power! The wild ones, the extreme ones, the ones
who saw nothing but the fact that the North had won in battle,
thought they saw how to get it. Give the freed Negroes of the
South the vote. If the Southern states were allowed back in the
Union without the hobble of the Negro vote, it was inevitable
that they would send a solidly Democratic contingent to Congress again, just as they had before the war. And a solidly Democratic contingent from the South could undo all the pleasing
and profitable legislation in regard to the tariff and banking and
railroads, which the Republicans had achieved in their heyday.
But give the Negro the vote, and a Republican majority would
be more than safe, insured by the millions of votes of the freedmen who owed their freedom to the Republicans. It was nothing
to the wild ones, urging this Negro franchise, that most of the
Negroes of the South were illiterate, with no notion of how to
use a ballot. They could be taught enough to vote Republican.

"The Negro must have the vote," they insisted. And in the
North there were humanitarians and liberals, firmly committed
to justice for the black man, who shut their ears to any hint that
there might be selfish motivations in this demand of the radicals.
Theodore Tilton, the idealistic young editor of the *Independent*,
ran a new slogan on the masthead of the paper: "The slave a
man, the man a citizen; the citizen a voter." It was easy for the
radicals, draped in the mantle of justice, to hide their real goal
from many. Horace Greeley, always in the liberal vanguard, was

for immediate suffrage for the Negro. Edward Beecher, who had helped Elijah Lovejoy long ago in Illinois, was for it also.

But Harriet Beecher Stowe was not so sure. She had gradually lost her vindictiveness toward the South in the months after the war ended—vindictiveness was never very lasting with her—and was following her brother Henry Ward Beecher's course.

"Henry takes the ground," she was writing her friend, the Duchess of Argyll, "that it is unwise and impolitic to endeavor to force negro suffrage on the South at the point of a bayonet. His policy would be, to hold over the negro the protection of our Freedmen's Bureau until the great laws of free labor shall begin to draw the master and servant together; to endeavor to soothe and conciliate, and win to act with us, a party composed of the really good men of the South. . . . Charles Sumner is looking simply at the abstract *right* of the thing. Henry looks at actual probabilities. We all know that the state of society at the South is such that laws are a very inadequate protection even to white men. Southern elections always have been scenes of mob violence *when only white men voted*. . . . If negro suffrage were required as a condition of acquiring political position, there is no doubt the slave States would grant it; grant it nominally, because they would know that the grant never could or would become an actual realization. And what would then be gained for the negro? . . ."

Harriet Beecher Stowe was looking at the South and its problems with more tolerance and understanding, forgetting the atrocity stories she had heard during the war, remembering the Negroes she had known, in Cincinnati. She knew they needed schooling, education, practical experience in fending for themselves before they were grafted, all unprepared, into a brandnew role in the body politic.

In the South, the wounded South, there were men ready to accept the fact that one principle they had fought for was dead. The slave was not a piece of property, but a man. They were ready to do what they could to help him move toward meeting his new responsibilities, they were ready to start schools for him, help him find a new place in society.

But the Radical Republicans had their way. And now, between the newly joined halves of the Union, began a new sort of traffic, not a healthy back-and-forth circulation, but a furious coursing toward the South of all those elements most likely to incite fever. Military governors traveled southward, to "restore order" in the "conquered provinces," and with them went Federal troops. Drifting, scheming men, sensing brand-new innocents to exploit, and political spoils to gain, packed their carpetbags and headed for the South. An era began in the South when no man could vote who had been an officer in the Confederate army, or who had held office in the Confederate government, or who had ever held any Federal office before 1861, including coroners, constables and sextons of cemeteries—but every Negro could. An era began when the most cynical and calloused elements of the North ruled the South for one purpose alone, individual gain.

But corruption, extravagance, cynicism released into the Northern bloodstream in the struggles of the war did not all drain southward. There were enough and more to flush the victorious Northern half of the Union with unwonted opulence. Any man cunning enough, daring enough, could make a fortune, as the North flung itself into a frenzy of railroad building, mining, timbering, factory building, oil-well drilling, all the activities the war had proved so easy and profitable. The North had not had any of its physical resources harmed, as the South had. It was as though the North had just begun to discover them, and just begun to discover what unhampered exploitation of them could mean.

Politics paid in the North too. In New York City, William Marcy Tweed, Grand Sachem of the Tammany Ring, was managing to steal seventy-five million dollars from the city in the little space of two years, simply by having all contractors doing work for the city double their bills and then hand him the overcharge. While this was going on, an appropriate number of city and state officials were growing rich on the necessary bribe money.

There was a wasting fever in the South. There was a raging, euphoric fever of overstimulation in the North. With such fevers burning, of course men began to think somewhat differently, to find their visions blurred in certain directions, to discover in themselves strange, new appetites that could be satisfied as no one had ever dreamed. With such fevers burning, a President could come within one vote of being impeached, merely for trying to uphold the Constitution; a couple of unscrupulous men named Jay Gould and Jim Fisk could print their own stock for a railroad and sell the stock interminably, their only worry being whether the printing press would break down; with such fevers burning, anybody, anywhere, could find himself talking publicly about things that would have seemed the rantings of delirium, ten years before.

Free love, for instance. It was hardly to preach and practice free love that Isabella Beecher Hooker, Harriet's handsome half sister, had recently joined with Elizabeth Cady Stanton, Susan B. Anthony, and the other respectable, if aggressive, women who had begun to agitate for women's rights some twenty years before. They, and she, wanted women as well as Negroes to be citizens with a right to own property, serve on juries, and vote. It was part of the same urge to better the world and to right injustice which had been the main impetus of the antislavery movement. Free love? None of those sober, decent women dreamed of such a thing.

But somehow or other, extremists and radicals climbing aboard the women's rights bandwagon, were entangling the right to practice free love with the other basic rights women were demanding, and what newspaper reader could resist the pleasant shock of making that the *whole* issue?

Two energetic sisters, Tennessee Claflin and Victoria Claflin Woodhull, were foremost in capturing everyone's attention. Given to visions, disciples of spiritualism, devotees of magnetic healing, they had come out of the West after the war, with a varied entourage which included a lover and ex-husband of Victoria's. Somehow they had won the confidence of old Commodore Cornelius Vanderbilt in New York. It was Tennessee (she often spelled it Tennie C.) who became the Commodore's special pet, and he would have married her if he could. Instead, he was persuaded to establish both Tennie C. and Victoria as stockbrokers, with a fine office on Broad Street. Soon they had their own weekly magazine as well. In the magazine they could expound on every subject that interested them—spiritualism, magnetic healing, Communism (their weekly was the first in America to publish Karl Marx's Manifesto), and free love. Victoria paid not the slightest attention to the old taboo about women speaking in public, and was a talented and spellbinding orator in behalf of all her causes.

Decent people might shudder, decent people might think Victoria Woodhull a disgrace to womankind, but decent people were suddenly *talking* about the subjects she flaunted before them. And Victoria and Tennessee were getting rich. Even on Black Friday, September 24, 1869, when the gold market collapsed, thanks to some more Gould and Fisk shenanigans, the panic that swept Wall Street hardly touched them, shielded as they were by their connection with Commodore Vanderbilt.

It was another world from the one people had known before the war, a world in which Harriet Beecher Stowe herself could have a kind of Black Friday of her own in 1869, when all the gold of her success almost turned to dross—a world in which the Claflin sisters would suddenly cross her path, and Henry Ward Beecher's too, wreaking destruction as they happily denounced everything they thought "humbug," in a raging fever of euphoria and progress.

Chapter 30

Room fragrant with violets, banked up in hyacinths, flowers everywhere, windows open, birds singing . . .

1866–1869

Fred's trouble was what led Harriet to Florida and to a new enterprise there. For once he had come home from one of his excursions to a Hartford tavern with something more than too much to drink. He had met with two young veterans of the war who had told him an interesting story. At the end of the war they had been mustered out in Florida, where they had been impressed by the possibilities of growing cotton. Land was cheap. There were plenty of ex-slaves willing to work for very little. As a result, they had rented a big, rundown "plantation" and tried to reestablish it. However, their money had run out before much progress could be made, and so they were home again in Connecticut, looking for other ex-servicemen to join them and add their money to the venture.

"Laurel Grove Plantation" was the name of the place, Fred told his mother. It was on the west bank of the St. Johns River, a wide and beautiful river that ran northward from the interior of Florida to the sea, at Jacksonville. The men, farmers bred, were sure a cotton plantation in that location could become a profitable enterprise in a very short time, once they had sufficient capital to hire enough workers. If Fred felt a thrill of interest in the project, he hardly dared to voice it. What capital had he, still living at home, dependent on the bounty of his mother and father?

But Harriet caught fire with the idea, leaping to the conclusion that the project was just the thing to cure Fred's difficulties.

What could be better for him than a healthful outdoor life on a plantation, far from the temptations of city taverns? Echoes of Lyman's old preachments in favor of physical exertion, memories of her own long-ago physical activities at the water-cure establishment, merged to make the plantation idea seem ideal. To make it even more reasonable for her to invest in such a venture and send Fred to oversee it, she saw it as a project that offered decent employment to ex-slaves and helped the Negro, in whose cause she had spoken, at an especially critical time.

She suggested that Fred invite the young men he had met to Oakholm, so she could discuss the venture with them. She had money to invest. Perhaps she might be able to advance the whole amount of capital needed, in which case, Fred could become the superintendent of the venture.

The young men came to see her. She was soft-voiced as always, but as firm and imperious as she had learned how to be. In no time it was arranged as she wished. Within a month Fred was packed and gone, to seek a new life in Florida.

Harriet saw him off feeling happier about him than she had since his return from the war, and wishing with all her heart that she was going with him. It had been a long time since she had taken a trip. The new land as described by the young men beckoned her enticingly, full of sunshine and flowers. The new venture intrigued her.

But there were a thousand things she had to do before she could think of a journey anywhere. She could draw upon the investments Thomas Perkins had made for her for money to invest in the Laurel Grove Plantation, but it was hardly right to do that for the day-to-day running expenses of her family and her home. And the running expenses of Oakholm were more than just running—they were racing, constantly threatening to get completely beyond her control. What had gone wrong? In spite of her careful overseeing of its construction, had careless contractors used inferior materials, shoddy workmanship? It was impossible to know, but pipes were forever bursting, windows jamming, cellars flooding, and other wholly undreamed of difficulties were always arising. When bills for repairs were added to the high cost of simply maintaining the house, the lawns, and the greenhouse, the result was staggering.

Calvin had predicted the house would be too much for them from the beginning. As the difficulties mounted, his gloom was becoming insupportable. He had talked of the poorhouse and a penniless old age before Harriet's success. Now he dwelt on those themes incessantly.

Partly to divert him, and partly because she really had a deep pride in his learning, Harriet began urging her husband into working on and completing the magnum opus that was to have filled his days after leaving Andover. She had James Fields's help in these efforts. Mr. Fields had written to Calvin telling him he was eager to publish any work of his on the history of the books of the Bible, and after that Harriet had been happy to see Calvin applying himself to its composition. By the time the wonderful opportunity for Fred came along, Calvin had actually completed two-thirds of the proposed work. But Harriet knew she did not dare relax her prodding till it was finally complete, and now she thought of a new scheme for urging Calvin on.

"Mr. Stowe and I shall come to Boston next week," she wrote Mr. Fields. "He will bring two thirds of the volume ready for the printer and engage to furnish the other third as fast as it is needed. . . . In regard to Mr. Stowe, you must not scare him off by grimly declaring that you must have the *whole manuscript complete* before you set the printer to work. You must take the three quarters he brings you and at least make believe begin printing, and he will immediately go to work and finish up the whole; otherwise, what with lectures and the original sin of laziness, it will all be indefinitely postponed. I want to make a crisis, that he shall feel that *now* is the accepted time, and that this must be finished first and foremost."

So she had to forgo any journeying if Calvin's book was to be finished, and beyond that, with all the bills to be paid, there was no need to manufacture a crisis for herself.

She had finished the magazine assignment of biographical sketches on the "Men of Our Times." To what writing project should she turn next? She remembered the idea that had come to her during the war years, a book based on the tales and legends that were Calvin's heritage from Natick, Massachusetts. She wrote to Mr. Fields about it, and he responded enthusiastically. He had not had a novel from Harriet Beecher Stowe since 1862, when he had published the romantic *Agnes of Sorrento*. Since then there had only been the "House and Home Papers," which had gradually come to be called "Chimney Corner Papers."

So Harriet began the book that would ultimately be *Oldtown Folks*. But this, she soon discovered, was a labor of love, unlike the journeyman writing she did for the "House and Home" sketches, or the biographical pieces. The story went slowly. She liked to let it linger in her mind, developing as it would. What else could she write, better yet, what had she already written, that might be turned into money? She remembered all the poems and hymns she had written, and published in her columns, and wrote to Mr. Fields suggesting that he publish a collection of these.

This time Mr. Fields responded reluctantly, almost as reluctantly as he had about *Agnes of Sorrento*. The truth was that although Harriet could spin out rhymes as easily as she could columns of everyday comment, she was not really a poet, but a sentimental versifier. Fields, who had known the weakness of *Agnes*, knew the weakness of Harriet's poetry, too. But just as she had doted on *Agnes*, seeing no fault in it, so she doted on her poetry. Hundreds of women had written her during the years, thanking her for it, telling her it expressed just what they felt. She insisted on the poetry collection to Mr. Fields, and Mr. Fields bowed to her determination.

With the winter, came letters from Fred down in Florida, where the sun shone and the air was mild. The letters sounded optimistic and eager. He and his partners were hiring laborers and making all sorts of plans. Harriet was very pleased and more than ever eager to travel to Florida to see it for herself. But still there was too much to do, too many bills to be paid.

She allowed herself a quick trip to New York to visit the Howards, and an extra pleasure in any Brooklyn visit was the opportunity to see and talk with Henry and hear the latest news about his activities. On this visit, he told her that he had contracted to write a novel, and Harriet was dazzled to hear that he was receiving twenty-five thousand dollars for it, an absolutely unheard-of sum. But no jealousy of her famous brother seemed to enter her heart. If Henry Ward suddenly decided to enter the field of fiction—her field—and if, in so doing, he was at once offered a price greater than any even she commanded for a serial story, it was undoubtedly as it should be. Only one thing hurt her a little. His story, *Norwood*, was a New England story also, like the one she herself was writing. She would have liked to read some of his pages and to share her manuscript with him. But Henry thought it would be better if they both kept their writing to themselves until they were finished. If anyone felt some hidden streak of jealousy, perhaps it was Henry. He was always glad to see Harriet, yet he never seemed to have much time for her, and only rarely since her great success had she been invited to stay at *his* house while she was in Brooklyn. But Harriet never even hinted that she felt a slight. Whatever Henry Ward did was perfect. She would not allow him an unworthy emotion.

Harriet buckled down to her story when she returned home, and dreamed of Florida. It was a day calling for celebration when Calvin finally, at last, and completely, finished his huge Biblical history. Harriet's pleasure was not dampened even when he gloomily insisted the book would be a massive financial failure.

A brand-new opportunity to make money arose fortuitously enough in Hartford. Ever since the war, the subscription book business had been booming. Book salesmen took to country roads all over America and sold farmers' wives large volumes lavishly illustrated with steel engravings to ornament their parlor tables and give witness to the culture of their homes. Hartford had become the publishing center of that boom, with more publishing houses being established every year. How long could such publishers overlook the name of Stowe, particularly when the famous Mrs. Stowe was a resident of Hartford?

Calvin and Harriet both were asked by an energetic representative to write books for the Hartford Publishing Company, and neither book sounded as though it would be difficult to produce. The representative suggested to Calvin that he make a collection of his old sermons and lectures, and promised the resulting book would sell one hundred thousand copies—every book the company published did that, or better. Harriet bethought herself of the biographical sketches of "Men of Our Times," which Mr. Fields had not cared to publish as a book, and was delighted by the vision of royalties from one hundred thousand copies rolling in, with no further work on her part. Unfortunately it was not to be so easy. Before long, the publishing company discovered the sketches Harriet had written would not be sufficient for a full-length book. A dozen or more new sketches would be needed, and those already written needed expanding.

Oldtown Folks was still far from completion although Mr. Fields had advanced her a great deal of money on it. The publishing company wanted *Men of Our Times* as soon as possible— if not by the spring, by fall at the very latest.

Was Harriet never going to have the chance to see the wonders Fred wrote about—the wide sweep of the St. Johns River, almost an inland sea at the bend where Laurel Grove was located, the fabulous live oaks, the orange trees—never feel the Florida sun warm on her head in midwinter?

Suddenly Harriet—who had always loved the winters of New England, who had bloomed like a Christmas rose in the snowball fights at the Vermont water-cure, who had scribbled half of *Uncle Tom's Cabin* while the icy winds of Brunswick whistled around the house—found she could not think in cold weather. It was impossible to write when she was forever in the state of a "froze and thawed apple." She had to go south.

She was simply Harriet, the runaway, again, fleeing obligations and commitments, the steady grind of work and responsibility without end, and was going! She would travel by boat from New York to Charleston, South Carolina, and there make a steamer connection that would take her farther south and up the St. Johns River to Laurel Grove.

Since 1852, the very name Harriet Beecher Stowe had been a symbol, south of Mason and Dixon's line, of everything the South detested. In many places, before and during the war, to own, or to read, her infamous book, was to risk being lynched or run out of town. Before the war was over, everyone in the South knew the rhyme of the Richmond sidewalks.

"Go, go, go,
  Ol' Harriet Beecher Stowe—
  We don't want you in Virginny."

Somehow it never occurred to Harriet that she might meet any unpleasantness or lack of welcome in the South now. Happily wondering if it was really possible she would be needing the light summer dresses she was packing, she made ready for the trip, and then took off for New York and the steamer.

In just a few days, there was Charleston!

"Could I tell you one-half what I have seen and see!" she wrote lyrically to Annie Fields. "Room fragrant with violets, banked up in hyacinths, flowers everywhere, windows open, birds singing!" Harriet felt the same warmth and beauty she had known in Italy.

And her lack of concern about the kind of welcome she would receive was surprisingly justified. No one was hostile. No one spoke unkindly. It was 1867. Charleston was still slowly, painfully, digging itself out of the rubble and destruction the war had left. The heartbreak, the tension and conflict of radical reconstruction were all around. But everyone was friendly.

Harriet looked about her and her heart swelled with sympathy. No letter from there could be wholly a paean to flowers and sunshine.

"I wish you could know of the sorrow and suffering I see, among people that one cannot help pitying," she went on to Annie. "Yet a brighter day is breaking for both *white* and black," she concluded firmly and optimistically.

Then she boarded the steamer and went on to Florida, and up the wide river with its green banks, and she was in the South beyond the ravages of the war and could give herself up completely to its spell.

Fred met her at the steamer landing at Mandarin, a settlement on the eastern bank, across the river from Laurel Grove Plantation. He looked tanned and healthy, and dazzling in white linen. Above the landing and the little wharves, the land was a bower of roses and greenery and those great, strange trees, the live oaks, with their huge, umbrella-like spread, and their mystical drapings of Spanish moss. The balmy air, the glossy green foliage, the massed glow of Cherokee roses, and underfoot, the silken, white sand—Harriet took one look, one deep breath, and lost her heart to Florida.

All was not felicity. After Fred had rowed her across the river, it was disappointing to see that the plantation buildings still looked rough and unkempt, and that the fields hardly seemed to have been planted. But she managed to stifle her worry. Fred and his partners were just getting started. They were working with untrained, disorganized labor. It would begin to take shape soon, she told herself. And Fred did look well. Surreptitiously she watched for signs of the old trouble, but either Fred was being very careful, holding himself firmly in check on this, her first visit, or he was actually better. His mother preferred to think that he was better, that the move into open, physical life, away from temptation, was curing him.

Breathing the soft air, gazing out at the pine woods beyond the cleared fields, reveling in the greenery and flowers springing even here, on a rundown plantation, it seemed to her that this was all one needed for earthly well-being, and that all one's cares and anxieties must surely melt away under the warmth of such a beneficent sun.

She took another trip with Fred across the river to Mandarin, where mail for the plantation was left by the Charleston steamer. Rambling up and down the soft sandy roads of the town, she fell even more in love with the village. Her walk brought her to a small, empty house, situated so beautifully she stopped to admire it. From the front of the house, the broad vista of the river was visible. Over the house arched the branches of an ancient live oak. Behind it was a glorious orange grove, the trees starred with golden globes of fruit. The air was full of the scent of orange blossoms, blooming simultaneously with the ripened fruit, and everywhere birds were singing.

Harriet hardly dared admit that what she wanted was to own this little cottage and the land around it for herself. She already had one dream house in the North, a dream house that took all her efforts to keep up with its demands. But someone had to have this cottage in Mandarin, someone she knew, someone in the family. Who? Which one of her brothers and sisters could she persuade? She thought of Charles, in Massachusetts. Charles had cleared himself of the heresy charges brought against him during the war, but he still was not happily settled with any congregation. She thought of her own vague plans to help establish a small church, especially for the local Negroes—an Episcopal church because that church was home to her now, and also because she thought it offered "the best system for training immature minds." A church . . . Charles . . . all began to be worked out in her mind. Charles had only to transfer his allegiance to the Episcopal Church as she had, come south, establish a small church in Mandarin, and *he* could live in this charming house with its view and orange grove. It seemed a perfect solution and she could hardly wait till she went north again and began to convince him.

With her imagination already settling Charles in the cottage, she could not quite give up some share in this pretty town for herself. Wandering farther down the road, she saw another orange grove, bordered by date palms, and found out that grove was for sale also. Perhaps that could be hers and one day she could build a little cottage on the land. Charles just up the road, herself and her family here—the future arranged itself happily in her mind.

The hours in Mandarin were too short. The weeks at Laurel Grove were too short. Suddenly they were over. She was saying good-bye to Fred and was on her way north again. But she was full of plans for returning. There was not the slightest doubt about it. Somehow, some way, she would come back to Mandarin, not just once, but again and again.

The pattern of Harriet's future winters was set for a long time. Just as she hoped, winter after winter she would return to Florida, until finally she, and Calvin too, would seem to be old settlers in Mandarin. In her youth, she and her family had pioneered in what was then the West, and now in her middle years, she was pioneering again, one of the earliest residents of the North to discover Florida as a winter playground.

She wrote to Charles as soon as she was back in Hartford, describing her plans for him. But he could not be swung from the Congregational to the Episcopal Church quite so easily. She did not argue with him. If he would not be persuaded into the Mandarin cottage, she would have to buy it herself, which was what she wanted all along.

Then she had to banish Florida to the back of her mind and *write*. There were the biographical sketches to finish for the subscription book people. There was the New England story, *Oldtown Folks*, and both the sketches and the book were overdue.

She interrupted writing to pack her young son Charley, still avid for a sailor's life, off to sea for another voyage. And then she was back at her desk again, to stay there all summer long, alternating her two assignments, depending on which publisher was urging her more persistently. The subscription book publishers turned out to be the most demanding, and so, before very long, it was *Oldtown Folks* which was pushed aside until the fall. But she wrote brightly to Mr. Fields that it was not cooling, but "boils and bubbles daily and nightly and I am pushing and spurring like fury to get to it."

The surprise of the summer was learning that Calvin's book, *The Origin and the History of the Bible*, so carefully wheedled from him, was selling extremely well. Calvin was first incredulous at the news and then accepted it as a matter of course. His collection of sermons for the subscription book people had already been completed, was published, and reports came that it too was selling nicely. Nodding sagely, Calvin retired among his books and papers, full of a satisfied sense of achievement.

Harriet could enjoy no such retreat. There would be royalties from Calvin's books, and royalties from all of hers still brought them a steady income. But periodically she had to send money to Fred for Laurel Grove Plantation, there was the cottage in Mandarin she was buying, and she had the constant bills for greedy Oakholm.

Men of Our Times was finished at last. She could turn to *Oldtown Folks*, but Mr. Fields, almost despairing of that book by now, suggested that she revise her "Chimney Corner Papers" for immediate publication as a book. She worked on those, and all the while there were her monthly tales for the young people's magazine which must be done somehow.

Christmas brought a short break in the grind of effort. At Christmas, Oakholm seemed to justify its expense, wreathed and decorated, and breathing a summer warmth in the green lushness of the conservatory. Harriet's family was gathered around her. Young Charley was home from the sea, and it was good to hear that his longings for a sailor's life were ended. He was ready to prepare for college as his parents wished. Georgiana and her doting husband were there from Stockbridge, Massachusetts, and Georgie was as gay and sparkling as ever. The twins, cheerful and competent, looked after things in general for their mother. Only Fred was absent, but already Harriet had begun to plan her winter trip to see him and to take possession of the little house in Mandarin. One face and figure forever vanished from the circle caused Harriet to look at the portrait of the young and handsome Henry—the portrait she had had painted soon after his death—and sigh and wish once again that somehow her earnest prayers and efforts would bring her some hint of the true "Biblical spiritualism," so she might have some word from him, "beyond the veil."

Then Christmas was over, and it was time to pick up work on *Oldtown Folks*. Harriet picked it up with little heart, all her thoughts directed toward Florida. Soon she gave up and started making plans. She would take young Charley with her this time, and instead of traveling by sea from New York, they would make the trip as guests of the government on a military train. Friends in Washington had arranged it.

"The little woman who had started the big war," traveling through the South in a government transport that spoke most bitterly of the South's defeat—was it possible she would find again the same lack of vengefulness toward herself that she had met the year before?

It was. She found even more friendliness this time, and met a unique gesture of courtesy in Charleston. Her arrival in that city was heralded in the newspapers and getting off the train, Harriet and Charley were met by an unknown young man. He greeted them in the name of his mother, who hoped they would be her guests while they waited for the St. Johns steamer. Harriet and Charley went with him, to meet a gentle woman in a gracious old Charleston house, a woman eager to meet Mrs. Stowe and to thank her for an act of courtesy and protection tendered her during the war by a young Union officer—a Lieutenant Beecher, one of Harriet's nephews.

Harriet felt a happy glow at this evidence of old enmities being forgotten. The glow increased when she and Charley boarded the St. Johns boat, and met new courtesy at the hands of the captain, a onetime rebel and blockade-runner, who was now showing an almost "pathetic solicitude" for Mrs. Stowe's safety and comfort. Then they came to the Laurel Grove Plantation in Florida. And the happy glow evaporated.

Fred had not even been able to sober up to meet his mother and young brother. He was thin and shaking, his eyes bloodshot, and the plantation was a shambles. Grinning, half-drunk Negroes lounged about in the midst of the confusion. A small amount of cotton had been harvested, but even that had been improperly stored and was spoiled by mildew.

It was ruin she stared at, ruin of all she had hoped for and worked for. She had poured ten thousand dollars into the plantation, but it was not the loss of the money that concerned her. It was Fred's collapse. Fred stared at her with a false defiance that did not hide the terror and bewilderment lurking underneath. He had tried. She knew that. In a sense it was not his fault. He had become "the victim of a sort of periodical insanity in which the power of the will was overwhelmed by a wild, unreasoning impulse."

She took a deep breath and considered what to do. She would not blame all the confusion around her on Fred's condition. The young men who were his partners might know something about farming in Connecticut, but it was clear they knew little about growing cotton. She wondered if there was any way in which she could reorganize the plantation into a productive operation. Day after day, she moved about the buildings and fields, a small, dauntless figure, trying to assess the situation, and she sought out neighboring farmers and anyone else who might be able to tell her what had gone wrong and how it could be righted.

Finally she had to realize that for all her determination, a talent for growing flowers was not enough to help her here. The situation at the plantation was hopeless so far as she was concerned.

She thought of the cottage and land across the river in Mandarin that was hers now. The orange grove there had once been a profitable operation, or so she had been told. Day after day, she had Charley row her across the river to Mandarin while she studied the situation. She looked at the house and considered how it might be enlarged and improved to become livable. She engaged workmen to begin the alterations. She looked at the grove and talked to people who had some knowledge of orange culture.

The air was as balmy as it had been the year before, the flowers as massed and lovely, and the birds sang in the shrubs and trees. But Harriet had no time for such delights this year.

Three months had gone by and Calvin and the girls were writing her plaintively from Hartford. Mr. Fields, in Boston, was wondering why he had heard nothing about the progress of *Oldtown Folks*, why he had heard nothing at all from Mrs. Stowe for so long.

She realized she had done everything she could in Florida at the moment. She said good-bye to the young men at the Laurel Grove Plantation, and wished them the good fortune they needed. She packed up Fred's things and Charley's and her own, and then she and Fred and Charley left for the North.

A sea voyage was her first plan for Fred, after returning to Hartford. A sea voyage would really remove him from temptation and strengthen him in both body and mind. It was impossible for her to take him herself. She simply had to finish *Oldtown Folks* soon. She had to apply herself to earning money from other sources as well. Calvin would have to take Fred.

Calvin, two successful books to his credit, had settled down to a scholar's life, resting massively all day long in his big chair, surrounded by books. He had grown a beard in the last years, a luxuriant frame for the lower half of his face that was in fine contrast to the pale, bald curve of his forehead. He had also taken to wearing a little black skullcap on the top of his bald head, and the whole effect caused Harriet teasingly to call him, "my Rabbi."

It was not easy to coax her Rabbi from the comforts of his chair and study, off into the rigors of a sea voyage. There were sighs and groans and alternate suggestions from him, and then more sighs and frowns when these were rejected. But Harriet had devoted three desperate months to Fred in Florida. It was Calvin's turn.

At last, she could write Annie Fields, "My Rabbi and Fred have gone to the Mediterranean—in a sailing vessel, for the benefit of being at sea." In the quiet house, she could get to work.

By the time Calvin and Fred returned, Harriet had accomplished a good deal. *Oldtown Folks* was almost finished, delayed only because she had taken on other assignments for articles. And because, during the summer, she had not been able to resist delving into the new "planchette boards," which seemed to offer further tantalizing evidence that there *were* some kind of physical manifestations in the world that could only be explained psychically. Perhaps, she thought, this was the way in which she might have a word from Henry some day.

Buoyed up by her busy months, she greeted Calvin and Fred, ready to believe that this time the miracle had been effected. Fred looked much better than when she had brought him North. When she learned that there had been no miracle after all, that Fred had been sober enough on shipboard, but still could not resist the "wild, unreasoning impulse" when on shore, she stiffened her back and started to plan Fred's future anew.

She prevailed upon a young cousin on the Foote side of the family, who had also fought in the war and had still not settled on a career, to take over the management of the orange grove in Mandarin. He and Fred were on their way south by the end of January, and Harriet was hopeful that with the enterprising Spencer Foote in charge, Fred would be moderately safe and that the orange grove might be made to pay.

Oldtown Folks was finished, after more than two years of work. It had turned into a book much longer than she had planned, and was far more profound. "It is more to me than a story," she

wrote Mr. Fields. "It is my resume of the whole spirit and body
of New England." She was rejecting James Fields's idea of serializing it, insisting that it be printed in its entirety. It would take
too long to serialize it, for one thing, and she wanted the book
to have an impact as a whole. Besides, she was not sure the
Atlantic Monthly's readers would altogether appreciate its flavor
of New England Calvinism. She remembered all of Dr. Holmes's
mocking comments on the followers of the old faith that the
Atlantic had published, and while she herself could smile at
the breakdown of the "wonderful one-hoss shay," she was still
loyal to those stern and rugged "orthodox" among whom she
had been raised. "Dr. Holmes has stung and irritated them by
his sharp, scathing irony, and keen ridicule;" she wrote Mr.
Fields, "and after all, they are not ridiculous, and the estimate
of New England life and principles and orthodoxy, as dramatically set forth, must be graver and wider than he has revealed it."

Her faith in *Oldtown Folks* was so great that she also wanted
to make sure it would be copyrighted in England. The law had
been changed somewhat since the publication of *Dred* had neces-
sitated her taking a trip to England for the British copyright.
Now it was only necessary for an author to be standing on
British soil anywhere in the Empire at the moment his British
publisher was taking out a copyright in his name in England.
A quick trip to Canada would enable Harriet to meet that re-
quirement. She would only need to stay there a few days, waiting
till word came by Ocean Telegraph that the copyright had been
secured.

She would not have to go to Canada till the book was off the
presses in May. In the meantime, she could go to Florida again.

Once upon a time, when she had been a slight, unhappy little
schoolteacher of twenty-one, she had felt herself "withered and
exhausted," her emotions all burned out. The years had wheeled
past her since then, twenty, thirty, thirty-five, and with each one,
as new responsibilities had fallen on her, her energy had grown
greater and her emotions had burned more brightly.

"I have worked so hard I am almost tired," she wrote to Fields
now, after a strenuous year of writing and planning for Fred and

Calvin and supervising a home in the North and investments
in the South. "Almost tired." She did know a real and healthy
fatigue as she started south, but it was the fatigue of energy
well used and needing only a brief banking to burst forth again.

The scene in Mandarin was as encouraging this year as the
scene at Laurel Grove had been discouraging the year before.
Spencer Foote had plunged to work with a will. The orange
grove was a busy place, with new trees being planted, other
fruit trees being added, and the packing shed repaired. Everywhere there was evidence that the grove would soon be a functioning enterprise, and Spencer Foote was businessman enough
to have prepared stencils for the orange crates that read: Oranges
from Harriet Beecher Stowe, Mandarin, Fla.

Harriet reveled in the atmosphere of purposeful activity for
almost two months, reveled in the sunshine and the flowers and
trees. Energy flowed back and new plans bubbled in her mind.
The Freedmen's Bureau was erecting a schoolhouse for Negro
children near her land in Mandarin. She was interested at once
and thought of ways in which she could help to make it a good
school for "the poor people whose cause in words" she had once
pleaded.

Then it was time to say good-bye to Fred and Spencer and
head north again. She stopped briefly in Hartford, and then
was on her way again, for she had to be in Canada by mid-
May. Waiting for her train, in Boston, she looked for books to
read during the uneventful days she must spend in Canada
till she had word that the copyright on *Oldtown Folks* was
secured. A new book caught her eye at once—*My Recollections
of Lord Byron*. Ostensibly anonymous, a quotation inside made
it clear that the book had been written by Countess Teresa
Guiccioli, the woman who had been Byron's mistress during
the last years of his life in Italy.

The name "Byron" would always catch Harriet's eye. Lady
Byron had mentioned the Countess to Harriet in the course of
relating some of the events of Byron's life after she had left him.
Harriet had to have this book, written by someone who could
only have seen Byron with a far different vision than her saintly
friend's. What had this immoral, unprincipled Italian made of

the man who had inflicted such a long martyrdom on his wife?
Did she condone him and hold him guiltless? Had Byron made
any confessions to her that showed any remorse on his part?

She began to read the book on the train and continued it in
her hotel room in Canada. And as she read, a dozen conflicting
emotions began to rise in her, shaking her with their intensity.

The Countess was telling again the old, old story, insisting
again, page after page, that it was Lady Byron's cruelty that
had caused Lord Byron's exile, Lady Byron's obdurate silence
in the face of all his pleas for reconciliation that had broken
the poet's heart.

She felt fury at the countess for repeating the story, and
even greater fury at Byron, who had mouthed the lies over and
over to his mistress, even as he fondled her and indulged his
own perversities. There rose in her a rage at life, wherein men
could so distort the truth and trample on the spirits of pure-
hearted women like Lady Byron. Rage, frustration, a surging
up of the old rebellion that had beat through *Uncle Tom's Cabin*,
a surging up of the old fearful fascination with the dark aspects
of lust, which had also found its way into the open in that book—
all these shook her.

But by the time she was ready to go home, she was calm and
purposeful. By the time the Ocean Telegraph wired the news
that the copyright on *Oldtown Folks* had been properly entered
in England, the energy and determination that had been building
since the success of her first great book had asserted themselves.

The true story of Lady Byron's martyrdom and her reasons
for enduring it, had to be told sometime. The lie could not go on
and on. Surely now, with the provocation of this Guiccioli book,
the time was ripe for the truth. "Both were gone," both Lord
Byron and Lady Byron. All who might be injured by the story
were gone. Someone had to step forward and tell the truth "due
to *justice*." If no one else did, then Harriet would have to.

Chapter 31

*I want, not your advice, as to whether the main facts should
be told, for on this point I am so resolved that I frankly say advice
would do me no good. . . . But you might help me . . . to make
the* manner of telling *more perfect.*

1869–1870

Harriet was fifty-eight. But she was not old, certainly not old
as Calvin was. She was still dark-haired, handsome and vibrant,
full of energy and passion. And for her energy she had more
than enough outlets—her writing, her family, her homes, north
and south, and her various enterprises in Florida. But for her
passions it was a different story. She had released them once,
in an irresistible outpouring, in *Uncle Tom's Cabin.* The cause
of the slave, while he was still in bondage, had been another
outlet. Then her idealized love of Lady Byron had been a channel
into which she could pour the "strange, yearning, throbbing feelings" reminiscent of her youth, and all her capacities for wor-
shiping someone who seemed finer than herself.

But Lady Byron had been dead nine years. There was only
her memory to cherish, a memory growing paler even as the
pressed rose from her garden had paled, growing more brittle
each year.

Then, suddenly, the book by the Countess Guiccioli gave Harriet's passions a focus again. Lady Byron was no longer a fading
memory but a near and immediate spirit being slandered anew
by her husband's lies, and gone now where she could not defend
herself even if she wished.

Was no one in England who knew the true story of Lady
Byron's life going to answer the calumnies in the book? Harriet

hardly waited to find out. Somehow, she was sure no one was. The friends who did know the story were dying, one by one. Soon there would be no one to clear the stain from Lady Byron's name.

"Please, Hattie, no," Calvin pleaded, after her return from Canada, when she told him what she planned. "No, no. It can only lead to trouble." But Calvin protested in that fashion about almost any proposal, predicting disaster at the start of any new undertaking. His voice was just an anxious whisper to Harriet, lost in the whirlwind propelling her.

Her idea was simply to write an article stating the facts. The article could be published by the *Atlantic Monthly* in America, and the *Atlantic* could make arrangements to have the same article published in England so the slander could be answered there at the same time.

She began the article with a review of the canards against Lady Byron that were being given new currency by the Countess Guiccioli's book. The Countess was saying once again that Lady Byron was a coldhearted wife who had left her husband for inadequate cause, a wife who had then allowed public sympathy for her to so nearly ruin her husband that he had been driven, "a sensitive victim," to the continent. After that, she had been a wife obdurately silent to all her husband's pleas for an explanation, for forgiveness, or for a reconciliation.

Harriet went on to indicate how very widespread this view of Lady Byron's conduct and character was by recalling conversations she herself had heard as a small child at the breakfast table in Litchfield. She recalled too the way the girls at the Female Academy there had sobbingly sung Byron's lament.

"Fare thee well! and if for ever,
    Still forever, fare thee well;
Even though unforgiving, never
    'Gainst thee shall my heart rebel. . . .

Though my many faults defaced me,
    Could no other arm be found,

Than the one which once embraced me,
To inflict a cureless wound? . . ."

She gave other instances of the way Byron, in his poetry, had
encouraged a picture of a wife who was cool, calculating and
cruel.

"Her favorite science was the mathematical,
Her noblest virtue was her magnanimity. . . .

Some women use their tongues, she *looked* a lecture,
Each eye a sermon and her brow a homily . . ."

Then, having reviewed the general picture of Lady Byron that
seemed so confirmed by her husband's poetry, she came to the
point of her article. "By a singular concurrence of circumstance,"
she knew the *true* story, and knew why Byron had been at such
pains to paint a picture of a wife, overbearing and unforgiving.

In the beginning, when Byron had first met the young lady who
would later become his wife, he had written a far different kind
of poetry to her, Harriet declared, and quoted examples of that
rhapsodical, almost worshipful verse.

"Her spirit seemed as seated on a throne . . ."

But then, he had asked her to marry him, and she had refused
because she was unsure of her ability to cope with a nature as
tumultuous as his. After this refusal, came the disaster. "From the
height which might have made him happy as the husband of a
noble woman, he fell into the depths of a secret adulterous in-
trigue with a blood relation, so near in consanguinity that discovery must have been utter ruin and expulsion from civilized
society."

Thus guardedly Harriet told the secret at last, naming no
names. She had no thought of scandal-mongering as she wrote
the fateful paragraph, no idea of being deliberately salacious.
She *had* to tell the secret of incest to explain why everything that
happened afterward had happened as it did.

"From henceforth this damning guilty secret became the ruling
force in his life, holding him with morbid fascination, yet filling
him with remorse and anguish and insane dread of detection."

All these emotions, Harriet's account continued, then

prompted him to write to several young ladies, proposing marriage. Among the young ladies to whom he wrote was the once-
worshipped one whose "spirit seemed as seated on a throne."
And that one, Anne Isabella Milbanke, having discovered she
did love the reckless and gallant poet enough to try to help him
release the nobility of his nature, wrote him an acceptance of
his proposal, freely expressing her love in her answer. To Byron,
reading her letter, "the discovery of the treasury of affection he
had secured was like a vision of a lost heaven to a soul in hell."

Harriet went on recounting the story just as Lady Byron had
told it to her that shadowy November afternoon in 1856. She told
of the tormented wedding day, with the guilty poet half fainting
at one point, then recovering to cry out in fury at his bride for
marrying him. She told of the young bride's bewilderment and
mounting fear, and her attempts to understand and pacify this
half-demented man. She told of how the poet's awful secret
had at last been revealed to the young wife, and how, shattered
though she was by the revelation, she had rallied her forces to
wrestle for her husband's soul. She told of the way Byron had
resisted his wife's efforts, of how he had launched into long and
terrible defenses of incest, finding philosophical, historical, even
Biblical sanction for it—all, all just as Lady Byron had related it
to her, through the course of that long afternoon.

Then there was the young wife's realization that the awful in-
trigue was still going on—there was Byron's hysterical demand to
her, that she leave him, a demand made even as he sat on the
edge of a bed, the object of his guilty love beside him. There was
the separation at *his* insistence—not hers, as public opinion later
held—and there was, for a while, public opinion turning against
Byron, and his flight to the continent. Byron had written *Manfred*
then, the poem Harriet had innocently quoted to brother Charles
and sister Sarah when she was in Switzerland, the poem that in
certain passages was such a fevered defense of guilty love.

After that Byron had begun his campaign to prove that the
separation from his wife had been her doing and her fault, not
his, and had argued that her silence, no matter how he appealed
to her, was further proof of her cold, unrelenting nature. Her
silence, Harriet cried out now, had been Lady Byron's only way

of protecting the guilty poet and giving him every opportunity
to feel remorse and repent. But repentance was beyond him.
Harriet told of how other women had tried to reason him from
the wild excesses of his life in Europe, Madame de Staël among
them, but Byron could repent just so far and no further. He was
half in love with his guilt, trapped in the need to justify it.

Meantime, in England, his wife was quietly trying to restore
some calm and order to a life that seemed shattered beyond repair, caring for the daughter to whom she could never explain
why her father was gone, making generous gestures of friendship
and help to that other one whose life had been so nearly ruined
by the poet, busying herself with all kinds of good works.

At last, at last, Harriet was able to paint the picture of Lady
Byron as she saw her, strong, unwavering in her belief that
her husband would some day be redeemed, a woman admired,
respected, loved by all who knew her, a woman whose life had
been one long prayer in action until the day of her death. Triumphantly Harriet finished her article with a paean of praise to
the woman who had truly been an angel on earth, and triumphantly she titled it, "The True Story of Lady Byron's Life."

Her faithful secretaries, the twins, copied the article for her,
and Harriet showed it to a friend or two in Hartford. She was
startled to find her friends so very shocked at the story of Byron's
incest, so appalled at the thought she planned to have the story
published. Impatiently she tried to tell them that the incest was
not the main theme of the article. It was not such a secret, anyway, but had long been known among aristocratic circles in England. The main burden of her article was clearing Lady Byron's
name, she told them. Could they not see the need for that, she
asked? Was it not time that a noble woman had justice done her
memory? When they still shook their heads in alarm, she took the
manuscript back from them, unhappy at their attitude, but not
at all dissuaded in her plan to send the article to the *Atlantic*. It
had been impossible for her *not* to write *Uncle Tom's Cabin*,
when that story was pouring itself out of her; it was impossible
for her not to tell this story now.

There was a certain amount of resistance from the *Atlantic
Monthly* offices too, when something was learned there about the

nature of the new article she was proposing. But the resistance was not coming from her old friend, Mr. Fields, whose opinion she might, perhaps, have heeded. Mr. Fields and his wife were in Europe for the summer, and so Mr. Fields knew nothing about the project. James R. Osgood, whom Fields had recently taken on as a junior partner, wrote Harriet his doubts about the wisdom of such a piece. But Harriet overrode his fears as easily as she overrode Calvin's.

She did have to realize by now that the article was going to "make a good deal of sensation," so she wrote Mr. Osgood that she wanted plenty of time to revise the proof sheets of the article. And she wrote to her friend, Dr. Holmes, sending him a copy of the manuscript.

"I want, *not* your advice as to whether the main facts should be told, for on this point I am so resolved that I frankly say advice would do me no good. But you might help me, with your delicacy and insight, to make the *manner of telling* more perfect; and I want to do it as wisely and well as such a story can be told."

Dr. Holmes, who was also a person not easy to dissuade from any chosen course, and a man who had been amused and charmed by Harriet since the beginning of their acquaintance, accepted Harriet's dictum about "no advice" calmly. Nor did he seem to be as shocked as the others who had read the article. A man of the world, shrewd, curious, observant, there were times when he himself would gladly have spoken or written of subjects generally prohibited in his circle of Boston Brahmins. Perhaps he looked forward to the kind of stir Harriet's article would make. He had only one suggestion. Harriet had given no indication as to her source for her story, no indication as to how she had come into possession of it, sweeping by all that with the sentence, "By a singular concurrence of circumstances, all the facts in the case, in the most undeniable and authentic form, were at one time placed in the hands of the writer of this sketch, with authority to make such use of them as she should judge best." Dr. Holmes suggested that for a story so extraordinary, she might better be more exact.

Harriet found this suggestion reasonable and wrote a postscript to her article, telling how, on her first visit to England she had

formed "a friendship with Lady Byron which was always regarded as one of the greatest acquisitions of the visit"—a friendship that had finally led to the confidence she was now making
public. She wrote of Lady Byron's "perfect conviction that her
husband was now a redeemed spirit," and her conjectures as to
whether a public confession might wholly free his soul from guilt.
She told of how Lady Byron had asked her advice and of how
it had been decided that nothing be said till "both were gone."
Both were gone now, so here was the truth at last.

Harriet sighed with relief and satisfaction when the manuscript
and its postscript were sent off to Mr. Osgood at the *Atlantic*,
and then she and her family departed for a vacation at the seashore. She realized that the disclosure of what a monster Lord
Byron had been might cause a sensation for a while in America
and England, but once the sensation had died down, she was
sure that her aim would be accomplished. Lady Byron would be
freed from the prison of lies in which Byron had forced her to
live her life. The bright eminence could be restored to her name
that Harriet knew it deserved.

So "The True Story of Lady Byron's Life" was published, first
in England, where Mr. Osgood had arranged for its publication
by *Macmillan's Magazine*, and then, in the later part of August,
in the *Atlantic Monthly*.

The thunder rolled, the lightning flashed, in England first. The
article had scarcely appeared before the whole British press
seemed to be screaming its protest in chorus, denouncing the
once-adored Mrs. "Beecher-Stowe" for her incredible, unwar-
ranted, well-nigh obscene attack on a poet who had become a
national idol.

Harriet was staggered when the news of this reception came by
Ocean Telegraph. An *attack* on the *poet?* That was not what she
had written. She had gone out of her way to emphasize Lady
Byron's faith in the "angel" in her husband, struggling with the
demon. She had emphasized all the circumstances of Byron's life
and heritage that might in some measure extenuate or explain
his behavior. There were strains of insanity in his family, a
wretched upbringing had been even more damaging because his

nature was the high-strung, oversensitive one of genius. Harriet had even indicated how religion might have helped to ruin him. "Lady Byron expressed the feeling too, that the Calvinistic theology, as heard in Scotland, had proved in his case, as it often does in sensitive minds, a subtle poison. He never could either disbelieve or become reconciled to it, and the sore problems it proposes embittered his spirit against Christianity. . . ." Appalling as his behavior was, she had *defended* him in the article.

But the British press was declaring that none of the story was true. That it could not be true. That it had all been the diseased invention of Lady Byron's imagination.

This was the incredible part to Harriet. The English still wanted to believe Byron's lies. Even when the truth was told they denied it, in terms of the falsehood Byron had given them. In a kind of panic she sat down to write Mr. Osgood at the *Atlantic Monthly*. Something should and must be done about "the infamous course of such papers as 'The Times,'" which persisted "in believing the story of an avowed libertine against that of a pure, noble woman, whose whole life shows not one record of duty unfulfilled." Someone should write a letter, an answer, a rebuttal—but who?

Then the article appeared in America, and the storm in England paled to the dimensions of a local disturbance compared to the hurricane in the United States.

Byron had become a classic in America in the years since 1815. His image shone for almost everyone as brightly as it had first shone for Harriet when she was ten. He was a poet everyone felt he could understand, a wild and reckless poet-cavalier who offered an ideal of romance in an age when there seemed little enough romance in the world—almost a necessary ideal for that reason.

Harriet was a well-loved national figure, and had been since the days of her triumph in 1852. Not one of her books failed to sell to a wide and eager audience. Her articles, her columns, her poems, her stories for children, were popular staples wherever they appeared. Her very name as a contributor had helped to launch the *Atlantic Monthly*. Her name was a household word, seeming to signify everything that was good, womanly and sincere.

And that made what she had done more appalling. What she stood for did not weigh in the scales of public sentiment against what *he* stood for. Comfortable, homely virtue against a romantic ideal? It would not do. Suddenly, to everyone, Harriet was transformed. She was not what people had thought. Instead of standing in a bright, domestic glow, she was enveloped in a smoky, sulfurous glare, an evil and malicious old gossip, flinging mud at a dead and noble genius.

Day after day, she arose in her rich and expensive house, went down the wide, carpeted stairway with its carved railings and into the breakfast room where the table was always set with flowers. And, her voice soft, she talked of all kinds of things to Calvin and the twins, funny happenings, odd misadventures, plans for the future, the weather. She would not look at the articles and reviews in the papers and magazines. Calvin and the twins had looked at them. The stunned, bewildered expressions on their faces made that clear. But Harriet would *not* read them. She ran away from even thinking of them.

Black Friday brought panic to the stock market, and everyone's attention should have been diverted to the financial holocaust. But no. Jay Gould and Jim Fisk simply joined Mrs. Stowe in her notoriety. Her scandal was not one the public could relinquish so easily. In the midst of money worries, it was a relief and a titillating pleasure to turn to discussing the article Mrs. Stowe had written about Lord Byron, and to speculating on why, why on earth she had done it.

Run away as frantically as she would, Harriet could not ignore letters from Mr. Osgood. He was writing in a kind of desperation. Subscriptions to the *Atlantic Monthly* were being canceled, a flood of cancellations came in with every mail, and Mr. Osgood saw the magazine that Mr. Fields had left in his charge destroyed by the Lady Byron article. He sent Harriet a bundle of clippings to read.

Tightening her lips, Harriet read what Osgood had sent her. What *had* gone wrong with the world? How could everyone ignore so completely the chief aim of the article to glue down on the revelation about Byron and her own scandalous reasons for making it. Over and over, the writers of the articles speculated on *why* she had done it. Perhaps Mrs. Stowe had seen her money and popularity waning, and so had turned to sensationalism to recoup her fortune. Perhaps it was simply a dreadful kind of snobbery, someone else suggested, whereby she could publicly parade her intimacy with a lady of title. The reviewer in the *Independent,* assuming as a matter of course that the story was a fabrication of Lady Byron's, which Mrs. Stowe had swallowed whole, developed that theory.

"She was evidently ready to believe anything. Her rapturous enthusiasm for Lady Byron rendered her childlike in her incapacity to doubt or criticize. Mrs. Stowe, as we all know, has a weakness for ladies of title. She fairly melts, dissolves away, like Mrs. Pendennis, into her pocket handkerchief, over Lady Byron."

Why indeed had she done it? Not only the critics of her own time, but every one of her biographers since has worried with the same question. There are those inclined to the same theory as the *Independent* reviewer, ready to believe she wrote and published her impetuous article out of a shameful, middle-class need to proclaim her friendship with someone like Lady Byron. But she had been a familiar of lords and ladies since 1852, and everyone knew it. She had not even mentioned her own friendship with Lady Byron in the original manuscript, but had added that fact in a postscript, suggested by Dr. Holmes.

Another rather obvious theory is that the article was evidence of a deep sexual repression suddenly manifesting itself in the need to make a public revelation of such an unsavory secret. Certainly there must have been sexual repression in Harriet's character. There was a degree of sexual repression in everyone in the sentimental and prudish nineteenth century, a repression that caused a concern with sex to manifest itself in many unlikely ways. All through *Uncle Tom's Cabin* and *Dred,* there were undercurrents speaking of the sexual abuses of slavery. No one had raised any outcry against those, and few of her biographers make any point of them either. But in the Lady Byron article, accusing a specific person of a specific crime, the sexual element was all most people could see at the time, and it continues to haunt the interpreters of Harriet Beecher Stowe. Was she, the mother of seven, really so frustrated and repressed she could not resist the pleasure of writing out a salacious story and rationalizing it as a necessity of justice?

There is, of course, the simple motive for her act, which Harriet herself gave, over and over, her eyes wide with surprise—a desire to see Lady Byron vindicated. One may wonder why this particular noblewoman filled Harriet with such a sense of identification. Was it Lady Byron's piety, her brilliant intelligence, her meticulousness, or had Harriet simply identified with her in the shock of betrayal—the betrayal of a love that had begun, in Harriet's case, when she was ten? The fact remains that Harriet once had identified herself to a remarkable degree with the plight of the slave, and so she wrote a book about the evils of slavery. The consequences had involved war and bloodshed, but the world had understood her, and ultimately the slave had been freed. This time she had identified herself just as passionately with the cause of a friend, a friend who seemed pure ideal, and had written an article about what that friend had endured in silence, and the world had not understood at all.

The clamor beat around her. She saw—she could not help seeing—the vicious cartoons of herself that were appearing. There was one in *Harper's Weekly* that pictured her as a horrible old woman in bonnet and shawl, swarming up a statue of Lord Byron, leaving muddy tracks on its smooth, marble surface. The caption read: "Now then, old gal, if you want to make yourself conspicuous, you had better go elsewhere, and not leave your dirty marks there."

James Fields came home from Europe and was so appalled by the damage that the "Lady Byron" article had done to the *Atlantic Monthly* that it was months before he dared communicate with Harriet, and even longer before their old friendship was resumed.

A few friends stood by. Dr. Holmes, who had carefully given her "no advice" as to whether the article should be printed, and who had seen it stir up a tempest beyond anything he anticipated, wrote her sympathetically. He had been meaning to write for some time, "but in the midst of all the wild and virulent talk about the article in the 'Atlantic,' I felt as if there was little to say until the first fury of the storm had blown over."

He went on encouragingly to say that "no sensible person could believe for a moment you were mistaken in the essential character of the statement" Lady Byron had made. And: "The fact that her statement is not peremptorily contradicted by those most likely to be acquainted with the facts of the case, is the one result so far which is forcing itself into unwilling recognition. . . ."

Harriet was cheered by that letter, and the Howards in Brooklyn were steadfast. "It's worth while to have trouble," Harriet wrote to Susan Howard, "to have friends stand by one as mine do by me. Depend upon it, the spirit of the Lord didn't pitch me into this seething caldron for nothing, and the Son of Man walketh with me in the fire. Eternal right and justice are with me, and I shall triumph by and bye on the other side of the river—and here too."

The extremity of her situation was forcing her to the same conclusion in which she had found refuge when the success of Uncle Tom's Cabin had threatened to overwhelm her. "The Lord had written that book," and that conviction had sustained her through everything. Now she was insisting that "the spirit of the Lord" had "pitched" her into this "seething caldron."

Armed with that belief, she was suddenly ready to fight back, as she had once fought back against the critics of Uncle Tom's Cabin. The world wanted to know why she had written the article? Very well, she would tell it. What other motive was more basic than uttering the truth? The world did not believe that the story she told was true? It had never occurred to her to doubt Lady Byron's story. But the world did doubt it, suggesting that Lady Byron was a mad old woman, bent on revenge against the poet, and that she had brooded on a few extravagant remarks made by her husband until she had built up the story for herself. Harriet found it incredible that people could reason that way, but they did. They did not consider Lady Byron's words enough. Very well. She would give them more. Somehow, somewhere, she would find other verification of the story. Many people did

know it in England, after all. The anger at Mrs. "Beecher-Stowe"
aroused by the publication of Harriet's article in *Macmillan's* had
provoked a small counterstorm of depositions and assertions af-
firming her charges against Byron. Mrs. Follen, who had been the
first to give Harriet an outline of Lady Byron's history, was dead.
But Harriet could write to her son, who should be able to corroborate the story. The more Harriet pondered, the more sure she
became that she could gather proof for her case. She would gather
enough for a whole book on the subject, a book that would silence
her critics and vindicate both Lady Byron and herself, once and
for all.

She had misstated the duration of the Byron marriage by a
year in her article and so had given her critics a weapon that
they used tirelessly. She decided to hire a lawyer to check her
material from now on. The lawyer was in New York, and Harriet
realized that it would be easier if she were there too. She found
rooms in New York and plunged into the task.

Writing this book was a tangled, nerve-racking project, far
more difficult than compiling the *Key to Uncle Tom's Cabin*. She
was dealing with something that could rest only on either complete faith in Lady Byron's veracity, or indirect evidence. Long
passages of Byron's work had to be scanned for the most minute
references that would seem to corroborate her charge. One reference had to be checked against another and another. Statements from England, passages from biographies of Byron that
quoted personal letters, other contemporary biographies, all had
to be studied. Facts eluded Harriet in the maze. Books and papers piled up around her and she darted from one to another,
losing her place, finding herself with one book when she wanted
another, rummaging in one pile after another for some item she
remembered, finding that only to lose the reference she had been
checking originally.

She had allowed herself headaches and weakness when the
difficulties started. But she was in a stubborn, fighting mood now,
and disregarded headaches, working feverishly. Henry Ward
came over from Brooklyn every day or so to read her copy and
advise her. Thomas Perkins, sister Mary's husband, came from
Hartford to help. Calvin hauled himself out of his easy chair and

came too. John Hooker, Isabella's husband, came. Isabella was already in New York, busy with her activities in behalf of women's rights. But in this moment of Harriet's need, Isabella put aside her own concerns to join the clan in helping sister Hattie.

Harriet read and wrote and arranged, the family read, checked references, offered advice and encouragement and bundled up manuscript or proof to send to Boston. Byron, Byron, Byron—the name began to have no meaning at all. It was just a counter in a desperate game. Incest, adultery, illegitimate child of an incestuous union—words that all of them would have hesitated to speak a year before were the common coin of their daily conversation. They were inured to the meaning of the words, except as they fitted Harriet's purposes.

By the end of the year the book was finished, or enough so that Harriet and Calvin could return to Oakholm. Harriet had done her best. Would the world listen and believe her? Or would there simply be a renewed outburst of criticism rising from prejudice and Byron-mania? Harriet hardly even wondered. She had proved her case, so far as she was concerned. She was finished with the matter.

Had she proved her case? The answer is simply, how could she have? How could anyone, short of presenting explicit signed confessions by both the allegedly guilty parties, Lord Byron and his half sister, Augusta Leigh?

In the years since Harriet Beecher Stowe's impulsive revelation of what Lady Byron told her, scores of Byron biographers have ransacked what evidence there is and studied it with far more scientific and scholarly eyes than hers. And the net result of their efforts is to make it seem quite probable that what Lady Byron told Harriet was true. It seems probable that Byron succumbed to an incestuous passion for his half sister one lonely, distracted summer in London, before his marriage to Anne Isabella Milbanke, and that he drew the loving, submissive Augusta into a liaison with him. In the cool light of distance, with all the available facts lined up, it seems probable. It was only *after* that interlude in London, during which Byron and Augusta were alone together for weeks, that Byron, in what looked like panic, proposed for the second time to Miss Milbanke, and rushed into marriage with her. It all seems to fit, emotionally. And there was the child borne by Augusta Leigh, the requisite time after the London interlude. Most biographers are ready to believe that the facts indicate Byron guilty as charged. But proven so? For all the evidence that points that way, there are those who find it possible to hold the opposite view, and to maintain the story was fiction, encouraged by Byron's exaggerated confessions, and clung to by Lady Byron, grown paranoiac and obsessive under the pressure of the wild and destructive acts Byron did commit during their marriage.

So the case rested in 1870, after Harriet's book, *Lady Byron Vindicated*, was published. Those who had believed the story as Harriet presented it in the original article continued to believe it. Those who had resisted it continued to resist. There was no clear-cut verdict either way.

And either way, there was no change in the image the world had of Lady Byron. If that image was all Byron's creation, as Harriet believed, Byron had done his work well, too well for her to undo it. She made a great effort to show how Lady Byron had been martyred and in noble self-sacrifice kept silent, and this portrait of a passive sufferer was all Harriet offered as a new portrait to replace the old one. Skilled as she was in creating "types" for her fiction, she always failed in attempts to portray a "good woman." So she failed again. Even to those who believed Harriet's story, Lady Byron remained an enigma. Painting with the "vivid lights, gloomy shadows and grotesque groupings" that were her specialty, Harriet had made the white too white in this case, and the black too black. The story telling instinct that gave dimension to her fictional characters deserted her in dealing with this material from real life, and she aroused no sympathy for the Lady Byron who simply bowed her head and submitted to whatever happened.

Lady Byron's image was basically unchanged. Only Harriet's was irretrievably damaged. Never again would she be to the world what she had been, a writer whose "style is always fresh, attractive, and charming, whose wit and humor are genuine, whose depiction of human nature is apt and true, and the at-

mosphere of whose writings is invariably wholesome, clean, stimulating to the moral sense." Her publishers might so advertise her,
and her books might indeed continue to sell, almost as well as
they had. But a smoky tarnish was on her name. And somehow,
even when the Lady Byron scandal was forgotten, the tarnish
still lingered, so that people heard her name or looked at her
picture with a faint distaste, unaware of why they felt as they
did.

If Harriet knew this was so, she gave no hint of it. She had
done what she was determined to do. The consequences had
been astonishing, but she gave no indication of regret for having
done it. Many friends whom she loved and respected felt regret
for her, but she took no notice of that either. In the year before
the Byron scandal, she had established a long-distance friendship
through letters with George Eliot, the brilliant English novelist.
George Eliot wrote her:

"My dear Friend . . . In the midst of your trouble I was often
thinking of you, for I feared that you were undergoing a considerable trial from the harsh and unfair judgments, partly the
fruit of hostility glad to find an opportunity for venting itself,
and partly of that unthinking cruelty which belongs to hasty
anonymous journalism. For my own part, I should have preferred
that the Byron question should never have been brought before
the public, because I think the discussion of such subjects is in-
jurious socially. But with regard to yourself, dear friend, I feel
sure that, in acting on a different basis of impressions, you were
impelled by pure, generous feeling. . . ."

Harriet read the letter gratefully and saved it, but had no
thought of writing George Eliot to explain further. Explanations,
once she had made it clear she was simply telling the *truth*, were
as foreign to her nature as regrets. There was no looking back to
analyze and wonder. There never had been, since the days of
her sin-haunted adolescence. Life was action, and moving on to
what had to be done next.

And what she had to do immediately, she realized, was to accept the fact that Oakholm, the house she had built with such

care and at such expense just six years before, was a mistake. It had been a dream since her school days, a house just where that one was. But once built, it had not been a dream come true. The maintenance and repair bills remained enormous. Commercial and manufacturing aspects of Hartford were crowding closer and closer to the grove around Oakholm. There were factories and their corollary slums nearby now, and there was sewage in the river.

It was time to put the house on the market and be finished with it. After that, she and her "old Rabbi," and the thirty-four-year-old twins could go to Florida for the winter. The orange grove and the little house loomed as such a pleasant retreat, Harriet thought Florida might become their permanent winter home, with summers spent visiting friends and relatives in the North. If that did not work out, later she might buy a smaller house in Hartford, or some other familiar city, any kind of small, comfortable place that would be more in keeping with the needs of Calvin, herself and Hatty and Eliza.

There were no long lamentations about saying good-bye to Oakholm, nor any self-recriminations for having involved herself with such a white elephant in the first place. Harriet supervised the closing of the house for the winter, and if there was some regret as she moved for the last times around her conservatory, it was faint. The roses and blue skies of Florida would be taking its place. Twin Hatty, who had some of Harriet's own skill with flowers, was arranging to have some of the favorite plants from the conservatory moved south with them. She would miss nothing.

Very soon, they were steaming up the broad smooth waters of the St. Johns. Then the steamer was landing at Mandarin, and Fred was greeting them. After the first embrace and kiss, Harriet drew back to look at him with that anxious appraisal she had never been able to avoid since he came back from the war. He was sober at the moment. He was tanned, as he had been since coming to Florida, and that gave him a general look of health. But Harriet sensed the same nervous tension in him as before, a tension that meant he still did not trust himself.

She stifled her worries in the pleasures of returning to Mandarin. These were doubled as she introduced Calvin and the girls to Florida's beauties. Her "old Rabbi" beamed with delight at the mild weather, the sunny skies, and the greenery all about. He gazed approvingly at the wide veranda that ran all around the Mandarin house, and made plans at once for where he would settle with his big chair and books. The girls too were thrilled by Florida, exclaiming endlessly over the flowers and trees. And it was very satisfying to see that under Spencer Foote's management, the orange grove was thriving, though it still had to make a profit.

Harriet made arrangements for further improvements and enlargements of the house, hired Negro girls to help with the cooking and washing and housekeeping, and even succumbed to the temptation of buying more land up the river from the orange grove. Florida was so completely hers now, it was difficult to remember that only accidentally—through the need to help Fred— had she first found her way to it.

The winds blew around the big, closed house in Hartford, but Harriet shut her mind to memories of that. Her book, *Lady Byron Vindicated* had come out, and was provoking new controversy in the North. But she shut her mind to that too. That was over, finished; and her domestic arrangements attended to, she settled to her writing again, taking up exactly where she left off when the Countess Guiccioli's book had interrupted her.

More *Oldtown* stories were what engaged her. Calvin had remembered so many legends and stories from his boyhood in Natick that she had been unable to use in *Oldtown Folks,* that she saw another book in the material—*Oldtown Fireside Stories.*

She wrote, and enjoyed her house and orange grove, and she went "owling about" along the river or into the countryside. The Howards came from Brooklyn for a couple of weeks, partly for a holiday and partly to get Harriet interested in writing for a new religious paper Mr. Howard was backing, in cooperation with Henry Ward. Mr. Howard's eagerness to have a serial story from her was further help to Harriet in closing the door on echoes of the scandal that had concerned her so recently. She grew enthusiastic about the new paper, to be called *The Christian Union*, and promised a serial.

But as week followed week in her sunshiny retreat, there was one trouble on which she could not close the door. Fred had not been cured. He had been sober when they arrived, and had remained so for days. Then had come the slip. He had vanished for hours and returned in the dazed, blind state that was such anguish to his family. Afterward, when he was sober again, there were the same heart-wrenching scenes of remorse and resolution that there had been so many times before, and a week or so of sobriety, and then again, the slip.

Watching helplessly, but still refusing to give up hope, Harriet pondered on what more she could do. Surely there was some way she could reach him, some way his own resolution could be strengthened so he could resist the first drink. It was that which led inevitably to each downfall, Harriet noticed. One drink, even one swallow, of "ardent spirits," and Fred was a changed man, unable to resist the impulse for more and more.

It was inevitable that Harriet, watching, brooding, suffering, should begin to wonder how she could protest against this particular kind of misery in writing. Fred's trouble was a kind of bondage, a bondage that held him and all his family in thrall. Harriet turned over in her mind ideas for some kind of story that would make the evils of that bondage plain.

She wrote to Mr. Howard, back in Brooklyn again, hinting at the thoughts in her mind. "There is a misery—a desolation—an anguish deeper than that of the slave; there is a cause where every good soul ought to be roused—but how to do it? Temperance stories have been thick as pigweed in rich land. I think I see how a better one could be written, but am not sure yet."

May came and June, and still she had "composed" no story on the theme. It was time to go north for the summer with Calvin and the girls, time to say good-bye to Fred until next winter, when they would return to Mandarin. Harriet held her son to her briefly before getting aboard the steamer for Charleston. As the boat moved away, she watched him, standing on the landing, a slight figure, waving, growing smaller, becoming finally just a blur of white, and then disappearing.

It was the last sight Harriet ever had of her second son, the young lieutenant who had fought at Gettysburg, and emerged from the battle with a private demon he could not conquer, no matter how desperately he fought.

Arrived in the North, Harriet and Calvin went first to Cambridge. Georgie and her husband, expecting their first child, lived there now, and young Charley was also there, attending Harvard, the school that had been anathema to his grandfather, Lyman Beecher, because of its Unitarian tendencies. Harriet had a letter from Fred while she was in Cambridge. He wrote that he felt his efforts were not contributing very much to the operation of the orange grove. He had heard talk of Chile being a land of opportunities, and so he had signed on for a voyage around the Horn to that country, to investigate for himself.

It was the last letter Harriet ever had from Fred, though it would be years before she stopped expecting one.

No shipwreck swallowed Fred. There was nothing so simple and final to which the heart and mind could ultimately adjust. Fred simply disappeared. Much later, Harriet and Calvin heard part of the story from acquaintances Fred had made on the voyage. He had not debarked in Chile, after all, but stayed aboard the ship to San Francisco. There he had gone ashore with the shipboard acquaintances and gotten drunk. The acquaintances made an effort to take him to a hotel. He eluded them and vanished. Police tried to locate him but found no trace. He had simply run away, it seemed, from a life in which he could not help disgracing and breaking the hearts of those he loved.

When Harriet's son Henry was drowned, thirteen years before, it had been a crushing blow. Hysterically and desperately, Harriet had reached out in all directions for some kind of comfort. She was still secretly clinging to the belief that some kind of spiritualism might put her in contact with him. But she *knew* he was dead and in Heaven.

Fred's disappearance was no such instant blow to send her reeling, but which she might finally learn to accept. It was rather the kind of wound that is hardly recognized as a wound at first, but continues to bleed, month after month, year after year, till the heart is drained.

When Fred vanished into the mists of San Francisco, his disappearance rounded out a year of disaster, disgrace and loss in his mother's life. Just a year before Harriet had been afire with a youthful zeal to tell Lady Byron's story to the world and establish that friend's shining image for all to see. She had, instead, stepped headlong into catastrophe and seen her own reputation almost ruined. The dream house built on her fame and fortune had shown itself to be a mirage, and was gone, sold at a tremendous loss. But it was Fred, her soldier boy, gone to where her heart could not yearn over him, gone to scenes and sufferings that her imagination could only make ceaselessly various and terrible, who had cast the darkest, longest shadow over the year, and changed something in his mother forever.

She was only fifty-nine. She looked much as she had a year before, still youthful, dark-haired, handsome. Her small frame was still packed with energy. She would write nearly a dozen more books, one of them a New England tale as delightful as any she had done. There would be joys and friendships. Her first grandchild, Georgie's son, would fill her with the love that only grandparents know. And there would be adventures and mischances to fill her with outrage and anger.

But the particular kind of passion that had impelled her to Lady Byron's defense in the summer of 1869, the particular kind of passion that had smoldered under all her conventional activities since she was a child, erupting most dramatically in *Uncle Tom's Cabin,* would be gone.

Chapter 32

During the passage of this story through The Christian Union *it has been repeatedly taken for granted by the public press that certain of the characters are designed as portraits of really existing individuals. . . . They are not. . . .*

1870–1875

It was a brand-new sort of disclaimer to introduce a work of fiction, but unfortunately, when Harriet wrote it, as part of the preface to the book edition of her newest novel, *My Wife and I,* she was a little late. A serialized version of the story had been appearing for the previous year in the new religious paper, *The Christian Union,* and, just as she wrote in the disclaimer, a great many people had been leaping to their own conclusions. One character especially had not only struck many readers as a portrait of a "really existing individual," but had also convinced the free-love evangelist, Victoria Woodhull, that it was a most unflattering caricature of herself. And by the time Harriet wrote the preface to the book edition, Victoria's annoyance had already helped impel her into revealing a most damaging bit of gossip that she knew about Harriet's famous brother, Henry Ward.

The great Henry Ward Beecher scandal would have erupted even without Harriet's lighthearted spoofing of the women's rights movement in *My Wife and I,* and without her cheerfully mocking portrait of a "new woman," that Victoria took as a portrait of herself. But it was certainly another of the ironies of Harriet's life that she should have contributed, even in a minor way, to the breaking of the story that almost ruined her best-loved brother.

Repercussions from the disastrous exposé of Lord Byron's sexual behavior were still sounding when the first ripples of the story about Henry Ward Beecher began to ring slowly outward in the summer of 1870. Harriet was in Cambridge crooning over her new grandson, and wondering when she would hear from Fred—or she was in Hartford, attending to the last details of selling Oakholm—or she was in New York, visiting the offices of the new paper being backed by the Howards and Henry Ward—but no place she went that summer did she hear any hint of the story. Henry Ward himself was completely unaware of any bomb about to burst in his life. Preaching, lecturing, writing, attending to the affairs of America's most famous church, spending a few days whenever he could on his farm in Peekskill, taking off for the mountains of New Hampshire in the hay fever season, he was living the life he had led for years, enjoying the pleasures and satisfactions of being America's best-paid, most widely worshipped preacher.

He had no notion at all, yet, of a tearful and dramatic conversation that had taken place one hot July night between Elizabeth Tilton and her husband, Theodore Tilton, his longtime protégé and dear friend. Sobbing, Liz Tilton had confessed to her husband that for the two years just past she and Mr. Beecher had been lovers, indulging in adulterous intercourse on various occasions, both at his home and her own.

Mr. Beecher had told her it was no sin, she said, and that they shared a divine love, in which physical intimacy was as pure and sinless as a handshake. The physical relationship had now been ended. Still, the burden of the secret had finally troubled her conscience so that she was led to confess, but she begged her husband to tell no one what had happened and to take no revenge against the Reverend Beecher, who was the dearest friend either of them had. And, stunned and shaken, Theodore Tilton had agreed to say and do nothing.

Henry Ward had gone happily on his way that summer and fall, cultivating his fruit trees and flowers at Peekskill, collecting books and paintings, fondling the uncut opals he liked to carry in his pockets, and preaching the gospel that God was love, and that beauty and luxury had their own moral uses.

And Harriet was busy "composing" her new serial for *The Christian Union*. She planned a bright, sparkling, up-to-date story, and nothing could be more up to the minute than the theme of women's rights, a topic continually spilling into the newspapers and magazines as the militant leaders in the fight dramatized their cause in every way they could.

Harriet was no enemy of the movement. Catherine, as opinionated as ever at seventy, might consider it an outrage to think of women voting. Her younger half sister, Isabella, romantic, intense and egocentric, might take the opposite extreme, not only joining with Miss Anthony and Elizabeth Cady Stanton in lecturing and publishing declarations, but becoming a disciple of the flamboyant Victoria Woodhull. But Harriet, and Henry Ward were somewhere in the middle, convinced that women needed more avenues for self-sustaining careers, more rights and privileges in general, and some day, the vote too, but not necessarily right this minute.

So Harriet plotted her story to convey her convictions in the dramatic style that was always easiest for her. She would make the story a first-person narrative of an earnest and high-minded young man come to New York to seek his fortune as a journalist. As a journalist in a weekly newspaper office, a scene familiar to Harriet for years, he would meet all sorts of people, "types" of every kind; as a newcomer to New York, he could be an observer and commentator on the current topics, fads and foibles of the day. And, of course, he could meet and woo and ultimately win a heroine of the type Harriet and everyone else liked best, a beautiful and petted child of a newly rich New York family, who was still unspoiled, wholesome and full of moral purpose at heart.

Choosing *My Wife and I* as the title for her book, Harriet was able to start off in a fine, light vein.

"I trust," she wrote, "that Miss Anthony and Mrs. Stanton, and all the prophetesses of our day, will remark the humility and propriety of my title. It is not I and My Wife—oh no! It is My Wife and I. What am I, and what is my father's house, that I should go before my wife in anything?" And so she was off, relating the adventures of Harry Henderson.

Meantime, in real life, Theodore Tilton was sitting in his own editorial offices at the *Independent*, brooding on what his wife had told him. Theodore was as extreme in his ideas about love, marriage, and the rights of women, as he had once been in his views about suffrage for the freed slaves. He was a good friend of Susan Anthony and Elizabeth Stanton, and frequently ran editorials in the *Independent* advocating more lenient divorce laws, the right of women to vote, and so on. In theory, he should have been able to accept his wife's confession of adultery with calm— a true, pure love was the one legitimate basis for any relationship between a man and a woman, and denying a relationship based on that sort of love was more sinful than indulging it. But there was the inevitable gap between theory and practice, especially when it was his pious, birdlike wife, who disapproved of his more emancipated friends, who had confessed to acting in such an unexpected fashion.

Theodore brooded to the point where he could contain himself no longer and had to speak of his misery to someone. He chose as his confidant, Henry Bowen, the owner and publisher of the *Independent*—Bowen, who, for years, had been whispering to one person or another of a similar confession involving Henry Beecher made by his wife on her deathbed. Henry's editorial connection with the *Independent* had ended soon after that earlier confession, and Bowen had looked at the Reverend Beecher with narrowed eyes ever since. Still, Bowen had never taken any open action against Henry, mindful of the esteem in which he was held and his powerful influence for good. He counseled Theodore to keep silent about his wrongs also.

But it was impossible. The worm was in Theodore's heart. His jealousy and outrage growing, he began to be abusive to his wife and erratic in his domestic behavior. Soon he again poured out the story, this time to Elizabeth Stanton and Susan Anthony. By this time, his conduct toward his wife had so incensed his wife's mother, a half-demented old lady, that she decided to take a hand in matters. She had never liked Theodore Tilton anyway. Now she began to spread stories that he was unfaithful and cruel to his wife and she urged her daughter to leave him.

Still Henry Ward had no idea of Elizabeth Tilton's confession to her husband. Unable to bring herself to tell him what she had done, Elizabeth passively allowed her mother to expound on her domestic troubles to Henry Ward and his wife. Still giving him no hint, she received the self-righteous advice from Henry and Eunice that she and Theodore should separate.

The explosion was bound to come soon. Theodore, obviously, considered himself the injured party. Finally it was Mr. Bowen, his first confidant, who encouraged the eruption. Having done a little brooding himself, Mr. Bowen had reversed his original stand. He was not too pleased with the radical Theodore Tilton as editor of the *Independent*. He was still vengeful toward the Reverend Beecher. Perhaps, if the two of them fought it out together they could relieve his displeasure by destroying each other. Accordingly he encouraged Theodore Tilton to write Henry Ward an abrupt note, demanding that he resign his pastorate and leave Brooklyn, "for reasons which you explicitly understand." Falsely, Bowen promised Theodore he would stand by him in any charges he made against Henry Ward Beecher.

At last, Henry Ward knew the confession Elizabeth Tilton had made, and he had some inkling of the whispering that had been going on. He could now deny his guilt and the whole story. Or he could affirm it, and in all shame and humility, ask Theodore Tilton's forgiveness.

For reasons never quite clear, Henry did not do exactly either—and so inaugurated the reign of scandalous confusion that would last for so long.

Henry read Theodore Tilton's note and cried, "Why, this man is crazy; this is sheer insanity." Shortly thereafter, when Elizabeth Tilton wrote to him, admitting the confession to her husband, and recapitulating its details, Henry rushed to her and obtained a statement in which she declared the original confession a falsehood, forced from her by her husband.

But then, before the same night was over, Liz Tilton recanted her recantation, in a letter addressed to her husband, saying the confession *was* true. And from then on, as the story of Henry Ward's alleged adultery with Mrs. Tilton threatened to break out into the open and wreck both Henry and his church, there would be a blizzard of new confessions and new recantations. There would be a letter of contrition from Henry to Theodore Tilton, which sounded as much like a confession of his own as anything could. And then a letter denying any contrition or confession. Henry and Theodore would be bitter enemies, Henry and Theodore would be vowing eternal friendship. Henry would threaten to resign his pastorate and commit suicide. Henry would refuse to resign anything or give quarter in any way to his enemies. And all the while, with the issue so constantly agitated, the story would be going on its whispered way. And some time, during the early winter of 1871, Mrs. Stanton, who had heard it from Theodore, would tell it to Victoria Woodhull.

Harriet's serial, *My Wife and I* was now rolling merrily along in *The Christian Union,* delighting its readers, winning new subscribers to the paper by the thousands, and proving to Harriet's complete satisfaction that the Lady Byron scandal had not really harmed her.

She had brought her hero, Harry Henderson, out of the New England town in which he had been raised, through his first shattering romantic experience with a flirtatious, mercenary belle, and effected his accidental meeting with the lovely creature who would be his fate, Eva Van Arsdel. Eva was a character with little trace of the "new woman" in her makeup, but she had a more strong-minded sister, eagerly working to carve out a career for herself and pursue it, despite social disapproval. Harriet was sympathetic to this dedicated young woman, but then, "it being the author's purpose," as she wrote later, in the preface, "to show the embarrassment of the young champion of progressive principles, in meeting the excesses of modern reformers, it came in her way to paint the picture of a modern emancipated young woman of advanced ideas and free behavior."

And so she came to the painting of the picture of "Audacia Dangyereyes," the picture that Victoria Woodhull—and a great many other readers too—were unalterably convinced was a caricature of "The Woodhull" herself.

"I heard," Harriet wrote, as she penned Harry Henderson's narrative, "a light footstep on the stairs, and a voice saying, 'Oh yes! this is Mr. Henderson's room—thank you,' and the next moment, a jaunty, dashing young woman, with bold, blue eyes, and curling brown hair, with a little wicked looking cap with nodding cock's-feather set askew on her head, came marching up and seated herself at my writing table. I gazed in blank amazement. The apparition burst out laughing, and seizing me frankly by the hand, said—

"'Look here, Hal! don't you know me? Well, my dear fellow, if you don't it's time you did! I read your last "thingumajig" in the "Milky Way," and came round to make your acquaintance.'

"I gazed in dumb amazement while she went on.

"'My dear fellow, I have come to enlighten you,'—and as she said this she drew somewhat near to me, and laid her arm confidingly on my shoulder, and looked coaxingly in my face. The look of amazement which I gave, under these circumstances, seemed to cause her great amusement.

"'Ha! Ha!' she said, 'didn't I tell 'em so? You ain't half out of the shell yet. You ain't really hatched. You go for the emancipation of woman; but bless you, boy, you haven't the least idea what it means—not a bit of it, sonny, have you now? Confess!' she said, stroking my shoulder caressingly."

Harriet was having great fun as she envisioned the interview, the bold and fearless young woman pressing closer and closer to her earnest and high-principled hero.

"Now, I ask any of my readers"—she had Harry saying in an aside—"what is a modest young man, in this nineteenth century, —having been brought up to adore and reverence woman as a goddess—to do, when he finds himself suddenly vis-à-vis with her, in such embarrassing relations as mine were becoming? I had heard before of Miss Audacia Dangyereyes, as a somewhat noted character in New York circles, but did not expect to be brought so unceremoniously, and without the least preparation of mind, into such very intimate relations with her. . . ."

Her hero's plight underlined, Harriet allowed the determined young woman to start enlightening him:

"You've been asserting, in your blind way, the rights of woman to liberty and equality; the rights of women, in short, to do anything that men do. Well, here comes a woman to your room who takes her rights, practically, and does just what a man would do.

I claim my right to smoke, if I please, and to drink if I please; and to come up into your room and make you a call, and have a good time with you, if I please, and tell you that I like your looks, as I do. Furthermore, to invite you to come and call on me at my room. Here's my card. You may call me 'Dacia, if you like— I don't go on ceremony. Come round and take a smoke with me, this evening, won't you? I've got the nicest little chamber that ever you saw. What rent do you pay for yours? Say, will you come round?"

Her hero properly stunned by all this and a good deal more, Harriet finally rescued him by bringing a friend and co-worker of his onto the scene. The friend, whose name was Jim, came to the door, saw Audacia, and cut a silent pirouette in the air behind her. After which, she turned her head and he advanced.

"Fairest of the sex (with some slight exceptions)—to what happy accident are we to attribute this meeting?"

"Hallo, Jim! is this you?" she replied.

"Oh, certainly, it's me," said Jim, seating himself familiarly. "How is the brightest star of womanhood—the Northern Light; the Aurora Borealis; the fairest of the fair? Bless its little heart, has it got its rights yet? Did it want to drink and smoke? Come along with Jim now, and let's have a social cocktail."

"Keep your distance, sir," said she, giving him a slight box on the ear. "I prefer to do my own courting. I have been trying to show your friend here how little he knows of the true equality of women, and of the good time coming, when we shall have our rights, and do just as we darn please, as you do."

Harriet let Audacia rant on a while longer, and then Jim arose, banteringly requested that she "withdraw the confusing light" of her bright eyes from them for the moment, as they had work to do, and attempted to steer her to the door.

"Stop!" she cried. "I ain't going to be put out that way. I haven't done what I came for. You both of you have got to subscribe for my paper, 'The Emancipated Woman.'"

"Couldn't do it, divinest charmer," said Jim. "Couldn't do it; too poor, mill runs low; no water; modest merit not rewarded. Wait till my ship comes in, and I'll subscribe for anything you like."

"Well now, you don't get rid of me that way. I tell you I came in to get a subscription, and I am going to stay till I get one," said Miss Audacia. "Come, Hal," she said, crossing once more to him, and sitting down by him and taking his hand, "write your name there, there's a good fellow."

So Harry wrote his name in desperation, and when the satisfied Audacia had finally departed, "Who," he asked his friend Jim, "Who, and what is this creature?"

"Oh, one of the harbingers of the new millennium," said Jim. "Won't it be jolly when all the girls are like her?"

It was not an ill-tempered portrait Harriet had drawn, only a one-dimensional humorous sketch, even though she had her hero, Harry, and his friend continue discussing Audacia after her departure in generally unflattering terms.

"Well"—said her hero—"if I believed that granting larger liberty and wider opportunities was going to change the women we reverence to things like these, you would never find me advocating it. . . ."

And, "Well, my dear Hal"—his friend replied—"be comforted; you're not the first reformer that has had to cry out, 'Deliver me from my friends.' Always when the waters of any noble, generous enthusiasm rise and overflow their banks, there must come down the driftwood—the wood, hay, and stubble. Luther had more trouble with the fanatics of his day, who ran his principles into the ground, as they say, than he had with the Pope and the Emperor, both together. As to this Miss Audacia, she is one of the phenomenal creations of our times; this time, when every kind of practical experiment in life has got to be tried, and stand or fall on its own merits. . . . For my part, I always said that one must have a strong conviction for a cause, if he could stand the things its friends say for it, or read a weekly paper devoted to it. If I could have been made a pro-slavery man, it would have been by reading anti-slavery papers, and *vice versa*. I had to keep myself on a good diet of pro-slavery papers, to keep my zeal up."

So Harriet had her fun with the "new woman" of the day and the radicals of the women's rights movement, all unaware that one extremely fearless new woman now knew some appalling gossip about her brother.

Still, it was not entirely Victoria Woodhull's irritation against Mrs. Stowe that prompted her to do what she did. For all her follies and excesses, all her trances and clairvoyant predictions, Victoria was a woman of raging sincerity when it came to exposing what she thought was "moral sham" or "humbug." And both her sincerity and her very real charm had won her some unlikely friends and unlikely triumphs as well. Mrs. Stanton and Miss Anthony, unhappy about her spiritualist leanings and free-love doctrines, could not resist her sincerity in their cause, and had only been able to bow before Victoria's superior talents, when she had achieved an unheard-of audience with a congressional committee, and had then enthralled the legislators with an impassioned but dignified plea for women's rights. She *was* sincere —about anything she felt led to "Progress! Free Thought! Untrammeled Lives!" which was the slogan that ran at the masthead of *Woodhull and Claflin's Weekly*.

But in spite of her sincerity and her success in presenting the cause to Congress, even in spite of the friendship of Mrs. Stanton and Miss Anthony, the rank and file of the suffragist movement were shocked by Victoria Woodhull. Finally those members met to censure her for the disorders of her private life, and more or less read her out of the movement.

Victoria Woodhull was irked by this, as well as by the patronizing jibes of Mrs. Stowe. Hypocrisy in general was aggravating her. And she was in this mood when she bethought herself of some hypocrisy in particular, of which Mrs. Stanton had informed her.

She wrote an open letter to the editor of the New York *World*, a letter that appeared in the paper in late May of 1871.

"Sir:," she wrote, "because I am a woman, and because I conscientiously hold opinions somewhat different from the self-elected orthodoxy which men find their profit in supporting, and because I think it my bounden duty and my absolute right to put forward my opinions, and to advocate them with my whole strength, self-elected orthodoxy assails, vilifies me, and endeavors to cover my life with ridicule, and dishonor. . . .

"But let him that be without sin cast the stone. I do not intend to be made the scapegoat of sacrifice. . . .

"I advocate free love in its highest, purest sense as the only cure for immorality, the deep damnation by which men corrupt and disfigure God's most holy institution of sexual relation. My judges preach against 'free love' openly, and practice it secretly. . . . For example, I know of one man, a public teacher of eminence, who lives in concubinage with the wife of another public teacher of almost equal eminence. All three concur in denouncing offenses against morality. 'Hypocrisy is the tribute paid by vice to virtue.' So be it; but I decline to stand up as the 'frightful example.' I shall make it my business to analyze some of these lives, and will take my chances in the matter of libel suits.

"I have no faith in critics, but I believe in justice.

Victoria C. Woodhull."

Victoria looked at the letter with satisfaction when it appeared, and then sent a message to Theodore Tilton that she would like to see him as soon as possible.

Henry Ward Beecher and Theodore Tilton were still engaged in their frantic round of secret meetings, almost daily letters and constantly changing attitudes toward each other. A "mutual friend," Frank Moulton, had entered the picture. With his help, Tilton had been persuaded for a while that the scandal he had originally tried to break open must, at all costs, be squashed, both for the sake of the enormous influence of Plymouth Church and Henry Ward, and also to protect the honor of his own wife and children. But the course of self-abnegating silence was not one Theodore could follow for long. Any new injury caused the old outrage to blaze forth. During the winter Mr. Bowen had finally fired him from the *Independent*. Plainly, Theodore's sense of outrage had blazed at this injustice. But Henry had hastily helped to raise funds and contributed five thousand dollars toward founding a new paper for Theodore to edit. As matters now stood in Brooklyn, Theodore had his new paper, *The Golden Age*, and he, Henry Ward, and even Henry Bowen, were in precarious accord, all sworn to protect each other, each one pledged to stop saying anything slanderous about any one of the others.

With things at this point, Theodore Tilton came to see Victoria Woodhull, whom he had long known by hearsay, but had never met. She asked him if he knew whom she meant by the "public teacher of eminence, who lives in concubinage with the wife of another public teacher," and when he faltered in his answer, she told him sweetly that she meant none other than the Reverend Henry Ward Beecher and himself.

What she then proposed to do, no one ever knew. For, after pleading with her not to reveal a cruel story that would hurt so many innocents, Theodore raced back to Brooklyn for counsel with the "mutual friend," Moulton, and with Henry Ward. Soon Theodore was busy establishing the warmest kind of friendly relations with Victoria. She was invited to dinner at the Tilton and Moulton homes and Theodore began eulogizing her in the editorial columns of his paper: "If the woman's movement has a Joan of Arc, it is this gentle but fiery genius . . . a woman who in moral integrity rises to the full height of the highest." He began visiting her frequently at her home, taking her rowing, or strolling in Central Park. Did they also become lovers? Later, Victoria would at one time say yes, and at another time no, which was often Victoria's way, and did nothing to damage her newsworthiness.

Henry Ward later admitted that he had thought it perfectly proper for Theodore to show Victoria kindness and attention. Later Victoria would claim there had been "many friendly discussions and correspondence" between herself and Henry. But this he would deny.

So the summer passed, with the threat of open scandal always a low and distant muttering, like a thunderstorm hovering at the horizon, but somehow, miraculously, never moving much nearer. Inevitably, a great many people knew the story now, knew that Theodore Tilton had charged his pastor with sexual intimacies with his wife, knew that Bowen had made the same charge against the Reverend Beecher in connection with his own first wife. Inevitably the story grew as it spread, so that some versions claimed the Reverend Beecher had been having clandestine affairs with his female parishioners ever since coming to Brooklyn, and that there was a small room behind his study in the church, to which some woman always had a key. And those who heard the stories believed them or disbelieved them, ac-

cording to their own natures and their previous opinions of
Henry Ward Beecher.

The whole Beecher clan had heard the stories by now. Catherine had heard of Henry's alleged adultery from Victoria Woodhull shortly before Victoria's letter to the *World*, Victoria having
taken her on a surprising carriage ride in the park to discuss the
situation. Catherine, her gray side curls bouncing, had angrily
told "The Woodhull" she would personally undertake to vouch
for Mr. Beecher's wedding vows. But that had hardly impressed
Victoria.

Harriet was also shocked when the story came to her ears.
And outraged at the idea that anyone could believe such slander.
Nor did it ever occur to her that she was showing a certain inconsistency in this attitude. She had instantly believed the worst
Lady Byron could tell her about Lord Byron, and had ultimately
revealed that worst to the world, finding, even after all her
efforts, little more substantiation for the charge than Lady Byron's
statement. Some people, like Lady Byron, were saints, whose
word could not be doubted. Some people, like Lord Byron, were
morally corrupt and did incredible things. Even after the searing
bath of her own scandal, there had been, for Harriet, no dawn-
ing awareness that people might be a little morally corrupt and
a little saintly both at once, and sometimes pitifully confused
as to which aspect of their nature they were exhibiting at any
given time. To Harriet, Henry was everything good, fine, noble
and generous—a masculine ideal almost parallel to the feminine
ideal Lady Byron represented. And so it was inconceivable to
her that he might have yielded to any sensual and emotional
urges that would trap him in situations too damaging for a man
in his position to admit. To Harriet, Henry was simply the victim
of a terrible conspiracy among small jealous men, Theodore Tilton, Henry Bowen, even Frank Moulton.

As her story, *My Wife and I*, began winding to it conclusion
as a serial, she went out of her way to make more explicit attacks
on Victoria Woodhull in her periodic columns for *The Christian
Union*. Victoria had helped to spread the slander about Henry.

Henry Ward insisted that the scandal itself had to be ignored
in print. All his devoted friends urged him to publish a firm

denial of the gossip to end the spreading rumors. Henry Ward
flatly refused. Thomas Perkins, sister Mary's husband, wrote
him from Hartford, where stories about him were circulating.
And Henry wrote back, "If my friends put their foot silently
on any coals or hot embers and crush them out *without* talking,
the miserable lies will be as dead in New York in a little time
as they are in Brooklyn." The "miserable lies" were not dead in
Brooklyn. Henry was simply whistling to keep up his courage.
But he remained committed to his course of public silence.

Harriet saw Henry in the early fall, at the Twin Mountain
House in New Hampshire, which had long been one of his favorite retreats and now was one of hers. Sick with sympathy for
him, trembling with rage at those who were attacking him, eager
to fight back at them, Harriet listened as he poured out his
feelings and conclusions about the sordid situation. In his worry
and need, he was grateful at last for the presence of this small,
devoted sister, glad to talk to her, hour after hour.

He told her how he believed the scandal had had its start,
and to Harriet, it seemed like Henry that, innocent as his
story was, he took onto himself a great burden of guilt in connection with it. Sitting near her, his head bowed so that his hair,
so long it almost touched his shoulders, fell forward across his
cheeks, he told her that he feared Elizabeth Tilton had indeed
become unduly fond of him. He blamed himself for that. He
blamed himself for all the visits he had made to the Tilton house,
both when Theodore was there, and when Theodore was away
lecturing. It made no difference that Theodore had begged him
to visit Elizabeth in his absence so that she would not be lonely.
Henry knew that Elizabeth, a sensitive, beauty-loving little
woman, had a childlike nature, eager to worship and adore. He
knew that she admired him extravagantly as her pastor. In the
greater knowledge that was his, he should have realized when
her admiration began subtly changing into something more
dangerous. But he had not. He had gone on visiting her, almost
as much at home in the Tilton house as his own, romping with
the Tilton children, laughing, teasing, kissing Elizabeth as if she
had been one of the children herself, or his own younger sister.
So she had grown more and more fond of him until, her emotions

inflamed, she had confessed something to her husband—who could know exactly what? And it was all his fault, Henry Ward said again, lifting his head to look at Harriet so that she saw the tears running down his cheeks.

Harriet protested violently. He had no reason to feel guilt. How could he have prevented it if Liz Tilton had grown "unduly fond" of him? Everyone knew the tremendous emotional appeal he had to the women of his congregation. And much as one might deplore the emotional folly of women losing their heads over their pastor, looking at Henry, knowing Henry, Harriet could understand how it might happen. At fifty-eight, Henry was still a handsome man, not tall, and grown somewhat corpulent, but an imposing figure all the same, who radiated power. His head was a lion's head, and the long, waving gray locks a lion's mane. His face constantly reflected the play of emotion and Harriet never tired of looking at it. Small wonder that foolish women whose lives were without purpose fell under the spell of one whose every word and glance were full of thought, emotion and meaning. It was ridiculous of Henry to blame himself for an electric vitality that made him what he was.

How could he have dreamed his visits to the Tilton house were dangerous? Harriet knew that Eunice, virtuous woman that she was, had become somewhat austere, offering Henry none of the laughter and gaiety he craved in life. She could remember way back to Cincinnati in the thirties, when Henry had been a golden-haired excitable boy, moving open-hearted and open-handed toward everyone. He had been so much in love with Eunice then, he could hardly wait until he had won a church and could bring her west. Finally he had been able to send for her, and she had been young and eager as he. But Eunice had changed through the years. And Henry had not changed as she had. So of course he sought gaiety and laughter somewhere, and if it had seemed to him that he found them among the Tilton children, and with Mrs. Tilton, how was he to have dreamed that his friendliness would be misconstrued, and ultimately used so horribly against him?

Harriet heard his story and interpreted it in the only way that seemed possible to her and told him he was blameless. In her fiction writing, she often showed great skill in analyzing facial characteristics, but gazing at her brother in a passion of sympathy, it never occurred to her that his face, strong and noble though it was, had a sensuality about it that could, to a less prejudiced observer, offer some support to the Tilton and Bowen stories. Henry's lips were full and curved like her own. Hers, in fact, had grown more firm through the last years than his. But she gave no thought to that, nor to the emotional impulsiveness that was the very essence of Henry's nature. She gave no thought to anything that would cast the slightest doubt on what he said and what she wanted to believe.

She stifled any bewilderment when he insisted on his considered belief that the only way to fight the slander was to ignore it and keep silent. And when he told her that attacks on his attackers simply added fuel to the fires, she agreed to make no more comments on Victoria Woodhull in her columns. She was sorry that the portrait of the "new woman" in *My Wife and I*, which so many had taken as a caricature of Victoria had annoyed Victoria, and she would do what she could to correct the damage.

She was preparing *My Wife and I* for publication as a book now. She would write a preface for the book insisting that no character in the book had any real-life model. And shortly thereafter, she sat down at a desk in the Twin Mountain House and did just that.

"The novel-writer does not profess to paint *portraits* of any individual men and women in his personal acquaintance," she wrote. "Certain characters are required for the purposes of the story. . . . A slight incident, an anecdote, a paragraph in a paper, often furnishes the foundation of such a character; and the work of drawing it is like the process by which Professor Agassiz from one bone reconstructs the whole form of an unknown fish. But to apply to any single living person such a delineation is a mistake, and might be a great wrong both to the author and to the person designated. . . ."

So Harriet tried to soothe Victoria Woodhull, and Mrs. Stanton too, for many readers believed Mrs. Stanton the original of another more fleeting caricature in the book—a handsome, popular, lovable reformer named Mrs. Stella Cerulean, who felt the world could be saved by free reliance on woman's instinct.

She wrote her disclaimer, she promised Henry that she would do what she could to end the gossip by ignoring it, and if there was anything else she could do to help him, she assured Henry she would do that too. He had only to call on her.

There was something more she could do, it soon turned out. Not all of Henry's brothers and sisters took such an unwavering view of his innocence as his older sisters, Catherine and Harriet. His much younger half sister, Isabella Beecher Hooker, was not at all sure of it. Sister Belle was thoroughly under the spell of "The Woodhull." In one of her clairvoyant trances, Victoria had predicted that the millennium was near at hand when the world would become a matriarchy, and who had she seen as the great female leader of this new age? None other than Isabella. If Belle could be convinced by Victoria that such glory did lie in wait for her in the future, it was hardly likely she would doubt Victoria's version of the Beecher-Tilton affair. Isabella became so sure of Henry's guilt that she began to wonder if she was participating in his crime of hypocrisy, by not speaking out the truth. She wrote to Thomas, the next to the youngest of the Beecher clan, and her own full brother, asking if he did not agree.

Thomas replied in alarm. "You have no *proof* as yet of any offense on Henry's part," he counseled his emotional sister. "Your testimony would be allowed in no court. Tilton, wife, Moulton & Co., *are* witnesses. Even Mrs. Stanton can only declare hearsay. So, if you move, remember that you are standing on uncertain information, and we shall not probably ever get the facts—and I am glad of it." Thomas, quiet, thoughtful, with a love of science that had almost—but not quite—triumphed over Lyman's determination to have him in the ministry, had always been one of the least disputatious of the Beechers. But Thomas' advice had no effect on Isabella. She wrote to Henry:

"I can endure no longer. I must see you and persuade you to write a paper which I will read, going alone to your pulpit and taking sole charge of the service."

And so during December and January, Harriet was sitting in a front pew in the Plymouth Church every Sunday morning

and evening, keeping guard against any surprise appearance of
Isabella. Harriet was the only one in the family who had always
been able to awe Isabella. If she appeared, Harriet must quell
her with a glance.

It was a strange experience for Harriet to sit there, Sunday
after Sunday, in the huge, crowded church that was the pride of
Brooklyn. The crowds had nothing to do with the dreadful
gossip. Henry had been drawing crowds like this for years, so
many people coming over from Manhattan to Brooklyn for the
services that the ferries that brought them were called "Beecher
ferries." And because of Henry's "ten-minute rule" which allowed
no one but pewholders into the church until ten minutes before
the start of the service, there were always eager crowds of non-
pewholders lined up in the streets before the church.

The unsettling thing was to see Henry, at the proper moment,
open the small door back of the platform, walk briskly and
firmly up onto the platform, stop briefly by the flowers banked
there to take a whiff of their fragrance, and then send his
sweeping glance across the congregation, just as always. When
the time came, he rose to preach with the same eloquence as
always too—just as though no hysterical half sister might be lurking in the anterooms, preparing to march down the aisle to deliver an appalling pronouncement, just as though no horrible
story was seething and coiling through the city, and farther,
threatening everything he was and did.

While Harriet kept her vigil, Henry was taking other steps
to try to quiet Isabella. It was somewhat bewildering to Harriet
that it was Theodore Tilton whom he sent to Hartford to talk
to Belle. So far as Harriet was concerned, Tilton was one of the
arch-villains of the conspiracy against Henry. And she would
not know for two years and more, not till the tangled details
of the Beecher-Tilton scandal would be related, day after day,
in a packed courtroom, for the ears of the nation, that Theodore
Tilton had won Isabella's promise of silence by threatening her
with a past adultery of her own. *Were* all these things possible,
Harriet would wonder then? Had the world gone mad?

All that Harriet knew in January 1872 was that sister Belle
had finally listened to reason. There was no more need for her

to stay in Brooklyn and take her post in Plymouth Church every Sunday. Perhaps, she told Henry, with Isabella come to her senses, there would be an end to the whole ugly business at last, and Henry agreed there might be, if everyone continued to keep silent.

Harriet was free to take herself and her family to Florida now, to the house in Mandarin. It looked lovelier and more welcoming than ever before to Harriet and Calvin and the twins. If only there had been some word from Fred, it would all have been perfect.

And now Henry's scandal was quiescent for almost a year. And during the interlude, Harriet was busy and generally happy. She was writing—there was never a time when she did not have some writing assignment to fill her mornings. That winter she was occupied with a series of travel sketches describing Florida for the unfortunate Northerners who had never known its tropical beauties. The sketches were appearing one by one, in *The Christian Union.* Later, they would be collected in a book called *Palmetto Leaves,* one of the first books to picture Florida as a winter playground. In her free time, she enjoyed picnics, parties, and excursions on the river.

A surprising and rather alarming offer came from a lecture-booking bureau in Boston, proposing that she make a tour with a program of readings from her own books. It was a startling idea to Harriet, brought up in the tradition that no decent woman spoke in public. But times had changed, and the compensation that the booking agency offered was very tempting. Should she do it—shouldn't she? "Kind o' love to—hate to—wish I didn't—want ter," she wrote to her friend, Annie Fields. Finally the "love to" reaction won out and she signed for a tour of forty readings in the fall of 1872, through forty New England towns.

She and Calvin and the twins went back north in the summer and visited with family and friends. There was a visit with Georgie and her husband and the wonderful baby, Freeman Allen, in Cambridge. There was a visit filled with sadness at Mary's home in Hartford. Thomas Perkins, Mary's good, kind husband, and Harriet's longtime adviser, had died in the spring. His death had been a blow to Harriet. "Nowhere in the world had I a truer friend," she wrote.

Then she braced herself for the new ordeal of the lecture platform. Harriet was sixty-one, and in the last year her hair, brown for so long, had turned white. Tiny, white-haired, wide-eyed, she hardly seemed a figure to step out onto a stage and capture and hold an audience. Her first appearance, in Springfield, Massachusetts, seemed to prove the whole venture had been a mistake. She was so gripped with stage fright her voice had been a whisper. Her audience had been restless, bored, disappointed.

But the initial failure was just what she needed, it seemed. She pulled herself together, and the talent for miming and clowning, with which she had delighted friends in private for years, and the dramatic instincts inherited from the eloquent Lyman, came to her rescue. Before her next reading, she stood in front of a mirror and combed her white hair into a high, cockatoo crest, such as Lyman had worn. Then she turned to Annie Fields, who was with her, and said, "Now, my dear, gaze upon me. I am exactly like my father when he was going to preach." And she gestured in an imitation of one of Lyman's old-time flourishes.

After that, it was all triumph. She stepped out onto the platform of Tremont Temple in Boston and read portions from *Uncle Tom's Cabin*, her voice alive and full of power, and she had her audience as Lyman used to have his, as Henry had his. Hundreds in her audience lived again the emotions they had first felt almost twenty years before, when the words they were hearing had raised the call to right a great wrong. Children and young people, to whom the words already belonged with history, felt their emotional excitement for the first time, and realized how they might have helped lead a generation to war. After Boston, she went on to Cambridgeport, Newburyport, Westfield, on and on through Massachusetts and up into Maine, then down into Connecticut and Rhode Island. Everywhere she had the same kind of success. No echoes of the terrible things that had been written about her at the time of the Lady Byron affair seemed to trouble her audiences. They had forgotten those to remember her as she had been. She expanded her program, reading portions from her other works, from her New England story, *The*

Pearl of Orr's Island, and from some of her shorter pieces. But everywhere, it was the little lady who had written *Uncle Tom's Cabin,* whom people came to hear and see, riding long distances from their farms, struggling through rain or snow storms so as not to miss her. After her reading, they would crowd around to meet her, to touch her, to introduce children to her, named after characters in her book, or after her, and to tell her what her most famous book had meant to them.

Calvin, staying with Georgie and her husband in Cambridge, had been sick while she was on tour. It was the first really serious illness that longtime hypochondriac had ever known. Harriet felt anxious about him, and now it seemed to her that the plan to have only the house in Florida, and to visit with family during the summer months, would not work. She must buy another house in the North, a neat, comfortable, ready-made house where they could spend their summers without the agitation of visiting. She fussed over Calvin, and then she took a quick trip to Hartford, still the city they preferred, and, with little trouble, found what she wanted, a pleasant, foursquare, gabled house, with plenty of rooms upstairs and down, and enough lawn for a garden. The house, on Forest Street, had still another attraction. The land where it stood adjoined the property on which the successful young writer of *Innocents Abroad* had just built a rich and beautiful home. Harriet met and talked with Samuel Clemens and his wife, Olivia, a tie between them already established. Harriet's younger brother, Thomas, had married them, in Elmira, New York, and they were extremely fond of him.

A new house to plan for, new friends, Calvin's convalescence, arrangements to take him to Florida as soon as possible—it did not matter how many activities there were to engage her, Harriet still could not run away from the catastrophe that had just befallen Henry Ward.

Victoria Woodhull, for reasons as tangled and personal and seemingly whimsical as everything else in the confused Beecher-Tilton difficulties, had suddenly decided to publish the complete story of the scandal, embellished with every lurid detail she had ever heard or imagined, in *Woodhull and Claflin's Weekly.*

Overnight the story became the sensation of New York. *Wood-*

hull and Claflin's Weekly was sought so eagerly that single copies
of the crucial issue were bringing as much as forty dollars. Victoria, and her sister, Tennie C., had been clapped in jail, through
the efforts of a young reformer named Anthony Comstock, for
sending obscene matter through the mail. And everywhere,
wherever Harriet went, people were either rapaciously discussing
the gossip about Henry Ward Beecher, or tactfully falling silent
upon Harriet's appearance and questioning her with their eyes.

It was more than unnerving to Harriet—almost beyond belief.
And in a curious sort of way, which Harriet herself did not seem
to notice, the bafflement that assailed her was actually the bafflement she had felt in the Lady Byron situation, in reverse.
When she had published Lady Byron's story, people had cried
out against her for believing an eccentric old lady's wicked nonsense about a great poet. They had doubted Lady Byron almost
by reflex instinct. But now, when a notorious woman came out
with a story that was obviously baseless slander against a good
and famous preacher, it was as though they were eager to believe the notorious woman's lies. Why? Why in one case was there
such instant doubt, and in the other such an instant willingness
to accept?

One great trouble undoubtedly was Henry's refusal to make
any denial of the story, or to refer to it in any way. *The Christian
Union* came out week after week with no mention of the scandal
at all. Victoria Woodhull, in jail and out, dared Henry Ward
Beecher to sue her for libel and he made no move. The story
spread and spread, across all of the East, across the country
where Henry's name had been famous for twenty years and more,
across the middle states of Kansas and Missouri, where the rifles
called "Beecher's Bibles" had helped in the fight for free soil,
on and on it spread, to the farthest coast. And still Henry said
nothing publicly.

Harriet and Calvin and the twins, stopping in New York on
their way to Florida assured Henry of their unwavering faith
and support. Harriet reiterated her loathing of "The Woodhull"
and her eagerness to have the woman shut up in jail permanently,
but Henry remained quietly determined to stand by the course
he had chosen.

Then the Stowes were off for the South and Harriet knew nothing about the various distracted and desperate activities of her brother, Theodore Tilton, Henry Bowen and Frank Moulton during the rest of the winter. The secret meetings, the letters, and the endless attempts to bury the scandal while still leaving *everyone* with honor intact and feelings unruffled, had started up again more violently than ever, a secret writhing in Brooklyn, going on far below the public gossip. Now and then, in misguided attempts to quiet the public talk, various documents did get into print, always with repercussions that required one or another of the group to answer with some retaliatory document that led to more' repercussions. One of Henry's sympathizers made the mistake of publishing the covenant between Henry, Theodore Tilton and Bowen, whereby they promised to say nothing slanderous about each other. Tilton, feeling that this made him out the scapegoat, rather than the injured party, angrily threatened to release for publication Henry's original "letter of contrition," which sounded so much like a confession of adultery. Henry was again threatening suicide.

Finally, two and a half years after the story had first begun to spread, Henry wrote, for publication in the Brooklyn *Eagle*, the firm denial of the story for which his friends had pleaded so long. ". . . the stories and rumors which have, for a time, been circulated about me, are grossly untrue, and I stamp them, in general and in particular, as utterly false," he concluded ringingly.

It should have been the end.

Harriet, returned with her family and settled down in the new house on Forest Street in Hartford, was sure it must be the end.

Then she spent some days at the Twin Mountain House in New Hampshire, while Henry was there, and was dismayed to find him newly alarmed. His overzealous friends were causing the difficulty. Eager to see their minister's name cleared *completely*, they had decided they could accomplish this by publicly branding Theodore Tilton as a bearer of false witness. This could be done by reading him out of membership in Plymouth Church. Harriet could not understand why their plans to do this

worried Henry so. Mr. Tilton *was* a bearer of false witness, was
he not? But Henry was frantic. Theodore must not be expelled.
He did not want to *hurt* Theodore. He was doing all he could
to prevent any rash act by his congregation.

Harriet marveled anew at her brother's goodness in trying so
hard to protect such a false friend as Mr. Tilton, and wondered
at Henry's reiterations that expelling Theodore would start the
trouble up again.

Then she had to depart on another lecture tour. This year the
bureau had planned a tour that took her west, through Illinois
and Ohio. The audiences were as enthusiastic as the ones of
the year before, and she enjoyed the readings, but the traveling
was wearing.

This tour took her to Cincinnati. For the first time in twenty-
three years, she returned to the city where she had lived so long
in exile, where all her children but the youngest had been born,
and where so much of the material for *Uncle Tom's Cabin* had
unconsciously been gathered.

Any emotions she had about her brief and dramatic return as
a highly paid lecture-circuit performer to the city where she
had lived in such obscurity were kept inscrutably to herself.
Any emotions that Cincinnati aroused were also buried. She
wrote to young Charley, in college at Harvard, that she had taken
a drive up into Walnut Hills and had seen the Lane Seminary
buildings, and the house where she had lived and his sisters had
been born, and that was all.

The tour completed, she came east determined it would be
her last venture of that kind. The endless, jolting train travel,
the discomforts and loneliness of hotel rooms, the strain of the
readings, were too much for her. She contracted for another
serial for *The Christian Union,* a sequel to the popular *My Wife
and I,* which she thought of titling *We and Our Neighbors.*

And she learned that despite Henry's efforts the congregation
of the Plymouth Church had expelled Theodore Tilton from
membership by an overwhelming vote. Henry was fearfully
awaiting the next move of an angry Theodore, now publicly
censured as the slanderer of his pastor.

She never asked herself why Henry seemed positively afraid

of Mr. Tilton. It was enough to tell herself that Mr. Tilton was such an unprincipled villain, of course Henry feared him. After pressing his hands in sympathy, and assuring him that no one as good as he could ever really be hurt by anyone like Mr. Tilton, she had to hurry on about her own life.

Calvin and the twins were already in Florida. She went south to join them, and again knew little of the further turmoil in Brooklyn. Just as Henry had feared, Theodore Tilton was enraged at being made a figure of guilt. In retaliation, he enlisted the support of various Congregational ministers, who agreed he had been read out of the church in a rather high-handed manner. There being no Presbytery, Synod or other general supervisory body in the Congregational church structure, an Advisory Council of Congregational Ministers was summoned to review the matter.

There was little sting in this counterattack by Theodore. The council met, voted a mild reproof to Plymouth Church and adjourned. But again, Henry's friends became his worst enemies, refusing to rest content with a partial victory. Theodore Tilton must be totally condemned in the public mind, Henry Ward Beecher completely exonerated and free of any blame whatsoever. Prominent men began making public statements about Tilton, calling him "out of his mind," and worse. A well-known theologian came out with a series of articles and lectures on the case, defending the Reverend Beecher and dismissing Tilton as "a dog."

Then, the badgered Theodore Tilton blew up completely and made good on his threat of a year before by publishing Henry's incriminating "letter of contrition."

Henry had finally embarked on some positive action to stamp out the scandal by the time Harriet and her family returned. Admitting publicly that there had been rumors, "insinuations and charges respecting my conduct," he had arranged for Plymouth Church to stage a sort of trial and examine the evidence and come to a decision. It was an odd trial in some respects. Henry had chosen the members of the examining committee before whom the key figures in the scandal were summoned to appear, but this did not seem to bother anyone. Theodore Tilton appeared before the committee, and though he had wavered until the last moment as to exactly what his charge would be, on the stand he firmly accused Henry Ward Beecher of adultery. Elizabeth Tilton, who had confessed and unconfessed a dozen times by now, finally made her choice too, and denied that there had ever been anything improper in the relations between her and her pastor.

The hearings were lengthy, and though they were supposed to be secret, Harriet and her family in Hartford could read all about them, and everyone all over the country could too. News was forever leaking into print from both the examining committee members and the witnesses. There were stories about the testimony, about the documents in the case, about the home life of the Tiltons, the home life of the Beechers, and any other topic that bore even remotely on the scandal.

Would the horror never end? Henry had been groaning the question from the beginning. Everyone who loved him was groaning it now, feeling that it had gone on interminably.

Then, even before Henry's handpicked committee of Plymouth Church members announced its verdict—the Reverend Beecher was completely innocent and had been woefully slandered—Theodore Tilton had realized *his* honor would never be upheld in Plymouth Church. He swore out a civil complaint in the Brooklyn City Court, charging the Reverend Henry Ward Beecher with having willfully alienated his wife's affections, and demanding one hundred thousand dollars as a recompense.

Years of meetings and pleadings and confessions and retractions and avowals and disavowals had been in vain. What had begun as a whispered confession of adultery had exploded at last into the glare of nationwide publicity.

Harriet ran away to Florida and Mandarin in October, earlier than she had ever gone before. She was in Florida when the Beecher-Tilton trial began, in January 1875, and she stayed there through three of the six drama-packed months that it continued. But there was no real running away from its poisonous immensity. Every newspaper in the country was pouring forth column after column to report each detail of the trial. Every newspaper in the country was taking sides, lining itself up for or against the Reverend Beecher. The pro-Beecher papers worked themselves into righteous hysterics, warning that a verdict against the Reverend Beecher would be a verdict against everything good and fine and holy in American life. And they did their best to explain away the evidence that seemed truly damning to the minister. But Henry had always had enemies. Impulsive, extravagant gestures had alienated thousands of the strictly orthodox. The very sweep of his fame and his own easy assurance in the midst of it had aroused hostility. And so the anti-Beecher papers were just as clamorous. A verdict *for* Beecher would be a verdict for hypocrisy, cant and what Victoria Woodhull called "moral humbug." The anti-Beecher papers played up the damning evidence for all it was worth and wrote scathing portraits of Beecher and his "Gospel of Gush" and of his idolators, rushing about trying to whitewash him.

Harriet was out of the reach of most of this and glad to be, and relied for her information on sympathetic reports from her long-time friend, Susan Howard. Mrs. Howard attended the sessions daily in the packed Brooklyn courtroom and wrote accounts of the proceedings to Harriet.

Harriet could not really concentrate on anything else. She waited tensely for Susan Howard's letters. "Faithful friend," she wrote her, when she had looked in vain for a letter across a span of several days, "cease not to write, for your letters are as cold water to a thirsty soul."

Harriet and her family headed north again in April, and stopped in Brooklyn to see Henry. But the excited crowds, the hordes of newspaper reporters and artists and the general carnival atmosphere, made a prolonged stay unthinkable. Harriet saw that Henry seemed to be bearing up extremely well. He had, once the civil trial started, adopted an almost debonair attitude, smiling, laughing and joking as he listened to the proceedings. And he refused to show anything but a kind of candid bewilderment on the witness stand, when the opposing lawyers managed to trap him, over and over, in contradictions. Harriet was relieved to see him so resilient in the face of attack, the image of his father, Lyman, who had never been so confident as

when he was defending himself against heresy charges. But the
heat of the drama was too much for her.

She, Calvin and the twins went home to follow the rest of
the proceedings by letter.

In a summer heat so intense that one of the jurors fainted,
the case that had begun in the freezing cold of January came
to an end. After the long and impassioned summations of the
opposing attorneys, the judge charged the jury carefully, warning them not to be influenced by the extraneous testimony that
had crept into the trial concerning Theodore Tilton's idiosyn-
crasies, or by any previous clearing of Beecher's name by Plymouth Church. "In any view of the case," the judge said, "you
may be disposed to ask why Mr. Beecher, if innocent, should
have garnered up in his heart all that pain and fear so long, when
he might have made proclamation to the world and trampled
out the scandal as with iron boots."

The jury withdrew and began its deliberations. For eight days,
while the nation waited, and reporters hung out over the roof
of the courthouse, trying to peer into the room where the jury
was closeted, the deliberations continued. At last, after fifty-two
ballots, the exhausted jurors dragged themselves into the courtroom to report—no agreement. At the beginning, they had been
eight to four against a verdict for Tilton. At the end, they were
nine to three against him. They could do no more. They had
reached a stalemate.

It was over. But not quite over. It was a victory for Henry,
but not quite a victory for Henry, depending on one's point
of view. Harriet and Calvin felt that it *was* a victory, considering
the careful, devious machinations of the conspirators against
Henry, and considering how even a member of his own family
had tried to betray him. (In 1874, Isabella had refused to be
silent any longer and had released for publication all her letters
to and from Henry concerning the scandal. Since then, the
Stowes and the Hookers were no longer enjoying the old amiable family relationship.)

But the public in general was not satisfied. The public
clamored for a definite conclusion. Within the course of the

year, a great church council would be called to reexamine the
millions of words of testimony. In this great church trial, Henry
Ward Beecher would be exonerated without a dissenting voice.

It would be over. But still not quite over. It would be years
more, and Henry would have expended all the charm and eloquence at his command on lecture tours, in articles, and in his
own pulpit, before he would begin to repair the damage done
to the public's picture of the Reverend Beecher as the country's
most brilliant, most lovable and gifted man of God.

The long, long preoccupation of the whole country with the
scandal—which "nothing since the outbreak of the Civil War"
had exceeded in interest—had changed something forever too.
Henry, who had done so much to lead his fellow men from the
old iron disciplines of Calvinism to the warmer, gentler gospel
of Love, had, all unwittingly, led them also to a new skepticism
in regard to the men who preached any gospel. No longer would
there be the blind reverence for the minister there once had
been. The age of cynicism was inaugurated for churchgoers now,
as well as for manipulators of the stock market.

Nothing had changed for Harriet. At sixty-four, she was too
fixed in the old pattern for the new cynicism to make any mark
on her. Things would continue to be what they seemed. And
it would have seemed inconceivable to her that later generations,
looking back on the Beecher-Tilton struggle would find a certain
wild comedy in it all, an extravagant cartoon quality in the self-
deluding, self-saving activities of the principals in the case.

There would never be anything the least bit amusing to her in
a tragedy that had "drawn on my life, my heart's blood." Henry,
she wrote to George Eliot, "is myself. I know you are the kind
of woman to understand me when I say that I felt a blow at
him more than at myself."

Once the struggle was over, Harriet would close her mind on
it and run away from any memory of it, recalling just the fact
that Henry had been nobly vindicated.

And only for later generations would there be a tantalizing
doubt as to what might have inspired Harriet's friend, Dr. Oliver
Wendell Holmes, to write his most famous punning limerick:

"The Reverend Henry Ward Beecher
Called the hen an excellent creature.
　　The hen pleased with that
　　Laid an egg in his hat,
And thus did the hen reward Beecher."

Chapter 33

*I feel myself as one who has been playing and picnicking on
the shores of life and has waked from a dream late in the afternoon to find that everybody, almost has gone. . . .*

1876–1882

Harriet was sixty-five as she penned that wistful comment in
a letter to George Eliot, and, being Harriet, she was exaggerating.
It was not so late in the afternoon as she thought. A good many
hours of daylight remained, hours that might not be filled with
the same kind of breakneck activity she had known so long, but
hours full of satisfaction and accomplishment.

The patterns of life were set, winters in Mandarin, summers
in the North, in the Forest Street house, with vacation weeks at
the Twin Mountain House or some seaside spot. "The girls," the
forty-year-old twins, Hatty and Eliza, ran the households, Eliza
taking charge in the North, Hatty in the South. There were often
visitors, both in Mandarin and Hartford, friends like the Howards, or members of the family, and these gave opportunities for
picnics, river excursions, croquet games. There were only a few
real worries.

One constant worry about Fred continued. It was almost six
years now since he had disappeared, and hardly a day passed
that Harriet did not think of him. She could not believe he was
dead. He was somewhere, surely, fighting his sickness, and one
day, with the "wild, unreasoning impulse" in check, he would
return.

She had a new worry that had arisen during the wretched
days of Henry's public humiliation. Her daughter, Georgie, had
suffered some sort of nervous collapse, slipping from her usual

liveliness into haunted, sleepless depression. Harriet had joined
in consultations and suggestions and anxious advice when she
was in the North visiting with Georgie and her husband and the
incomparable grandson, Freeman. Then a doctor seemed to know
just what to do. Georgie improved and became her old self. Only
gradually had it become apparent that there was something false
about her brightness, a feverish quality in her liveliness. The
doctor had prescribed morphine to lift her from the original depression. It was quite a customary prescription, except that it
had not worked quite as it should have with Georgiana. The
cure had become its own illness. Georgie burned with a flame
that was lighted only by the drug. In its absence, she plummeted
into a state from which she could only be rescued by more
morphine.

The daughter most like her in wit and talent, caught by drug
addiction—her soldier boy a slave to alcohol—Harriet, who reacted all her life against any kind of bondage, could not escape
the ironies that pursued her.

But the twins, so good, and efficient were a comfort. The
career of Charley, her youngest, born so auspiciously at the end
of her exile in the West, offered satisfaction. Charley had finished
Harvard, and like a true son of Harriet and Calvin, a true grandson of Lyman, had decided to go into the ministry. He had
warmed Calvin's heart by the further decision to get his theological training in Germany, at Bonn. Harriet and Calvin could discuss Charley's future happily, proud that the old torch was being
rekindled, to be carried on in his hands. Calvin, visionary as ever
in his seventies, had moments of alarm in the night sometimes,
when it seemed he saw the Devil, coming to tell him that Charley, the son who was his last, bright hope, was dead. But Calvin
was steeped in Biblical quotations and soon was able to worst
the Devil with paralyzing rejoinders.

Late afternoon or no, there was little that Harriet could do
for her children now. They were grown and beyond her. Suddenly, in a characteristic sort of contrariness as a writer, she
began to think about her childhood.

Autobiography is the first form of expression, for many writers, the emotions of their childhood lying nearest and most in need of ordering and clarification. And in one sense *Uncle Tom's Cabin* had been an emotional autobiography for Harriet, with its great central theme of bondage and escape. But she had, all unconsciously, chosen to embody her emotions in characters wholly foreign, against scenes often imaginary.

Now she began to think about the real scenes of her childhood. The real emotions, of passion and terror and love, had burned themselves out in the "vivid lights, gloomy shadows, grotesque groupings" of *Uncle Tom's Cabin* and *Dred* and *The Minister's Wooing*. What she could remember was the happy residue of the early days in Litchfield, the placid rhythms of life there, and a little girl enjoying them in the years before a realization of bondage had darkened them.

She began to write her last, full-length book, a book that would be a gentle reflection of what life had been in Litchfield, long ago. "Poganuc" was the name she gave to Litchfield for her story. *Poganuc People* was the book's title, and she wrote along on it in Florida and in Hartford, recalling the Litchfield characters she had known, Judge Tapping Reeve of the Law School, the Revolutionary War veteran, Colonel Tallmadge, the other figures of importance in the town, and all the rustics, the farmers, the storekeepers, the ebullient stage driver. The heroine of her story was a small girl named Dolly, a softened and sentimentalized version of herself, and she was turning her story on the simplest of themes. Dolly, daughter of the town's minister, and so being raised in the bleak atmosphere of Calvinism, would discover the warmth and glow of the Episcopalian Christmas after an Episcopalian church was established in Poganuc. There would be more to the story. As it unfolded, Harriet could review the importance of the old religion in towns like Litchfield at the beginning of the century. She could touch lightly on the historical and emotional reasons for its importance. But lightly. The struggles to understand had been over long ago. In the long light of the afternoon, she could look back with clarity and affection. At the very end of the book, the little girl, swiftly grown up, could find both her love and her faith in the warming, somehow more human, arms of the Episcopal Church.

The story began in one of Harriet's favorite settings. "The scene is a large, roomy, clean New England kitchen of some sixty years ago." They had laid a spell on her, those kitchens with their wide fireplaces, tall black clocks in the corner, "scoured tin and pewter," and everything shining with whiteness and neatness "as if work were some past and bygone affair, hardly to be remembered."

But along with the nostalgia for the vanished whiteness and neatness, there were memories of laughter, of drawling Yankee wit, and pungent New England expressions. A "strapping, buxom Yankee maiden" named Nabby presided over the kitchen. A handsome member of Poganuc's "democracy," who was definitely too proud to work as a servant, Nabby was "able to compromise her pride in working for 'the minister,'" and Nabby's colloquies with Hiel Beers, the dashing stagecoach driver who was courting her, were rich with humorous insult.

"Hiel Beers," said Nabby at one point, "don't give me none o' your saace, for I won't take it. Jim Sawin said last night you was the brassiest man he ever see. He said there was brass enough in your face to make a kettle of."

"You tell him there's sap enough in his head to fill it, anyway," Hiel responded imperturbably.

Rustic witticisms sparkled through the book. There was the farmer so stubborn that the "only way to get that fellow to heaven would be to set out to drive him to hell; then he'd turn and run up the narrow way full chisel." The same stubborn fellow was so aggravated at the "gittin' up and sittin' down" in an Episcopal church that "he comes out o' church as cross as a bull in fly-time."

Events that had starred her childhood came back to Harriet. For purposes of the plot, the first event of the story would be the fascinating Christmas "illumination" of the new Episcopal church in Poganuc, so thrilling to Dolly. After that there was the great election day of 1817, when the Democrats had smashed the Federalists "all to flinders," and "everything that could stand on its hind legs had voted, and the hogs had won." There would be the Fourth of July celebration on the Green. There would be "tea-drinkings," "apple-bees," and expeditions to the woods for chestnuts. There would be candle-making days, and trips to the woods to gather herbs and simples, and one summer Sunday, there would be Dolly's own "conversion," and her father saying to her tenderly, "Now has a new flower bloomed in Heaven." Everything she remembered most fondly went into *Poganuc People*.

Everything that had really hurt her or given her pain was left out, glossed over, or turned into a gentle parable. Oddly enough, though the little Dolly of the book was described as one of the last of a large family of children, there was almost no sense of brothers and sisters in the story. The brothers were away at school, or busy with their own affairs. There was no older sister, like the domineering Catherine, who had left such a mark on Harriet's life. There was no companionable little brother, as Henry Ward had been, whose recent troubles had caused her such grief.

About the time *Poganuc People* was concluding its run as a serial in *The Christian Union*, and while Harriet was still enjoying the winter months in Florida, there came the news that Catherine, aged seventy-eight, had died suddenly of an apoplectic stroke at the home of their half brother, Thomas, in Elmira, New York. This was a shock. Catherine had been as vigorous and opinionated as ever, in her seventies, sending out letters and declarations with her usual authority. Harriet might leave her out of a book, but to think about life without Catherine was unreal.

It *was* afternoon. Not everybody—but a great many had gone. Harriet was as "one picnicking, waking late," to discover she was more and more alone.

Still, there were activities in behalf of the living to claim her interest and attention. Charley was back from his studies in Bonn, and announcing his engagement to a pretty young lady named Susie Munroe. Harriet was stirred into all kinds of plans by this news, and was eager to see how she could help Charley obtain a good church for his first post.

There were always writing projects. *The Christian Union* was a ready market for anything she wrote. William Dean Howells had become editor of the *Atlantic Monthly*, and was inviting her to contribute to that magazine again.

One day after her latest book had been published, she was sending Dr. Holmes a copy of *Poganuc People*.

"Dear Doctor: I wish I could give to you and Mrs. Holmes the exquisite charm of this morning. My window is wide open; it is a lovely, fresh, sunny day, and a great orange tree hung with golden balls closes the prospect from my window. . . ."

She loved flowers as much as ever, and often when she left her desk she would become absorbed with oils and brushes and canvas, trying to capture, with the richness of paint, the "vivid lights, gloomy shadows," of a magnolia blossom with its dark leaves, or some other dramatic Florida bloom.

She and Calvin and the girls were in the North in 1879, for Charley's wedding to Susie. After that, Harriet was busy for weeks, helping them get settled in the new parsonage in Saco, Maine, where Charley had his first pastorate. She was easier in her mind about Georgie, for Georgie seemed less nervous and blind-eyed in her excitements.

The afternoon grew later, broken only by the realizations that another friend had taken leave. George Eliot, somehow very dear, although Harriet had never met her, was one who departed in 1880. At the end of the year, her former editor, and long-time friend, James T. Fields, was gone.

1881. . . . And on June 14, Harriet was seventy.

"I am come to those years where I may hope before long to join that circle of friends beyond the river, that is every day growing larger and more inviting," she wrote to Annie, James Fields's widow.

It had been a habit of hers to contemplate her own death with varying emotions ever since she was a schoolgirl, and writing Catherine, "I wish I might die and let the memory of me and my faults perish in the grave." At thirty-nine, she had resolved to write something about slavery "if I live." At seventy, the eventuality was a good deal closer, but she was still the Hattie she had always been, lively, energetic and impetuous most of the time, and then periodically retreating into those moods when she contemplated everything "in relation to eternity."

It was pleasant to have Samuel Clemens and his wife Livy as neighbors in Hartford. Mr. Clemens was world-famous now, as the author of *Tom Sawyer*, and his house, so huge and ornate, with porches and balconies, turrets and gables, paneled rooms and leaded windows and special effects, might remind Harriet a little of the folly she herself had built, at the height of her success, but she never said so. She liked to drop in for chats and laughter, liked having "Mark Twain" drop in at the Stowe house just as easily. He had asked her to design and arrange for the planting of his conservatory, and so she spent weeks arranging great banks of potted plants and flowers and baskets of ferns, with all the drifting, floating water-plants clustered around its central pool.

The tensions with Isabella were easing. Harriet, still secretly interested in spiritualism, could not approve those aspects of it that fascinated Belle—the seances, and table-rappings and unseen controls. But Belle was her sister. So they visited again.

The ties with Mary and her children had never been strained. Charles Dudley Warner and his family were neighbors and good friends. There always seemed to be visitors, good friends passing through the city, or literary acquaintances, or simply those who knew her as the famous writer of *Uncle Tom's Cabin* and wanted to see her and shake her hand.

Then there was one last public triumph. The editors of the *Atlantic Monthly* had inaugurated a custom of honoring the original contributors to the magazine with parties on their seventieth birthdays. It was in keeping with the inconsistencies in Harriet's life, and all its unexpected absurdities, that the editors, in conclave assembled to plan a tribute to Mrs. Stowe, should have gotten the date of her birthday wrong, forgetting the day completely the year she was seventy, and then scheduling their fete for the year she was seventy-one.

Harriet could be tactful, especially since they had erred in the right direction, making her younger rather than older. She accepted with pleasure their invitation to a seventieth-birthday party gala.

A garden party was planned, to be held on the lawns of the home of one of Massachusetts' ex-governors, near Boston. Invitations were sent out to the literary great of the day, several hundred invitations in all, and, of course, to the widespread Beecher clan.

And so, on the appointed day, it seemed to Harriet there was a small multitude starred about the grass, clustered about the gaily striped marquee, or moving toward her and Calvin, when it became known she had arrived.

Thirty years before, when *Uncle Tom's Cabin* had been published, women would have billowed and floated about like vast flowers in their crinolines. The look was different now. Women wore narrow, tubular dresses, swept back to small bustles. Tiny bonnets, nodding with flowers and plumes, tilted forward on their heads. As the ladies moved across the lawn, they appeared to slant forward slightly, the very fashions giving them an eager, expectant look. Bright parasols, fringed and striped, flickered among the silk hats worn by the gentlemen, who were elegant in slim trousers, and high-buttoned, long-tailed coats.

Not all the literary great who had been invited were present. Thirty years had changed more than fashions in clothes. It had long since become fashionable among writers to dismiss *Uncle Tom's Cabin* as a book with no literary pretensions. The days were gone when such figures as George Sand, Heinrich Heine and Tolstoi had praised it as a masterpiece. Harriet's popular scribbling "for the pay," with its careless grammar, loose construction and frequent sentimentalizing had further destroyed her reputation with those who were interested in literary artistry. Memories of her impetuous disclosures about Lord Byron lingered in many minds. Still, there were enough well-known and distinguished figures, enough men and women who admired Harriet, to make it a brilliant gathering.

After the music and the collation, when everyone was assembled under the marquee, the tributes began. Just as long ago, when she had sat quietly while someone else rose to respond for her, Harriet sat quietly today. Calvin felt himself too old for such duties now, so it was her brother, Henry Ward, who responded to the address of welcome for her. Paying tribute to his sister's talent, he referred humorously to his own one attempt at novel-writing, which had been a failure as excessive as the great advance he had received. He had written *Norwood*, he said now, to scotch the rumors that had once claimed that *he* and not Harriet had written *Uncle Tom's Cabin*. After that, he grew sentimental, summoning the ghosts of Lyman Beecher and Roxana to hover over the gathering.

Then it was time for the poems.

John Greenleaf Whittier, seventy-five years old, with his own memories of the long fight of the Abolitionists, had written a poem for Harriet. Too shaky to read it himself, he gave it to someone else to read.

> "Thrice welcome from the land of flowers
> And golden-fruited orange bowers
> To this sweet, green-turfed June of ours,
> To her who in our evil time
> Dragged into light the nation's crime
> With strength beyond the strength of men
> And, mightier than their sword, her pen; . . ."

For forty more lines, it went rhyming on, to conclude:

> ". . . the unending years
> Shall tell her tale in unborn ears.
> And when with sins and follies past
> Are numbered color-hate and caste,
> White, black, and red shall own as one
> The noblest work by woman done."

Dr. Oliver Wendell Holmes was at the gala, and he too had written a poem for his friend. As a matter of fact, he had written two, but the first had evolved into a serious work, and remembering that the occasion was a garden party, and remembering Harriet, whose gaiety had always pleased him, he put that effort aside to revert to his old punning self.

He had once made a lovely pun on Henry's name. This time he had been inspired to a learned pun on Harriet's, taking off from Archimedes' ancient pronouncement that if he had a lever big enough and a fulcrum for it, he could move the world. The Greek word for lever, spelled out in English letters, was *sto*. What could be better?

And so, by the fourth stanza of his tribute, he was declaiming, with twinkling eyes:

"When Archimedes, long ago,
Spake out so grandly, 'Dos pou sto;
    Give me a place to stand on,
I'll move your planet for you now,'—
He little dreamed or fancied how
The *sto* at last should find its *pou*
    For woman's faith to land on.

Her lever was the wand of art,
Her fulcrum was the human heart,
    Whence all unfailing aid is.
She moved the earth! Its thunders pealed;
Its mountains shook, its temples reeled;
The blood-fed fountains were unsealed,
    And Moloch sank to Hades."

There was a great deal more, but in those phrases he had summed up Harriet's accomplishment as aptly as anyone could in rhyme, and as irresistibly. Everyone smiled in appreciation and looked toward Harriet, sitting so composedly on the platform. She looked very small and rather old-fashioned, but she had been the lever that moved their generation, their whole century.

More poems were read as the shadows lengthened across the lawn. There were letters of tribute that had come from some who had been invited but could not attend—from Rutherford B. Hayes, from Edward Eggleston, George W. Cable, Joel Chandler Harris.

Then there was a pause in the program, and everyone looked toward Harriet again, and rose and began clapping. They wanted her to speak. She hesitated a moment, then rose and moved to the front of the platform. The clapping stopped, but everyone remained standing.

"I wish to say that I thank all my friends from my heart—that is all," she said. But then she had a further thought.

"And one thing more—and that is, if any of you have doubt, or sorrow, or pain—if you doubt about this world—just remember what God has done. Just remember that this great sorrow of slavery has gone—gone by, forever. I see it every day at the South, I see these people growing richer and richer. I see men very happy in their lowly lot; but, to be sure, you must have patience with them. They are not perfect, but have their faults, and they are serious faults in the view of white people. But they are very happy, that is evident." Then she went on to give two instances of Negro happiness she knew from Mandarin. A Negro friend in their neighborhood had done very well, and one day told Calvin, "I have got twenty head of cattle, four head of hoss, forty head of hen, and I have got ten children—*all mine, every one mine.*" She spoke of an evening festival at this same man's home, to raise money for the church. She and her family had attended the festival and she told of what a successful evening it had been. They were homely incidents, painting pictures for her listeners, as she had once painted other homely pictures to move the world.

"That is the sort of thing I see going on around me," she concluded. "Let us never doubt. Everything that ought to happen is going to happen."

She made a small gesture of gratitude and went back to her chair.

"Everything that ought to happen is going to happen. . . ." It was, in her quiet, but still firm voice, the faith of all the nineteenth-century seekers after a better world, all those brave and dedicated liberals, reformers, and crusaders who were sure that if men only tried hard enough, everything could someday be made right and perfect. And it was, in a curious sort of way, the old faith of Calvinism, which had ushered in the century, turned inside out. Things *were* predestined, only no longer did people believe that the plan had evolved in wrath. The plan of their coming into being sprang from a will toward the good, which a God of love had put into men's hearts.

"Everything that *ought* to happen is going to happen. . . ."

Chapter 34

It was a different world entirely from the world into which Harriet Beecher had been born almost a century before. Seventy years before, eighty years before, when the United States themselves were still very young, life had been a personal and private thing between a man and his God. Each man stood alone under the arches of infinity, unique in his character, unique in his destiny.

No one was alone like that anymore.

The United States had grown up. The wound that had almost split it in two was not healed completely. It had been too much aggravated for that. But the United States was one country, a giant, pulsing with power and arrogance, every part of it linked to every other part in a nervous network of communication and transportation. Trains thundered from coast to coast and from one section of the country to another, creating new wealth wherever their narrow tracks were laid, parallel lures to the horizon. The lazy days of shipping by canal boat were over. The great days of river steamboating were almost over. Trains went faster. Trains went everywhere. Trains carried everything, meats and vegetables in refrigerated cars, people in lavish Pullman cars, and there were appropriate cars for heavy machinery, oil, lumber, grain, whatever people wanted to transport. It had taken almost two weeks to make the trip from New York to Cincinnati when the Beechers made their western hegira in 1832. The same trip could now be made overnight.

Transportation within cities had changed. No longer were horse-drawn carriages, omnibuses or wagons the only way to move people or goods from one part of the city to another. Electric railway cars, in the form of streetcars or elevated or subway trains, were whirling people to their destinations with new speed, new noises, and exhilarating showers of sparks. The bicycle had suddenly taken the country by storm. Everywhere people were riding bicycles, for pleasure, for romance and for exercise, as well as more utilitarian reasons.

The telegraph, invented in the 1840s, had been improved, and a transatlantic cable had been successfully laid at last. In 1876 at the great Centennial Exposition in Philadelphia, Emperor Dom Pedro II of Brazil had stopped at the booth of young Alexander Graham Bell and picked up a cone-shaped instrument on display. "My God, it talks!" he said in surprise. Since that time, the telephone had invaded offices and homes everywhere. No longer would it have been necessary, in the 1880s, for Henry Ward Beecher, Theodore Tilton, Frank Moulton and all the others involved in the Beecher-Tilton scandal, to write such a mountain of letters to each other. By telephone, they could have denounced, shown remorse, confessed, recanted, and in every other way expressed their day-to-day emotions, and their words, writ on air, would have been gone, leaving no piled-up heap of evidence to make a six-month sensation of the trial.

Newspapers had changed. They were no longer the small partisan journals they had been before the war, mere vehicles of personal opinion. The emphasis was on news, news that was so much easier to gather, thanks to all the new means of communication, easier to set up in type on the new linotype machines, easier to print swiftly on the new rotary presses.

Thomas A. Edison's experiments with the dynamo, which had led him to perfecting the electric railway car, had also inspired him, by 1880, to invent the incandescent lamp. In no time, there would be a new kind of light in homes, offices, factories.

No one was alone quite as people had been before. Everyone was dependent on everybody else for something, and everything that had once been absolute had shifted into being relative to something else.

Darwin's theory of evolution, first announced back in the 1850s, was the bombshell that had toppled the old pillars of creation, the whole vision of a self-inclosed universe within which John Calvin had built his creed. Religion, science, philosophy—none could ever be the same again. Political theory, law—everything was changed by this idea of organic evolution. If the relationship of the states to the Federal government and the Union had *not* been fixed immutably by the ideas of 1787 (as John C. Calhoun so firmly believed they had been), then the character of the Federal government not only could, but must, be continually modified in relation to the organic growth of the country as a whole. Law itself was not immutable logic, but the outgrowth of experience—or so wrote young Oliver Wendell Holmes, the brilliant son of Harriet's old friend, the Doctor.

There were many who felt that religion was swept away entirely if the new doctrine was accepted, and to save their religion they rejected Darwin. How could one believe both the Biblical story of creation and Darwin's theory that man had evolved through billions of years from a single cell? Never mind how— Henry Ward Beecher could. Always one who moved swiftly with the tide, Henry could believe both things at once, just as his father, Lyman, had been able to believe in both free will and predestination. The laws of Nature were the laws of God, Henry had always insisted. And he was untroubled also by the new "higher criticism" that was subjecting the Bible to critical tests long standard in every other field of scholarship, using new historical, geological or archaelogical facts to assess its validity. Henry had come instinctively to the conclusion, long ago, that the Bible must be read figuratively and allegorically, not literally.

But there were philosophical problems not to be solved so easily as Henry settled them. The nation, full of power and arrogance, no longer had the conscience that once had directed it. No longer was man required to see himself as a worm before God's mighty throne. God's words, God's laws, were not to be interpreted literally, but figuratively, as they applied to changing times, changing needs.

But how? How? Figurative interpretations can be as many and as varied as there are imaginations to figure them. There had to be some kind of philosophic test. In the 1860s, and '70s and

'80s, Charles Peirce, William James and John Dewey were formulating one. "Does it work?" was the essence of their test for any truth. "The ultimate test for us," William James wrote, "of what a truth means, is the conduct it dictates or inspires . . . The effective meaning of any philosophical position can always be brought down to some particular 'consequence.'"

Truth, in other words, was always changing, mutable as any other fact in life. It might not be so difficult for Henry Ward Beecher to accept, Henry, who for years had taken what he wanted from the Bible and ignored the rest, taken what he wanted from life too, and justified it later. But Henry, for all his position as a leader, was adaptable as water, far more adaptable than his sister Harriet could ever be to the pressures of life around him. Her skill was in reflecting that life, his to move with it. The truth—had he told the truth finally, on the witness stand, when he denied ever having had any improper relations with Elizabeth Tilton? Was he justified in the way he had abandoned her at the time of the trial, and ignored her completely from then on, even as her life sank to lower and lower levels of poverty and misery? No one ever knew for sure.

In 1884, when the Republicans, glutted with wealth and riddled with corruption after twenty-four years of uninterrupted power, nominated James G. Blaine for President, Henry Ward Beecher shifted from his long allegiance to the Republican party to support Grover Cleveland, "Grover the Good." Then when a scandal about an illegitimate child Cleveland had sired threatened to ruin his chances, and Cleveland determined the "truth" should be told, whatever the cost—what did Henry Ward Beecher think? He went on campaigning for Cleveland, even more vigorously than before. He cried, "When in the gloomy night of my own suffering, I sounded every depth of sorrow, I vowed that if God would bring the day star of hope, I would never suffer brother, friend or neighbor to go unfriended should a like serpent seek to crush him. . . . Because I know the bitterness of venomous lies, I will stand against the infamous lies that seek to sting to death an upright man and magistrate."

But Cleveland had already told the truth, had confessed that years before, he had been intimate with a widow who bore a child and gave the child his name. Although there was no proof of his paternity, even doubt about it, he had undertaken the financial support of the child.

And finally, in Cleveland's case, sympathy swung to the "singularly honorable" course he had taken, and he was elected. The pragmatic "consequence" of telling the truth could hardly have been happier. Did Henry Ward ponder any different courses he might have taken, had his own disaster struck ten years later?

"Does it work?" It was a truly American philosophy for a country where the future was always new and no one's life was set in the patterns of the past. It was a fit conscience for a giant just growing into maturity. And there was no reason to think it would not work as well for those whose hearts were set on the good, the true and the beautiful, as for those who simply considered the expediencies of the present.

"Does it work?" It would impel the young giant out of the nineteenth century into the twentieth, into new riches, new inventions, new wonders, new excesses—and new reforms too, when the liberals could prove that it did *not* work, in the long run, to let children labor in sweatshops, or to underpay and ignore the vast forces of adult labor, or to let great business monopolies take over the resources of the country.

"Does it work?" would serve the young giant well, for quite a while.

But it would never be a credo for Harriet Beecher Stowe, born almost at the beginning of the century, Harriet, who in the clear bright light that had shone then, had seen right and wrong, utterly different, utterly uninterchangeable, once and for all, confronting man with the need to choose.

Still, it would not matter, for even as the century was growing old, so was she. She would not have to live too long in this strange, loud world, where only machines were immutable, and values could shift like clouds.

Chapter 35

I wander at will from one subject to another . . . Now and then I dip into a book . . . Pictures delight me . . . Of music I am also very fond . . . Blessed I have been in many ways . . . Sorrows also I have had . . . But they are all passed now. . . ."

1883–1896

A decade and more after her seventieth birthday party, Harriet sat at her desk, writing to her old friend Dr. Holmes. She looked very small and frail. Her hair, snow-white and gently curling, was bound back with a black velvet ribbon. Her great, heavy-lidded eyes were no longer luminous, but dimmed with age. She was eighty-two, and there was a gentleness about her face, a repose, as though she were looking at life from a long distance, seeing all its storms as remote. She was content with little things, sunshine and flowers and pictures and music.

Sorrows there had been in the last ten years. The very year after the great garden party, in 1883, Calvin had fallen dangerously ill of Bright's disease. He had recovered enough to spend the next winter in Florida, as usual, but during the next year, it became clear that he could travel no more. The winters in Florida were over. His illness was incurable. It was simply a question of waiting for the end. He suffered no pain. Harriet was grateful for that. She arranged her life so as to spend most of her time with him, and there had been one last interlude for the two of them, long, quiet hours, when all that had bound them together for so many years held them as content in each other's company as they had ever been. Calvin's mind stayed clear. "He is as competent as ever to explain a text or instruct me in the merits of a verse," Harriet wrote to Susan Howard.

His old drollery and rustic humor had remained unextinguished too. Moonfaced, white-whiskered, round as a butterball, he lay propped up against the pillows, or, on good days, sat in the chair by the window, and he and Harriet made little jokes and laughed, or were simply silent.

The twins ran the house as efficiently as always. There were frequent visitors, visits from sister Mary and her children and grandchildren, or sister Belle and her family. Mr. Clemens ran in and out with jokes and stunts to amuse Harriet and Calvin. A book signed with Harriet's name came out, another subscription book from one of the ubiquitous Hartford companies. It was called *Our Famous Women*. But the company had farmed out most of the writing. Harriet was through writing, except for letters to friends.

She wrote to Dr. Holmes, in the summer of 1885, reporting on Calvin's decline. "I am thankful that the passage downward is mostly painless, though sure. He is longing to depart to a higher rest; or as you said to have inscribed on his grave:

'Not Finis, but End of Vol. 1.' "

Still, it would be another year, a year very much like the one just past, before the volume would close. It was August of 1886 when Harriet's "old Rabbi" died quietly, murmuring "Peace with God! Peace with God!"

The cemetery at Andover, where their young son Henry had been buried almost thirty years before was the place where both Harriet and Calvin had chosen to be buried. The twins and Charley took charge after Calvin's death and arranged everything. Harriet had only to follow along, from Hartford to Andover, from chapel to graveside, lost in a haze of memories.

There had been more sorrows the next year. On a Sunday night in February, Henry Ward Beecher preached his last sermon. Four days later he suffered the stroke he had feared since the days of his campaigning for Frémont, when dizzy spells had periodically gripped him. He was gone within a week.

It was hardly grief Harriet felt. Her brother had simply been translated to a higher, more glorious life. But now, it really was late, late in the afternoon, and almost everyone was gone.

Another loved one left the picnicking ground on this side of the river to cross to the other bank. It should, perhaps, have been more shocking than it was to Harriet, for this was her daughter, Georgiana Allen. But, haunted by morphine, Georgiana's life had been a nervous torment in the last years. Besides, after Calvin's death, a calmness had come over Harriet. There were no more spasms of grief to rack her. Emotions had burned out. She was simply waiting to greet all those she loved someday soon. She would see Georgie again, and both the beloved Henrys, her son Henry and her brother Henry, and the baby who had died in the cholera epidemic in Cincinnati, and Calvin, and Lady Byron, and—so many. They had just gone on ahead.

There had been joys in the decade just past. While Calvin still lingered, Charley and his wife, and his two babies, had come down from Saco, Maine, to Hartford. Fortuitously, and perhaps not so accidentally, Charley had received a call to the pastorate of a Congregational Church not two miles from the house on Forest Street. With her son preaching in Hartford, Harriet went no more to the Episcopal Church, but went each Sunday to "Charley's church"—the Congregational Church, into which she had been born. Visits from Charley and his family, moments of joking with his two sturdy grandsons, had helped brighten the last year of Calvin's life. With Calvin gone, Harriet found even more pleasure in their appearances.

Charley had been putting together her "autobiography" ever since his arrival in Hartford. She got out the letters she had saved across the years, and reminisced about her childhood for him. Reading the letters, sorting them, putting some aside as too private for the eyes of others, had given her very "peculiar feelings."

"Reading old letters, when so many of the writers have gone from earth, seems to me like going into the world of spirits— letters full of the warm, eager, anxious, busy life that is *forever* past. . . . It is affecting to me to recall things that strongly moved me years ago, that filled my thoughts and made me anxious—when the occasion and emotions have wholly vanished from my mind. . . . The romance of my youth is faded, it looks to me now, from my years—so *very* young. Those days when my mind lived only in *emotion*, and when my letters were never dated, because they were only histories of the *internal*. But now that I am no more, and never can be, young in this world, now that the friends of those days are almost all in eternity, what remains? . . .''

What remained? Only a vague wonder at having once felt so much and so deeply, and no more strength or even desire to evoke those emotions in the hearts of others. So there came about the last little irony in Harriet's life, an "autobiography" so cool and remote that it hid almost completely the passionate creature who had "lived only in emotion," and whose history was mostly internal. Faithfully following his mother's instructions, Charley chose among the letters those that reflected her in her loftiest, most moralizing vein. Names and dates and events were there to give the outline of her life, but the letters that marked its course appeared like small, official monuments, most of the gaiety and mischief, the contrariness and passion that had made her Harriet somehow missing. She who had been a runaway all her life, running away into moods and books, running off on trips and junkets, had run away one last time from a world that might have wanted to know what she was really like.

"It is the true story of my life," she wrote in the preface for Charley's manuscript and the collected letters, "told for the most part in my own words, and has therefore all the force of an autobiography." Then she concluded, "If these pages shall lead those who read them to a firmer trust in God and a deeper sense of His fatherly goodness, throughout the days of our earthly pilgrimage, I can say with Valiant for Truth in the Pilgrim's Progress . . .

" 'I am going to my Father's and tho' with great difficulty, I am got hither, yet now, I do not repent me of all the troubles I have been at, to arrive where I am.

" 'My sword I give to him that shall succeed me in my pilgrimage and my courage and skill to him that can get it.' "

She signed it, "Hartford, Sept. 30, 1889, Harriet Beecher Stowe," writing her name "fully and euphoniously" just as Calvin had advised her to so long ago.

She was suddenly and acutely ill soon after that. Was it a stroke, the same kind of lightning that had struck down both Henry and Catherine? Perhaps so. At any rate, though she made a quick physical recovery, she was never again quite the same mentally. There were days when her intelligence was as quick and interested as always. There were other days when she retreated from awareness so completely she was like a child.

Her eightieth birthday came. Here and there, the newspapers noticed it, generally with a few light and contemptuous comments. The country that she had helped to lead to war had grown beyond her, and looked back on her with impatience and annoyance, almost as though embarrassed that a little woman, burning with her own emotions, could have had such uncanny power over it.

The *Independent,* the religious paper for which Harriet had written so many hundreds of columns and one of her best serial stories as well, marked her birthday with comments that reflected the general disdain:

"'Uncle Tom's Cabin' was the output of a very inferior artist. Mrs. Stowe is famous, and her novel has had a great triumph, but it is a mediocre piece of sensational romance, and more than mediocre, viewed from a just, critical point of view. . . . Her style was of that flamboyant kind grateful to the crude, popular, and vulgar taste. She made hysterical folk have fits, and politicians caught up her hysterical wail and made the very most of it."

A few comments were fairer and more honest. Another critic wrote: "Not only does she stand in the foremost rank of famous women of the world, but in shaping the destiny of the American people at a most critical period of their history, her influence was probably greater than that of any other individual. Charles Sumner said that if 'Uncle Tom's Cabin' had not been written, Abraham Lincoln could not have been elected President of the United States."

Whatever they wrote, it hardly mattered. Harriet had run away into a world of her own. Now and then she had rational days when she knew exactly what her condition was. "My mind wanders like a running brook," she wrote Susan Howard on one of those days. "I have written all my words and thought all my thoughts, and now I rest me in the flickering light of the dying embers. . . ."

It was another rational day, in 1893, when she answered a letter from Dr. Holmes.

"My Dear Friend Dr. Holmes;" she wrote in her fine, still racing script, "Your more than kind—your most charming, really lovely letter of January 31 was to me the profoundest surprise and the greatest pleasure I have had in many a day—I might say, year. That you should remember and think of me and write me so at length, with your own hand too, is a kind courtesy and an honor that I sincerely appreciate.

"I must tell you, my dear friend, if you do not know it your-self—and I say it not to flatter but because it is true—your lamp burns as brightly as ever. The oil in it has not run low, leaving but a feeble gleam, as mine has done. . . . I am glad to know how you pass your time, and that you have such a peaceful, cheerful happy life. That you make others happy, I know, for your presence always was like sunshine. . . ."

She went on to tell him of her life, how her physical health had been excellent since the alarming illness four years before, and how she was almost always cheerful and happy. But "my mental condition might be called nomadic," she told him. "I have no fixed thoughts or objects. I wander at will from one subject to another. In pleasant summer weather I am out of doors most of my time, rambling about the neighborhood and calling upon my friends. I do not read much. Now and then I dip into a book much as a humming bird, poised in air on whirring wing, darts into the heart of a flower, now here, now there, and away. Pic-tures delight me and afford me infinite diversion and interest. I pass many pleasant hours looking over books of pictures.

"Of *music* I am also very fond. I could not have too much of it, and I never *do* have as much as I should like. The street bands, even organs, give me great pleasure, but especially the singing and playing of my kind friends, who are willing to gratify me in this respect.

"I make no mental effort of any sort; my brain is tired out. It was a woman's brain and not a man's, and finally from sheer

fatigue and exhaustion in the march and strife of life it gave out
before the end was reached. . . ."

She thanked him again for writing her and thinking of her,
and signed herself most sincerely his friend. "A woman's brain
and not a man's," she had apologized, after all that brain had
accomplished—for she was still Hattie who could never resist
some touch of martyrdom or melancholy.

Soon there were no more rational days. She moved through a
house filled with mementos of her greatest achievement. The
library shelves had a collection of foreign editions of *Uncle Tom's
Cabin*, book after book, in one strange language after another,
testimony to the way she had once spoken in a voice that carried
around the world. The silver inkstand given her in England still
stood on her desk. Porcelain figures of Uncle Tom and little
Eva stood on tables and shelves. Somewhere there was the gold
slave bracelet she had been given in England too, engraved on
one link with the date that Great Britain had freed her slaves,
on another link with the fateful date of January 1, 1863, when the
United States had done the same.

But none of those things meant anything to Harriet anymore.
She had forgotten about them.

Out of doors, one sunshiny day, a strange gentleman approached her and asked to shake her hand. He had read *Uncle
Tom's Cabin* with "satisfaction and instruction." She looked at
him wonderingly, and then she remembered: "Ah yes! That was
a great book. God wrote it." And she smiled. It had nothing to
do with her.

One obsession linked her to past sorrows. She became convinced that Fred, her soldier boy, who had vanished twenty-three
years ago now, was coming home again. She returned from her
rambles in the garden or down the streets around the house, her
arms filled with flowers. She wanted to decorate the house for
his homecoming. If she saw anyone in the street in a uniform,
she would run up to him and call him Fred.

Except for that wistful sense of anticipation, everything was
happy. She darted out across the backyard to the Clemens' house.

She drifted down the street to Charles Dudley Warner's and slipped inside to play the piano there.

She was like quicksilver. Her twin daughters could not keep up with her. They hired a kind, strong Irish nurse to be with her all the time.

And so three years and more passed from the time she sat, small and frail, to answer Dr. Holmes's last letter to her. Dr. Holmes was dead, but she did not know. So many were dead, but she had forgotten. They seemed to be with her whenever she wanted them. Except for Fred, and he would return soon.

She grew still frailer. There was no more wandering, no more singing and picking flowers. She lay in bed.

Almost at midnight on July 1, 1896, two weeks after her eighty-fifth birthday, she opened her eyes. Her Irish nurse who was sitting nearby, rose and came to give her medicine. Harriet tried to smile at her—a smile that went back across the years, greeting everyone who had been dear. "I love you," she said, and then lay back again with a little gasp. As simply, as easily as that, she was gone, escaped at last from the final bondage, into eternal freedom.

They buried her in the Andover Chapel Cemetery, between her husband, Calvin, and her golden son, Henry. There were few enough left of those she had loved most deeply to stand beside the grave. There were only three of her children, the twins and Charley. There were Charley's family, his wife and two sons, and the first, handsome grandchild, Georgie's son, Freeman Allen. There was sister Belle, and her good friend, Annie Fields. Still, Harriet's grave was banked with the flowers she had loved, and on the casket was a wreath that had been sent by the Negroes of Boston. The card read: "The Children of Uncle Tom."

Epilogue

A compound of contradictions—deep feeling and sentimentality, laughter and melancholy, self-righteousness and humility, dark fears and clear visions—she had written the book that helped to change the course of history.

A miracle, an enigma, grown greater through the years. But should we wonder at that?

Here we have no continuing city . . .

Sources and Acknowledgments

Any new study of Harriet Beecher Stowe obviously must rest on the accumulated literature and research into her life. Grateful acknowledgment is made of the help given by various books about her. *The Life and Letters of Harriet Beecher Stowe*, compiled and edited by her son, Charles E. Stowe, is the authorized biography. Another *Life and Letters*, written by her good friend, Annie Fields (wife of one of Mrs. Stowe's publishers, James T. Fields), gives some of Mrs. Fields's personal impressions of her friend. *The Life-Work of the Author of Uncle Tom's Cabin*, by Florine Thayer McCray, written during Mrs. Stowe's lifetime, and published in 1889, was never approved by the Stowe family, but gives an interesting contemporary viewpoint of the author. A centennial biography in 1911, by her son, Charles E. Stowe, and her grandson, Lyman Beecher, and a lengthy study of Mrs. Stowe in that same grandson's book about the Beecher family in general, *Saints, Sinners and Beechers*, give further family memories and impressions. *The Autobiography, Correspondence, etc., of Lyman Beecher*, her father, which she helped to prepare, also includes chapters of her own reminiscences.

More recent works include *Harriet Beecher Stowe*, by Catherine Gilbertson, published in 1937, and *Crusader in Crinoline*, by Forrest Wilson, published in 1941. Especially grateful acknowledgment is made to this last book, a definitive biography of Mrs. Stowe, which not only includes various letters previously unpublished, but presents the results of much careful detective work to fill in missing details for a meticulous chronology of her life.

The aim of this portrait being to reassess and reinterpret the facts already known, Harriet Beecher Stowe's own voluminous writings were also a chief source of study. These include more than thirty published books, novels, collections of essays and columns, biographical sketches, children's stories, travel letters and poems, as well as hundreds of columns written for various religious papers and weeklies. In these writings, Harriet Beecher Stowe revealed herself in all her contradictory moods, as well as in her special kind of constancy.

The further aim being to present her against the background of her century and to trace her history in terms of the history of her time, there was an equal, or even greater amount of supplemental research. To summarize for another era the special doctrines of Calvinism as they affected her in her childhood, the works studied included: *Calvin: Theological Treatises*, translated and edited by the Reverend J.K.S. Reid; *Portrait of Calvin*, by T.H.L. Parker; *Jonathan Edwards*, by Perry Miller; *Yale and the Ministry*, by Roland Bainton and various histories of Congregationalism in America. The manners and tastes of the early half of the nineteenth century were reflected in a variety of books, of which grateful acknowledgment is especially made of *Domestic Manners of the Americans*, by Frances M. Trollope, first published in 1836. Russell Lynes's *The Tastemakers*, of our own day, was also helpful. Mrs. Stowe's writings on the Lord Byron affair were studied in relation to such works on Byron's life as *Byron*, by André Maurois, and *Lord Byron's Marriage*, by G. Wilson Knight. *Free Love and Heavenly Sinners*, by Robert Shaplen, offered valuable material about the Henry Ward Beecher scandal, supplementing the contemporary newspaper records that were consulted. The standard biographies of such figures as John C. Calhoun, Oliver Wendell Holmes, Abraham Lincoln, Eli Whitney, and other personalities who figure in her story, were also vital aspects of the research.

Selected Bibliography

Biographies

The Life of Harriet Beecher Stowe, by Charles Edward Stowe
    Riverside Press, Cambridge, Massachusetts, 1889
The Life and Letters of Harriet Beecher Stowe, by Annie A. Fields
    Riverside Press, Cambridge, Massachusetts, 1897
The Life-Work of the Author of Uncle Tom's Cabin, by Florine Thayer McCray
    Funk & Wagnalls Company, New York, 1889
The Autobiography, Correspondence, etc., of Lyman Beecher, D.D., edited by Charles Beecher
    1864
Harriet Beecher Stowe, by Catherine Gilbertson
    D. Appleton-Century Company, New York, 1937
Crusader in Crinoline, by Forrest Wilson
    J. B. Lippincott Company, Philadelphia, 1941

Supplemental

Calvin: Theological Treatises, translated and edited by J.K.S. Reid
    Westminster Press, Philadelphia, 1954
Portrait of Calvin, by T.H.L. Parker
    Westminster Press, Philadelphia, 1955
Jonathan Edwards, by Perry Miller
    William Sloane Associates, New York, 1949

Yale and the Ministry, by Roland H. Bainton
    Harper & Brothers, New York, 1957
Byron, by André Maurois
    D. Appleton-Century Company, New York, 1930
Life and Letters of Anne Isabella, Lady Noel Byron, by Ethel
    Colburn Mayne
    Charles Scribner's Sons, New York, 1929
Lord Byron's Marriage, by George Wilson Knight
    The Macmillan Company, New York, 1957
The Tastemakers, by Russell Lynes
    Harper & Brothers, New York, 1954
Domestic Manners of the Americans, by Frances M. Trollope
    Dodd, Mead & Company, New York, 1927
Free Love and Heavenly Sinners, by Robert Shaplen
    Alfred A. Knopf, New York, 1954
John C. Calhoun, An American Portrait, by Margaret L. Coit
    Houghton Mifflin Company, Boston, 1950
Yankee From Olympus, by Catherine Drinker Bowen
    Little, Brown & Company, Boston, 1944
Main Currents in American Thought, by Vernon L. Parrington
    Harcourt, Brace & Company, New York, 1927
Sunshine and Shadow in New York, by Matthew Hale Smith
    J. B. Burr & Company, Hartford, Connecticut, 1868
The Growth of the American Republic, by Samuel Eliot Morison
    and Henry Steele Commager
    Oxford University Press, New York, 1942

INDEX